VACATION PLACES RATED

March 6, 1996

To Steve Wilson

Happy travels as
you traverse this
broad and diverse
globe of ours!
Steve Plog

Fielding Titles

Fielding's Alaska Cruises/Inside Passage
Fielding's Amazon
Fielding's Australia
Fielding's Bahamas
Fielding's Belgium
Fielding's Bermuda
Fielding's Borneo
Fielding's Brazil
Fielding's Britain
Fielding's Budget Europe
Fielding's Caribbean
Fielding's Caribbean Cruises
Fielding's Caribbean East
Fielding's Caribbean West
Fielding's Europe
Fielding's European Cruises
Fielding's Far East
Fielding's France
Fielding's Freewheelin' USA
Fielding's Guide to the World's Most Dangerous Places
Fielding's Guide to Kenya's Best Hotels, Lodges & Homestays
Fielding's Guide to the World's Great Voyages
Fielding's Hawaii
Fielding's Holland
Fielding's Italy
Fielding's Las Vegas Agenda
Fielding's London Agenda
Fielding's Los Angeles Agenda
Fielding's Malaysia and Singapore
Fielding's Mexico
Fielding's New York Agenda
Fielding's New Zealand
Fielding's Paris Agenda
Fielding's Portugal
Fielding's Rome Agenda
Fielding's San Diego Agenda
Fielding's Scandinavia
Fielding's Southeast Asia
Fielding's Southern Vietnam on Two Wheels
Fielding's Spain
Fielding's Thailand Including Cambodia, Laos, Myanmar
Fielding's Vacation Places Rated
Fielding's Vietnam
Fielding's Worldwide Cruises
The Indiana Jones Survival Guide

VACATION PLACES RATED

**The hottest travel
tips of the year
based on a survey
of 13,500 travelers**

Stanley C. Plog, Ph.D.

Fielding Worldwide, Inc.
308 South Catalina Avenue
Redondo Beach, California 90277 U.S.A.

FIELDING WORLDWIDE INC.

PUBLISHER AND CEO **Robert Young Pelton**
PUBLISHING DIRECTOR **Paul T. Snapp**
ELEC. PUBLISHING DIRECTOR **Larry E. Hart**
PUBLIC RELATIONS DIRECTOR **Beverly Riess**
ACCOUNT SERVICES MANAGER **Christy Harp**

EDITORS

Linda Charlton   **Kathy Knoles**

PRODUCTION

Gini Martin   **Chris Snyder**
Craig South   **Janice Whitby**

COVER DESIGNED BY **Digital Artists, Inc.**
COVER PHOTOGRAPHY BY **Zephyr Pictures**

Inquiries should be addressed to: Fielding Worldwide, Inc., 308 South Catalina Ave., Redondo Beach, California 90277 U.S.A., Telephone *(310) 372-4474*, Facsimile *(310) 376-8064*, 8:30 a.m.–5:30 p.m. Pacific Standard Time.

ISBN 1-56952-062-3

Library of Congress Catalog Card Number

94-068324

Printed in the United States of America

Letter from the Publisher

In 1946, Temple Fielding began the first of what would be a remarkable new series of well-written, highly personalized guidebooks for independent travelers. Temple's opinionated, witty, and oft-imitated books have now guided travelers for almost a half-century. More important to some was Fielding's humorous and direct method of steering travelers away from the dull and the insipid. Today, Fielding Travel Guides are still written by experienced travelers for experienced travelers. Our authors carry on Fielding's reputation for creating travel experiences that deliver insight with a sense of discovery and style.

Many of us who are bitten with the travel bug have never really sat down and figured out why we had such a good or bad time on our last trip. Stan Plog is the first person I have met who can make sense out of the travel experience and what makes it enjoyable. Great trips are not just dumb luck, lack of rain, sunsets and great margaritas. They are a combination of knowing who you are, what you expect and what the destination really delivers.

Why haven't you seen this material anywhere else? Because Stan has spent his career researching, interviewing and summarizing what travelers want for the travel industry. After much coaxing and cajoling we finally convinced Stan to publish this information for the first time. Inside this book you will get firsthand knowledge of how 13,500 experienced travelers rate specific destinations.

This book should be any traveler's first step in picking a vacation destination.

Today the concept of independent travel has never been bigger. Our policy of *brutal honesty* and a highly personal point of view has never changed; it just seems the travel world has caught up with us.

Robert Young Pelton
Publisher and CEO
Fielding Worldwide, Inc.

DEDICATION

To my two sons, Stephen and Gregory, with whom my wife, Georgia, and I have shared many great trips and hope to experience even more.

A WORD OF APPRECIATION

As is true with most books, a variety of people helped to make it all happen. In most cases, it may seem self serving to thank your publisher. But it is truly deserved in this case. Robert Young Pelton had great ideas that I believe have contributed to the usefulness of this book. He suggested the inclusion of maps that appear at the beginning of each vacation place rated, the use of color codes and icons to illustrate where various personality types might like to visit, and he enlarged the book to include more of the topics that I have learned about through years of continuous research on travel experiences. Also, his editorial comments helped to enliven and smooth out various chapters and sections.

In my company, Shelley Sasson deserves special praise and comment. She shepherded the document through its various stages, helped to correct and clarify sections throughout the book, and assisted heavily in the editorial review and style for the section that is the main focus of the book-Section II: Vacation Places Rated. Shelley, you know how much I appreciate your assistance and how difficult it would have been to complete this assignment without your presence. David Steininger did most of the word processing, either smoothing out my rough word processing documents or struggling through my difficult handwriting when I reverted back to my old habit of using paper and pen. Not to be forgotten are the various researchers and staff members of Plog Research who directed many more studies than I could personally handle. I have learned from each person and I want to offer my thanks. They are too numerous to mention, but their help is deeply appreciated.

ABOUT THE AUTHOR

Harvard trained Stanley C.Plog, Ph.D., CEO and chairman of Plog Research, Inc. in Los Angeles, is the travel industry's top guru and marketing consultant. For nearly 30 years, he has provided in-depth research and insights to travel industry leaders. These include most major U.S. airlines (such as American, United and Delta) and international carriers (British Airways, Lufthansa, Swissair), various hotel chains (Holiday Inns, Marriott, Hilton), rental car companies (Avis, Dollar, Budget), cruise lines (RCL, NCL, Costa, Silversea), numerous resorts and destinations (Hawaii, Switzerland, Portugal, Beverly Hills), tour operators and other travel related companies.

Plog Research interviews thousands of travelers each year to find out what they like, don't like, and where they plan to travel next. The American Travel Survey is the company's annual study on travel, from which Plog and his staff have gleaned hundreds of facts, figures and conclusions—information he shares now with you to make you a happier, smarter traveler.

Fielding Rating Icons

The Fielding Rating Icons are highly personal and awarded to help the besieged traveler choose from among the dizzying array of activities, attractions, hotels, restaurants and sights. The awarding of an icon denotes unusual or exceptional qualities in the relevant category.

RATINGS: Fielding Award, Author Selection, Money Saver, Expensive, Quality, Warning, Danger, Inexpensive, Mild Disapproval, Spacious, Cramped

CULTURAL: Museum/Art, Interesting Architecture, History, Book Reference, Artistically Important, Musically Interesting, Cultural Archeology, Crafts, Theatre

SIGHTS: Picturesque, Great Scenery, Market, Beaches/Resorts, Cultural, Fortress, Castles, Church

WHERE TO STAY: Simple, Luxurious, Cottage, Bed & Breakfast, Scenic, Business, Honeymoon, Chateau

TRAVEL TIPS: Arrival/Departure, By Air, By Water, By Train, By Car, Bus/Local Transit, Barge, River Boat, Calendar, Itinerary, Compass, Kids

ACTIVITIES: Downhill Skiing, X-country Skiing, General Sports, Water Sports, Sailing, Scuba Diving, Snorkeling/Diving, Deep-sea Fishing, Freshwater Fishing, Swimming, Hiking, Walking, Relaxing, Golf, Tennis, Horseback Riding, Cycling, Workout

SPECIAL INTEREST: Mystery, Singles, Romantic, Nude Beaches, Lecture, Spectacular Cuisine, Wine Tasting, Shopping, Nightlife, Cafe Stops, Gardening, Pro Sports, Festivals

TABLE OF CONTENTS

Section III:
Travel Smarter, Not Harder

LIST OF MAPS

Top 25 Domestic Destinations

Top 25 International Destinations

THE RESEARCH METHODS

Most of the information presented in this book comes from a study called the American Traveler Survey (ATS). It is an annual study conducted by my company, Plog Research, Inc. on the travel habits of Americans. To conduct the research, we draw a random sample of all U.S. households and send out a mail questionnaire with a postage paid return. The sample is balanced not only geographically for area of residence and household income, but also includes all ethnic groups. In addition, the survey includes approximately an equal number of men and women. The use of incentives, based on awarding prizes of free travel (cruises, airline tickets, some hotel and rental car awards), produces a return rate of approximately 50 percent—the 13,500 respondents reported on in this book. The study seeks in-depth information about both leisure and business travel habits and characteristics. It covers where people have traveled, mode of transportation to get there, sources of information used to plan the trips, who in the households contributed to the decision to go there, who selected the mode of transportation, and a variety of issues on what makes a pleasurable vacation and what can spoil it. More important, ATS obtains information used in this book on the destinations visited, hotels, airlines and cruise lines used, and which of these destinations and services these leisure travelers especially like. This latter set of questions allows me to develop the Satisfaction and Loyalty Indexes referred to in various chapters.

In addition, other large research projects also reported on in Vacation Places Rated include Hotel-Agent, Cruise-Trak and Tour-Trak. Each of these is also based on mail surveys, with incentives used to increase return rates. Hotel-Agent is a survey of 2000 full time travel agents and provides information on their views of the services provided by hotel chains to travel agencies and their clients. Cruise-Trak contacts over 2000 past cruisers and those who have never cruised to determine their images of various cruise lines and why some people either do or do not plan to cruise again or never will cruise. Tour-Trak is based on a continuing survey of persons who go on fully escorted tours, with over 14,000 returned questionnaires. It evaluates their tour experiences by country, with detailed information collected on the degree to which they liked or did not like various aspects of the services they received (the tour program, quality and location of the hotels, quality of the meals, etc.).

Finally, an untold number of other studies and experiences in my nearly 30 years as a travel researcher in dealing with the problems that all travelers face contribute to my conclusions throughout the book. It's a great field in which to do research and one which has kept my interest in high gear during this period of time. Fortunately my company has now risen to the position of dominance in the area of travel research and consulting. Each year we do more studies for more companies than any other organization. Throughout this time, my staff and I have always tried to convey very clearly to our clients what travelers really want in a vacation experience. We feel elated when our clients listen carefully and we can see improvements in their products and services, and dejected when they sometimes do not. Overall, we feel very satisfied because most of our clients don't call unless they want to make something better. We will continue to work toward the goal of providing you, the traveler, with a more enjoyable set of experiences wherever you travel, especially in protecting the natural environments of so many beautiful vacation places around the world.

If you have had a travel experience you would like to tell me about to help illustrate some of my points, or something that you disagree with, you can write to me at the address below. More than anything, however, I want to wish you a good trip. My overriding purpose in preparing this travel guide is to share what I have learned so that you will select the right place for your vacation and have a good time while you are there.

> Stanley C. Plog, Ph.D.
> Chairman & C.E.O.
> Plog Research, Inc.
> 18631 Sherman Way
> Reseda, California 91335

Section I: Guaranteeing a Great Vacation

PLAN YOUR VACATION THE RIGHT WAY

If vacations are important to you, more like a necessity than a luxury, then you need this book. I'll try to save you from making bad decisions and help you make the right ones. In addition to telling you about the best places to visit and the ones to avoid, you'll discover your travel personality so that you can make even better choices. I have included a simple quiz that tells you what kinds of vacations you'll enjoy the most and which places are most likely to make you happy. With this knowledge, you can choose the best destinations in the U.S. or elsewhere in the world that fit your personality. For the first time, you can leave town with greater confidence that the journey you take will provide the happiness and satisfaction you want. You should experience more emotional highs when you travel, and fewer disquieting lows. Do everything possible to make your dream trip a success!

Leisure travel requires making terribly important choices. If you select the wrong destination for that week or two, you've thrown away a lot of money and wasted precious vacation days. You may return home feeling disgruntled and out of sorts for some time to come. Nobody told you that everything wouldn't be idyllic. The city looked quaint in the promotional pictures, with smiling people and open spaces. The hotel's brochure displayed an attractive lobby and clean, handsomely decorated rooms. What you found was a dirty town that did not live up to its description, indifferent or hostile local citizens, and a run-down hotel featuring old beds and worn out carpeting. You won't go there again, but what place will you choose for your next vacation? It could have some of the same problems, unless you learn in advance about its qualities from a reliable source.

When most of us think about our next vacation, just the anticipation can make us feel excited weeks in advance and, sometimes, for days after we return. We dream about visiting new and exciting places, renewing old friendships, or enjoying a romantic getaway. We can also recharge our psychic batteries by getting rid of pressures and time schedules, contemplate the meaning of life in a quiet forest, be mesmerized by the waves at beachside, or gain a new sense of self-importance because of the respectful and courteous manner in which others now serve us throughout our travels. Or, we can simply let go and have a wild time from morning to night, or just collapse on the sands of a warm beach and "pig out" on great food.

Whatever the reasons, leisure travel is growing in importance in people's lives. A travel boom started in 1994 that will continue throughout most of the '90s. Why? Because, the recession, Gulf War, and belt tightening that corporate America forced on its workers led many people to postpone vacation plans, or take shorter trips closer to home during the last several years. But that can only last so long. After awhile, a sense of cabin fever sets in and most of us begin to say to ourselves, "I don't know how much longer the economy will be bad, but I'm not getting any younger. Who knows what tomorrow might bring? So, I'm going to enjoy myself while I've got my health and can still get around." That sense of, "I've gotta do something before I explode" has been building, and now the travel bubble is popping.

How do I know this is true? Through my company, Plog Research, Inc., I interview literally tens of thousands of travelers each year. My job is to find out what they want and what makes them unhappy, and then give straight advice to most major airlines, many hotel chains and cruise lines, a variety of rental car companies, various destinations, escorted tour operators and many travel publications. Based on solid research, I track trends in leisure travel habits and preferences for the services provided by these travel companies. My staff investigates what people like, why they like it, what they don't like, and where they plan to travel next. In short, I learn a ton of things about what makes a good vacation trip and a bad one. I want to pass that on to you. Leisure travel is expensive, in time and money. So, you should think about it and plan your trip as carefully as buying a new car. This book can greatly help you reduce your chances of having a bad vacation because you went to the wrong place—a destination that doesn't live up to its reputation or doesn't fit your personality. Or, perhaps you chose the wrong cruise line or got a travel "bargain" that turned out to be a rip-off. If you have only one vacation a year, don't blow it. Learn about the places you are more likely to enjoy, and know why in advance of your trip.

Most of the information I'll present in this book comes from my company's very large annual, rigorously executed study on travel, called the American Traveler Survey (ATS). It collects more information on travel than any other project of which I'm aware. Based on more than 13,500 completed questionnaires from Americans in all 50 states, it plumbs the depths of people's experiences. I've learned about which destinations send the greatest number of visitors home happy and contented, and which ones don't. I also discovered which destinations will grow in the future because these provide what travelers want and still possess a unique charm, and which ones are likely to decline because they are getting old and tired. I focus on the elements that make up a good trip, and the things that can spoil it. All in all, it's a pretty good way to plan your next vacation: learn from the mistakes of thousands of others, and benefit from their good experiences at the places they've told me about.

I'll include facts, figures and conclusions from a number of other studies I regularly direct—to round out the picture and give you more perspective on how to make better choices. I'll also throw in personal observations gathered from more than 25 years of learning about travel from people like you. I've learned how to travel better—and smarter—and I'll share those insights with you.

Let's get started and venture forth together as we explore the many opportunities of travel. It's exciting and addictive, and we should approach it with the state of mind suggested by Ralph Waldo Emerson who said, "Nothing great was ever accomplished without enthusiasm."

WHY YOU NEED A GREAT VACATION

A great vacation is your reward. You earned it! You deserve it! Don't let anyone make you feel guilty for taking the time to get away—or for having so much fun while you're there. You need vacations. Why?

- You'll probably live longer because you reduced stress and strain in your life. Somehow, memorable vacation experiences create lasting memories that are pleasant to recall and can help us get through bad days because we know another great trip is coming up—it's a fact. Dr. Harry L. Johnson, past president of the Life Extension Foundation, says, "Vacations are essential to health. But sitting around home is not enough. Health deteriorates when leisure time is marked by decreased physical activity, by social isolation or lack of mental stimulation. Medical records of 3000 men employed by ten companies revealed that, over several years, those who never got away from their jobs were 75 percent more likely to suffer heart attacks than their vacation-going coworkers."

- It can also help your mental health. The pressures of daily work seem less important while traveling. Knowing you have planned a great vacation can help you survive unpleasant experiences both at work and in home life. You'll probably find that relationships with your spouse and others around you also become "kinder and gentler."

- People who travel regularly do better at their jobs. James W. Bruskotter, previously the manager of personnel development at Marathon Oil, says, "I can't imagine a man with much potential who hasn't traveled. That applies to various levels— to people who become supervisors as well as executives." A senior midwestern businessman responsible for reviewing promotions explains, "When you need a man who can disengage himself, stand back and see all sides of a problem, you may

7

decide that a man who has been and seen and done will be able
to make the fast, difficult decisions. He'll get the nod."

- Children who go along with their parents on trips tend to stay
  ahead in school. Most of us believe that leisure trips can
  broaden our children's perspective on the world. But it's also
  true that travel helps them achieve better grades. An Illinois
  teacher with 23 years experience in elementary grades states,
  "I think experience is more valuable than what children read in
  books. And the ones who travel do seem to make better
  grades." Conney M. Kimbo, who was Associate Dean of Stu-
  dents at Grinnell College in Iowa strongly agrees. "A background of travel tends to be a significant advantage to a
  student's whole educational program. Logically, then, such a
  background is one of the factors considered on any application."

There are many reasons to consider vacations away from home as a necessity,
not a luxury. The payoff comes in so many ways that you probably hadn't
thought about, but it's there. Like me, I'm sure you can recall many times when
a fellow worker returns from a leisure trip and just bubbles with excitement in re-
counting the great experiences. You've probably done the same.

Travel: The New Giant Among Industries

You're also helping the economy when you travel, especially since many others
share your interests. The next time you lock your house to start a vacation, you'll
join more than 2.8 million Americans who, on average, also will begin their trips.
That's like moving all residents out of San Francisco—every day of the year! This
amounts to well over a billion vacation trips by Americans a year, each averaging
more than four nights away. Those numbers are growing. By the turn of the century, you and others like you should stretch the figures to 1.5 billion yearly trips,
if estimates provided by the U.S. Travel & Tourism Administration prove correct.
U.S. airlines will carry almost 330 million leisure passengers in 1995, just within
our 50 states, numbers that are also now increasing after several years of stagna-
tion.

International travel adds to the total. The U.S. Department of Transportation
estimates that 97 million people passed through U.S. airports last year on their
way to or from foreign destinations, about half of them Americans. Cruise line
passengers should total 5 million in 1995. All of the above figures are projected
to grow by four to five percent each year, compounded, for the next decade. If
true, almost all categories of travel will double in volume by the year 2005. Travel
and entertainment, as an industry, is big business—so big that it is the second
largest employer in the 50 states, and projected to become the largest within five
years. That means it will soon exceed agriculture, the automobile industry, or big
oil in size. About the same time, it will also become the largest employer in the
world.

Nearly 47 million foreigners visited the U.S. in 1994. They now contribute a $23 billion surplus to our balance of payments. If that sounds big, it's just a trickle compared to what will happen. As economies improve throughout the globe, especially in the Far East and third world countries, another 4 billion people could start traveling before the end of the century. At that time, it might seem a little crowded, at least compared to now, at many of the popular places you planned to visit—in the U.S. and elsewhere.

Are We Running Out of Places to Visit?

Have no fear that there won't be enough warm and sunny beaches, or exotic locales to provide you with the proper backdrops for your vacations. Throughout the year, I get calls from investors who want to know about the feasibility of developing a new luxury resort in Venezuela, complete with a five star hotel and private, natural tide pools for guests to swim in; or, someone inquires about the prospects for a billion dollar resort in Brazil; or, a new Caribbean hideaway wants to know how to get air service to bring in guests from North America and Europe. I also hear from existing destinations that ask how to freshen up their locales to get rid of the old, tired feeling that their own resorts now have. They hope that, if they spruce up the surroundings in the right way, their places will now appeal to a younger and more affluent group of travelers.

There will be plenty of destinations for you to choose from for a long time to come. It's just that you may not want to go to many of them because of their inherent problems. Some are very crowded; their popularity means that many tour programs include them as standard attractions in their itineraries. Others now look a little seedy and shopworn because success often does not foster a drive to keep up appearances. Or the locals may be rude and discourteous. They've learned that tourists keep coming, regardless of how badly they treat them. You too could receive surly and disinterested service. Also, it may be that the place just doesn't fit your personality, but you didn't know about that in advance. I want you to avoid these places, so I've also included places that rank lower in preference in this book.

Leisure travel did not always place as high on the list of alternatives as to how people spend their money. As recently as the late 1960s, only 25 percent of Americans had ever taken a trip on a commercial airline. Now those figures have reversed dramatically. Approximately 78 percent of the population has flown in a jetliner, according to Gallup trend studies released by the Air Transport Association (ATA). In fact, more people fly each year (about 35 percent) than had ever flown before, up to as recently as 1970. The basic psychology of the nation has changed. The American work ethic reigned supreme from the time of our founding fathers until nearly 40 years ago to the point that we considered vacations away from home to be a luxury that often could be skipped.

I can recall studies I conducted for clients in the early 1970s in which the primary research questions centered around how to get more people to take vacations, especially by air. At the time it was more popular to save money in order to buy a new living room set, kitchen appliances, or a new car. Or, perhaps put the money away for a down payment on a house, or save it for a rainy day. At the time, popular belief held that vacations were expensive and their benefits temporary—vanishing shortly after you returned home. You enjoyed the trip while you were on it, but the pleasure disappeared quickly. The money spent for something frivolous like vacation trips, it was believed, could buy something much more valuable for the house that could be enjoyed for years to come. Thus, leisure travel provided only temporary pleasure; material things offered long term enjoyment.

Oh, what a difference a few years can make. A majority of Americans now believe that material goods deteriorate over time and, ultimately, lose most of their original value. But, a wonderful trip with the family, or a special friend, can provide memories that can be savored for a lifetime. These memories are irreplaceable, whereas you can always buy a new and better dining set, a prettier sofa, or a new car with improved performance. Since leisure travel also offers opportunities for personal growth and important learning experiences that could change your life, it no longer is seen as a luxury that must compete against more important items in the family budget. It's a necessity that stands on equal footing against expenditures for food, rent, clothes and other necessities.

The world has awakened to the American experiences. Others want to enjoy what we have come to take as an inherent right. Europeans now travel more internationally than we do, a reversal of a pattern that was prevalent until the mid 1970s. Asians have taken to the skies in record numbers during the past decade, not just the Japanese but the newly affluent Koreans and millions from other "Asian tiger" nations. I can't leave out Latin America, where dictatorships have given way to more prosperous democracies with emerging middle classes that can now afford to fulfill some of their dreams by visiting foreign lands. Peace in the Middle East, along with the growing stability of an increasing number of nations in Africa, will also produce more and more travelers. As a result, various commercial airplane manufacturers confidently predict that the number of airplanes in the sky will double within a decade, even if U.S. airlines do not place another order.

Travel Now While the Time Is Still Ripe

These trends lead to a few simple conclusions:

1. The best known destinations in the world may be filled with wall to wall people before too long because new travelers typically want to visit the most popular places they have seen on TV or have read about in newspapers and magazines before they go to lesser known spots. They also have dreams and they want bragging rights in their neighborhoods. If they are the first to visit a famous city or resort, they can be the star attractions at business and social gatherings. Thus, if you have always longed to go somewhere that is well known, you may want to do it soon before you have to elbow your way through the crowds and confront even more souvenir shops and fast food places than currently exist. Destinations have a nasty habit of changing their character over time (I'll tell you why later on).

2. In general, costs of leisure travel will rise more rapidly than inflation during the coming decade, especially at these popular spots that can play the laws of supply and demand to their advantage. Hotel rates, held down by low occu-

pancy rates during the recession, are inching upward. Occupancies are now up, and most hotel chains are bumping up room rates several times a year. Again, the message is to visit that dream spot first, before you think about lesser known destinations, because you may be shocked at how expensive it will be in a few years.

3. Although there will be many new destinations coming on line during the next decade, expect most of them to be sun 'n fun spots (sandy beaches and warm water) or sports locales (ski areas, golf resorts, tennis camps) since these are man made. All it takes is investor money and a sunny location. There's still plenty of both in the world. But you can't design or build in tradition when you develop a resort, or add a sense of history and ambience with an architect's pen. These require decades, if not centuries, to achieve. If history and tradition are part of your special interests, you have another reason to begin planning that long awaited trip—now, and not later.

4. Finally, let's emphasize once more that a great vacation can turn you into a new *you*—healthier, happier, wiser, and probably better able to perform at your job and take on more responsibility.

Whatever your choice, go to your dream place first or save it for later, just make sure you go someplace now and don't delay. You need vacations, and you'll discover you're a better person for taking the time to escape from your daily cares.

WHY DO YOU WANT TO TRAVEL?

Answer a simple question—a question you probably have not thought about before. Why do you want to take a vacation trip, anyway? Does the answer seem self obvious to you? Or, can you only stumble and say, "Because... because..." ? Robert Louis Stevenson, in *Travels With a Donkey* (1878), commented, "For my part, I travel not to go anywhere, but to go. I travel for travel's sake. The great affair is to move."

Perhaps you too have itchy feet. You must be on the move, going whenever you can to any place that happens to appear on your personal radar screen. Nothing wrong with that except that you probably are missing out on a lot of enjoyment that comes from the anticipation of thinking about a well planned trip to a great place. Even worse, you've wasted a lot of money going to destinations that don't measure up to your expectations because you galloped off into the sunset with little thought about where you might end up. If you gain some understanding about your own travel motives, you can select better destinations and seek out more interesting activities while you are there.

Some Travel Motives: Which One Fits You?

In some research I conducted, I developed five basic travel motives that are worth listing to point out their relative importance. Decide which motive best describes you, and then see how many people are like you. Better yet, rank order these motives in order of importance because each of them fits everyone to some degree. It'll give you even a little more understanding of who you are. I purposely omitted the most popular choice—to be with friends or family members you love—because it doesn't say much about the inner you.

These travel motives are:

1. *To add interest and excitement to one's life*—especially true for people whose work-a-day world is not as challenging as they would like. Vacations take on special importance because they make work more bearable—there's always something to look forward to or to reflect on long afterwards.

2. *To add a sense of self-discovery or a sense of finding one's self*—the idea that many of us often search for the meaning of life and wonder about our position in the universe. Contact with people in other cultures, or viewing historic places, or quiet solitude in a forest can help us gain perspective as we address these cosmic-like questions.

3. *A chance to unwind and relax*—the need often expressed by busy people who simply want to get away to some enchanting place where they can slow down and once again "smell the roses." How many times have you also said this to yourself? This need is a temporary need, however. Once you've spent a couple of days recovering, one or more of the other motives will become dominant.

4. *Ego support*—travel provides reassurance to our bruised egos that are pounded daily by people and situations who challenge our basic feelings of self-worth. The experiences of others waiting on us while traveling, and being gracious to us and catering to our needs and demands, can help undo the damage inflicted by a "cruel world." Don't be afraid to admit the fact; it feels good when someone pays attention to us... even if you're paying for the gracious services you receive.

5. *Life is too short*—the idea that we all must face up to our own mortality, sometimes as a result of events that abruptly bring home the temporality of the human condition (for example, the death of a friend or relative). "I'm not getting any younger and I had better do some of the things I have always wanted to do before it is too late" is a statement we have all heard many times and have probably thought about ourselves. Life shattering experiences can make us reorder our priorities, often with a focus on enjoying things more while we're here.

When I prepared this list of motives in the form of test questions and presented them to travelers, the results surprised me. The rank order and relative importance of each of these motives can be seen in Figure 1. Before you look at it, remember to decide which one **best** describes why you like to travel, and rank order the rest, so that you can find out how many people share your motives. You'll learn a little bit more about yourself.

Figure 1	
Life is too short; travel while you can	32%
It adds interest to one's life	30%
Just need to unwind/relax	29%
Want ego support (care from others)	5%
It provides a sense of self-discovery	4%
	100%

The largest number of people (32%) show some concern about the brevity of their existence and feel they should *enjoy life* before something unforeseen happens. If this motive hits you, then taking that one big vacation you have dreamed about for a long time should happen soon. You'll be surprised at how much you'll enjoy it, with memories popping into mind at odd times long after the trip is completed. Plan on another excursion later in the year because you need these getaways to help maintain a sense that your existence does not just consist of work, work, work. The older you get, the more you begin to recognize that life should be approached one day at a time; enjoy it, savor it, and make certain you use time (vacation days) to do what you want to do.

If you selected a desire to *add interest to your life,* the second most popular choice, my research indicates that you may not be working in the job of your choice. It has become routine and boring and you don't see a way out of the situation in the near future. As a result, you will relish your time away from the job. For you, the best solution is to take frequent but shorter vacation trips. A weekend here; a four day trip there. Many of the places you go will be close to home, and you will probably jump in the family car a majority of the time. Although you won't spend more time away from home than someone who takes a couple of longer trips each year, frequent getaways provide something to look forward to, and memories to cherish long after your return.

Of almost equal importance to the first two items is the need to *unwind and relax* (29% choose this motive). If this fits you, then your work life is probably very intense, or problems at home catch up with you and add to your stress. Most often, your vacations should come at irregular times of the year—when the pressures build and you feel a need for a break. The tendency will be for you to make decisions on the spur of the moment as to where you'll go on that next trip. But you'll be better off if you do good planning in advance and write out a list of preferred spots. That way, you will have a better chance of ending up somewhere new (rather than the same old tried and true place) that is both interesting and relaxing. Find out about your travel personality (see section entitled, "What Kind of a Traveler Are You: A Quiz) and then look up which destinations fit your style.

If you belong to the small number of people (5%) who select wanting *ego support* as your primary motive, have no fear—you're not alone. It's a secondary reason for most people. We all enjoy being cared for and waited upon, though some people are less willing to admit it. A specific destination choice should be less important to you than making certain you select better quality hotels and restaurants where service is an art, and anticipating your every need is considered de rigueur. You might want to think about taking a cruise, especially with a luxury line, since they can envelope you with kindness and attention every waking moment. It can be a grand feeling.

Finally, if you seek a *sense of self discovery* when you travel (4% of travelers), you probably already know that places of quiet solitude meet many of your needs. Such times of reflection can offer a duality of deeper understanding. You can recognize that, in the eons of history, your personal troubles now seem unimportant. At the same time, you are likely to gather a greater sense of self esteem because you are also part of that history—and of nature in all its diversity and mystery. It's a chance to drop some of your excess emotional baggage and personal hang-ups. You should also consider going to somewhat isolated locations in foreign countries where the exposure to different cultures makes you think more about who you are and what you want to do with your life. These experiences can put more of your life in perspective and send you home refreshed, ready to tackle those problems you consider most important. Not many people may think the way you do, for you live on a somewhat higher plane. Selecting the right place to visit will take more careful thought and planning because fewer places provide the solitude and opportunity for reflection that you require.

Let's put some perspective on these travel motives because travel is addictive. If you haven't done it for awhile and then take a trip, you'll probably want to go away again—soon. If you're like some people, you may start traveling almost full time after you retire. So why does it capture people's imaginations to such a degree? When you talk to people in depth about why they like to travel, as I do, you get the feeling that it changes all the rules about how they live their lives. Everything gets tipped more in their favor, provided it was a good trip.

1. First, you can usually expect to raise your standard of living when you take a vacation. To see and do things you can't experience every day; eat better meals than you usually get at home, sleep in nice places with interesting histories and attractive decors. Vacations mean all this, and more. Cruises and resorts/spas have grown greatly in popularity in recent years because they dramatically raise those standards for most people through the care and attention that are provided.

2. You can relax—really relax. You don't have to get up for a job. You can be around and not do a thing without feeling guilty because there's yard work or housework to do. Your schedules are your own and not set by someone else—your boss, regular meetings at the P.T.A. or your church, the need to visit relatives you haven't seen for awhile. Forget about obligations and concentrate on enjoying yourself. That's the essence of a good vacation. The vacation days you spend at home usually don't provide the same sense of escape.

3. You don't have to take guff from anyone. Since you're paying the bills, you're in charge. You can make demands on other people and expect them to do your bidding. If they don't, you can yell at them, and they're not supposed to yell back because they're paid by you. That's a nice sense of power.

4. Let's face it, pampering feels good. We all need it. It helps us recover from the stresses and strains we feel constantly. Enjoy good service and the attention you get when others wait on you. That's part of life's simple pleasures. If you don't feel you're getting that extra bit of attention you want, then demand it.

All of this adds to your feelings of self worth. Many people won't admit directly that they need to feel better about themselves, but we all do. It's a universal human condition. Constant love and attention can make us all grow personally, even if that attention comes mostly when we travel.

TEN GOLDEN TIPS TO MAKE SURE YOU HAVE A GREAT VACATION

Travel is really a simple pastime. Just get in your car and drive someplace, or hop on an airplane and enjoy the exotic and unusual things that a faraway destination can provide.

Or is it all that easy? Without giving much thought to what kind of a trip you want to take, what you want to do when you get there, and whether the destination will really satisfy everyone who's going along with you, your hopes and dreams could be turned into a shambles. So here are a few tips to make sure you don't waste your time or your money the next time you leave home to start that great vacation.

1. **Find out who you really are.**
   You already know that you have a unique personality, and you also know that you've enjoyed some places more than others. Therefore, take the little quiz in this book (see "What Kind of a Traveler Are You: A Quiz") to define your personality and then determine which destinations in the U.S. and the world are most likely to provide you with the vacation experiences you desire (see "Vacation Places Rated"). Follow this rule and you are likely to have more great vacations and fewer bad ones.

2. **Do what you've always wanted to do.**
   As I said earlier, vacations offer that unique opportunity to get away from always having to conform to others' wishes. Now you can be the real you, enjoy what you like most, and even do things that others would not have expected of you. Just do it and don't delay. This is especially true when you think about the more exotic or expensive trips that you have put off because of the difficulty of getting there or the costs involved. The older you get, the less likely you will have the energy or the health to do those odd things. So, start working on those kinds of trips now.

   You face a special problem when your spouse or friend is a different type of personality than you, as based on the quiz in this book. However, that can be solved by making sure that the places you select rate seven or higher (on a ten point scale) for each of your personality types (again, see "Section II: Vacation Places Rated"). If so, that destination is likely to provide enough of the kinds of activities that each of you will enjoy. Then you'll both have a great vacation, even if you do somewhat different things while you're there.

3. **Read, read, read.**

   To really enjoy a place, you need to know more about it. The more you know, the more you'll be able to select the things that appeal to you and the better you'll understand the interesting culture, people, or unique sense of history of those destinations. Your sense of enjoyment will be multiplied immeasurably. That way you'll not miss that great little winery in Napa Valley, California or the Bordeaux region of France, the museum in Europe that targets your special interests, or the special events that will happen while you're there (music festivals, historic pageants, local celebrations).

   Many sources of information exist. Once you've selected a place, travel guides provide in-depth perspective that unquestionably enhance the value of your trip. Fielding has more than 40 of these, and other publishers also provide a number of well researched titles. Travel magazines, Sunday newspapers, and some national newspapers and Sunday supplements also feature stories by travel writers who can give you many new insights about what's going on at various places. Don't forget visitors bureaus in the U.S. and foreign government tourist offices located in some of our major cities. They have tons of information available, along with willing, helpful staffs. I've listed the addresses and telephone numbers for the bureaus for each of the destinations evaluated (see "Vacation Places Rated").

   The important point is to spend time getting the information necessary to ensure a fabulous vacation.

4. **Plan, plan, plan.**

   Not all of your time will be devoted to reading. A lot of it should go into planning and coordinating your activities so that, once there, you don't waste precious hours trying to find out where to go, how to get there, what transportation to use, or how long all of these activities might take. Even such little details as not being aware of national holidays in a country can foul up an important part of your trip because you may not be able to visit a museum you had planned for that day, many of the restaurants have closed, or public transportation stops running just at the time you want to get back.

   Lay out the most logical path for your trip, how many miles or places you want to cover in one day (or you may decide to settle in just one spot), the most important things that you want to see or do, and the days that would be best to pursue them. Cover all of the little details about where to get a rental car (if you plan on one), the train schedules, or when some of the sightseeing activities take place and how expensive they are. The more you prepare, the more you'll enjoy. Typically you will find that good planning allows you to increase the number of things you see and do by 50 percent, while lowering the amount of stress you feel while doing them.

5. **Don't take the cheapest price.**

   How many times have you been warned to be careful of those bargains that are too good to be true? As is usually said, they probably are too good to be true. Travel scams are the fifth largest source of consumer complaints, after problems with new and used car dealers, home improvement scams, auto repair rip-offs, and mail order and telemarketing fraud. These data come from a joint 1994 report by the Consumer Federation of America (CFA) and the National Association of Consumer Agency Administrators (NACAA). If you're concerned that you may have encountered a possible rip-off, get in touch with Call For Action, an international nonprofit organization in Washington, D.C. at their toll free number, ☎ *(800) 647-1756.*

Especially in travel, good bargains are everywhere. But you should usually try to get the best rates only from well established names, like major airlines, recognized hotel chains, cruise lines that your travel agent or friends tell you about, etc. If you stay with names you recognize, or that have been recommended to you, and then shop for bargains, you'll typically come out ahead. Read the chapter entitled, "Getting the Best Travel Bargains" to know more about how to be a smart shopper.

6. **Start your vacation from where you sleep.**
Don't make the silly mistake of a friend of mine. He's bright, well traveled, normally has a lot of common sense, and sufficient income to take the kinds of trips he desires. He discovered an incredible price on a round trip to Italy for his wife and himself (about one-third the normal cost), so he suddenly decided to go. All fine and good, except that since the airfare was so cheap, it also put him in the mood that he should choose bargain hotels. He paid an average of $65 a night and bitched and moaned the whole time he was there (and afterward). He could have upgraded for $20 to $30 more each night and really enjoyed himself. Much of the trip seemed to be wasted because the poor hotels cast a pall over all of his travels.

Your hotel room is your refuge, your haven, and your place to relax after a day of heavy activity or some stress. A nice room just makes you feel better about yourself and the world around you. At a resort, you may spend half or more of your time in it, so its importance cannot be overlooked. Select a number of good hotels, and then look for which one currently offers a great price.

7. **Variety is the spice of life.**
People I classify as *venturers* tend to choose a different spot each year for their vacations. Therefore, they need little of this advice. But *dependables* are more likely to find a spot they like and return to it each year to immerse themselves in the things they enjoy most. As long as you read, plan well, and select destinations from this book that fit your personality type, you have reduced the possibility that you're going to have a bad trip. Therefore, get out and do something different each year so that your life has more spice and nice in it. Even your personality will probably seem to be a little more lively by doing different things each year.

8. **Get the right equipment.**
Getting the right equipment for your trip is the least expensive part of travel. Luggage that costs $100 to $150 will last more than twice as long as that costing $50. You'll be surprised at how well quality gear is designed to pack

many of the odd things that you need when you travel and how you can get more into a small suitcase. Also, good luggage with its side pockets and dividers takes less time to pack when you're getting ready to leave. How much is your time worth? I personally learned long ago that I don't like to get up earlier in the morning just to spend more time packing for a trip because of inadequate luggage. I'd rather be out enjoying things.

Also, get yourself a good camera. The inexpensive throwaway camera almost should be declared illegal for serious travelers. Cheap lenses don't get good pictures. Therefore, consider buying one of the new quality "point and shoot" 35mm cameras, especially one that has a zoom lens. These cameras require no adjustments from you for either focusing or setting the shutter. They do all of that automatically (in contrast to the fixed focus lenses on cheap cameras). Many of these have now been designed to be small pocket versions that sell for $100 to $150 at discount and they take excellent pictures. Not only will you have better travel memories, but the camera will serve you well for all the other photos you take throughout the year. One little hint as you shoot away on the trip: get closer to most of your subjects in order to make them more recognizable and particularly help them come alive in your photos. Remember, the grand vista that you take in with your eyes will probably be reduced to a small 4" by 6" print. This advice especially applies to taking pictures of people. The most common mistake is to stand too far away with the result that you do not truly capture the expressions of your subjects' faces or you lose the sense of what you were trying to photograph.

Finally, don't forget good walking shoes. You'll spend a lot of time on your feet. A pair of good leather shoes is usually more comfortable than jogging shoes over an extended period of time.

9. Think right; pack light.

If you've traveled a lot, you've probably learned this lesson on your own. If you haven't, learn from the mistakes of others.

Wise travelers take fewer clothes and belongings with them than they think they will actually need. They choose flexible coordinates that will get them through many situations. If need be, they'll wash a few things in the sink in their hotel room or send them out to the hotel cleaners on their trip. If you move around much, you get tired of carrying the extra baggage that, after the trip is over, you find you really didn't need. The lighter you travel, the more you'll enjoy everything because you have a greater sense of personal freedom and movement as you go from place to place. The more you have to pack or unpack, the more you just get disgusted with yourself for not having thought about that in advance.

10. Take the hand of an expert.

Unless you are really into the Internet or you use a CD-ROM (a very small minority of the population), spend some time seeking out expert advice. Travel agents generally know more than you do about how to get bargains, what kinds of things you can do at various places, and the ways to ensure that you don't get ripped off wherever you go because that's what they do every day. They have lots of information sources at their fingertips. I talk more about this later on in the book, but you need to make sure you select someone whose personality seems to mesh with yours and whose experience and judgement you trust.

Also, talk to representatives at city or state visitors bureaus or foreign government tourist offices, especially in person, if you can. The Los Angeles office of the Swiss National Tourist Office once helped plan a trip for me through Switzerland in which train connections sometimes were only four minutes apart. I would never have tried that without their advice (trains always run on time there!). My wife and I had a better time because we saw more each day and spent less idle time sitting around train stations.

Most experienced travelers probably already follow a third to a half of these tips, but forget or don't think about the others. The more you take into account all of them, the more you will probably enjoy your vacation.

WHAT CAN MAKE A VACATION TRULY HEAVENLY—OR ONE THAT'S MADE IN HELL

Many things can ruin a vacation. The restaurants you chose weren't up to the quality you expect, the weather was bad for most of the trip, the hotel was dirty, or you missed your flight connection and the cruise ship sailed without you. Nature's disasters lie beyond the control of even the most careful planners. But, let's do what we can about those areas in which you should be able to take charge of your life on that all important trip. Make the right decisions, based on good knowledge, and more things should go right for you.

What Makes a Vacation Great

The 13,500 people who participated in my company's American Traveler Survey were asked about what they like most about their favorite destinations. Although their choices of great places vary from Maine to Tahiti, from New Orleans to the heart of Africa, the answers given as to what makes a place great and, therefore, the vacation truly memorable, are relatively limited in number. Even more striking is the fact that two qualities are so very fundamental and dominate everything else by wide margins.

Figure 2 summarizes what these travelers said. It shows that the beauty and scenery of a place lead the list, followed by the feeling or ambience that the area radiates. Still important, but further down, are such items as good weather, friendly or interesting people, the availability of good sports facilities, great restaurants and good food, and the opportunity to pursue historic or cultural interests. Measuring at very low levels are such items as good local transportation, that the area offers good value for the money, and that it has good accommodations.

Something is missing in this list of top ten—something that used to be very important a couple of decades ago—good shopping, which translates as lots of things to buy at reasonable prices. It is mentioned by only three percent of travelers. Very few places in the world offer bargains for Americans anymore. As a result, it's not very important as a motivating factor for travel. So, don't expect shopping to be great at most of the places you'll visit.

Let's take a closer look at those items that are most important. You should raise a few questions about the destinations you are considering for your next trip to determine how well they measure up on fundamental characteristics.

When travelers talk about beautiful scenery, their most frequent references are to beautiful countryside (pretty valleys, majestic mountains, multi-colored landscapes) and attractive beaches (lots of white, soft sand, clear blue or green water, small waves, and attractive coves and inlets). In addition, they tell me that they want a place where they can drive around, without encountering big crowds, to see the natural sights. This desire is especially important if it is an area that has maintained its natural and unspoiled qualities. Lakes, national parks, and big trees can all add to this overwhelming feeling of natural beauty, which creates its own sense of serenity. So, the question remains: when you think about your next destination, just how much beauty and scenery does it really have?

When we examine qualities of ambience or the "feeling" a place creates, a very close second in order of importance, we now introduce some of the man-made qualities that can truly make a vacation spot great. To travelers, ambience or atmosphere typically refers to the fact that there are many things to do there. Lots to do can vary all the way from enjoying quaint villages that invite travelers to stroll and enjoy the sights, sounds, and aromas, to a drive through the countryside that is rich in history and traditions. Although you may feel you just want to unwind on your next trip, that feeling typically lasts only a couple of days. Select places that offer many appealing activities so that you don't get bored.

Also part of the ambience or atmosphere, and growing in importance in recent years, is whether the environment seems to be healthy and clean. Leisure travelers are becoming more conscious about pollution and waste wherever they go. For example, visitors often comment on the cleanliness of the rivers, lakes, and the air in Switzerland. Even an industrialized nation can provide a clean and wholesome environment if it works on the problem with Switzerland's dedication.

One final point on ambience or atmosphere: some people also mention that they do not want a place to be too crowded. Crowds obviously can contribute to an oppressive feeling and a desire to leave in order to get more personal breathing space. The bigger the city you choose, the more likely you will encounter heavy traffic, crowded sidewalks, and busy department stores—some of the things you may be trying to escape by leaving home.

If I asked you what good weather means to most people, the third item on the list, you would undoubtedly give the right answer. By an overwhelming ratio (more than twelve to one), people state that they want a place to be warm and comfortable, without rain, so that they can be outside and participate in all the things that they want to do every day while on vacation. Warm, predictable weather usually enhances any vacation. Only a small number, about two out of 100 to be exact, state they would rather have a place that has cool, fall-like temperatures. Unless you have other reasons to visit a place at a special time, go there only when you think you can enjoy great weather. I once caught a cold because I hadn't dressed adequately for the damp, cold weather in the English countryside in November. Being sick spoiled part of the vacation for both my wife and me.

One out of five travelers state that they must have good sports facilities and activities available if they are to be happy. Surprisingly, no sport category dominates this list. Golf, tennis, fishing, skiing, hiking and camping broaden the appeal of a destination. This reflects very personalized interests. You have to decide what sports you want to pursue, if any, when you're traveling. In addition, about one out of seven travelers indicate that the availability of great restaurants and a chance to eat well contribute to making vacations memorable.

Finally, cultural and historic interests dominate choices for about one out of nine travelers. This may be somewhat surprising since some of the top travel destinations in the world, such as the popular countries and cities of Europe, have an appeal based almost entirely on the culture and background of the area. For that minority of travelers, however, their strong interests in the sense of history derived from the buildings, monuments and museums that go with such history, will lead them to return again and again to these famous spots.

A few items have very low levels of choice (5% each), such as good local transportation, the area offers good value, or the accommodations are especially good. Although some of these qualities may not contribute greatly to the memorability of a vacation, their lack can quickly spoil a trip, as we will see in a moment.

Figure 2

What Makes a Vacation Memorable

(Answers From Leisure Travelers)

Scenic beauty	53%
Good ambience/atmosphere	48%
Good weather	27%
Friendly/interesting people	22%
Availability of sports/personal interest activities	19%
Great restaurants/good food	14%
History and culture present	12%
Good local transportation	5%
Good value for the money	5%
Good accommodations	5%

The most important point growing out of this discussion is that you should make certain that your interests, and those of others traveling with you, can be covered very well wherever you're planning to visit. Scenic beauty and the feeling or atmosphere of a place dominate all choices. If you concentrate most on whether or not these two characteristics can be satisfied at your choice of spots, then you probably made a good decision. You and everyone in your traveling party will return home happy and satisfied.

What Can Ruin a Vacation

Having looked at the characteristics of a destination that can make a trip truly memorable and enjoyable, let's turn to the factors that can give you a vacation from hell. In planning your next trip, you should also ask yourself whether you have thought about the important things that could make you and everyone else traveling with you very unhappy.

In Figure 3 we can see what travelers tell me bothers them the most. The striking fact is that almost everyone mentions their distaste for dirt and filth—a dirty hotel room, the area around the hotel seems dirty and run down, or that poverty is evident almost everywhere they go. How many times have you actually asked yourself before taking a trip, "Did I really select a hotel that is clean and attractive?" Or, "is there lots of poverty and filth there?" You should. We already discussed why you need to think carefully about getting a comfortable, clean hotel room. It is your base of operations and your place of repose when you want to relax after a heavy day of sightseeing. It's a place of refuge and retreat when you are tired or not feeling very well, and you will probably remember your experiences in it more clearly than many of the other things you did on the trip. Also you will sleep much better if your room feels clean, safe and secure from the bad elements that are present in every locality. You don't want to walk outside of your hotel and see more dirt and filth. That's not what vacations are supposed to be.

Can you really enjoy a place where people constantly beg on the streets and the stench of unsanitary conditions and crowded ghettos permeates the air? Each of us is concerned about poverty, but it's not something we try to do something about when we're on vacation. When you're on vacation, you're supposed to have the opportunity to forget about the world's problems, not be reminded of them. Avoiding dirty cities or places that have lots of visible poverty is worth thinking about in your future travel decision making.

Further down the list, but still important, are those items that make you feel on guard all the time, with the result that you have lost the ability to be relaxed and comfortable. When a place is very expensive, you have to watch what you spend. High prices make you scrimp and cut back on what you really would like to do. As a result, your trip is less fun. The prevalence of many tourist traps also adds to the feeling that you need to keep your guard up. Combine that with unfriendly or indifferent local people, and you have the ingredients to make a stew consisting of some very unpleasant travel experiences. Too much commercial development can spoil the ambience of an area, a topic we will talk more about in a later section. The fact that few people speak English can often make it difficult to get around for some people who are less comfortable traveling on their own. Again you may not feel totally relaxed because you wonder how you can get from one place to another without getting lost, or you may not be able to order what you want in a restaurant since you can't read the menu. Either situation can make you feel more tense.

Figure 3

Factors That Can Spoil or Ruin a Vacation Trip

(Answers From Leisure Travelers)

Hotel is dirty or run down	77%
It is dirty everywhere	72%
The locals try to "rip you off"	58%
It is rainy or cold/bad weather	46%
Poverty is evident everywhere	43%
It is very expensive	40%
Too many tourist traps	36%
Local people are unfriendly	35%
There is too much commercial development	24%
Few people speak English	21%

Just as we talked about the small number of things that contribute to making a great destination great, only a few things have to be considered regarding what can make it seem like a trip to hell. You should ask, is the place dirty and unkempt, particularly the hotel you will be using? Or is it so expensive that you will feel you have to constantly watch your spending? Are the local people accommodating and friendly, or do they offer indifferent and even hostile service? Do the locals try to sell you cheap and overpriced trinkets at the many tourist traps and souvenir shops, or can you trust most of what they tell you? Read enough travel guides or travel articles in magazines and newspapers and you'll get some hints. But, first start with the vacation places that most people say are great—those places we review later in this book.

WHAT KIND OF A TRAVELER ARE YOU: A QUIZ

On the surface, it makes a lot of sense: different destinations should appeal to different types of people. Marketing executives for most travel related companies believe this, but they develop very few strategies to cope with their conclusions. They make most of their decisions on how to buy advertising space in magazines or time on television and radio based on the income levels of the audiences of those magazines or TV and radio stations. Their simple assumption is that people with bigger incomes also travel more.

When travel marketers rely on demographic characteristics such as age, income, sex and marital status, they can learn a limited number of things about you. But, sometimes the findings are so self evident that they don't predict much at all. Higher income families (and individuals) live in more expensive homes, buy more goods and services (and also buy **more expensive** items), and send their children to better schools. Older persons tend to be less active in life; men buy more sports equipment than women; and, single people eat out more often than married couples, and so on.

These characteristics also predict travel patterns to some degree. Expensive resorts place a greater share of their advertising in very upscale magazines to reach the very affluent. Tour operators tend to target empty nesters (no children at home) and retired persons. Adventure tour operators go after younger, very active single persons when they sell their treks through the rain forest or biking caravans in the Swiss Alps.

But these are such crude measures. Consider your own neighborhood. By definition, most of your neighbors share relatively similar incomes (to afford a house or rent payments equal to what you pay), and a relatively similar degree of marital status and occupation also probably exists on your block (professionals, or middle management, or blue collar, etc.). But, among all the people you know on your block, **it will be surprising if any two families—or individuals—experienced similar kinds of vacations** during the past year. One family may have gone to the Caribbean to be on the beach; another charged off to a jazz festival in Newport,

Monterey or Sacramento, other neighbors just returned from a two week escorted tour of Europe; a fourth explored the beautiful old mansions of the deep South. This lack of commonality points out the problems of using demographics to predict behavior. General trends can be noted (high income people spend more and travel more), but specific behaviors, habits and preferences largely remain hidden. In order to predict with greater accuracy what you as a consumer are likely to do, I need to inquire into your personality makeup. *The more I can help you know about you as an individual, the greater the likelihood that you will select and plan a more satisfying trip.* Without understanding the type of person you are, you could be convinced by friends and associates, or by a travel agent, to select vacation trips that are not very satisfying because the people you listened to have personalities quite different from your own. So, if you can learn something about yourself, you should be able to make better choices about where to go on that next trip.

But personality research always proves difficult. The hundreds, if not thousands, of individual traits, preferences, motivations and behaviors that make us unique also mean that finding a common thread to present a simplified description of personality patterns can be very difficult. I have spent over 25 years perfecting a system that I used increasingly in my company for a variety of clients. It predicts not only people's travel preferences, but their media tastes, beverage choices, and a host of other tendencies as well. It can work for you. Since it forms the cornerstone of the building blocks for helping you make better travel decisions, take a few moments of your time to answer the questions and determine your final scores. There are no right or wrong answers—or personality types. Just different people with different interests. You can still understand most of the book without completing the list but you will learn much more about travel—and about how to choose a better vacation for you—if you take the plunge and complete the test. Whoever travels with you on trips should probably also complete the test and see if his or her personality matches yours. It might explain why you like the same places, or why each of you typically selects a very different kind of destination.

Your Travel Personality Quiz

It only takes a couple of minutes of your time, but you can probably learn a lot about your travel personality and the places that you'll like the most for your next vacation. So, answer **every** question (the test isn't valid, if you don't).

Please indicate the degree to which *each* of the following statements applies to you. Does it apply very much, somewhat, a little, or not at all?

	Very much	Some- what	A little	Not at all
1. I prefer to visit places that have not been discovered, especially before hotels and restaurants are built.	☐	☐	☐	☐
2. I will hurry to get to places, even when I have plenty of time.	☐	☐	☐	☐
3. I am actively involved in a rigorous physical fitness program.	☐	☐	☐	☐
4. I would generally rather go for a walk than read a book.	☐	☐	☐	☐
5. I have more energy than most persons my age.	☐	☐	☐	☐
6. I get very frustrated when I'm stuck in traffic.	☐	☐	☐	☐
7. I make decisions quickly and easily	☐	☐	☐	☐
8. Crowds in shopping malls have always bothered me.	☐	☐	☐	☐

How to Score Yourself

For each of the questions, give yourself points as follows:

If you answered:		Score yourself:
Very much	=	4 points
Somewhat	=	3 points
A little	=	2 points
Not at all	=	1 point

Two different personality measures are contained in this quiz—the **A** scale and the **B** scale. The A scale consists of all of the odd numbered questions (1, 3, 5 & 7). So, count up your total on these items. You can have anywhere from 4 points (answered all as "Not at all") to 16 points (answered all as "Very much"). When you tally it, remember your total on the A scale.

Depending upon your point total on the A scale, your personality is classified as follows:

A Scale

Point total:	Travel Personality Type:
4 to 8 points	Dependable
9 to 12 points	Centric
13 to 16 points	Venturer

Score the B scale the same way. It consists of the even numbered questions (2, 4, 6, 8). Tally up your points on it and determine what type of person you are.

B Scale

Point total:	Travel Personality Type:
4 to 9 points	Mellow
10 to 16 points	Active

With this information, you can now determine which of six personality types you are. So, you can be:

Active Venturer

Mellow Venturer

Active Centric

Mellow Centric

Active Dependable

Mellow Dependable

Read on because you'll now learn some things about yourself—what you are like as a person and the kinds of vacation places you will probably enjoy the most. We describe the A scale types first, the *venturers, centrics* and *dependables*, followed by a review of the meaning of the B scale—the *actives* and *mellows*. And, when we talk about the top destinations later on in the book, we separate them into the spots that will be enjoyed most by the various types of groups listed above.

The A Scale:
Venturers to Dependables

The three personality types we just mentioned actually represent separate places on a continuum as follows:

Dependables	Centrics	Venturers

Thus, *venturers* and *dependables* place at opposite sides on this personality trait scale and prefer very different kinds of vacations and activities while on a vacation. *Centrics* fall in the middle and generally can swing one way or the other to some degree to please their travel partners. If you and your partner place at opposite ends of this scale, you will face greater difficulty in finding places that seem mutually interesting and exciting. Wherever you decide to go, you will probably often end up pursuing very different kinds of activities and interests. This *venturer-dependable* scale, as we call it, is the more important of the two scales on which you tested.

So, let's get into describing each of the personality types.

Venturers
(Scale A: Score of 13 to 16 Points)

Leisure travel occupies a central place in your life. If you are a typical *venturer*, you go to more places—and more often—than anyone else. That's why we call you a *venturer*—someone who ventures forth very eagerly and excitedly.

You'd rather fly than drive to where you're going because driving takes too much of the time you could spend at the destination pursuing the things you like to do. Then you want to rent a car and start out on your own, almost without a plan—and **without** a tour guide—to discover the unexpected sights, sounds and culinary delights that every new travel experience can bring. You definitely do not like to travel with a group or by following a heavily determined itinerary. If you ever joined an escorted tour, it probably was by accident and you will not willingly make that choice again. You want freedom, glorious freedom, to follow your interests of the moment. You are happiest when you feel unfettered and unrestricted by the dictates and commands of others.

Typically, you like to visit relatively unknown and uncommon destinations long before travel writers have discovered them and encouraged hordes of people to come. You listen to the unique travel tales of your friends and associates, and eagerly read about hidden, but interesting, places that someone has discovered. You will even put up with inadequate hotels and food if you can be there before commercial development—and the crowds of tourists—consume the place. Above all, you want a sense of spontaneity in your trips, a feeling that something new and fresh will happen every day, and perhaps several times a day. That adds a sense of *joie d'vivre* to your travel experiences.

Unique cultures especially attract you. The opportunity to meet people of different backgrounds, languages and social standards holds a special allure. Even when you don't speak the language, a frequent occurrence for someone with your venturesome spirit, you'll get around just fine. Sign language, a handful of words you've picked up, a lot of pointing (to pictures of where you want to go or of food you want to order), and even some laughing moments will help you get comfortably through just about every situation you encounter. No trinkets or souvenirs for you. Rather, you will buy only authentic arts and crafts, clothes or other reminders of your grand escapes. Everything must be real, with no sense of falseness.

History may hold a great fascination. But you will avoid Buckingham Palace, the Eiffel Tower, and Paul Revere's New England stopping places in favor of lesser known old cities and buildings that exude their own sense of importance and romance, even if they're not listed in guidebooks. You prefer to discover an ancient monastery, old fort or historic building quite by chance, wander through its quiet interior unhampered by crowds, and try to figure out for yourself what mysteries it holds.

From this little personality quiz, we also know a lot more about you—beyond your travel habits. What you do on a trip, in many ways, is a reflection of your daily life-style. Again, the higher your score on the scale, the more you are likely to pursue activities described below.

You love to experiment with life. That can take many forms and options. New products, especially technology, often hold a special fascination. You may be the first one in your neighborhood to own a new type of stereo sound system for your home, or buy a brand new model of a sports utility vehicle, or to experiment with a new personal digital assistant (PDA) that has just been released in the marketplace. You are quite willing to try out new products long before these become popular or more reasonably priced. The joy of discovery far outweighs the risks associated with buying products that don't live up to their promise or that will soon become more reasonably priced after more competition takes over in the marketplace. Searching, seeking, probing, looking for something new and different, always wanting something new in your life—these are characteristics that friends and relatives would probably say are part of your personality if asked about you by outsiders.

This constant interest in what is new also has a flaw. You can experience some difficulty in stabilizing your life. With such varied interests, pursuits and hobbies, you might lack a central focus that can help provide a sense of direction and stability. If everyone was like you, society might not have that central tendency of beliefs and social mores—the virtues most of us believe in—and could veer off course within a generation. Even you can experience the discomfort, at times, of wondering who you really are.

Even your media habits don't follow the norm. Typically you read more than most—books, magazines and newspapers—and watch TV less. When you turn on the "tube," you are much less likely to prefer any of the top ten sitcoms or "soaps." Instead, you'll seek out dramas, special news magazine format shows, and selected sports (football and basketball; you have less interest in baseball or hockey). You hold definitive opinions about much of what you see happening in the world, strongly prefer commentators who agree with your views and are relatively comfortable and at ease with the decisions you make. This low level of anxiety about how you are handling your life's affairs adds not only to creating an aura of self confidence that is evident to your circle of friends, but also helps to make you relatively successful in your occupation and various other pursuits in your life. Confidence breeds success because others will accept what you say or otherwise follow your lead. But, if you haven't found the right job, you may feel somewhat like a misfit because others don't quite seem to catch on to what you're thinking. That feeling, of having ideas others don't understand, often leads *venturers* to go out on their own to start up new businesses.

Most likely you convey a friendly personality to others, but part of that amiable exterior is only skin deep. You tend to be a bit of a loner. Because your ideas are often different from the people around you, and the fact that you can be very contemplative or reflective, means that you frequently seek personal space. You'd rather be alone, or doing things on your own with no schedule or commitments. That's a formula for a truly great vacation. Just wander around and take whatever time seems warranted to explore the interesting sights of the day, or to pursue personal sports and other activities. You may put on a pleasant face, and appear to be enjoying the company of others who are with you, but that often is just a "cover." You might wish they'd go away so you could pursue a schedule of your own making.

Exercise and good health habits—proper diet, some use of vitamins and supplements, and following a disciplined routine to get enough sleep and exercise, even when you travel—are likely to be part of your daily commitment. Participation in individual sports, like skiing or tennis, are more likely for you than social sports, such as golf or bowling. You might even own some exercise equipment at home, a treadmill or a stair climber.

So, in conclusion, we have a travel personality who likes to explore more than average, is willing to risk taking a less than satisfying vacation by choosing a place that's off the beaten path, and may read a lot of books and magazines to learn about where else to go that is truly different from the last place visited. All in all, that's a definition of a venturesome personality. Look for destinations in this book that achieve ratings of 7 or higher. You're more likely to end up with a great vacation.

Dependables
(Scale A: Score of 4 to 8 Points)

If you read the descriptive section on *venturers*, you reviewed a personality quite the opposite of yours. You prefer a life that is more structured, stable and predictable. You would rather follow some set patterns or routines in your life so that you are more likely to know what will happen during each day and, therefore, can plan or prepare for it much better.

A boring life? Hardly. A sense of routine can make all of the changes in your life seem much more interesting and exciting. Besides, your type of personality provides an extraordinarily important function in this or any other nation. Through your commitment to consistency, you help keep society from being pulled off course by *venturers* who constantly want to try something new and different. Without the stability that you provide to daily social life in your community, there would be few constant, common values that hold us all together and give the nation a sense of direction and purpose. For this reason, we have labeled your type, *dependables*. At work, in your church (if you attend), or in your lodge group, you are often the one that many people ask to get things done because your relatively quiet and easygoing manner, coupled with your commitment to doing everything well, means that they can count on you for your unfailing follow-through. You have qualities that many other people wish they had, but admit they don't have the patience to learn. Your travel habits tend to follow a more easy to understand pattern since you would rather go to places that have earned a well deserved reputation, rather than experiment with more recently discovered and, potentially, less satisfying destinations. These better known places can offer much of what you want, including interesting things to do and predictable quality for hotels and restaurants. Since they are well established destinations, they usually have attracted a number of major hotel chains at all price levels, a good selection of restaurants (particularly family style), and probably a few of the entertainment facilities that you may not have time to use very often back home—miniature golf courses, arcades, movie theaters, etc.

When given a choice, you often prefer to travel with a group of people, rather than alone. You tend to be much more of a social person than a *venturer* and, as a result, you enjoy the company of others. Interesting people that you meet on a trip can add to the overall quality of your experiences. Fully escorted tours are chosen more often for your trips, especially when you go to Europe or someplace else quite far away. You see the many advantages of these tours. These ensure that you hit all of the important spots, good hotels are selected so there's no risk in your choices and, since restaurants are largely predetermined, you need not give much thought to the possibility of getting sick on local food. You enjoy most of the sightseeing activities considerably, and it is especially helpful to have a guide serve as an interpreter and someone who can handle any problem situations you might encounter.

There is a lot to talk about when you come back from trips: so much that you have seen, so much that you have done. You hope to retain the excitement of all this to some degree by picking up some of the visual reminders of where you have been, silver sugar spoon sets from various places in England to add to your collection at home, a matched set of Hawaiian shirts, or a desk-size copy of the Statue of Liberty or the Eiffel Tower.

You tend to do less traveling than *venturers*, taking fewer vacations, not going as far from home, and not spending as many nights away on those trips. Also, you often have a great preference for destinations you can drive to, rather than having to get there by airline. When you find a place you like, you would much rather return to it on a regular basis than seek out a new and different spot each time. In this manner, you have reduced some of the risks associated with selecting a new spot for each vacation, a typical pattern of *venturers*.

Crowds at places you visit tend not to bother you greatly. This simply means that lots of people are having fun, much like you, and it can be interesting to see so many different people from other parts of the country or from around the world.

For your media habits, you contribute heavily to the rankings and importance of most of the top ten or twenty shows on television. Because you are a sociable person, you very much enjoy the type of humor that permeates many sitcoms. Baseball is often your favorite sport, with your interest growing in intensity during pennant races and world series playoffs. Because you like the more captivating feel of television, you tend to read fewer magazines and books than *venturers*.

An important goal in life is to reduce risk and make sensible choices. Therefore, you tend to be a late adopter of new products. You prefer to wait until competing technologies have sorted themselves out, the winning products or brand name have established themselves, and prices have declined to the point that they now seem stable and offer very good value. In this manner, you are much better at saving your money than your opposite counterpart who likes to try many new un proven products when they first come out, and when they're at their most expensive point in product life cycles. Thus, you can be considered a strong price/value shopper. In your daily shopping, you tend to select more popular well known brands. Their popularity means that they must be good or so many others would not be using them.

In summary, if you fit the typical personality type of a *dependable*, you are a very valued person because you help to keep society on course. Your travel habits are more predictable than is true for a *venturer*. In general, you want to choose places that are better known, have a history of providing good experiences and good value for the money to travelers, and at which many of the services and facilities you enjoy back home (good hotels and restaurants, entertainment and games) have been put in place. Your preference for escorted tours grows out of the fact that they ensure that you see all of the important and interesting places at a price that is highly competitive, and because you also enjoy being with people.

The Centric Personality
(Scale A: Score of 9 to 12 Points)

By definition, you fit between *venturers* and *dependables* on the scale. It would be easy to assume that you are simply an "average" personality and do not go to extremes on most things. The partial bit of truth hidden in that statement covers over your much more unique personality characteristics and behaviors. You comprise the largest segment of travelers. As a result, the majority of travel providers—airlines, resorts, rental car companies, tour operators, cruise lines, and others—typically place you at the top of their list of persons they want to reach and motivate to travel. Your significance lies not just in how many people are like you, however. It also grows out of the fact that you are easier to motivate to take a trip or buy a product than the personalities that lie more on the extremes on either side of you. *Venturers*, almost self-consciously, will ignore advertising. *Dependables* pay attention to advertising but their commitment to a regimen and daily routine makes it more difficult to change their habits and get them to take a trip. In contrast, you are more flexible and adaptable, with a willingness to sample new destinations if a travel promoter presents enticing advertising.

Also more than other groups, your travel relies on mixed modes of transportation. In the same year, if you are an active traveler, you are likely to fly to one or two destinations and drive to two or three others. In contrast, your counterparts prefer either to fly *(venturers)* or drive *(dependables)*. Although air travel saves tremendous amounts of time when the distances are great, the convenience of auto travel (take everything that you want with you) and the ability to go at your own pace provides its own inherent interest.

Unlike *venturers*, you prefer at least some quality commercial development before you visit an area. A good bed in a nice hotel, food that can be trusted, and a transportation network that can help you get around are what you consider to be basic necessities that you would like to see firmly in place before you visit. But, when overcommercialization sets in, signified by too many souvenir shops, the intrusion of fast food outlets, and the diesel smell coming from too many tourist buses, you will move on to some other place that has not yet lost its qualities of freshness and uniqueness. The kinds of things that you like to buy on trips to foreign lands are the products that various countries specialize in as part of their national heritage. Thus, wool sweaters and skirts in Scotland or England, crystal in England, Germany or Scandinavia, pottery and silver in Mexico, or semi-precious stones from various countries around the world —these all serve not only as reminders of a great vacation, but they can be used when you return home.

The great capitals of Europe were once a favorite goal for an extended trip for your type. Now, however, most of them seem overcrowded, far too expensive, and quite unfriendly in terms of how local citizens treat tourists. Therefore, when you go to Europe you might visit smaller towns and enjoy leisurely drives through the countryside. And, when you go into villages, you frequently prefer to stay at quaint little bed and breakfasts (B&Bs) far more than the other two types of travelers.

The diversity of the kinds of places that would be of interest to you opens up many more travel destinations of potential interest than is true for either *venturers* or *dependables*. You could enjoy a cruise in the Greek Isles, a car trip through gold mining ghost towns in California, or a shopping spree in New York City equally well. You will probably return to a place that you particularly like every two to four years, interspersing other new destinations (for you) in between. In some respects, you can have the most satisfying travel experiences because of your ability to absorb, and like, such different types of places.

If you follow the typical pattern for your personality, you have traveled both independently (probably with a spouse or a friend) and have taken more than one fully escorted tour. Since you have nothing against tours, you are likely to sample one of these every three to four years, and occasionally more frequently if some special offer presents itself. This includes tours for international travel and also domestically where it's possible to see New England's fall colors, visit Southern mansions, or travel historic routes as part of a tour group. Depending upon your age, the Elderhostel program is largely made up of your type.

Cruising has experienced double digit growth in the past several years and you are the main reason. You have decided that it is affordable, much more interesting than you ever thought, and so easy and comfortable because your hotel room goes with you wherever you are and you don't have to pack and unpack every day. You may also own a time share, the concept of owning one or two weeks of vacation time in a specific condo or hotel setup in an attractive resort area. Time shares tend to offer excuses for travel and most of these owners travel very regularly.

You have mixed media habits, combining both TV and reading. You enjoy quite a few shows on TV, read an occasional book, and magazines such as *Reader. Digest*, *People* and *National Geographic*.

In summary, you constitute the most important travel segment available. With the largest numbers of people just like you, the fact that you are generally easier to motivate for travel through advertising, and that you are willing to visit a variety of destinations, most travel companies desperately try to focus on you and your needs. They offer lots of special deals and incentives to get you to travel. You use mixed modes of transportation to get there, tend to return to a place you like every three to four years, and you also mix up the kinds of lodging that you use even on the same trip—a three or four star hotel, along with an economy/budget motel and a B&B.

The B Scale:
Actives and Mellows

Some people start a vacation running. From the moment they arrive at their destination, they jump into things—visiting historic sites, shopping, swimming, tennis or golf, enjoying the nightlife. They crowd as many things as they can into each day to get maximum enjoyment from the trip and to return home with their heads crammed full with the sights, sounds and feelings of where they have just been.

Others pursue the opposite path with equal devotion. They want to relax at every opportunity. They'll get in some sightseeing, shopping, and perhaps some personal sports, but at a much more leisurely pace. A vacation can only be a vacation if you don't have to hurry. Otherwise, you would feel like you are still back at work facing daily pressures and stress.

Sound familiar? Which one fits you? Perhaps both do because we can all change our mood from one vacation to the next. Sometimes, the strains from our jobs lead to a feeling that we just want to get away and unwind. No time demands, no daily schedules, and no obligations to meet. Just kick back and take it easy. Get up when you wake up, eat when it seems convenient, take a nap if it suits you, and perhaps play a little golf in the afternoon—if you don't have to work hard to get a convenient starting time. You may stay in one place, or wander off to a new city every couple of days depending upon your mood. For many, that's a true vacation. General Jonathan Wainwright survived the Bataan Death March of the Japanese in the Philippines during World War II and three years in a concentration camp. After he was freed, a reporter asked him what he planned to do when he returned to the U.S. "When I get home," he replied, "I'm going to sit on my front porch in my rocking chair. After three weeks, I'll start rockin'... but just a little bit at first." Haven't we all felt like that at times?

But, if you didn't just leave a pressure cooker at work, and you're reasonably rested, you may want to charge into your vacation with vigor. Take advantage of every minute. Come alive and enjoy the variety of things to do that most vacation spots offer. Explore, learn, and try out everything you can discover. You get charged up this way and, when you do, you forget about almost everything back at the office. In fact, you may forget to call in periodically to see if any client needs to talk with you because your head has gone elsewhere. You have completely, successfully put your mind and body into another space zone—one where it almost seems surreal because it's so different from your daily life. The flurry of activity energizes you and for a week or two you feel much younger and very invigorated.

Most of us can probably identify with both vacation experiences because we've had a need for each at different times in our lives. That will also continue in the future. But, the fact is that we tend to express more of one need, or pursue one type of vacation, than the other throughout our lives because our personality has consistency. Most often you apply the maximum energy you can to your vacations; or, you want to soak up energy by lying around the beach so that you can return to work feeling refreshed and invigorated.

So, read on and learn a bit more about yourself. To keep it simple, we've divided this scale into just two types: the *actives* and the *mellows*.

The Actives
(Scale B: Score 10 to 16 Points)

You have more energy than most people, and you've probably noticed that. At work, others don't keep up as well or get as much done as you. At home, you like to keep going. Rather than sit comfortably in a chair, you'd rather do something related to your career or pursue a hobby. Or, perhaps you just spend time puttering round the house, keeping the yard up and otherwise fixing things that may not even need fixing... yet. The higher your score, the more likely you feel a bit edgy if you're not actively involved in some activity. If you fit in the 14 to 16 range, you may have trouble adapting to a crowd. You want to keep moving, always stay in motion, to see and do more things than most people ever think about. If you apply most of that energy to your work, it can result in great success because "luck" is typically a fortunate by-product of the amount of dedicated effort. Your friends at your job may think you are a workaholic, not recognizing that you can't stand still like most people you know. You just have to keep moving, and that frequently means getting very committed and involved in your livelihood. Conversely, if you feel stuck in a not very interesting vocation, your boredom may reduce your day to day effectiveness and hurt your chances for career advancement.

For many of you, a little voice inside seems to nag at you and say that it's almost a sin not to keep active. We weren't put on planet earth just to sit. Since we have limited time here, make the most of it. Do something useful, purposeful—for yourself or for those in need. A lot of social good can come from people like you who have a concern about the things that are wrong in our society, or the world, and the boundless energy and enthusiasm to do something about it. Your type of personality can be found in lay leadership positions in churches and synagogues, or as heads of United Way and American Cancer Society fund drives. When you confront problems, at your job or in your volunteer work, you attack them, solve them, and get on to other things.

A drawback also can be apparent in your psychological make-up, primarily if you place very high on the scale. If you do not find an acceptable outlet for all of that enthusiasm, your friends, relatives and work associates may find it a bit difficult to adapt to your idiosyncrasies. You have trouble slowing down to their pace, and they cannot catch up to yours. Also, you may not be as reflective or introspective as could be good for you. If you can't sit still very long, you can easily miss out on the opportunity to think about who you are, where your life seems to be heading, and what you want to do about it. Is your job satisfying? Are you making adequate progress in it? Should you change directions and try something new? Are you adapting to your marriage or social relationships the way you should? Would it be better to start on new paths in this important personal part of your life? These and other fundamental questions of life need to be raised and answered periodically to make certain that you're taking as many right paths as possible. It's for your benefit.

If you don't measure at the extreme for an *active* personality, you probably adapt to people and difficult situations more easily. You tend to be somewhat less demanding as a person and, as a result, a bit more adaptive to whatever you encounter. Your energy still measures above average, but not so high that your constant activity bothers others—at home or at work. And you may think about the meaning of life more than persons whose energy levels seem boundless. Thinking is worthwhile, provided you come to some conclusions and do something about those conclusions. For you, the good news is that your type of personality can more easily find contentment in life than persons who score very high on the B scale.

Your personality as an *active* also carries over to your travel patterns. For the most part, you will hit the ground running. You have to see and do as much as possible on every trip, using most of your waking hours to get involved. Play a round of golf, tennis or ski, then see the local sights, perhaps shop a bit, and check out the local nightlife. Or, depending upon your interests, spend all day exploring historic sights, buildings and unique local attractions. Wherever you are, you want to be involved, exploring and learning about the things around you.

The Mellows
(Scale B: Score 4 to 9 Points)

Laid back, calm, easygoing, happy-go-lucky, unruffled, untroubled, informal, unceremonious, casual, carefree—a lot of these words probably apply to you. You've even heard them used by friends and associates to describe you in the past. The lower your score on the B scale, the larger the number of these adjectives that fit your personality.

Above all, you probably have been described as mellow, creating a feeling among friends that you are genial, calm in most of life's storms, cordial, affable, cheerful, pleasant, agreeable, and otherwise able to adapt to a lot of different situations—even those that would bother most people.

An easygoing approach to life wins a lot of friends, so your social circle can be very broad—at your choosing. Most of us like to be around people who allow us to be as we are, and your acceptance of almost anyone and everyone creates that comfortable feeling for others. Typically, your demands from life are not heavy. You don't have to buy fancy cars, or change them every two years, or live in a grand house, or brag about your accomplishments or the wonderful successes of your children. Life is rather good, just as you take it on a daily basis. If you have faced a lot of difficult situations in life, these have probably made you a stronger person and also better adjusted. You recognize more of what is good, cherish it, and come away with greater contentment.

If you also scored as a *venturer* on the A scale, your mellowness can signify the quality of being reflective. You might like to think about the meaning of life and where you fit in. In so doing, you can easily counter what can be the frenetic energy of some *actives* for a more thoughtful and playful approach. If you do, then you have a very good chance for success at work and in your social sphere because anyone who uses good thinking will usually race ahead of someone who simply works hard, but without much thought about why or where all of this activity might be leading.

There can be a down side to your personality. If you scored in the 4 to 6 range on the scale, you could be close to becoming a couch potato. Too much TV, too much sitting and eating, and too much talking with friends rather than getting involved in things. All of this nonactivity can make you into a pretty dull person. If that's the case, then you should think about doing something more purposeful and energetic in your life; lay out some plans for yourself and take action on them. You can actually change important personality characteristics by doing things differently on a daily basis. So, someone who approaches life too slowly

can become more alive and excited about almost everything, with a little concen
tration and self determination.

   Your mellow personality also relates to what you do when you travel. Most like
ly, you travel less than the very *active* person, but when you go you can get more
out of a trip than your frenetic counterpart. Your relaxed manner can mean you
enjoy almost everything you do—at a relaxed and leisurely pace. With a smile on
your face, you can enjoy the big and little moments in your trip almost equally. If
you are a *mellow venturer*, you may have the best of both worlds. This is because
you often want to read more about a place in advance of the trip, and end up with
a better understanding of what it has to offer. Then, during your visit, you are
more purposeful in seeing what's important, understanding what you see, and re
turning with memories that are more crystallized and long lasting. At the place
you visit, you can be more reflective, thinking about the meaning in your life of
everything you see and do on that trip. Visiting old churches or buildings where
historic events happened can be an almost mystical or magical experience.

   Now, read on and find out what kinds of places you are most likely to enjoy de
pending upon your unique personality characteristics.

Section II:
Vacation Places Rated

THE TOP 25 DOMESTIC DESTINATIONS—AND WHY THEY MAY SURPRISE YOU

In most statistical tallies, the top destinations are determined by counting the number of visitors each receives during the year. In these situations, Florida typically leads the list for domestic destinations, followed by Hawaii, with California in third position, and New York, Las Vegas and a mixture of other states rounding out the top ten. Internationally, the United Kingdom grabs the most mentions, followed by France, Germany, Italy and, typically, other European countries before parts of Latin America, Asia or the Mid-East appear on the radar screen.

But this is hardly a good way to determine what are the best places to visit since it is simply a restatement of the obvious. Those places that draw the largest number of visitors each year also have the largest budgets for advertising and promotion and, as a result, can continue to make their presence felt in the marketplace. Large destinations also have large budgets that help to self-perpetuate their size. Walt Disney World/Epcot Center, for example, registers about 30 million admissions each year. Through every travel agency that sells leisure trips, their promotion tentacles reach, octopus-like, in the form of advertising materials and special incentives for travel agents to sell Walt Disney World/Epcot Center. They also get favorable articles placed in family-oriented magazines, and they overwhelm local advertising and promotional programs with their ability to have special admission offers placed on coke cans, the backs of grocery shopping bags and through heavy TV advertising that often includes a super athlete who has just won something big and declares that, "The first thing I'm going to do is go to Walt Disney World," (or Disneyland). But measuring the most popular places, based on numbers of visitors, does not necessarily provide information on the best places to visit. Like a big flywheel in a giant piece of machinery, these most frequently visited places can continue to generate the advertising that will remind people that they should come, once more, to their own big corner of paradise.

In the American Traveler Survey, I devised a better reflection of what are the best places to choose for a vacation. I simply asked people to name the places where they had taken vacations in the past three years, and to indicate those that they especially liked. Then I determine what percentage of people who visited went home happy—stating they really like the place. The Plog *satisfaction* ratio shows how well each destination delivers on its promise. Does it send people away happy most of the time, or do very few say that it was really a great place? Not only does this offer a new and better measure, but it allows less well known places to compete on equal footing with the mega-destinations that otherwise dominate the promotional wars. I also asked people to describe, in their own words, why they liked the places they chose. This gave me a more personal feel for what makes a destination great.

This chapter presents the top destinations in the world, i.e., those that provide the greatest satisfaction to the largest number of visitors. You will notice that the ranking is quite different from anything you may have previously seen offered by "experts" because I changed the rules of the game. A more level playing field exists for competition between the big and the small.

How Destinations Are Ranked

This chapter provides a listing of the top 25 domestic destinations, rank ordered. The remaining U.S. destinations follow in the next chapter, also ranked but without detailed comments. I assign star ratings to these to let you know just how great travelers think each place is, based on the satisfaction scores provided by *all* travelers. My system is as follows:

★★★★★   Absolute best; far ahead of the pack in most characteristics; in a class by itself. Very few achieve this status.

★★★★   Excellent; among the best; will provide memorable vacation experiences for almost everyone.

★★★   A good-to-very-good destination; above average in most respects; generally will not disappoint.

★★   Suitable for some people, but not all; probably not much to do there, or weather is poor, or people not friendly, etc.

★   Be selective; very few people like it and you may not either; perhaps you have friends or relatives there. You better know what you want to do before you go there, otherwise it could be a bad vacation experience.

In general, destinations with 3, 4 and 5 stars will be described; the 1 and 2 star places will only be listed in the next chapter.

The star system rates destinations on an overall basis. But, to help you choose the best spot for you, I also include a 1-to-10 ranking scale that designates the degree to which a destination appeals to each personality type—*venturers, centric* and *dependables*. It is also based on the percentage of people who visit a place who also say they especially like it, as follows:

Scale Score	Percent of Visitors Who Especially Like It
10	50% and above
9	45-49%
8	40-44
7	35-39
6	30-34
5	25-29
4	20-24
3	15-19
2	10-14
1	9% and below

One final point of comment: U.S. destinations generally score very well. The top places score as high or higher than the best destinations elsewhere in the world. Very few states score at low levels. You'll also find more poor places to visit beyond our shores.

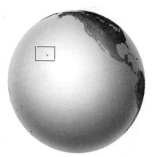

Hawaii

#1 RATING: ★★★★★+

Centrics	Venturers	Dependables
10	10	10+

Mauna Loa is the world's largest active volcanic crater.
Waves curl at 30 ft. on the North Shore in winter.
Iolani Palace (Honolulu) is the only royal palace in the U.S.
Captain James Cook named Hawaii the Sandwich Islands in 1778.
Don't take volcano rocks unless you want BAD LUCK!

What a perfect place! It seems to have all of the qualities that make a vacation trip truly memorable, and none of the problems that can spoil or ruin it, as based on travelers' own comments. One person said, "It is one of God's gifts to mankind." People just seem to gush when they talk about their rapture with Hawaii and what it offers. It scores a perfect 10 with all personality types so that we had to add something to its 5-star rating—a plus sign.

Its long list of items that make a vacation truly great, according to the visitors I've interviewed, include the best weather in the world (the most frequent reference), warm and beautiful beaches with some of the greatest swimming anywhere, lots to do, very friendly people, great food and restaurants and an unbelievable selection of sports facilities for golf and tennis enthusiasts. It also offers snorkeling, sailing, scuba diving, canoeing and many other water activities. Travelers frequently mention the absence of graffiti. There is no fear of crime, they say. You almost cannot get a bad hotel, and prices for hotels and food seem relatively reasonable. Hawaii seems to control all the things that could ruin or spoil a vacation. It envelopes you in a sense of peace and serenity that almost cannot be matched, and it immediately makes you feel relaxed and comfortable. Its scenic beauty is mentioned by almost every person who selects Hawaii as the favorite destination in the American Traveler Survey. Maui receives the largest number of superlative comments, followed by Kauai and then some of the other islands.

Helicopter Sightseeing

Kauai

Zoo and Sea Life Park

Lihue.

Oahu

Surfing

Kahuku

Wahiawa

Kar

Waianae

Climate

Honolulu

Scenery

Pearl Harbor

History

Beaches

Doing Nothing

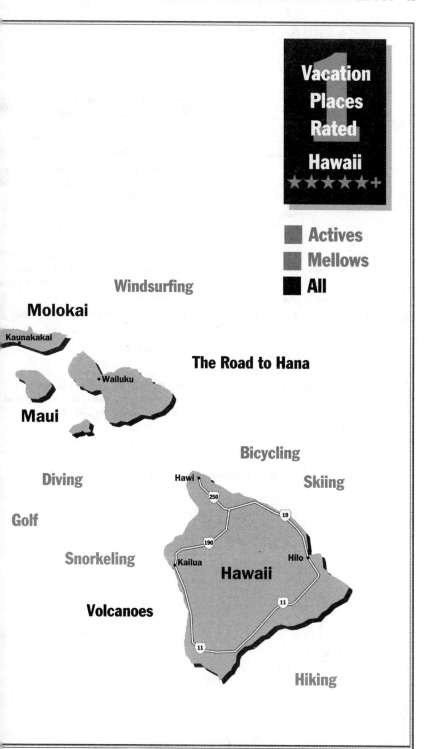

WHAT TO DO ON HAWAII

Actives	Mellows
1 Rent a jeep or car to explore any of the islands. Don't set a schedule. You can get around any of them in a day.	Visit the U.S.S. Arizona Memorial (sunk December 7, 1941 at Pearl Harbor by Japanese attack), Oahu
2 Swim at Hanauma Bay (Oahu) among the friendly fish. They'll eat from your hands. Bring a snorkel and mask.	See Bishop Museum and historic King Kamehameha Center (Honolulu). The islands' histories are intriguing. If you walk through Waikiki, pay attention to the mixture of races and cultures in Hawaii. Visitors always stand out from the crowd, don't they?
3 Tandem bicycle ride down Kilauea (Big Island of Hawaii). All down hill and lots of fun.	Hear authentic Hawaiian music and watch hula dancers (all islands at parks, in hotels, on beaches and the Polynesian Cultural Center, Honolulu).
4 Play some of the most scenic golf courses in the world, especially at Kaanapali and Wailea (Maui) or Kona (Big Island). Tennis is also great, with the ocean and mountains as a backdrop.	Explore Iao Valley State Monument (Maui).
5 Visit Hawaii Volcanoes National Park on the Big Island of Hawaii (fascinating, eerie). And drive around the back side of the volcanoes where you can see nature's process of reconstruction—new plants growing in recent lava flows	Visit Honolulu Zoo and Sea Life Park (also Honolulu) to get a feeling for the diversity of life on and around the islands.

For further information about Hawaii, contact

Hawaii Visitors Bureau
2270 Kalakaua Avenue
Honolulu, HI 96815
☎ (808) 923-1811

WHAT PEOPLE LIKE ABOUT HAWAII

Dependables

People whose personalities are classified as *dependables* seem to like it even more (note the 10+ score). They give me similar comments about the great weather and beautiful scenery. But, this sets the stage for them to relax, soak up the sun, and come back home with their psychic batteries recharged. Their comments include:

It has clean surroundings, friendly people, and the kinds of things I like to do—good entertainment, daytime tours and great restaurants.
37-year-old female medical technician, Grand Forks, ND

I especially like Kona, its beauty and peacefulness. You can really relax. There is very little traffic. It has great resorts, good food, and friendly people. It truly has the 'Aloha' spirit.
Saleswoman and buyer, Pleasanton, CA

It has a great climate and historic places. I especially like the pineapples you can get over there.
51-year-old housewife from Potomic, IL

It's Maui for me. It's seeing the sights, the weather, the people, ocean, sands, sunsets and sunrises. It has great food and the smell of clean air and beautiful flowers overwhelm you.
Female business executive, Pittsburgh, PA

Centrics

Read what *centrics*, who are the largest number of visitors, tell me about why they like the islands.

The people are wonderful, the scenery is breathtaking, and most hotels are within my price range. There is so much to do, and the food is excellent. The swimming is superb!
Female legal assistant, Upstate New York

Wailea on Maui has such great weather, fabulous beaches, and good restaurants. Also, it has fantastic recreational facilities and it's relatively uncrowded.
Retired male, Las Vegas, NV

Hawaii is such an easy place to drive around and see many new and different sights in an uncrowded and secure atmosphere.
Teacher from small town in New York

It has beautiful surroundings. It's peaceful, clean, no poverty, with great weather, good food, great beaches, and it's not a wild place. Also, it's not crowded or overdeveloped. There's just a lot to do.
Married saleswoman, Scituate, MA

Venturers

When *venturers* talk about Hawaii, they are equally as enthusiastic. Their most frequent references are to its unequalled weather that allows them to do almost anything they want—whenever they wish. Hawaii's warm, gentle breezes enhance every activity. Venturers want to be active and involved while they are there.

It's tough to find a place that has more than it has—beaches, mountains, whales, golf, weather, food, accommodations. You name it, it's got it.
Senior executive, Plano, TX

The people are great! The climate is wonderful! The culture is interesting! The food is good! It's great for outdoor sports!
Male, senior corporate manager, Cambridge, MA

It has beautiful scenery and a slow pace of life. It has plenty to do, if you choose. I especially like Maui and Kaui.
58-year-old female teacher, Wichita, KS

Maui has clean salt water and great beaches. It has coral and interesting fish, and it's not crowded.
51-year-old female middle manager, Churchville, MD

WHAT PEOPLE LIKE ABOUT HAWAII

Dependables

Centrics

Venturers

It was absolutely beautiful. The meals were great, the weather was terrific, and the entertainment fabulous. Everything was very enjoyable and reasonable.

30-year-old housewife, Madison, WI

The beauty of the islands, the warm, sunny climate, the peoples' friendliness. I just love all of Hawaii, but especially Maui the best.

Widow in Upstate New Jersey

It has natural beauty, great beaches, and fantastic snorkeling. There's much friendliness among the people, interesting history, and the weather can't be beat. Also, I appreciated having a wide choice of vegetarian food.

Housewife from Central New York

If you want to love Hawaii rent a jeep and go to the villages away from the tourists talk and deal directly with the people!

50-year-old male middle manager, Tampa, F

Get the picture? Recent visitors to Hawaii say that you almost can't go wrong. The Main Island, Oah and its primary beach, Waikiki, do not come up for many references, but a large number of places on other islands receive frequent superlative comments. If you haven't visited it before, pack your bags and s traveling. If you haven't been there for quite awhile, you may want to consider going back very soon. W it's that great, its peaceful serenity may be a welcome relief from the noisy commotion of your daily life

Alaska

#2 RATING: ★★★★★

Centrics	Venturers	Dependables
10	10	7

Mt. McKinley is the highest peak in North America. (20,322 ft.)

Caribou thrive in the Arctic tundra.

Smoke has been escaping Valley of 10,000 Smokes since Mount Katmai erupted in 1912.

104 million acres in Alaska are environmentally protected.

Ketchikan holds the U.S. record for the most totem poles and rainfall (160 in. a year!)

The last two U.S. territories to become states grab the top domestic destination ratings, as based on travelers' evaluations in the American Traveler Survey. How different they are. The warm weather and great beaches of Hawaii contrast sharply with the cold and frigid climate of our northernmost state. Yet, visitors are just as rhapsodic in talking about Alaska's virtues.

The most frequent mentions from *centrics*, by far, focus on Alaska's scenic beauty and its unspoiled qualities. Somewhat routinely these guests say that it's indescribably beautiful, quite unlike anything else they've ever seen, and difficult to comprehend unless you've been there. It offers sightseeing opportunities that cannot be matched anywhere. In the same breath they talk about its clean and unspoiled character, with a feeling that the state has done a lot to protect the environment and set aside preservation areas for wildlife and plants. Words like "natural," "wild," "untouched," "clean," "preserved" and "like things used to be" crop up frequently in these conversations.

Further, Alaska creates a sense of peace and serenity among many who journey there. They mention a feeling of being close to nature, and that its remoteness and lack of people immediately make you feel relaxed and at one with yourself. This ability to get close to nature and yourself at the same time sends some of its visitors home feeling better about themselves and more able to handle their pressure-filled lives because their problems don't seem so overwhelming anymore. Alaska creates a spiritual sense among many visitors, causing them to pause and reflect on the meaning of life.

If Alaska intrigues you and you're thinking about a trip, plan on getting involved in lots of activities. Almost everyone mentions that there are almost too many things to choose from every day. For sports, fishing comes in for superlative comments, but there's also hunting, hiking, mountain climbing and skiing. And just getting around to remote regions or some of its old-time cities can fill your days. As one person said, "There's so much to do and room to do it in." Helicopter rides and cruising also receive favorable comments. Friendly people do not get mentioned as often as for Hawaii, but it still is one of Alaska's many qualities.

Fly Over Remote Areas

Hiking

Kotzebue Arctic Museum

Fishing

Hunting

Iditarod Dogsleds

Cruise Coast

Canoeing
Camping

Aleutian Islands

Trans-Alaska Pipeline

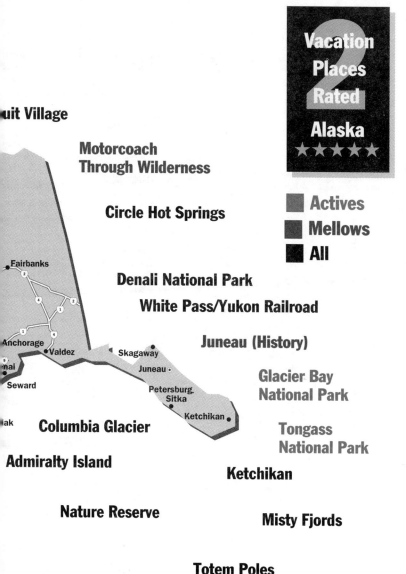

Vacation Places Rated

Alaska
★★★★★

Actives
Mellows
All

uit Village

Motorcoach Through Wilderness

Circle Hot Springs

Fairbanks

Denali National Park

White Pass/Yukon Railroad

Juneau (History)

Anchorage • Valdez   ◄ Skagaway

nai   Juneau ○

Seward   Petersburg

                        Sitka

                        Ketchikan ●

ak   **Columbia Glacier**

Glacier Bay National Park

Tongass National Park

Admiralty Island

Ketchikan

Nature Reserve

Misty Fjords

Totem Poles

WHAT TO DO IN ALASKA

Actives	Mellows
1 Fish in one of its great streams or lakes.	Sail up the Alaska Coast on a major cruise line; see glaciers and stop in native villages.
2 Rent a plane with a good bush pilot and let him take you to remote places (Indian villages, lovely lakes, lovely glaciers).	Walk the streets of Juneau; visit old taverns; see historic homes.
3 Come for the Iditarod dog races and enjoy the friendly rivalries, high spirits, and outgoing nature of native Alaskans.	Drive the AlCan Highway; some of the best sightseeing in the world.
4 Camp and hike around Mt. McKinley.	Take a motor coach tour of wilderness areas to get the feeling of Alaska's size, isolation and beauty.
5 Take a guided canoe trip down one of Alaska's mighty rivers; sleep out under the stars.	Sample Anchorage's diverse restaurants morning noon and night to experience its varied and lively foods; fish may be the freshest you have ever tasted.

For further information about Alaska, contact

Alaska Division of Tourism
P.O. Box 110801
Juneau, AK 99811-0801
☎ (907) 465-2012

WHAT PEOPLE LIKE ABOUT ALASKA

Dependables	Centrics	Venturers

A smaller number of *dependables* choose Alaska as one of their favorite places. Those who do tend to also comment on the state's beauty, but are less captivated by its opportunities for fishing and hunting. Instead they bring up the state's unique history and that it seems like a throwback to the spirit that built the 48 states during the 1800s.

The words of *centrics* can sometimes tell it best. They refer to the natural beauty and unspoiled environment again and again.

When *venturers* comment about the state, they often convey the feeling that they have been allowed to observe or become part of something quite magical and mystical. Alaska creates the sense of a time warp among many first-timers. It doesn't really exist. It can't be real.

Venturers' comments reflect their feelings.

It has a frontier atmosphere about it. It's expensive, but the scenery is priceless!
Retired salesman, Adamsville, TN

The vastness of the area, the environmental protection and the preservation of wild areas all add to a great feeling for the place.
50-year-old female teacher, Dallas, Georgia

The beauty of the country overwhelms you. It's unspoiled and its people are friendly. The wildlife is amazing.
74-year-old female, Tigaro, OR

It has scenery and interesting history and it offers great variety.
72-year-old female, Minneapolis, MN

It is so beautiful and so wild.
Retired housewife, Collinsville, Virginia

It's pristine and unspoiled with guaranteed good fishing and friendly guides.
43-year-old salesman, Marietta, GA

I simply like its open spaces.
Lawyer, Raleigh, NC

I love its great outdoors, the fishing, the sightseeing, and seeing people who are doing the old-time things—the things that the rest of the country used to do.
Retired housewife, Yakima, Washington

Wow! It has spectacular salmon fishing and great scenery. The people are unique enough for me to rescript 'Northern Exposure'.
Female physician, Golden, CO

It has scenery and good climate, along with friendly people. And it's easy to get there.
Homemaker (64 years), Atlanta, GA

It's wild, it's natural, and it has great fishing!
Male business executive, Boise, Idaho

It's beautiful country! It has fascinating native crafts and good recreation opportunities.
Married female executive, Eugene, OR

What beauty and how unspoiled it is.
Foreman, Elkhart, IN

It has majestic beauty, it's a water/ocean destination, and it has comfortable, cool weather that I enjoy.
Female teacher, Downers Grove, Illinois

No other place is as unspoiled and with so few people. It has just gorgeous scenery.
Female teacher, Green Bay, WI

WHAT PEOPLE LIKE ABOUT ALASKA

Dependables

It's a beautiful land, more like things used to be. And, it has excellent tours and accommodations.

Female teacher, Valparaiso, IN

Centrics

It's a great adventure place, but it has few risks.

Retired male, Olympia, Washington

It's relaxing and interesting. It's not crowded and it has beautiful scenery. Also, it has very nice people wherever you go. I like it a lot.

Male business executive, Keasaugua, IA

I just love its beautiful scenery. It's clean and unspoiled and so close to nature. It has so much geographical interest and it's so very different from home.

Married female, civil servant, Port Jefferson, NY

Venturers

I like its wild country and the Iditarod. Its scenery is unblemished. It's wilderness country.

Retired professor, Pennington, NJ

In this age of congestion, pollution, crowding, noise, drugs and crime, it seems there can't be a place so pristine and pure that it is a throwback to a more comfortable and relaxed era. Yet, Alaska invites you to come and experience it for yourself. Find out what it means to be close to nature; learn something about the meaning of life and your place in the grand scheme of things; understand what inner peace and serenity can do for your soul and then try to take it back with you and impose it on your everyday world! No other destination in the American Traveler Survey creates this sense of belonging and oneness with nature.

Colorado

#3 RATING: ★★★★★

Centrics	Venturers	Dependables
10	10	10

More than 1000 Rocky Mountain peaks are over 10,000 ft. high.
Denver was founded in 1858 after gold was discovered.
Boulder's Naropa Institute is the only accredited U.S. Buddhist university.
Beer lovers head for Golden for the Coors brewery tour.
You'll see more "A list" celebs in Telluride than Aspen.

In ancient mythology, when Atlas shrugged, he must have created the Rocky Mountains in Colorado because travelers describe the state's mountain scenery in terms that make it seem truly mythical and majestic. Colorado joins two other Western locations in the five-star category. Hawaii's warm sunny beaches are not for everyone, and Alaska may seem too far away. Colorado is the answer for vacationers who report treasured memories of great skiing, spectacular mountains and a variety of things to do in all seasons. The open spaces, clean air, and the glamour of its chic ski resorts entice travelers who want to play hard as well as those who want to relax and enjoy the view.

Centric personalities enjoy the myriad of outdoor activities in the crisp Colorado climate: snow skiing heads the list, followed by hiking, rock climbing, fishing, river rafting, horseback riding, and observing nature and wildlife. They rave about the variety of things to see and do, and they appreciate the unspoiled natural beauty that surrounds them as they pursue their favorite activities. These travelers talk about the mountains soaring into clean, pure air, and the very different and beautiful four seasons that are part of the environment.

Colorado is primarily seen as an outdoor state for adventure and involvement. But it also provides an atmosphere for more thoughtful reflection. As one woman from Grafton, Nebraska said:

It offers peace, quiet, beauty…it's unique. There is lots to do, or nothing to do. My family can enjoy nature and get to know each other.

For those who still like cities, it has good shopping, interesting museums and fine dining in Denver or the ski resorts of Aspen, Steamboat Springs, Vail or Breckinridge. Those who are price conscious, or who travel with families, talk about the reasonable prices of accommodations and restaurants, as well easy accessibility.

White Water Rafting

Vail

Coors Brewing Tours

Four Corners

Scenery

Downhill Skiing

Ghost Towns

Off-road Driving

Camping

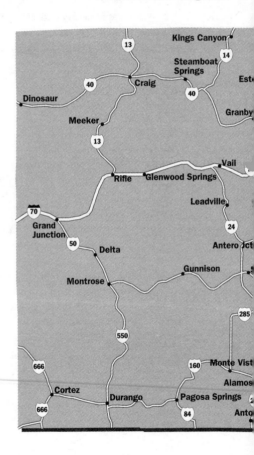

Ranches

Wide Open Spaces

teamboat Springs

Air Force Academy

Vacation
Places
Rated
Colorado
★★★★★

Actives
Mellows
All

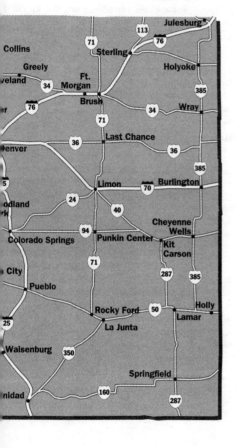

Hiking

Telluride

Aspen

Mesa Verde National Park

Old Railroads

Ski Resorts

ock Climbing

Black Canyon of the Gunnison

WHAT TO DO IN COLORADO

Actives	Mellows
1 Rafting is available and popular on almost every river in the state, and you can request your own "degree of difficulty."	If you are visiting near Denver in the summer, call ahead for information about the Cherry Creek Arts Festival in July ☎ *(303) 355-2787.*
2 Black Canyon of the Gunnison National Monument contains 12 miles of the earth's oldest base rocks, to a depth of 2700 feet. There is a visitor's center, camping and hiking, but caution is advised in some areas.	The well-known Coors Brewing Company in Golden, Colorado offers tours. Call ☎ *(303) 277-BEER.*
3 There are two railroad trips worth taking: First, the Cumbres and Toltec Scenic Railroad from Antonito to Osier to Chama, New Mexico. This is an all-day affair on an old narrow gauge, coal burning train, affording spectacular scenic views. The second is the Durango and Silverton Narrow Gauge Railroad, which suggests reservations a month in advance.	Central City is an old mountain mining town that offers all the charm of narrow winding roads, an opera festival, and more recently, legalized gambling.
4 Visitors interested in Native American history will enjoy Mesa Verde National Park in southwestern Colorado. Its cliffs and canyons contain some of the largest and best-preserved cliff dwellings of the ancestors of today's Pueblo Indians.	Allow two hours for a free tour of the Air Force Academy in Colorado Springs.
5 Take the family to Royal Gorge Bridge, near Canon City. The bridge is said to be the highest suspension bridge in the world, and the park features an incline railway, aerial tram, scenic trails and children's attractions.	Four Corners Monument is the only place in the US where four states meet (Colorado, Arizona, Utah and New Mexico). Beautiful scenery can be enjoyed, and Ute, Hopi and Navaho wares are available for sale.

For further information about Colorado, contact:

Colorado Tourism Information Service
1625 Broadway, Suite 1700
Denver, CO 80202
☎ (303) 592-5510

WHAT PEOPLE LIKE ABOUT COLORADO

Dependables

Dependables remember outdoor activities as well, in all seasons, and enjoy the relaxation of sitting by a fire contemplating the snow-capped Rockies, combined with the accessibility of nearby shops, restaurants and night life.

Centrics

Listen to what the *centrics* tell us. They love the scenery, the outdoor activities, the climate, plus the great restaurants and shopping.

Venturers

Both *venturers* and *dependables* mention the variety of activities, the scenery and the climate. The purer *venturers* emphasize the low population density, the uniqueness and the sense of adventure while on vacation. They picture themselves on uncrowded ski lifts, rushing down the slopes or touring the historic western sites, with old buildings, railroads and mines.

It's so beautiful there, and we have access to gambling.
Female office worker, Oklahoma City

The scenery is so beautiful. We're into camping, hiking and rock climbing, and now they have major league baseball!
42-year-old executive, Minneapolis, MN

We loved the railroad (near Durango), and the old buildings. There's a lot to see and tours to do.
Recently retired male, Brockway, PA

The countryside is unspoiled, the hotels and restaurants are reasonably priced, and the roads are good for traveling. It makes it easy to vacation with or without your family.
44-year-old father, upstate NY

There are few people. You can see beautiful wildlife in out of the way locations very easily. It's great for all outdoor activities.
Married professional male, Idaho Falls, ID

It's such beautiful country. There is so much to see and do, and it isn't overpopulated. We can have a great time, any time of year.
43-year-old teacher, Brecksville, OH

Snow, mountains and fireplaces—what a great memory I have of that state.
48-year-old nurse from Texas

It's being in the outdoors, in the majestic scenery of the Rocky Mountains that makes it so wonderful.
50-year-old male, Calden, NY

There are plenty of activities and wonderful weather.
33-year-old homemaker, Arlington, TX

It's gorgeous and I can relax. Also, it's convenient to home, but far enough away to feel like we're on vacation.
Homemaker, Wichita, KS

The climate is great and I love the atmosphere of the shops and restaurants. Those beautiful, beautiful mountains! There is nothing like them here.
Retired female, Owego, NY

The mountains are beautiful, the facilities are excellent, the outdoor activities are abundant.
Self-employed male from New York

WHAT PEOPLE LIKE ABOUT COLORADO

Dependables

Centrics

*You can get easy accommo-
dations at reasonable rates.
And mostly, it has such great
snow skiing!*

> 40-year-old lawyer,
> Buffalo, MO

*We like to hike and ski and
enjoy that mountain scenery.
Also, the shopping, museums
and dining in Denver are
great!*

> 34-year-old housewife,
> El Paso, TX

Venturers

*It's a peaceful, person
place to go. Nature's beauty
untouched. There are few
and fewer places like this. C
orado just never disappoints*

> Senior CP
> Georgetown, T

Northern California

Mount Whitney is the highest mountain in the lower 48 states.
Hearst Castle in San Simeon inspired "Xanadu" in Citizen Kane.
Yosemite's El Capitan monolith challenges rock climbers at 3591 ft.
Northern California boasts more than 250 wineries.
San Francisco's Lombard St. has 10 hairpin bends in less than 500 ft.

Because of its size, California has been divided into two destinations in my survey—Northern California and Southern California. Although they're both popular, the Northern area of the state comes out ahead.

People who love it seem overwhelmed by its diversity. They use more adjectives, and talk about more things to do, than for any other state or destination I surveyed. A larger number of Californians choose their own state as their favorite place than is true for any other place. People describe it as scenic and beautiful, although not quite as often as for Hawaii or Alaska. California also captures people's hearts with its sense of grandeur and majesty, words that do not occur as often for some of the other Western states. San Francisco wins the popularity contest among the three personality types I surveyed, followed by Napa Valley and various parts of the Sierras.

Centrics most often mention the mild and comfortable weather in the Northern part of the state. Then they talk about how much there is to do and the fact that you can do it all at your own pace because of the leisurely and relaxed life styles of Californians. No push and no pressure contribute to a good vacation atmosphere. For them, the state has it all. Mountains, the Pacific Ocean, great restaurants and good food contribute to a good vacation. But it also has areas that are still rustic and not overly commercial, great nightlife and culture (primarily in San Francisco), fabulous wineries, wilderness if you want it, great snow skiing areas, and an overall positive ambience that is difficult to describe to others. It can provide a peace and serenity not always found elsewhere.

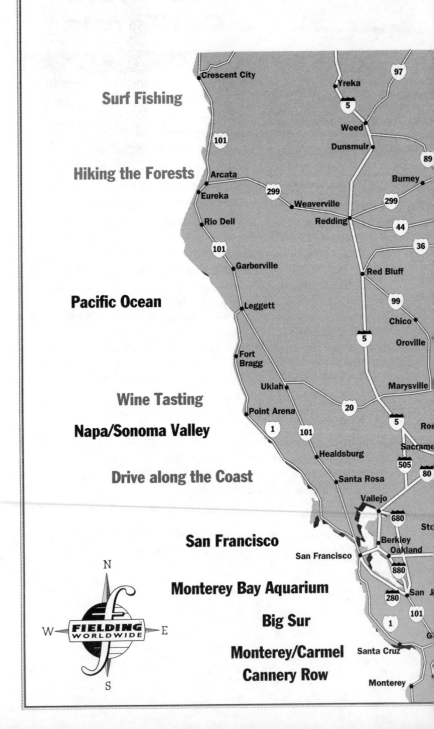

Surf Fishing

Hiking the Forests

Pacific Ocean

Wine Tasting

Napa/Sonoma Valley

Drive along the Coast

San Francisco

Monterey Bay Aquarium

Big Sur

Monterey/Carmel

Cannery Row

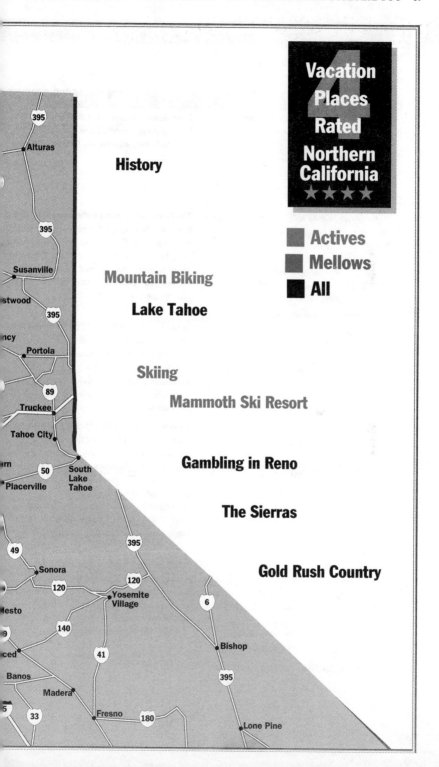

WHAT TO DO IN NORTHERN CALIFORNIA

Actives	Mellows
1 The University of California at Berkeley has often been ranked #1 among public universities in the country. Enjoy a walk or jog through the beautiful campus in the Berkeley Hills and later investigate the offbeat shops and people on Telegraph Avenue, just off the campus.	From San Francisco, take the ferry across to the charming community of Sausalito. Shop, dine and enjoy walking the hilly streets.
2 Put a flower in your hair, and visit the notorious '60s at the Haight-Ashbury district in San Francisco. This was a mecca for flower children and other radical types in that bygone decade. It has now been gentrified to some extent, but there is still lots of "hippie" memorabilia mixed in with the "yuppie" coffee houses.	The Napa and Sonoma valleys produce wines that many believe are the equal of fine French vintages. Drive through the beautiful rolling hills, take a couple of winery tours and enjoy some excellent food as well. Napa is more "developed" than Sonoma; a visit will stay in your memory a long time.
3 If you take your vacation in the winter months, ski the Sierras. Skiers tell me that California skiing and ski resorts are a little different from others. Mammoth and Lake Tahoe are two to try.	In the Presidio district of San Francisco is a jewel of an art museum called the Legion of Honor that is virtually unknown outside the city. It specializes in 17th and 18th century European art and the Presidio location is worthwhile on its own (under the shadow of the Golden Gate).
4 Spend a day in Marin County. "Hang out" at Stinson Beach, then visit the giant redwoods in Muir Woods. Hiking among those splendid trees puts human problems in a better perspective.	Spend a day in the Monterey-Carmel area. Monterey was built on the fishing and canning industries, and is very much part of Jack London country (which has also been developed as an industry!). The boardwalk is great fun and be sure to see the Aquarium. For Carmel, the words "quaint," "charming" and "gorgeous" fit to a tee. Its scenic beauty, restaurants and elegant shops are relaxing and refreshing.
5 Big Sur is a place for meditation amid the indescribable beauty of Northern California's rugged coastline. Not too far away, take the loop of the 17-mile drive off Highway 1, near Monterey. You'll see beautiful homes and the three magnificent golf courses of Pebble Beach, Spy Glass Hill and Cypress.	You'll be fascinated by Gold Rush Country, accessed by Route 49 (named after the famous '49ers). A tour should include the restored towns of Columbia and Auburn where you can buy authentic old medicine bottles sold to miners. Sacramento also has good Gold Rush displays.

For further information about Northern California, contact:

California Office of Tourism
P.O.Box 1499
Sacramento, CA 95812
☎ (916) 322-1396

WHAT PEOPLE LIKE ABOUT NORTHERN CALIFORNIA

Dependables	**Centrics**	**Venturers**

Dependables enjoy many of the same things about Northern California, including their favorite city San Francisco. But they describe it in more muted tones, preferring to soak up the atmosphere at a more leisurely pace. Their comments reflect these interests.

Listen to the enthusiasm of *Centrics* as they talk about Northern California's diversity.

Venturers especially emphasize the diversity of things to do in Northern California, and overwhelmingly lavish their praise on San Francisco. If you get tired of the city, you can jump in a car and drive for an hour in almost any direction to change the scenery and the kinds of activities you can pursue. Their comments express these feelings.

I just like all of Northern California. It has beautiful scenery, the people are friendly, and there's lots to look at.
Secretary, 28 years old, Springfield, IL

I love Napa Valley and the rest of the wine country. It's quiet and peaceful, an easy paced life-style.
44-year-old female executive, Burlington, NJ

San Francisco has such a variety of activities and it's so easy to get around. It's a beautiful city, largely unspoiled. It has great restaurants, many fabulous sights, and culture and the arts.
39-year-old male writer, Brooklyn, NY

San Francisco has beautiful scenery, good restaurants, and the wine country is so close by. I just love relaxing around that place.
46-year-old senior executive, Bronx, NY

The city (San Francisco) has such varied and beautiful terrain and a wealth of activities available.
Male CPA, age 35, Charlottesville, VA

There's so much to see and do there (in San Francisco). You can walk to everywhere, prices are relatively reasonable and the weather relatively O.K. BART (Bay Area Rapid Transit) makes the whole thing so accessible.
Executive, 59 years old, Bellerose Manor, NY

Morro Bay State Park at Morro is it for me. It has lots of trees in the campground, and lots of room on site. Everything is accessible by walking into town. And it's a great spot for scuba diving.
28-year-old CPA, Sacramento, CA

At Mt. Shasta, the people are friendly, you've got clean air and water, spectacular scenery, and you'll make such great friends with everyone.
41-year-old female executive, Idaho Falls, ID

The Sierras have open space, a beautiful environment, and they have a sense of remoteness and isolation. They provide a real physical challenge.
48-year-old executive, Encinitas, CA

WHAT PEOPLE LIKE ABOUT NORTHERN CALIFORNIA

Dependables

Centrics

Venturers

I'll take Napa Valley. It has relaxation written all over it. It's close enough to cultural activities and tours. And it's very nice even in November or December of the year when there are less tourists. The B&Bs are not crowded.
49-year-old entrepreneur, Nixa, MO

It's so peaceful on the seashore at Pajora Dunes . It's uncrowded, relatively undeveloped, and just plain beautiful.
67-year-old retired pilot, Oakland, CA

Carmel has everything. It's relaxing, scenic, has good food, good accommodations and great shopping.
45-year-old executive, Pleasanton, CA

Everything's good about Napa: 1. good scenery, 2. good weather, 3. good food, and 4. good tennis and golf.
Housewife and executive, Cambridge, MA

There's a cleanliness about San Francisco that I like. And, it has good weather, natural beauty, great food, and a variety of things to do.
33-year-old male pharmacist, Tucson, AZ

I don't know which I like better—my shrink's office or Northern California. It has scenic beauty and great people.
Single female motion picture producer, Beverly Hills, CA

The climate is moderate, people are mostly great, and there's lots to see and do. If you get tired of it, you can go to the Sequoia forest, the wineries or head across the Golden Gate. It's a beautiful city with great architecture and many interesting places within a hundred miles.
62-year-old middle manager, Lancaster, PA

Northern California scored just a fraction below the classification as a five star destination in my surve These comments reflect the sincere enthusiasm of the many people who visit the area. If you draw a hu dred mile circle around San Francisco, you'll cover most of the places they talk about, including several pa of the wine country, the lonely and isolated places in the Sierras, the quaintness and charm of Carmel a the Monterey Peninsula, the Sequoia and Redwood forests and some of the great golf resorts of the wor When you come, don't hurry. Take your time and enjoy the relaxed lifestyles that captivate its many visitc Plan on doing a lot of walking, wherever you go. The weather, the many different sights, and the gre shopping (also mentioned by many visitors) invite you to explore things on foot.

Maine

#5 RATING: ★★★★

Centrics	Venturers	Dependables
10	10	8

Maine is 89 percent forested.
Ninety-eight percent of the nation's blueberries come from Maine.
Resident "downeasters" disdain urban pretension, prefer practicality.
Mt. Desert Island is shaped like a lobster claw.
L.L. Bean in Freeport stays open 24 hrs, 365 days a year.

Those who choose Maine as a favorite vacation destination rave about the scenic beauty, the laid-back ambience and the great food. It may sound like many another spot in the United States, but Maine's attractions are very individual to this "Pine Tree" state. When Maine's visitors talk about the scenery, they refer to the famous rugged, rocky coastline rather than "sun 'n fun" kinds of beaches. People they meet are friendly, but uncrowded areas are singled out for mention, and more than one visitor noted their appreciation for, "nice people, and they leave you alone."

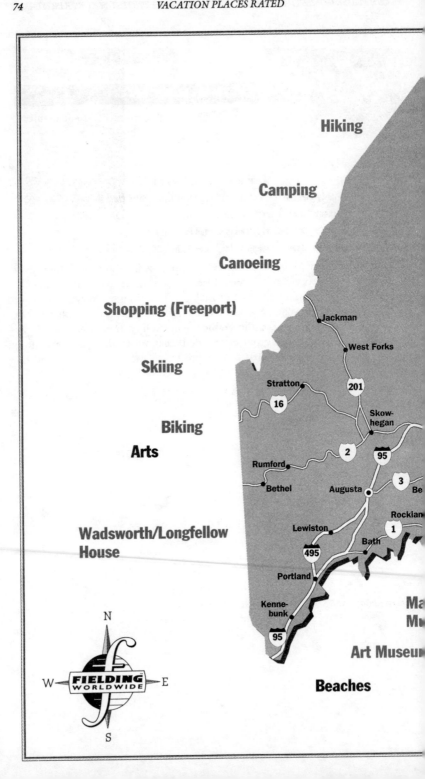

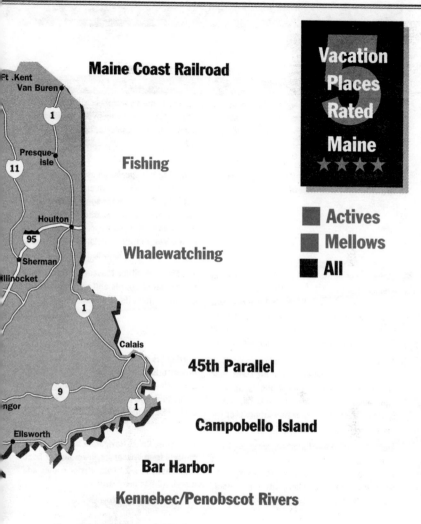

Maine Coast Railroad

Fishing

Whalewatching

45th Parallel

Campobello Island

Bar Harbor

Kennebec/Penobscot Rivers

Acadia National Park

Schooner Days

River Rafting

Vacation Places Rated

Maine

★★★★

■ **Actives**

■ **Mellows**

■ **All**

Ft .Kent
Van Buren
1

Presque-
isle
11

Houlton
95
Sherman
llinocket
1

Calais

9
1
ngor
Ellsworth

WHAT TO DO IN MAINE

Actives	Mellows
1 Acadia National Park offers an unusual scenic backdrop of ocean and mountains. All kinds and levels of recreation are offered: hiking and bike trails, watersports and cross-country skiing are examples.	One of Maine's special events is Schooner Days, held in early July in the Rockland/Thomaston area. For information ☎ *(207) 596-0376.*
2 Give white-water rafting a try on either the Kennebec or Penobscot Rivers.	Shopping is a special pleasure around Freeport. It offers not only quaint antique stores, but is headquarters for some of the finest outlet stores in the US. Your travel agent or library can point you to some of the best bargain areas, of which Rockport Shoes and L.L. Bean are the best known.
3 Maine is one of the most important lobstering areas in the world. Most of the coastal communities have lobster boats that will take you out on the water, teach you everything you want to know about lobsters and how to catch them. Then, by all means, eat one for dinner.	The Maine Maritime Museum in Bath includes two former shipyards and some children's activities within its 15 acres.
4 For camera buffs, a visit to Maine wouldn't be complete without shooting Nubble Light near York Harbor, one of the most photographed lighthouses in the state. Nearby is Wiggley Bridge, a restored suspension bridge over the York River.	Portland is Maine's cultural showplace. Among other attractions, visit the Wadsworth-Longfellow House and the Portland Museum of Art (displaying artists associated with the state, like Homer and Wyeth).
5 Maine is a good headquarters for quick trips into Canada. One notable historic site in New Brunswick is Campobello Island (across the narrows from Lubec) where future president Franklin D. Roosevelt spent most of his boyhood summers.	The Maine Coast Navigation and Railroad departs from Wiscasset. Train and/or boat tours last 1-1 1/2 hours. Historic sites and marsh wildlife are featured.

For further information about Maine, contact:

Maine Publicity Bureau
P.O. Box 2300
Hallowell, ME 04347
☎ (207) 623-0363

WHAT PEOPLE LIKE ABOUT MAINE

Dependables

Centrics

Venturers

Although *dependables* rate Maine lower than *centrics* or *venturers*, there is still plenty for them to explore and enjoy. Most important to this group of people is the scenic beauty, the quaintness of the small towns, and the general restfulness of the area. Many seem to have family and friends in Maine, and they feel at home there. One man remarked to me that he liked spending time in a place where tradition was in place and respected.

Vacations in Maine are perceived by *centrics* as offering a different pace of life. They like the casual life near the coast, or the camping and recreation of the more inland forests. New England hospitality seems more relaxed than in other parts of the country, neither formal nor overwhelming, which puts this group at ease. The more *active centrics* emphasize how many things there are to do in a small area, like viewing historic sites, museums and galleries, hiking, fishing, swimming and boating. *Mellow centrics* talk about shopping for antiques and gifts in quaint, picturesque towns, the wide range of good accommodations and the natural, unspoiled beauty of Maine's rocky shoreline. Here are some of their own words:

Maine, with its forests that grow to the rocky water's edge, its low density population, and its variety of activities and attractions, has designed itself for the *venturers* among us. When they mention scenic beauty, they emphasize the wilderness of Maine, the "natural, unspoiled" mountains and coastline, the abundant wildlife of the forests. These folks are busy! They follow the bike and hiking trails, they sail, they camp, they play golf and watch whales. Like all Maine tourists, they appreciate the inns and hotels, the shopping, and the delicious dining—especially seafood. There is nothing in the world like lobster pulled out of Maine waters, and onto your dinner plate in minutes. Read what the *venturers* say to us:

I have fond memories of staying near clear, clean water and sharing good meals with friends. We like to do a little hiking in the mountains, too.
Scientist, Chalfont, PA

The coast of Maine offers so much. It has beauty, history, lots of relaxing coastline, museums and galleries. We've always had good shopping and international food experiences. We find it accessible and economical. There is a lot to do in a small area.
Mid-level manager, 41, Porter Valley, CA

What I remember is the sound of the waves on the rocks, the foghorns at dusk and dawn, the unspoiled beauty of nature, and all the local crafts and the wide variety of people.
Human resources manager, female, Nederland, CO

I love that rocky coastline!
Female college student, Frederick, MD

We bought land there because we like the laid back atmosphere. Fishing, swimming, hiking and snow-shoeing in winter are hobbies we enjoy there.
Homemaker, Amesbury, MA

We stay at a wonderful old hotel (the Claremont in Southwest Harbor), and enjoy the peace and the beauty of the scenery. We go hiking, sailing, bird watching, whale watching and generally relax.
Female CPA, Bronxville, NY

WHAT PEOPLE LIKE ABOUT MAINE

Dependables

I go to one of the camps that is available to me. It's restful, scenic and full of tradition. I'm able to spend time with family and friends, and find it a very good way to get away.

Military man, Concord, NH

Centrics

The friendly community of Boothbay Harbor has a really relaxing atmosphere, good food and great gift shops. I love the ocean view and the way it smells.

Self-employed male, Baltimore, MD

I like the casual life on vacation. I go saltwater fishing, love to eat the seafood. Off season especially, it's uncrowded, and I enjoy the company of the natives.

Retired male, 79, Carmel, NY

Venturers

It's an unspoiled wilderness that has changed very little in 30 years. That's very appealing in this day and age.

Self-employed male, 38, Madison, NJ

It's rustic and "country" there. I feel the peace and quiet, and I'm glad that people tend to leave you alone.

Female office worker, Newton, MA

Las Vegas

#6 RATING: ★★★★

Centrics	Venturers	Dependables
9	6	9

During the Civil War Nevada silver kept the Union solvent.

Nevada claims the first use of skis in the U.S.

Nevada is a world supplier of turquoise and rare opals.

The discovery of 1 1/2 ft. long moccasins led archaeologists to think giants once inhabited Nevada.

The Hard Rock Hotel has invested $2 million in rock memorabilia.

Las Vegas belongs to Dependables and Centrics. It's their kind of town. If you're a Venturer, forget about the place. You might enjoy a drive through it to see the man-made miracles and to contemplate how something this unique could happen. But, after you've had lunch, you'll probably want to move on.

If you're a Dependable or a Centric, however, you'll love everything about Las Vegas. In my interviews, they state that three things make the town appealing to them. In order of importance, it's gambling, lots of entertainment and reasonable prices for hotels and meals. Occasionally someone will mention that interesting and attractive outdoor attractions exist nearby. But mostly they feel captivated by the sights and sounds of a city where miles of neon flash at you 24 hours a day, and where time passes unnoticed because no clocks or windows exist in the casinos to remind you of the real world outside or your responsibilities that await back home.

In my continuing surveys of Americans' leisure time pursuits, only four percent were interested in taking a gambling trip as recently as 1985. Now that figure has jumped to 16 percent, and it's still climbing. Among the eight states that have casinos (including Indian reservations), Las Vegas has always been the mecca, the leader on every dimension. It gets about 30 million visitors a year, has nearly 90,000 hotel rooms (the most in the U.S.), and is also the fastest growing city in the U.S. If you want to visit, you have to do some advance planning because hotel occupancies currently run at well over 90 percent, also the highest in the U.S.— and probably in the world.

To those who like it, Las Vegas offers excitement, 24 hours a day and seven days a week. You can choose from dozens of gaudy casinos to play the tables or pull one-armed bandits, see different big name entertainment every night you're there and eat in fancy restaurants at bargain prices. Also, your hotel room won't cost you an arm and a leg.

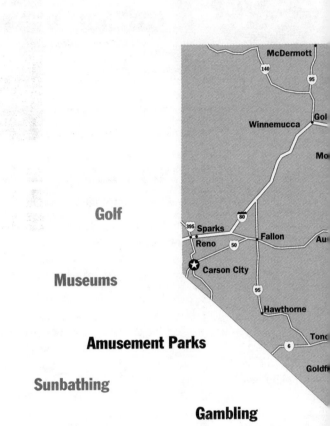

Golf

Museums

Amusement Parks

Sunbathing

Gambling

Tennis

All-you-can-eat Buffets

People-watching

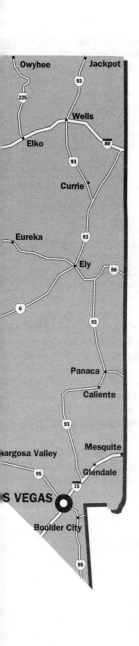

Vacation Places Rated

Las Vegas

★★★★

■ **Actives**

■ **Mellows**

■ **All**

Shows

Lake Mead/Hoover Dam

Boating

Water-skiing

Swimming

Getting Married

Shopping

WHAT TO DO IN LAS VEGAS

Actives	Mellows

1   Visit the new Hard Rock Hotel/Casino. See top groups in an intimate club atmosphere at The Joint. Or check out the Hard Rock Beach Club with whirlpools, spas, a sandy beach and a lagoon with underwater music. The collection of rock memorabilia throughout the casino/hotel is impressive.

Check out each of the new mega hotels that opened in late 1993. The MGM Grand (5005 rooms), has wax figures of Dorothy, The Tin Man, the Straw Man and the Cowardly Lion from Wizard of Oz and a 33 acre amusement park. Treasure Island (2900 rooms) has an outdoor 65 foot lagoon called Buccaneer Bay with replicas of a British Man o' War and a pirate vessel that sail to each other and do mock battle several times a day (22 actors, music, and lots of battle sounds).

3   Restaurants—you've got to try some. What you get for the price at some of the inexpensive "all you can eat" buffets in the big hotels will amaze you. Then, go to a few of the better known, pricier places on the strip. Ask your concierge for recommendations.

Lots of museums exist around the city, most with modest charges or free admission. Take a look at The Imperial Palace Hotel's auto collection, the U.S. bank note display at Binion's Horseshoe Casino, the Liberace Museum, the Guinness World Records Museum, and the Las Vegas Natural History Museum.

4   If you're in to golf or tennis, you've found your place. Golf courses are attractive and reasonably priced. Tennis courts at the better hotels are well-maintained and usually free to guests.

It's a grand place to shop. Caesar's Palace hotel has 70 very tony boutique stores; the Fashion Show Mall features Beverly Hills-types of stores, along with more conventional department stores and specialty shops. You'll find more unique kinds of items in Vegas than most places because the town's elite don't want to be caught wearing the same dress to a party (I know; I did a study for Neiman Marcus before it opened).

5   Escape to Lake Mead/Hoover Dam area (24 miles away) for boating, water skiing or swimming. Nearby mountains are especially good during the hot summers. Great for hiking, hunting, mountain climbing and winter sports.

Check out the gambling at as many places as you can (hotel owners prefer to call it gaming—it sounds less sinful). Each casino has a different theme. MGM Grand built four casinos, from informal to a Monte Carlo style.

For information about Las Vegas contact

Las Vegas Convention & Visitors Authority
Convention Center
3150 Paradise Road
Las Vegas, NV 89109
☎ (702) 892-0711

WHAT PEOPLE LIKE ABOUT LAS VEGAS

Dependables

Centrics

Venturers

In recent years, some of the big hotel and casino owners have tried to make Las Vegas into a family resort by adding children's attractions to the large, new hotels (MGM Grand, Treasure Island and Luxor, in addition to the older Circus Circus). They want to attract baby boomers who take their children with them on vacations. But, few people interviewed ever talk about how much fun it is to have the kids along. Rather, they still see Vegas for what it always has been—the best place in the world to kick back, gamble and forget about what's happening in the rest of your life. Listen to what *Dependables* say turns them on about Vegas.

Centrics also like gambling, but they put much more emphasis on the variety of entertainment available in Las Vegas, and the sense of excitement that the city creates. It amazes them and seems to invigorate their lives. Feel the enthusiasm in what *Centrics* say about this desert town.

Although some *Venturers* also like to gamble, they don't stick with it around the clock the way *Dependables* and some *Centrics* do. Rather, *Venturers* tend to get bored after awhile and then look for other action. Shows, especially with name entertainment, can amuse them, but not for long. They use simple descriptions like, "It's exciting," "It's got 24 hours non-stop activity," and "There's no shortage of things to see or do."

We love everything there. The weather's great. The food is wonderful and reasonably priced. And we just love to gamble.
52-year-old secretary, Springfield, OH

What I like is the awesome casinos and entertainment facilities. To me it's the eighth wonder of the world. And its got great food at great prices.
29-year-old single man, self-employed, Grandview, MO

It's got good food that's not expensive, it's got gambling which I like, and it's got great stage shows. And the hotels are nice.
41-year-old secretary from Trempleleau, WI

It's exciting and always changing. It has a happy, festive atmosphere. Its got excellent prices and a variety of entertainment. And there's an opportunity to gamble.
55-year-old male, middle manager, Bellaire, TX

For me, it's gambling! There's no stress. You can forget about problems right away. There's no concept of time. Most of the casinos' help are friendly and accommodating.
48-year-old male executive, Northe Platte, NE

There's something for everyone. It's a great escape. It has gambling of all kinds. And it's got good food and good entertainment.
Male Field Inspector, Arnold, MO 51 years old

WHAT PEOPLE LIKE ABOUT LAS VEGAS

Dependables

Centrics

Venturers

There's plenty of entertainment and you don't have to spend all of your time gambling. It's got very reasonable food and lodging costs. It's very clean and it has beautiful scenery.

36-year-old female student from South Easton, MA

The total cost of the entire package is great for someone like me. I'm retired and I enjoy the perks they give for senior citizens.

69-year-old male from Beaumont, TX

It has good food, great entertainment, wonderful night life, majestic scenery and, of course, gambling.

Male executive, 47, Saint Claire Shores, MI

It has excitement and casinos, as well as a beautiful variety of hotels. The food is good and inexpensive.

49-year-old female teacher, Baytown, TX

Wow it's got it all! Fine foods, clean accommodations, entertainment and shopping. And it has gambling. With all this you still get reasonable travel packages.

Retired homemaker, Denver, CO

Washington State

#7 RATING: ★★★★

Centrics	Venturers	Dependables
9	10+	7

Leads the world in apple production.

Early Seattle had a shortage of females.

Mt. Rainier is the fifth highest mountain in the lower 48 states.

Seattle's repertory theater community ranks second to New York.

Bruce Lee and Jimi Hendrix were born in Seattle.

The State of Washington seems to exist for the benefit of Venturers. They like the kind of excitement it exudes, the variety of life-styles that travelers can pursue, and the ability to get away from it all or get totally involved on the same trip. In fact, if they alone rated the state, it would be classified in the five star category.

Those who like it believe that it offers more diversity than practically any other destination in the world. Venturers and Centrics both sprinkle their conversations with comments about its scenic, natural beauty that is apparent almost regardless of where you drive. Tall, snowcapped mountain ranges provide the setting, they say, for outdoor fun, such as hiking, camping or personal meditation. Clean, clear water everywhere—oceans, harbors, lakes and streams—invites visitors to sail, powerboat, swim or just be mesmerized by its constant motion. Add to this the fact that Washington also has an abundance of man-made attractions, such as good ski resorts, fabulous restaurants and interesting, well maintained cities—without suffering from overdevelopment or excessive commercialism.

Although Washington sometimes gets criticized by outsiders for the amount of rain it gets each year and for its relatively cool climate, the Centrics and Venturers I've interviewed generally have no complaints. They believe that Washington weather borders on the ideal. They like its coolness; it contributes to an invigorating feeling that makes you want to get out and do things. It could be participating in active sports, or just walking around to take in the sights and sounds of one of its unique cities.

Although Seattle is the favorite in Washington for these travelers, most references are to other parts of the state. It's not that they don't appreciate Seattle's many charms. It's just that the state's natural beauty and the many opportunities to do things outdoors override most thoughts about city life. The area west of the Cascades dominates most people's imaginations. The eastern half hardly ever gets talked about by visitors.

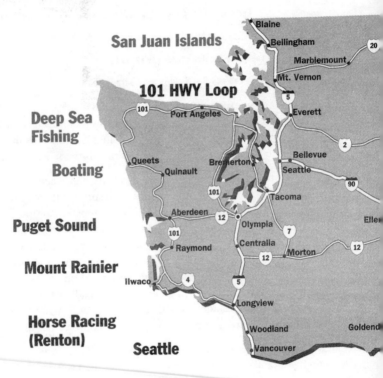

Mt. St. Helens
Volcanic Monument

Vancouver Island   Skii

San Juan Islands

101 HWY Loop

Deep Sea
Fishing

Boating

Puget Sound

Mount Rainier

Horse Racing
(Renton)   Seattle

Museums/Arts

Shopping

Space Needle

Vacation Places Rated 7

Washington

★ ★ ★ ★

ympic National Park

North Cascades National Park

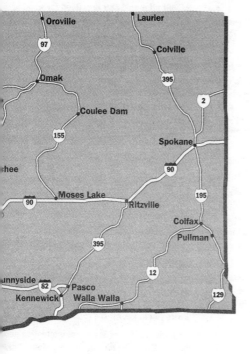

■ **Actives**
■ **Mellows**
■ **All**

Spokane Falls

Hiking

Camping

Bicycling

Snoqualmie Pass and Falls

WHAT TO DO IN WASHINGTON STATE

Actives	Mellows

1 Take the 101 Highway loop around Olympic Peninsula. It can be done in a day, but two days are more leisurely. Stop by the National Park's Visitor Center (Port Angeles), catch Ruby Beach on the western coast (rugged and strangely scenic), and don't miss the Hoh Rain Forest (up to 200 inches of rain a year; magical and mystical with moss on every tree, some of which reach nearly 300 feet). Plan on doing some walking and hiking.

Visit Pike Place Market at Pike Street and First Avenue. Overlooking the waterfront, the long narrow complex offers an enticing display of fresh seafood, produce and arts and crafts. Also take in Pioneer Square Historic District, just south of downtown, an area rebuilt after an 1889 fire. Good for walking tours.

2 Visit the San Juan Islands, a very different climate from most of Washington (warmer and with less rain). These vary from isolated Lopez Island (good for camping and bicycling), to Orcus Island (largest, most rugged of the islands), to San Juan Island which is very popular and offers a variety of activities from sightseeing to boating and taking interesting drives.

The Space Needle provides a view of the entire city. Choose a good, clear day when cloud cover's not too low so that you can see great distances and the snow clad tops of Mount Olympus and Mount Rainier. Bring along a good camera; the pictures can be stunning.

3 Use Seattle's closeness to Canada to visit Vancouver and Victoria. Both are fascinating cities with a British heritage (especially Victoria) and offer a cleanliness and feeling of safety and comfort not present in many U.S. cities.

Museums and attractions in Seattle are worth separate visits. In most cases, their names suggest their displays, as The Maritime Heritage Center, Nordic Heritage Museum, Museum of History and Industry, the Seattle Aquarium, the Museum of Flight

4 Visit Mount Rainier, a short drive from Seattle. A 14,410-foot tall volcano, it has a permanent glacial cap. Particularly attractive in the summer when wildflowers bloom.

Drive through Snoqualmie Pass (I-90), the main east-west artery through the state. Beautiful surrounding hills and quaint villages invite you to get off the road.

5 Tour Seattle by foot. It has a variety of interesting museums, outdoor markets and art centers. The city is cleaner and safer than most large cities, and has a more uniform architectural style that gives it a feeling of cohesiveness. As I said, the city is cleaner and safer than most which encourages people to walk around.

Boat tours of Puget Sound are interesting and informative. Take the longer excursions that include lunch, brunch or dinner on board to see more of the area and come away with a more relaxing feeling.

For further information about Washington, contact:

Washington Tourism Division
101 General Administration Building
AX-13
Olympia, WA 98504-9052
☎ (800) 544-1800

WHAT PEOPLE LIKE ABOUT WASHINGTON STATE

Dependables	**Centrics**	**Venturers**

Few good quotations can be gotten from *Dependables* in my surveys. They offer lukewarm comments, such as, "It's a beautiful place," "It has good shopping, food and climate," and "I like the state's basketball tournament." In general, outdoor attractions do not interest them as much. As we have seen, visitors who like Washington the most get captivated by the sense that the state has not lost its natural charm. It still has a pristine quality and has not become overly commercial, even though it also has a world class city—Seattle.

Washington captures the hearts and souls of *Venturers*. But *Centrics* also feel its pulse. Their comments may sound a bit more muted, but that's because their personalities also are somewhat less outgoing. Scenic beauty and a variety of things to see and do also capture the imagination of *Centrics*.

Venturers offer the most enthusiastic comments.

Seattle, Washington has lots to do. It's a big city with great food and nightlife. And there are mountains and nature nearby.
39-year-old self employed male, Witchita, KS

The San Juan Islands have everything I need, especially the uninhabited islands. You have water, serenity and weather that is warmer and not as wet as in other parts of the state. It's a good area for sailing, too.
Senior executive, 59 years, Chesterfield, MO

I like Wenatchee, Washington. It's scenic and the people are very friendly. The mountains and the water create a very relaxing feeling. It's just a beautiful place.
32-year-old female, also self employed, Carthage, TX

I like the back country of the Olympic Peninsula or the Cascade Mountains. It has solitude, clean air and clean water. It lacks the sounds and busyness of civilization.
53-year-old teacher, Bremerton, WA

Puget Sound has scenery and a mild climate. And it has minimal commercialization.
Male executive, 51, Fort Wayne, IN

Seattle and the surrounding area. There's a lot to do there. It's very scenic, you have good skiing, and you can go hiking in the mountains. It's a very clean city.
30-year-old housewife, State College, PA

WHAT PEOPLE LIKE ABOUT WASHINGTON STATE

Dependables

Centrics

Seattle has most of what I want...beautiful scenery and the people are nice. The summers are amazing there, they are just so nice.

27-year-old businessman, San Jose, CA

Seattle has much to offer. Lots of variety in outdoor activities and natural beauty. It has music, clubs and theater.

Grade school teacher, 41, Fairhope, AL

Venturers

Give me Whidbey Island. is still pristine and not crow ed. The people are friendly a congenial.

Male entrepreneur, 6 Mission Viejo, C

I always like Seattle. It b good restaurants and ther good sightseeing in the are There's boating on Lake Wa ington, and good golfing in area. And, you're near enou to Canada to be able to go there when you want to.

81-year-old homemak Ponte Vedra Beach, I

Vermont

#8 RATING: ★★★★

Centrics	Venturers	Dependables
9	9	8

In 1941 the people of Vermont declared war on Germany two months before the U.S. did.
Vermont leads the nation in maple syrup production.
American Museum of Fly Fishing displays the tackle of Gen. Patton, Daniel Webster and Winslow Homer.
Vermont boasts the Morgan, the only horse breed originating in the U.S.
At Haskell Opera House, Derby Line, the audience sits in the U.S. and the stage is in Canada.

If you don't have time to tour all of New England, Vermont is the state you might choose to capture the feeling of the entire area. It's New England exemplified, lacking only a seashore. The people I survey mention the scenic beauty, especially the changing colors of the fall foliage. They enjoy skiing, breakfasts with pure Vermont maple syrup, typical New England features like covered bridges and efficient but friendly service from hosts of chic bed-and-breakfast inns and from campground operators.

Destinations earn high marks when they offer something for everyone within their own unique environment and Vermont is no exception. These travelers particularly emphasize the state's rural environment, its lack of commercialization and the quiet, relaxation and peace they experience while there. Here is small town America, New England style, that is echoed on the West Coast by Oregon. That rural atmosphere does not mean there isn't plenty to do in Vermont, however. History exists everywhere, as well as scenic beauty, skiing in winter, fishing and watersports in the summer, and solitude or city amenities as you choose.

Lake Champlain

Watersports

Burlington Shopping

**Ben and Jerry's
Ice Cream Factory
(Waterbury)**

Sailing

Skiing

Mountain Biking

Killington

Fishing

Horseback Riding

Bed and Breakfasts

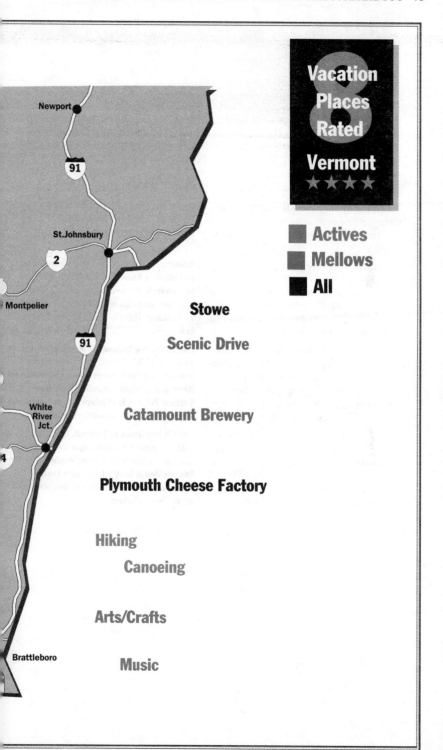

WHAT TO DO IN VERMONT

Actives	Mellows
1 Lake Champlain runs southward from the Canadian border and offers lots of sailing and watersports activities. Look for the fabled Lake Champlain monster, à la Loch Ness! If you'd like to just be a passenger sometimes, there are scenic ferry trips available.	Combine seeing the fall colors and a visit to the Stratton Arts Festival in Stratton Mountain. More than 200 Vermont artists participate.
2 Do you ride? The Killington Mountain Equestrian Festival takes place in July. You can see or participate in hunting, jumping or racing events.	One of the most famous resorts in the east is Topnotch Resort and Spa in Stowe. Play hard, or relax and renew yourself.
3 Both Stowe and Killington boast breathtaking gondola rides to the top of Vermont's highest peaks. Once there, hike, ski or just enjoy the view. Both also offer exciting alpine slides, where riders control the speed of descent as they take in the scenery.	Arlington is Norman Rockwell's home town and offers a Rockwell exhibit in a 19th century church. His fans enjoy viewing hundreds of examples of his work amidst a real Rockwell setting. There is also a Rockwell museum in Rutland.
4 For an exotic cultural experience, take a side trip into French Canada, just across the border to the north. The people and the ambience are different from the rest of Canada, from France and from the U.S.	The Shelburne Museum is an extensive reconstruction of 37 historic structures from all over New England. These house collections or items and artifacts depicting early New England life and is of interest to scholars and tourists alike. Formal gardens, too!
5 Camel's Hump State Park is one of the few undeveloped peaks among the highest mountains in Vermont. Investigated first by French explorers who settled colorful names on several areas, it can be an invigorating experience. Hike to the summit where rare alpine vegetation is found.	Food is important in Vermont. Don't leave without touring a maple sugar factory (Vermont is the country's leading producer) or the famous Ben & Jerry's Ice Cream Factory, whose advertising always features black and white Vermont cows.

For further information about Vermont, contact:

Vermont Department of Travel and Tourism
134 State Street
Montpelier, VT 05602
☎ (802) 828-3236

WHAT PEOPLE LIKE ABOUT VERMONT

Dependables

Dependables also visit Vermont, but in smaller numbers. They are less likely to choose it as a favorite destination (unless they ski), perhaps because it is in fact somewhat less commercially developed and farther from the coast than other New England States. Those few *dependables* who mention Vermont are particularly fond of the well-run hotels, inns and bed-and-breakfast accommodations available.

Centrics

Centric personalities go to Vermont for the scenery, especially in the fall. As a bonus, they discover the friendliness of the people, the pleasant accommodations, the variety of things to do outdoors and the interesting shops. One woman who stayed near Killington praised the local craft industry, commenting that Vermont stores offer distinctive items she can't get elsewhere. Camping, golf and fishing are activities specified by *centrics* as particularly enjoyable in Vermont's fresh air and crisp weather. Comments of *centrics* who like Vermont demonstrate their enthusiasm.

I had always heard about the changing colors of the leaves, but really didn't know what to expect. It's absolutely glorious, I couldn't believe it. There's something special about the climate, too. It makes you feel alive.
Homemaker, 45, Tucson, AZ

We enjoy a quiet atmosphere on vacation. Traveling with the family in Vermont, we feel we can do what we want, when we want and how we want. Kids can wander safely and still have a good time!
Construction worker, 27, Auburn, NH

Venturers

Vermont is a good vacation destination for *venturers* because it remains uncommercialized and uncrowded. That affords them the opportunity to spend time getting familiar with the real New England and its residents and also to spend time in comparative solitude when they wish. Venturers say that skiing dominates all sports in Vermont and their comments confirm that. They can choose from beginner or advanced slopes, and hardly have to repeat a location during a season. They single out Killington, Stowe and Sugarbush as special favorites for winter vacations. *Venturers* admire nature in all its forms, and they say that Vermont's mountains and forests are very fulfilling. For example:

The summer weather is perfect for lots of activities because it doesn't get too hot. We like a lot of water around for good fishing. The scenic background is beautiful. There is a lot to do outdoors, yet its close to city/suburban amenities.
Male government employee, Frederick, MD

We bought a summer home there, where we retreat whenever we can. We enjoy the wild and natural surroundings, and sometimes you just crave solitude.
Publishing executive, 42, New York City

WHAT PEOPLE LIKE ABOUT VERMONT

Dependables

Centrics

We enjoyed all of our New England vacation, but Vermont was my personal favorite. There is just something about the atmosphere that's special, especially around Lake Champlain.

Executive secretary, Canton, OH

We drove through so many pretty towns, I can't remember the names of them all. The backdrop of the Green Mountains is very impressive scenery. The food is very good, too. I had the best breakfasts of my life in Vermont—maybe it's the homegrown maple syrup!

Male insurance executive, Nashville, TN

Venturers

It's so clean and beautiful and quiet there. We go for the skiing, mainly, but like to break it up with day trips here and there. Things look like you expect New England to look.

Female lab assistant, Lexington, KY

It's beautiful, it's not overcrowded and the skiing is great.

Male student, Boston, MA

We like to ski, but there is a lot to see and do besides. Boats, fishing, hiking, festivals in the summer. My husband has gone hunting. Everyone is always nice . We like to get away from the "big city" atmosphere.

Office worker, Baltimore, MD

It's small in area, and somewhat far from the rest of the country, but Vermont packs a powerful punch in terms of tourist appreciation.

Oregon

#9 RATING: ★★★★

Centrics	Venturers	Dependables
9	10	5

Oregon has the only nickel smelter in the U.S.
The transcontinental railroad reached Portland in 1883.
Crater Lake at 1996 ft. is the nation's deepest.
Ft. Stevens was shelled by a Japanese sub in June, 1942.
Some sand dunes in Oregon are as high as 500 ft.

The great outdoors exists outside of the Pacific Northwest, but you would never know it, the way people talk about Oregon. Beautiful scenery is everywhere, but Oregon has special qualities imparted by an abundance of water—from the Pacific Ocean, from the lakes and streams, and from the rainfall. One visitor told me that her word association with "Oregon" was "green." This atmosphere inspires a wealth of outdoor activities, most of which take place along the Pacific Coast, within easy reach of the ocean. Enthusiasts mention camping, hiking, biking, horseback riding, whale watching, windsurfing and especially fishing. While it's true that these activities can be pursued elsewhere, there is no other place as "green."

Especially noteworthy is the fact that a very high proportion of Oregon residents choose a site in Oregon as their favorite place to vacation.

Portland Rose Festiva

Astoria Column (Scenery)

**Fort Clatsop
National Memorial**

**Mt. Hood
Scenic Lo**

River Rafting

Fishing

**Devil's Punch Bowl
State Park**

**Warm Springs
Indian Reservation**

Eugene Parks

Sea Lion Caves

Crater Lake National Park

Vacation Places Rated

Oregon

★ ★ ★ ★

Actives

Mellows

All

Cascade Range

Columbia River Gorge

Camping

Hiking

Wine Country Tours

WHAT TO DO IN OREGON

Actives	Mellows
1 Explore the Mt. Hood Scenic Loop, beginning in Portland and continuing through Mt. Hood National Forest (Mt. Hood is a dormant volcano) to the Columbia Gorge. It offers spectacular scenery and outdoor activities.	Although covered bridges are normally associated with New England, there are several in Oregon. Upper Drift Creek Bridge, Lost Creek Bridge and Lane County's Office Bridge are notable.
2 Crater Lake National Park on the crest of the Cascades features the brilliant deep blue lake and many recreational facilities.	Fort Clatsop National Memorial near Astoria features a replica of a fort built by the Lewis and Clark expedition in 1805. In the summer, rangers present a living history program. The Astoria Column nearby is 125-feet high on Coxcomb Hill affording a wonderful view.
3 Don't miss Oregon Caves National Monument where the stalagmites and naturally carved cave walls inside Mount Elijah offer a special experience.	Of special interest to gardeners, the Portland Rose Festival is held each June in that city. ☎ *(503) 227-2681*.
4 The Warm Springs Indian Reservation is home to several tribes. Powwows and other special events are held throughout the year, and there is a museum specializing in exhibits from the tribes.	Like much of the West Coast, Oregon has a well developed wine industry, mostly still family owned farms. Almost all welcome visitors for tours and tastings. Call the Oregon Wine Growers Association ☎ *(503) 228-8403*.
5 Curious to see a recently active volcano? Several air charter companies in Portland are happy to give you a look at Mount St. Helens from above.	In a state full of parks, Eugene, Oregon is especially noted for its fine ones. While visiting Eugene, don't miss the Hult Center for the Performing Arts, an architectural triumph for a small city. See a performance, an art exhibit or take a guided tour.

For further information about Oregon, contact

Oregon Tourism Division
775 Summer Street, NE
Salem, OR 97310
☎ (503) 547-7842

WHAT PEOPLE LIKE ABOUT OREGON

Dependables

Oregon offers one puzzling contradiction: although it achieves a four-star rating overall, it is in some ways still a vacation secret from much of the country. This may account for the relatively few *dependables* who reported on this destination, and why this group has lower interest in it. As we know, *dependables* tend to like places that are popularized and familiar, and Oregon attracts active, outdoor types who are more "rugged individualists." However, Oregon has recently attracted more attention thanks to TV shows and feature films set in the state. Once people discover its stunning coastline and pretty small towns, I'll have quotes from lots of *dependables* to share with you.

Centrics

It's easy to see why Oregon as a vacation destination appeals to the *venturers* among us, but *centrics* also enjoy its clean beauty and relaxing atmosphere. One feature that *centrics* talk about is the small towns that are scattered along the coast. There is something about a friendly, attractive little town that goes hand in hand with relaxation and good memories. *Centric* travelers to Oregon also give more-than-usual high marks to the accommodations, which promises lots of clean, pleasant, affordable hotels and inns. The *centrics* comment:

Our all time favorite place to relax is Eagle Ridge near Klamath. It has beautiful scenery, nature, and is close to home. You can relax and do nothing, or take your choice of a million activities.

Factory foreman, Portland, OR

The scenic beauty is unmatched. Everything is green, and there is water everywhere. The whole environment is very friendly.

Manufacturing manager, Escondido, CA

Venturers

Oregon is well liked by all its visitors, but it is the *venturers* who have elevated it to its high rank. They are the people who take advantage of all the outdoor activities, and they are the ones who really appreciate the pristine beauty of the state and the fact that its beaches and recreation areas are still uncrowded. We received several comments not only about the beauty of the scenery, but also describing the *variety* that is unique to Oregon. The ocean leads into mountain ranges, which descend into valleys that become desert, and back into a mountainous area—all in the space of relatively few miles. Here is what the venturers tell us:

Oh, what a wonderful culture they have there! (Eugene) For example, everybody goes to Saturday market, to get what they need and meet each other. I think the weather is wonderful.

Female student, Poway, CA

We had the best meal of our lives in Coos Bay. I picked blackberries while my husband went fishing. Later on we put everything together for a great fresh dinner. I'll never forget it!

Female executive, 35, Newbury Park, CA

WHAT PEOPLE LIKE ABOUT OREGON

Dependables

Centrics

Venturers

Black Butte Ranch was great. The climate is very different from home, and I liked how clean and quiet it was. We did all the things you can do on a ranch. The hospitality was super.
Female teacher, Lansing, MI

I'm a fan of the climate. It's cool in the summer, and not too cold in the winter. I don't like extremes, so it's perfect for me.
Accountant, Springfield, IL

North Umpqua River is on of the most beautiful scenic rivers in the Pacific Northwest. It naturalness is unspoiled an the fly fishing is just great.
Retired male
Brookings, OR

It's so nice that the beache are uncrowded. I like to watc the whales, and there is goo hiking nearby. Lincoln City a small town, with friendl people. We feel like we fit righ in there.
Manager, manufacturing
Mt. Laurel, N

I've been windsurfing on th Columbia River and hav gone cross-country skiing in th winter. All our past experienc have been good ones, so we fee positive about returning. Th accommodations were lovely.
Homemaker, 32
Prescott, A

The lack of commercial en croachment is very refreshing.
Attorney, Reno, NV

Arizona

#10 RATING: ★★★★

Centrics	Venturers	Dependables
9	8	9

The Arizona trout is only found in Arizona.

14 Indian tribes live on 20 Arizona reservations.

The Grand Canyon is one of the Seven Natural Wonders of the World.

Tombstone was the site of the West's most famous gunfight (O.K. Corral).

Kitt's Peak Observatory at Sells operates the world's largest solar telescope.

Arizona has a unique profile in the interviews. References to its warm and comfortable weather equal the number of comments about its beauty and scenery. At all other destinations, the beauty of a place tends to overshadow thoughts about pleasant temperatures and plentiful amounts of sun.

During the winter months, most of the state basks in warm days and comfortable evenings, with pleasant, dry air creating a feeling that all is well, according to travelers in my surveys. Gentle desert breezes help to cleanse each person of the internal pressures and stress that they brought with them to the state. This helps to convince them that they should enjoy each day's pleasant moments, without worrying about what will happen tomorrow. Balmy weather comforts and caresses even troubled souls.

Arizona also demonstrates another relatively unique characteristic. All personality types, *venturers*, *centrics* and *dependables*, give the same reasons as to why they like the state. As you'll see in a moment, no distinguishable differences exist in what each of these groups likes about the state, or what they want to do when they're there. Although golf and tennis abound at major resorts in the Phoenix/Scottsdale and Tucson areas, most people say they simply want to relax when they get there and lie back while others serve their every wish.

The favorite areas in the state, in terms of frequency of mention, run from north to south. These include the Grand Canyon, Sedona/Oak Creek Canyon area, Phoenix/Scottsdale and Tucson. Beyond this, occasional references appear for some of Arizona's big lake areas in the north (Lake Powell, Glen Canyon Dam Recreation Area and Lake Mead). Surprisingly, the beautiful open desert areas with Saguaro cactus and other native plants around Tucson, which bloom profusely after the summer rains, and the breathtaking Painted Desert region east of the Grand Canyon do not receive spontaneous comment from interviewees. Apparently, most visitors fly or drive directly to the specific location of interest and do not venture much beyond those confines.

Grand Canyon

Mule Riding

Hiking

Boating

Lake Havasu

Colorado River

Watersports

Tucson

Pictograph Rocks

Golf/Tennis

Phoenix

Oak Creek
Canyon

Sedona (Arts)

15

67

North Rim

Grand Canyon

93

Kingman   40   Ash Fork   Willia

40   Fla

89

Prescott

17

93

Wickenberg

60

10

8   Casa G

Yuma

N

W   FIELDING WORLDWIDE   E

S

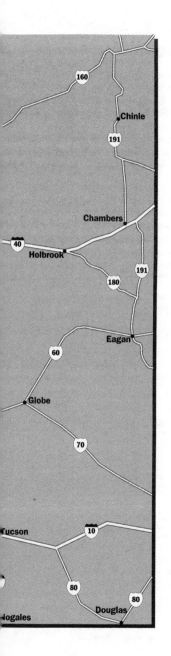

Lake Powell

Painted Desert

Petrified Forest

10
Vacation
Places
Rated

Arizona
★ ★ ★ ★

- Actives
- Mellows
- All

Cross Country Skiing

Montezuma Castle Monument

Indian Cliff Dwellings

Museums/Galleries

Saguaro National Monument

Horseback Riding

Tombstone/Jerome (History)

WHAT TO DO IN ARIZONA

Actives	Mellows
1 If you're in shape for it, a mule trip down to the bottom of the Grand Canyon is a memorable adventure. Ferde Grofé was so struck by it that he included the famous "On The Trail" interlude in his Grand Canyon Suite. You can't weigh over 200 pounds and must be at least 4'6" in height. When you return, have dinner at Angel Lodge. Good food in a magnificent old building.	If you haven't been there, the Grand Canyon is a must. Not only are the vistas stunning, but it offers so much more than is commonl known. The Kaibab National Forest surround it, and the Visitor Center has such interestin explanations of how it was formed. You'll se footprints dinosaurs left in ancient mud.
2 Watersports on the Colorado River are lots of fun. The western half of the state is a water wonderland fed by the Colorado. Tubing, river rafting, water-skiing, power boating, sailing and swimming are all excellent. Look to the Lake Havasu area, Glen Canyon Dam or Lake Powell regions for good locations.	Not far away, and another must see, is Oak Creek Canyon and Sedona. The canyon is lus and narrow, with very different kinds of vege tation from elsewhere in the state. The red rocks of Sedona offer a stunning backdrop pictures you'll take. Interesting art gallerie abound in the area.
3 Montezuma Castle National Monument contains the ruins of often-photographed prehistoric Indian cliff dwellings (built in 12th and 13th centuries). Makes you pause and think about their accomplishments. Located in the east, central portion of the state.	Arizona has many interesting old, small citie with intriguing histories. Try to catch Tombstone (south of Tucson where you can see humorous headstones and the graves of som famous people) and Jerome (a copper minin town that died and now attracts artists and others).
4 Winter sports also thrive in Arizona, from as far south as Tucson (Mt. Lemon), to the northern portion of the state. Cross-country skiing is great around the Flagstaff area.	Visit some of Arizona's natural wonders. The Petrified Forest (eastern portion of state, o of I-40) has rainbow colored remains of log that became mineralized. Nearby, the Painte Desert rivals all other grand vistas you may have encountered. Sunset Crater Volcano National Monument, also in the eastern (an northern) part of the state, has the remains of a once active volcano (a thousand years after Christ) and features multihue cinder c ors around its base.
5 Horseback riding is prevalent throughout the state, and is included as part of the package at dude ranches. These rides usually take you out into the desert, some with midnight rendezvous where cowhands set up tasty buffets for tired greenhorns.	If you golf or play tennis, you must bring yo equipment along with you when you visit. Large resort hotels typically have their own courses or courts.

For further information about Arizona, contact:

Arizona Department of Tourism
1100 West Washington Street
Phoenix, AZ 85007
☎ (800) 842-8257

WHAT PEOPLE LIKE ABOUT ARIZONA

Dependables

Centrics

Venturers

Dependables also provide similar kinds of comments that reflect the enticing nature of the state's comfortable climate and diversity.

We like the weather in the winter months and the activities that are offered that relate to some of our hobbies and interests. We also have made some very good friends there.

Retired male, 64, Outing, MN

Tucson has everything for us—great weather, natural beauty, friendly people, lots of churches, mountains all around, cactus and flowers and lots of good shopping.

55-year-old RN, Rockford, IL

Tucson has so much. It has good weather, historic sites, mountains, old home sites, historic churches, and interesting architecture.

Architect, 54, Chicago, IL

Sedona, Arizona is historic, beautiful country. Much of it is unpopulated, but it has good facilities there or close by in other towns.

Retired female, 65, Beech Grove, IN

I like the Grand Canyon. It reflects the beauty of God's creation, and it's so unspoiled.

39-year-old senior male executive, North Olmsted, OH

Note how enthralled visitors are with Arizona and the similarity of comments from different personality types. First starting with *centrics.*

I love the Grand Canyon and its beautiful vistas. And I really like the fact that it lived up to its advance billing.

42-year-old male office worker, Rockford, MN

Give me the Grand Canyon. It's just what the name implies—Grand! There are plenty of places to see and many places to spend the night, or however long you want to stay.

Retired female, 75, Johnson City, TN

The Grand Canyon has beauty, inspiration and good weather!

44-year-old minister, Lanett, AL

The Enchantment Resort at Sedona, Arizona is what its name implies. It has beauty and solitude, and the accommodations are excellent.

Housewife, 51, Phoenix, AZ

Tucson, Arizona has everything. Golf, tennis, great climate, good food and it's very convenient to get to.

Female executive, 61, Evergreen, CO

As for *venturers,* they seem to like the relaxed life-style of Arizona also.

I'll take any area of Arizona that gives me good golf courses and good food. The state has just really great weather, good food, good recreation and good nightlife.

58-year-old senior executive, Corona, CA

Lake Powell offers total relaxation. I have friends there, and it's also convenient to get to.

Senior executive, 43, Englewood, CO

Grand Canyon National Park is so great. It has scenery, hiking and camping.

31-year-old female chef, Miami, Fl

I like Tucson, Arizona. It has a dry climate with great resorts for golf, tennis and swimming. It also offers scenic areas for hiking and horseback riding.

Female physician, 40, Roanoke, TX

I'll take northern Arizona for either camping or staying at a bed and breakfast. It's quiet and cool in the summer, doesn't have many people and has natural, beautiful scenery.

33-year-old homemaker, Phoenix, AZ

WHAT PEOPLE LIKE ABOUT ARIZONA

Dependables

Centrics

The Grand Canyon has something for all members of the family to love. It is a beautiful spot. Good motel accommodations too. The food was too expensive, though.

45-year-old female government employee, Garland, TX

Venturers

In summary, Arizona creates a relatively uniform feeling among its many visitors. Although it offers many outdoor activities from which to choose (camping, hiking, swimming, boating, golf and tennis), most people immediately feel relaxed and without a sense of daily pressure or time urgency. They'll do everything and anything whenever they feel like it, or nothing if that also suits their fancy. If you're looking for that kind of a vacation, Arizona could possibly be your first choice.

Montana

#11 RATING: ★★★★

Centrics	Venturers	Dependables
8	10	6

Montana Indians said stealing horses showed a man's bravery.

One horse was the lone survivor at Custer's Last Stand.

A mountain collapsed across the Madison River in 1959 creating Earthquake Lake.

Ted Turner, Tom Brokaw and Harrison Ford have Montana homes.

Pompey's Pillar near Billings bears the only known graffiti from Lewis & Clark's expedition.

A line in a country-western song invites someone to, "meet me in Montana..." After talking with lots of people who chose Montana as their favorite vacation destination, I know what types might like to take up that invitation, and what they will do when they get there.

Most travelers who visit the popular western United States first mention the grandeur and beauty of its scenery, and Montana is no exception. If you go there, you will travel under the "Big Sky" through the wide open spaces that characterize much of the West. What makes it different from other favorites? The climate is cooler and drier than in Oregon, cooler and wetter than in New Mexico or Utah and it is more sparsely populated than these states. Like visitors to Colorado, Montana fans rave about the special quality of the mountains, but the great granite slabs of Montana provide a different "look" from the Rockies to the south. It seems that almost everyone who visits Montana spends time at Glacier National Park where the mountain scenery is especially breathtaking and there is almost no limit to the outdoor activities available.

Also worth noting is the fact that Montana attracts visitors from all over the United States (possibly attributable to its famous national park). Southerners, Midwesterners and urban travelers from the East make up most of those who appear in the American Traveler Survey. By contrast, Oregon, although more highly ranked than Montana, seems to be a secret limited to those on the West Coast.

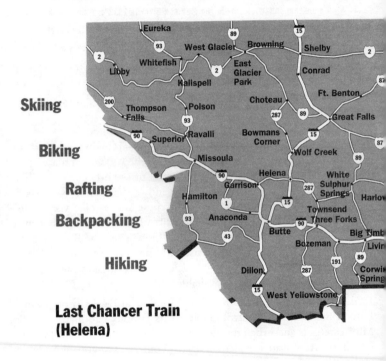

Glacier National Park

Camping

Skiing

Biking

Rafting

Backpacking

Hiking

Last Chancer Train (Helena)

Gates of Mountain Wilderness

Helena

Boating

Canoeing

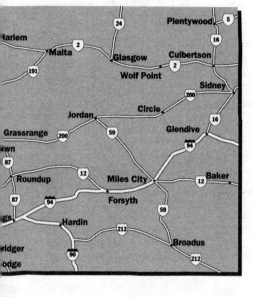

11 Vacation Places Rated

Montana
★ ★ ★ ★

■ **Actives**
■ **Mellows**
■ **All**

**Charles M. Russell
Museum (Great Falls)**

Billings Rodeo

Dude Ranches

Fishing

**Little Big Horn
Monument**

Hot Springs

**Pictographs Caves
(Billings)**

WHAT TO DO IN MONTANA

Actives	Mellows
1 The battle of Little Big Horn is one of the most dramatic episodes in the history of the West. For those who want a little more than your average sightseeing, Custer's Last Stand reenactment is held each year in late June. Call Hardin, Montana, Chamber of Commerce for information.	In Billings, Montana's largest city, attend the Billings Night Rodeo, almost every night from June through August. Food and beverages are on sale, and country-western dancing often follows.
2 Glacier National Park in the Northwestern part of the state is a "don't miss." Some attractions are: Going-to-the-Sun Highway, the brilliance and variety of its flora (and the hikes required to see some of the best), bus tours and lake cruises.	The Towe Ford Museum in Deer Lodge contains one of the more complete collections of vintage Fords and Lincolns in the world.
3 Another remarkable recreation area, the Gates of the Mountain Wilderness, near Helena, is reached by boat or trails. It features a canyon of 1200-foot limestone walls on the shores of the Missouri River, with lots of interesting nooks and crannies to explore.	Another museum worthy of a visit by art lovers is the Charles M. Russell Museum in Great Falls, specializing in the works of that noted cowboy artist.
4 Virginia City is a restored mining town with an interesting and sometimes violent history. Tours of the town, "old-time" entertainment, gold-panning, hunting and fishing are available.	Take a ride on the "The Last Chancer," an automotive train in Helena that takes you on a short tour of Helena's history.
5 Lewis and Clark Caverns State Park is a complex of vaulted chambers and passageways whose colors and formations make it one of the most beautiful in the country. Warning: it's cold down there, so bring a jacket!	Those interested in Native American history should visit the Pictographs Caves southeast of Billings. Many cultures have left pictorial records on the walls of the caves.

For further information about Montana, contact:

Montana Travel Promotion Division
Department pf Commerce
1424 9th Avenue
Helena, MT 59620
☎ (406) 444-2654

WHAT PEOPLE LIKE ABOUT MONTANA

Dependables

Centrics

When *centrics* describe their trips to Montana, they talk about the appeal of a slower pace of life. If they are not campers, they can enjoy the splendor of the scenery and appreciate Montana's history from the comfort of a first-class ranch-style resort. Even those who like a bit of "city life" seem to appreciate that this is one of the last areas of truly unspoiled, sparsely populated wilderness in our country. Here's what they say:

Everyone we met was friendly and "laid back." There's no glitz and glamour, but you'll never see rivers and lakes like that anywhere else. The excellence of the food is surprising, lodgings are good, too, and the costs are very acceptable.

Owner of printing business, Los Angeles, CA

Venturers

Not surprisingly, Montana attracts the *venturer* type of personality above any other. More so than most people, *venturers* appreciate the isolation of the parks, mountains and waterways of Montana. They think the lack of congestion has kept the sky and air clear, the waters clean and unpolluted, and the wildlife abundant. The words "natural," "unspoiled" and "wild" come up often in conversation. Perhaps another reason that *centrics* and *dependables* don't meet each other in Montana is that the activities are almost entirely geared to the outdoors. No one talks about quaint shops, great outlet buys or even cultural experiences; therefore *dependables* are not attracted to the area and have little to say. Montana is the place for fishing, backpacking, tracking bighorn sheep, and skiing in the winter. Listen to some comments from *venturers*:

Montana has a lot of historical interest for me. I also really like the beautiful scenery, the cool climate and the clean surroundings. I also like what it doesn't have: less people, no tourist shops, no fast foods and no toll booths!

Homemaker, 55, Rio Dell, CA

WHAT PEOPLE LIKE ABOUT MONTANA

Dependables	**Centrics**	**Venturers**

Centrics

Triple Creek Ranch has excellent food and accommodations. There is plenty of nature to enjoy, and plenty of activities. Everything is well thought out here, and details are taken care of. You're on your own, but someone is there when you need them.
Self-employed female, 39, Ft. Lauderdale, FL

Glacier National Park seems to be less heavily traveled than other national parks. The quiet is very appealing and relaxing.
Thirty-seven-year-old physician, Kalamazoo, MI

Venturers

Glacier National Park and Yellowstone have the greatest scenery. We have enjoyed great hiking trips, camping and the outdoor areas in general. Montana has very nice resorts and good restaurants, too. We also have friends nearby to visit.
Female dentist, Cary, NC

I went to a yoga workshop in Helena that I enjoyed. There is also good vegetarian food. I like to be able to enjoy the things that are important to me amidst those beautiful mountains. Everything and everyone is so likeable.
Episcopal priest, Chicago, IL

It's a nice experience to have a good time with your children without going to a theme park.
Attorney, St. Paul, MN

I have a great memory of driving the Sun Highway, and of Glacier National park. The views are outstanding, the pure beauty is almost overwhelming. The people are great and the cost for the trip is reasonable, well worth it.
Teacher, 47 Charlottesville, VA

If the rugged scenery and outdoor areas created by glaciers sound appealing to you, call your traveling companions and like the song says, meet them in Montana!

Orlando/Disney World/EPCOT

#12 RATING: ★★★★

Centrics	Venturers	Dependables
8	6	8

Disney World gets more visitors than any other attraction anywhere.
Cassadaga, near Orlando, is a mystic's mecca started by spiritualists.
Walt Disney World is spread out over 28,000 acres.
Friday and Saturday are the least crowded days at Disney World.
Winter Park has canals reminiscent of Venice.

Planning a family vacation? You've got the time and money saved to make it special? You want to go someplace where the children will be entertained (and maybe informed), where the adults will have a good time, where the weather is warm and where all the things you do and see will bring back good memories in the future? According to the people I surveyed, Orlando and the Walt Disney World/Epcot complex satisfy all those requirements, and more. In fact, if you choose that part of Florida to visit, it's probably because the Walt Disney Company lures you.

Theme parks of all kinds proliferate in the Orlando area. In addition to Disney World and Epcot, travelers enjoy parks with different emphases at Sea World of Florida, Universal Studios of Florida and Disney/MGM Studios. When you're ready for a change, you can easily find a beautiful beach, a boat to hire for sailing, water-skiing and fishing on various lakes, or sightseeing trips to the many other attractions in the Orlando area. This variety of activities entices adults and children, *centrics*, *venturers* and *dependables* to Orlando, and keeps them coming back. It's true that venturers evidence much lower interest levels than others because a theme park vacation is not appealing to their adventurous spirits. However, many adults who visit Orlando "for the children" surprise themselves by having a wonderful time in or outside the parks. All personalities also enthuse about how clean, safe and secure they feel in this area, while the tropical climate and lush scenery contribute to a "vacation" state of mind, far away from workaday problems.

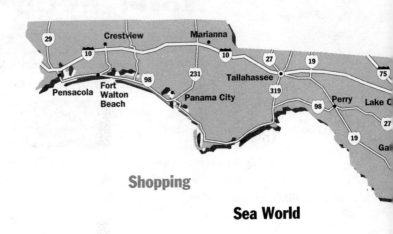

Shopping

Sea World

Hot Air Ballooning

Dog Racing   T
         Clearwater

         St Petersburg

         Sara

Boating

Fishing

Waterskiing

Universal Studios

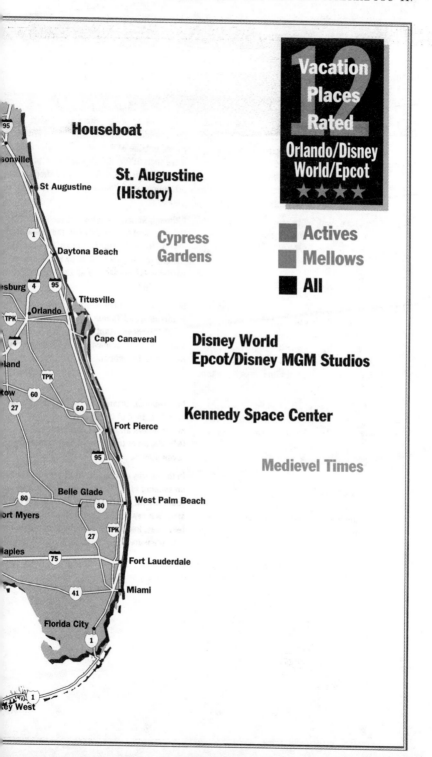

WHAT TO DO IN ORLANDO/ DISNEY WORLD/EPCOT

Actives	Mellows
1 Children and adults will have a good time at Weeki Wachee on the Gulf. A natural spring maintains a steady 74 degree temperature, and you explore a typical Florida ecosystem on a nature cruise down the river. Also enjoy an underwater theater performance, hiking trails, water and beach activities.	You'll seldom see anything to compare with the wonders of Cypress Gardens in Winter Haven outside of Orlando. The park contains more than 8000 varieties of exotic plants, a museum, rides of all kinds and other special attractions. It's a don't-miss experience.
2 Rise above it all, and see it all a lot better from a balloon. Inquire at your hotel or tourist information service about hot-air ballooning over Orlando.	Although St. Augustine is not too close to Orlando, find time to drive up the coast to the oldest city in the United States. You can tour the city by foot, by boat or by horse-drawn carriage. Be sure to see all the attractions in the Old City.
3 The Kennedy Space Center on Cape Canaveral is not far from Orlando and provides a very exciting experience. If your timing is lucky, you can arrange to watch a shuttle launch; otherwise there is still plenty to see and learn. There are guided tours, museums and films in two IMAX theaters.	In Orlando, or in the nearby cities of St. Petersburg and Tampa, you might take a flutter at the races—that is, greyhound racing. The dogs run in at least one of the three cities January to December.
4 How about renting a houseboat to navigate the active St. Johns River? You can be your own captain from Sanford, near Orlando, all the way to Jacksonville.	In November, Orlando hosts the Walt Disney World Festival of the Masters (displays from major American artists) and Light Up Orlando, an entertainment spectacular on seven stages.
5 Finally, you can participate in a variety of watersports on Orlando's waterways. Lakes abound in central Florida, so boating is especially popular. Fish, water ski and dive in Florida's warm waters.	In the nearby community of Kissimmee, spend an evening at Medieval Times Dinner and Tournament, where you will feast medieval-style in a replicated European castle. A few feet away, knights on horseback compete for your pleasure.

For further information, contact:
Florida Division of Tourism
125 West Van Buren Street
Tallahassee, FL 32399-2000
☎ (904) 487-1462

WHAT PEOPLE LIKE ABOUT ORLANDO/ DISNEY WORLD/EPCOT

Dependables	**Centrics**	**Venturers**

Dependables

If you remember that *dependables* are less adventurous than others, are more comfortable in familiar surroundings and like to travel to places that they know are popular, you'll understand why they endorse Orlando so enthusiastically. The Disney people, and those who operate the other theme parks, create a special world apart where visitors can forget their troubles, enjoy rides and shows with lots of other people, and expose their families to wholesome and memorable experiences. They don't have to leave the parks to feel their vacation is complete, but lots of other opportunities exist if they choose.

Disney World is very popular with many people and has so much family entertainment that is amazing for all ages. It's very clean, well staffed and well organized.

Teacher's aide, 35, Ellsworth, ME

We went because we wanted to see Disney World. Epcot was special because I felt I had visited foreign countries that I will never have a chance to actually go to. The entire Orlando area has more that enough entertainment for any one leisure visit.

Male department manager, Waukegan, IL

Centrics

Centrics especially appreciate that the wide range of activities offers something appealing to all age groups and interest levels. This might be a fair summary of what *centrics* tell me: At Disney World, everyone can disappear for a time into the fantasies that the Disney parks create so perfectly. You can leave Epcot with the feeling that you have not only enjoyed yourself, but have learned a great deal about modern technology and about other countries. Parents can allow older children to wander off on their own without fear of unpleasant occurrences. Even adults without children enjoy the parks, and also participate in beach life, watersports, shopping and nightlife.

Disney World is a very happy and safe environment. Everything is clean and pleasant for all family members. There is so much to do and see just in the park alone that you could spend days and not see it all. I'd like to come back if we can.

42-year-old police officer, Kalamazoo, MI

All of the Orlando area seems designed for family fun—lots to do, wonderful weather, places to eat, good shopping and constant entertainment.

Female office worker, Leominster, MA

Venturers

Although this destination appeals most to *centrics* and *dependables*, *venturers* satisfy their curious natures and high energy levels very nicely in Orlando. Here is exactly what they say:

Orlando has Disney World, and it offers many leisure activity options. The weather is great, so you can take advantage of lots of outdoor sports and sights. The hospitality is gracious and transport is easy so you get around to everything. Felt relaxed while I was there.

Male graduate student, Arlington, VA

Lots of entertainment—we can all be busy all the time. And great weather!

Homemaker, 33, Clarks Summit, PA

WHAT PEOPLE LIKE ABOUT ORLANDO/ DISNEY WORLD/EPCOT

Dependables

Disney World is great family entertainment. I feel the whole area is very clean, safe and friendly. It's central to Tampa and Daytona Beach for side trips.

Female salesperson, La Porte, TX

Orlando is like a second home to us. It's relaxing, fun and has everything.

Social worker, 51, Flemington, NJ

We enjoyed Disney World very much. It's lots of fun, there is lots to do, it's friendly, safe and a good value. Epcot is stimulating and educational for all of us. We also like the beach and enjoy just lying out in the sun when our daughter isn't with us.

Senior corporate manager, Cedar Grove, NJ

Centrics

It has so much to offer. We went to theme parks, there are great beaches, shopping and nightlife. It's also close to St. Petersburg, a city that we like very much.

Office manager, 27, Oconomowoc, WI

Theme parks for the kids and great golf courses for me! My wife likes it all.

Male manager, 45, Amherst, NH

We had a great time at Disney World and Epcot. Something for little kids and big kids, too!

Serviceman, 30, Silver Spring, MD

Disney World in Florida has such a great atmosphere. There is a big choice in accommodations and they all seem good. We like the variety of activities in the park and the surrounding areas. Weather, landscape, competent and friendly staff everywhere we went.

Male, 61, banker, Oklahoma City, OK

Venturers

I enjoyed seeing a very different part of the country. I think they go out of their way to show you a good time. You really feel like a valuable guest.

Male musician 38, Lansdale, PA

There are many, many things to do for the whole family. Having other theme parks nearby is great for the family and it's close to the Gulf Coast for other kinds of activities.

Supervisor, male, Smyrna, TN

People sound happy when they talk about their vacation in the Orlando area. It's theme park heaven with a lot of extras thrown in, such as warm weather, good golfing and watersports, and beautiful nearby cities. Families, this is for you!

South Carolina

#13 RATING: ★★★★

Centrics	Venturers	Dependables
8	8	9

South Carolina was the first state to secede from the Union.

137 battles in the Revolutionary War were fought in S.C.

Charleston has withstood five fires, 10 hurricanes and an earthquake.

South Carolina is second only to California in peach production.

The first shots of the Civil War were fired in S.C. in 1861.

If I hadn't been to South Carolina, I'd board the next plane! The reviews and descriptions from travelers who vacation there are that enthusiastic. Most of South Carolina's visitors head for one of the big resort areas of Myrtle Beach or Hilton Head. The attractions are beautiful, clean beaches, outstanding food and golf, golf, golf. It's worth emphasizing that the quality and variety of food and restaurants in South Carolina receive more mentions than most other popular destinations. The Charleston area draws its share of praise for its historic associations, architecture and its genteel Southern hospitality.

Centrics, venturers and *dependables* visit South Carolina in about equal numbers, and are equally ardent in declaring their appreciation for the area. As with some other destinations, the differences among the groups lie in what they do after they arrive.

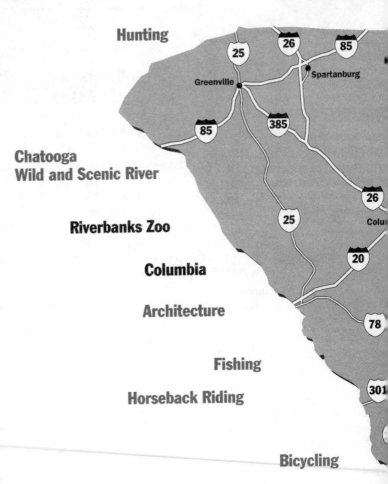

Cowpens Battle

Hunting

25

26

85

Greenville

Spartanburg

85

385

**Chatooga
Wild and Scenic River**

26

Riverbanks Zoo

25

Colu

Columbia

20

Architecture

78

Fishing

Horseback Riding

301

Bicycling

Camping

Watersports

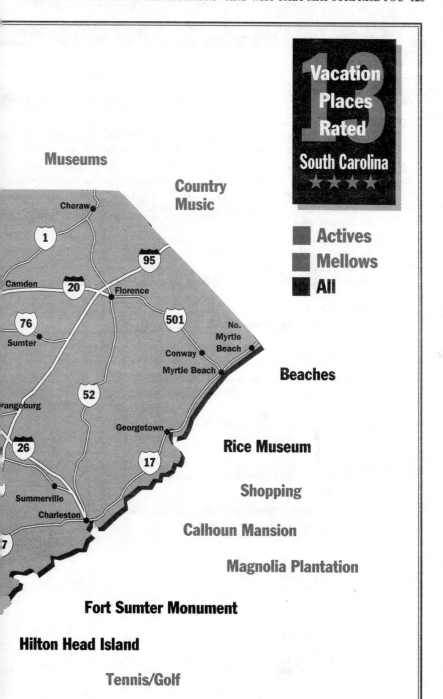

13

Vacation
Places
Rated

South Carolina

★★★★

Actives
Mellows
All

WHAT TO DO IN SOUTH CAROLINA

Actives	Mellows
1 South Carolina has an unusually long hunting season. Deer, wild turkeys, a variety of waterfowl and small animals are plentiful.	Enjoy Charleston signature dishes like she-crab soup and benne wafers at one of the city's sophisticated restaurants.
2 Walking is the best way to explore the charms of Charleston. There are several good walking tours, escorted or self-directed, which will allow the best perspective of a city that specializes in preservation.	The Sun Fun Festival takes place in early June, featuring sports and outdoor entertainment. Contact the Myrtle Beach Chamber of Commerce.
3 Hilton Head Island offers recreational facilities for golfers, tennis players, sailors, bike and horse riders, and more. In addition, explore wildlife and waterfowl habitats, learn about the Gullah culture that flourished on the offshore islands.	If time is limited for historic building tours, try these two different examples of fine old homes: Calhoun Mansion in Charleston and Magnolia Plantation and Gardens nearby.
4 J. Strom Thurmond Lake, named after South Carolina's longtime U.S. senator, lies on the western border, away from the main tourist areas on the coast. It offers nature programs and all kinds of water and outdoor activities. No commercial lodgings, but plenty of room for campers.	History buffs will enjoy Fort Sumter National Monument in Charleston Harbor, where Confederate troops began the Civil War by firing on, and subsequently occupying the island fort.
5 Fishermen will have a good time anywhere in the state, but they can combine excellent freshwater and saltwater fishing right in Charleston. Look into deep sea fishing out of Charleston Harbor and find good fishing in estuarine creeks.	The Myrtle Beach area has recently developed into the new easternmost center for country-western music. Visitors can drop in on clubs or investigate concerts and activities featuring this popular entertainment.

For more information about South Carolina, contact:

South Carolina Department of Parks
Recreation and Tourism
Inquiry Division
P.O. Box 71
Columbia, SC 29202
☎ (803) 734-0235

WHAT PEOPLE LIKE ABOUT SOUTH CAROLINA

Dependables

Centrics

Venturers

I know it sounds repetitive, but *dependables* who like South Carolina like it for the same reasons the other personalities do—they just don't pursue things to the same degree. Words like "relaxing," "calm," "clean and safe," and "easy access" appear often when they write or talk about their trips. For example, *dependables* play a lot of golf at Myrtle Beach or Hilton Head, but they are less passionate than some others. Their sightseeing is done at a more sedate pace and one homemaker mentioned enjoying the "more settled" crowd at Hilton Head. Here are more of their comments:

Myrtle Beach is comparatively close to home, which is convenient for us. Its beaches are clean and there are lots of family activities. We feel safe there. The hotel rooms are clean and appealing, and we like the variety of restaurants.
Teacher, 29, Taylor, SC

I like the atmosphere. All the nice hotels on the ocean present a pretty picture. Everyone seems to be having fun. It's quiet, peaceful and very scenic.
Male, field supervisor, Elkin, NC

There's something for everyone—for me and for the kids, too. The people are very friendly, the food is great and there are several nice hotels at reasonable prices.
Self-employed male, Livonia, MI

Golf is very important to *centrics*, and they also enjoy the rest of resort life: beaches, tennis, elegant restaurants, warm ocean waters. They like the fact that there are plenty of activities for the whole family. One man sounded especially relieved that his wife and children were able to keep themselves busy while he was out on the golf course! *Centrics* who include Charleston in their vacation report how immaculate and charming the city is, and how interesting they find the historic homes and other buildings. Here's what some *centrics* told us:

We like to go there at a time of year it's not crowded, but the weather is still good. The local people are quite friendly, and we always meet people from all over the United States. We play some golf, and we really enjoy the good food selections.
Retired male, Caledonia, NY

Myrtle Beach has great beaches and ocean-front activities. There are lots of restaurants and hotels to choose from, at a reasonable cost. It's convenient for us; we can drive there in one day.
Self-employed male, Mansfield OH

We like it so much that we bought a time share in a quiet neighborhood. We're near the beach and have access to lots of golf courses and places to eat.
Teacher, 34, New Freedom, PA

And, what do the *venturers* find appealing about South Carolina? They are also golf fanatics, even more so. But, they are also more active. At resorts, they swim, play tennis and volleyball and enjoy fine food at gourmet restaurants when their active day is over. Several from this group report taking jaunts to islands off the coast that offer different cultural experiences, and they are also energetic sightseers in the historical areas, like Charleston. Here's what they tell us:

Let me tell you what I like: beautiful beaches, nice weather, beautiful ocean water to swim in, nice people around you, relaxing, yet plenty of excitement and things to do, places to go. It's a good bang for your $buck$!
Male government employee, Yorktown Heights, NY

It's not commercialized. The atmosphere is laid-back and the people are friendly. Great weather here, at the edge of America, and fresh seafood all year long, you-all!
Female, self-employed, Charleston, SC

I fell in love with the long, white sandy beaches and the beautiful hotels. We enjoy golfing during the day, then trying out the great variety of restaurants and night spots.
Receptionist, Burnt Hills, NY

WHAT PEOPLE LIKE ABOUT SOUTH CAROLINA

Dependables

People are always nice in the South, but Charleston seems to have more than its share of graciousness. It's an easy city to explore and appreciate. It's not too big or overly commercialized, either.

Finance executive, Kansas City, MO

Centrics

I love to play golf and I love the beach. It's perfect!
Female counselor, Midlothian, VA

I went to college there, and I keep going back because it's so easy to relax there. The location is beautiful and the people are wonderful. The historical sites, especially in Charleston, really add to the atmosphere.
Attorney, 52, Houston, TX

Venturers

Myrtle Beach just shimmers. It has some special quality of air and water that impresses you. And, it's family oriented.
45-year-old self-employed female, Colorado Springs, CO

The golf courses are plentiful and challenging. Fortunately, there are plenty of things for my wife and kids to enjoy, too.
Salesman, Warrington, PA

If you are someone who loves to play golf and appreciates a variety of fine dining, please do try South Carolina. It should be a good fit.

Southern California

#14 RATING: ★★★★

Centrics	Venturers	Dependables
8	10	8

Los Angeles has 6500 miles of streets and 40,000 intersections.
McDonald's got its start in California in the 50s.
The Pantry restaurant, open 24 hours since the 20s, has no locks.
Will Rogers' historic house was built so he could do rope tricks indoors.
During a severe drought in 1916 San Diego hired a rainmaker; refused to pay him when floods came.

Every New Year's Day, Southern California residents worry that people watching the Rose Bowl will envy the warm weather and beautiful scenery they see on television and stampede in droves to swell the population. They might have cause to worry, because our travelers tell us that warm weather and beautiful beaches top off what they like about the area.

Surprisingly, the glitz and glamour of Hollywood are not the magnets for Southern California tourists. The Los Angeles area seems to have lost its charm for visitors. Rather, most head for San Diego or Disneyland. And, yes, they mention the temperate weather, the nearness of the ocean and the nice beaches more than any other features. San Diego and Disneyland also earn points for being clean and feeling safe, and for being located within driving distance of other attractive locations, such as Mexico or Palm Springs. In addition to the obvious attractions of weather and beaches, everyone in the interior of the country must have a relative or friend to visit in Southern California because they also mention that this gives them a good excuse to take a trip, especially in the winter months!

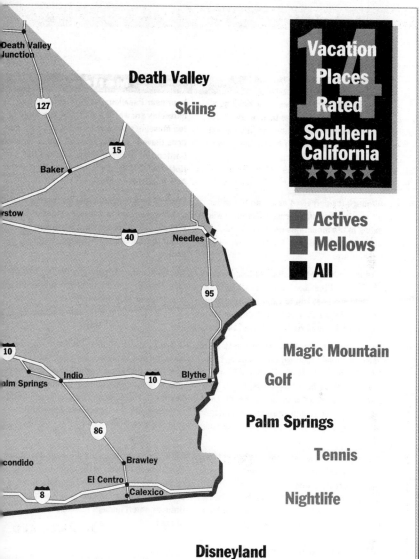

WHAT TO DO IN SOUTHERN CALIFORNIA

Actives	Mellows
1 Time your trip for the New Year Holiday. Stay in Pasadena and arrange to view the Rose Parade on New Year's morning. It's a great spectacle, and football fans can go to the game that follows.	In or near Pasadena, several gardens and museums are worth a visit. See the Huntington Museum's historic exhibits and rose gardens (have tea in the garden), tour Descanso Gardens for azalea displays and see the Norton Simon Museum (modern art) and the Asia Pacific Museum.
2 Although it's perceived as a warm-weather mecca, Southern California offers good winter skiing in the mountains near Los Angeles. Snow Summit and Bear Mountain are two popular areas.	Every major big-league sport is represented in Los Angeles, and to a lesser extent in San Diego. Look for celebrities, especially at Laker (basketball) and Dodger (baseball) games.
3 Visit Channel Islands National Park, a series of islands off the coast of Ventura, California. It involves a boat trip to explore interesting flora and fauna on islands that have been somewhat isolated from the rest of the state.	The Queen Mary is permanently berthed at Long Beach. Take a tour of this former luxury liner, dine or stay onboard.
4 For an opposite extreme, take a trip to Death Valley National Monument in the desert, the lowest point in the lower 48 United States. (A few miles away, in the Sequoias, is Mt. Whitney, the highest point in the lower 48). Overnight accommodations are good, and historic. See Scotty's Castle, but don't go in the summer.	In San Diego, don't miss Balboa Park. This beautiful and extensive complex houses not only the world famous zoo, but several museums, a well-known outdoor theatre, and the Reuben H. Fleet Space Theatre, specializing in documentaries shown on a huge 360-degree screen.
5 Although Los Angeles is not a "walking" city, it has interesting ethnic communities containing great restaurants, shopping and friendly locals to involve you in their culture. The Fairfax neighborhood where many Russian Jews have settled is one and the Monterey Park-San Gabriel area where Chinese from Taiwan and the mainland live is another.	Old Town State Historic Park near downtown San Diego is the site of the city's beginning. In addition to the park and memorials, there is a plaza of shops and restaurants worth touring. Outdoor entertainment is occasionally offered.

For further information about Southern California, contact:

California Office of Tourism
P.O.Box 1499
Sacramento, CA 95812
☎ (916) 322-1396

WHAT PEOPLE LIKE ABOUT SOUTHERN CALIFORNIA

Dependables

It's clear that Southern California offers something valuable to all personality types on vacation. *Dependables* prefer the same destinations as the others, San Diego and Disneyland, but they pursue somewhat different activities. *Dependable* personalities tell me they enjoy the theme parks (Disneyland, Knotts Berry Farm, Universal), the beaches and, of course, they appreciate the area's warm weather and the fact that friends or family reside in Southern California makes it easier to visit. Note in their own words how they are observers and sightseers rather than active participants.

We especially liked the tour at Universal Studios, and the shows. There is so much to see in Southern California! We can go at our own pace, and take lots of interesting pictures—we're camera buffs. It was a great vacation.

**Homemaker, 40,
Little Falls, MN**

Disneyland is a world in itself. It's clean and safe, the hotels are very good. There is a wide choice of restaurants and lots of different activities available.

**Systems analyst,
Concord, CA**

Centrics

The *centric* personality typically arrives in San Diego, sets himself up in one of the nice hotels he's heard about, and heads out for Sea World or the world famous San Diego Zoo. Another day he might cruise the harbor, sun himself on the beach, and shop at one of the picturesque centers on the water. He may take his family on a day trip to one of the Mexican beach communities or to Disneyland. An abundance of theme parks and seaside entertainment characterize the entire Southern California area and offer the variety so many people rave about, as can be seen in the following quotes:

I really loved San Diego. The weather is so great. You don't have to worry about keeping busy. The attractions, like the zoo and Sea World, are first class. The accommodations were very nice, and there is great shopping on the coast.

**Female project manager,
Bozeman, MT**

We have friends and relatives we like to visit there. We also enjoy the variety of the environment—the mountains, ocean and desert so near. The attractions are very numerous and we love the weather.

**Self-employed male, 61,
Morgan, VT**

Venturers

Venturers are not immune to the charms of beaches and the benevolent climate, but they like more action. In this group I found a few younger travelers who enjoy the Los Angeles area and its show business ambience. Here, too are those who delight in the varied entertainment and the nightlife available in San Diego, Los Angeles and even Disneyland. Venturers don't just lie on the beach; they sail and water ski and go snorkeling. They are interested in almost everything—theme parks, too—but it is the variety of activities and extremes of scenic beauty that appeal to them. Here are some of their own comments:

Wow! the variety of things to do—so many attractions, natural and man-made. We drove, so we saw great scenery, especially along the coast. The extremes of climate, scenery and activities are remarkable.

**Military man, 44,
San Antonio, TX**

The weather's great and we have friends near there (San Diego). We always enjoy the golf courses, and it's an easy drive to Los Angeles, Mexico or Palm Springs if we get restless. I know the area now, so we go to the best places to eat, the best beaches and so on.

**Male, 31, in sales,
Des Moines, IA**

WHAT PEOPLE LIKE ABOUT SOUTHERN CALIFORNIA

Dependables	**Centrics**	**Venturers**

Dependables

Spending time in the Los Angeles area is so much fun. I love TV and the movies, so I soak up that atmosphere. Beverly Hills is fantastic.
Female office manager, San Jose, CA

The area is very convenient for a lot of attractions. We stay near Disneyland, because we always find it clean and fun for everyone, but it's also close to nice beaches, and we have relatives who live nearby.
Male student, 22, Provo, UT

I'd like to recommend the Hotel Del Coronado in San Diego. It's a beautiful, clean resort, right on the ocean. The accommodations are luxurious, the food was excellent, and so was the staff.
Self-employed male, Farmington, IA

Centrics

It's close to lots of other attractions, with great weather and very good dining experiences. It's not too far away, so less planning is involved.
Writer, Fountain Hills, AZ

What wonderful restaurants and food! Imagine, dining under the stars in such beautiful weather. I loved it all: mountains, desert, even the malls!
Female personnel manager, Rochester, NY

It's a good family fun trip. We can do it by car, which makes it easy and inexpensive.
Teacher, 57, Pleasant Grove, UT

There is a lot to see and a lot to do. We found it very exciting. We felt a real vacation atmosphere.
56-year-old female office worker, Cleveland OH

It was like having three vacations in one, because there were so many things to see and do. I really enjoyed the variety of people we encountered there.
Office worker, Chicago, IL

Venturers

Los Angeles was very interesting and different to me. found great places to eat and shop. The beaches are nice, the people are nice and there is a lot of interesting sightseeing you can do.
Female office worker, Dunbar, West Virginia

You can do anything on Catalina Island—snorkeling, parasailing, sunbathing and hiking. The seafood is great, the locals are friendly and there is no crime. Can't beat the weather and the sightseeing, too.
Female department manager, Fridley, MN

Disneyland makes me feel like a kid again!
Self-employed male, 57, Great Falls, MT

I like being able to take short trips from San Diego into Mexico or Los Angeles. We also enjoyed Disneyland again. It good clean fun for all ages, the beaches are accessible when the weather's warm.
Female office manager, East Northport, NY

Do you like warm weather, lots of sun and surf and a wide variety of activities and entertainment? Next time you plan that kind of vacation, you might remember the words from the above travelers and try Southern California.

Wyoming

#15 RATING: ★★★★

Centrics	Venturers	Dependables
7	10	7

Wyoming is second in mean elevation to Colorado.

Wyoming women were the first in the U.S. to vote.

The state has the world's largest elk herd at Jackson Elk Refuge.

Yellowstone's Lower Falls (308 ft.) is higher than Niagara.

Pioneer-spirits can take covered wagons from Yellowstone to Grand Teton.

Wyoming, like several western states, evokes lyrical comments from its visitors about its breathtaking natural beauty. Most people who choose Wyoming as a favorite vacation spot are those who like spending time outdoors, usually being very active. If you hike, ski, fish or just relax, wouldn't you rather do so in a spectacular natural setting? One woman wrote that "Those majestic mountains and valleys have the most tremendous natural beauty I have ever seen." Praise indeed!

Wyoming has something truly special in the way of attractions that distinguishes it from nearby beautiful states like Montana and Colorado. It has Yellowstone National Park, a place so unique that visitors will come just to see it. Most of Wyoming's tourists start or finish their trips there and describe it as "different," "unusual" and "unique." What makes Yellowstone stand out for them are the steaming thermal pools and geysers that shoot scalding water high into the air, and the abundance of large, visible wildlife such as bears, elk, bighorn sheep and bison.

**Yellowstone
National Park**

**Buffalo Bill
Museum (Cody)**

**Grand Teton
National Park**

**Mountain
Climbing**

Bicycling

Jackson Hole

Snake River

Rafting

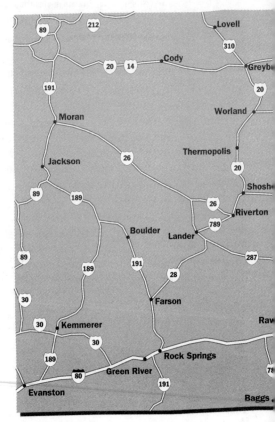

Rock Climbing

Skiing

**Devil's Tower
National Monument**

Scenic Drives

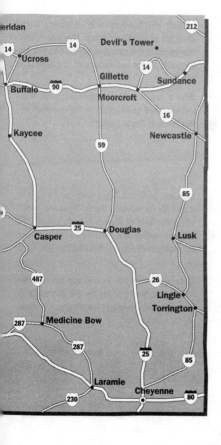

Actives
Mellows
All

Hiking

Hunting

**Thermopolis
Hot Springs**

**Arts/Crafts
(Casper)**

Photographic Ops

Dude Ranches

**Rodeo
(Cheyenne)**

WHAT TO DO IN WYOMING

Actives	Mellows
1 Yellowstone is not the only national park in Wyoming. Take a look at Grand Teton National Park, which includes Jackson Hole. In the summer, mountain climbing and hiking are popular here.	The state's largest professional rodeo is held in Cheyenne in July. Lots of food and western-style festivities last for a week.
2 Raft or float down the Snake River. The Snake is a popular venue for all kinds and lengths of water trips, and there are lots of companies to help you get organized.	In Cody, visit the Buffalo Bill Historical Center, good for at least half a day. There are four museums in the complex devoted to the history, art, crafts and culture of the American West.
3 Devil's Tower National Monument is the most conspicuous landmark in northeastern Wyoming, and has been featured in the film *Close Encounters of the Third Kind*. Rangers conduct nature walks, and other outdoor activities are available. The most active travelers can climb the tower.	After a day of active sightseeing, soak in a bubbling hot spring bath in Thermopolis in Hot Springs State Park.
4 Wyoming offers big game and trophy game hunting that is unbeatable. Prong-horn antelopes and mule deer are widely distributed; bear, elk, moose and mountain sheep are baggable. Or, you can hunt with binoculars and cameras.	Jackson, in Grand Teton National Park, is noted for its western flavor. Wyoming is definitely the land of the cowboy, so spend time there in spring and summer to catch one of the many festivals celebrating the Old West.
5 Winter or summer, take the Snow King Scenic Chairlift to the top of Snow King for panoramic views and nature trails. Descend when you like via an alpine slide that provides views of forest and meadow.	Casper, Wyoming is a good size town as Wyoming goes. Visit in June for the Cottonwoods Festival, featuring arts and crafts, country music and more.

For further information about Wyoming, contact:

Wyoming Division of Tourism
1-25 at College Drive
Cheyenne, WY 82002
☎ (307) 777-7777

WHAT PEOPLE LIKE ABOUT WYOMING

Dependables	Centrics	Venturers

Dependables

Like some other destinations where the outdoors is emphasized, Wyoming attracts fewer *dependables* than other personalities. They find much to do and to like in Wyoming, if they take a trip, and few are immune to the captivating charms of Yellowstone. Sometimes a *dependable* will discover something new in the experience:

That is just amazing scenery! On that vacation I experienced a sense of adventure I've never experienced before.
Female computer consultant, 34, Maple Heights, OH

Centrics

Most of the *centrics* who like Wyoming also talk about Yellowstone. They find it very different from other places they have visited, and they especially like to bring their families. Their children can enjoy the outdoors and learn about geology, geography and behavior of the wildlife from the Park Service rangers. All of Wyoming offers a tranquil setting where everyone can pursue favorite activities, such as hiking, camping, fishing, skiing and even rodeos, without fear of being overwhelmed by crowds. They tell me there is a "down to earth" quality about the state and its residents that is very appealing. Here are some of the things that centrics say:

It's clean and almost unspoiled by people. You feel like you are back in simpler, less complicated times—'Back to the good ol days'—and I'm only in my 30s! The air is clean, the water is pure, and it's just a good place to be.
Machinist, 37, Sarasota, FL

It has such scenic beauty and the air is so fresh. We particularly enjoyed the wildlife at Yellowstone. It's a very tranquil setting, away from the pressure of everyday work.
Female teacher, 27, Billings, MT

There is a lot to see, especially if you appreciate majestic mountains, open spaces and fresh air. Yellowstone is unique.
Male graphic artist, Arlington, IL

Venturers

Venturers mention skiing more often than *centrics* and more frequently than other outdoor activities. Jackson Hole is the Wyoming ski spot that *venturers* seem to appreciate because it's more rustic and rugged than other ski areas. Skiers endorse its great chutes, deep powder, high elevation and ungroomed slopes. Rafting the Snake also receives votes from these travelers, as do camping, boating, fishing, hiking and other outdoor recreation activities. The fact that Wyoming is uncrowded and uncommercial enables these individuals to get away and enjoy some solitude when they wish. They also love Yellowstone for its dynamic geysers and wildlife. *Venturers* continually seek different experiences.

I like to do active things on vacation, but I also want some peace and quiet. I don't like crowds. Wyoming lets me do what I want. It's totally beautiful, and I feel like I am really getting away from everything.
Regional manager, San Jose, CA

It's a totally different environment from where we live in the Florida keys.. The scenery and the climate are so different that it's very stimulating. The children really enjoy it.
Fisherman, 38, Marathon, FL

Here's what I like: Fishing. Taking lots of pictures. No people. No phones. No radio. No papers. That's Wyoming!
Female insurance underwriter, Denver, CO

WHAT PEOPLE LIKE ABOUT WYOMING

Dependables

Centrics

Venturers

It's not too commercial, so I can still afford it. Also, it's an easy drive from home.
59-year-old salesman, Salt Lake City, UT

I enjoyed the contrast between Wind Rivers, which is quite secluded with lots of wildlife, hiking and fishing, and Jackson Hole which is more sophisticated. I loved the shops there!
Female lab technician, Brigham City, UT

I love those majestic mou tains. Wyoming is blessed wi natural beauty that God ma just for us.
Teacher, 36, Chanute, I

If you haven't thought about it before, perhaps you should be tempted to see the wonders of Wyom

North Carolina

#16 RATING: ★★★

Centrics	Venturers	Dependables
7	9	7

Leads the nation in cigarette and furniture production.
The Wright Brothers plane lifted off the sands of Kitty Hawk in 1903.
North Carolina troops suffered the greatest losses during the Civil War.
When handkerchiefs are tossed over Blowing Rock Ridge, currents of air blow them back.
Blackbeard the pirate was killed in a NC struggle in 1718.

The Carolina cousins have a lot in common. They both have a seashore, attractive weather, lots of recreation facilities and the charm of the South. What distinguishes North Carolina, according to the people I surveyed, is its lack of commercialization and development. Words like "not crowded," "quaint," or "no rip-offs" come up frequently when people talk about what they like. North Carolina appeals to a wide variety of people across the personality scale, all of whom enjoy the peaceful beaches, fresh air and the variety of things to do and see in this unspoiled part of the U.S. But, it primarily grabs the attention of *venturers*, people who like to reach out and explore all the interesting things around them.

One of the reasons for North Carolina's wide-spread popularity, in the words of many visitors interviewed in the American Traveler Survey, is that it has something for everyone. The state offers extremes of geography, from the Blue Ridge and Great Smoky Mountains in the west, to the sloping coastal plains, where lakes, rivers and the Atlantic Ocean's islands and beaches meet. The area called the Outer Banks is one of the most sought-out vacation destinations in the eastern part of the country and is frequently cited by travelers as a favorite vacation spot.

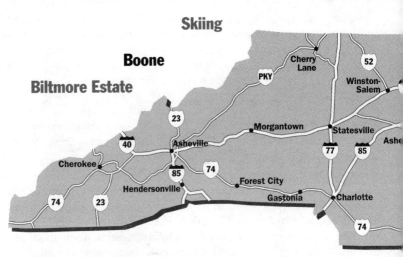

Actives
Mellows
All

Bicycling

Backpacking

High Country

Skiing

Boone

Biltmore Estate

PKY
Cherry Lane
52
Winston-Salem
23
Morgantown
Statesville
40
Asheville
77
85
Ash
Cherokee
85
74
Hendersonville
Forest City
Gastonia
Charlotte
74
23
74

Blue Ridge Mountains

Carowinds Theme Park

Smoky Mountains

Raleigh/Durha

Canoeing

Charlotte
Motor Speedway

N

W ——— E

FIELDING
WORLDWIDE

S

Whitewater Rafting

Vacation Places Rated 16
North Carolina
★ ★ ★

Grandfather Mountain

Wright Brothers Memorial

Devil Hills

Outer Banks

Nags Head

Cape Hatteras

Cape Lookout

Beaches

North Carolina Battleship

Cape Fear River

History/Museums

Hang-gliding

WHAT TO DO IN NORTH CAROLINA

Actives	Mellows
1	Adventurous souls have always found it romantic to search for buried treasure. How about searching under the sea? Lots of ships went down off the coast, and scuba divers can investigate to their heart's content.	If you are happiest at luxury resorts, head for Asheville. Surrounded by the Great Smoky and Blue Ridge Mountains, it boasts the Grove Park Inn Resort, one of the nation's finest.

1 Adventurous souls have always found it romantic to search for buried treasure. How about searching under the sea? Lots of ships went down off the coast, and scuba divers can investigate to their heart's content.

If you are happiest at luxury resorts, head for Asheville. Surrounded by the Great Smoky and Blue Ridge Mountains, it boasts the Grove Park Inn Resort, one of the nation's finest.

2 For a perspective from the air, go hang gliding off the dunes at Nag's Head.

Also in Asheville is the famous Biltmore Estate, originally built by the Vanderbilt family. The mansion is French chateau style and is surrounded by gardens, greenhouses and a winery. Not to be missed, especially if you can schedule your trip to coincide with the Festival of Flowers held annually in April.

3 Cape Hatteras National Seashore is the most extensive stretch of undeveloped seashore on the Atlantic. It includes the Outer Banks, Ocracoke and Hatteras Island, and is noted for its wild beauty and occasionally treacherous sands. Walk, fish, hunt, or just observe the terrain and wildlife. Look for dolphins!

Want to take the kids to a theme park you'll all enjoy? Paramount's Carowinds in Charlotte offers different facets of Carolina's past and present, along with cartoon characters, shows, rides and many other attractions.

4 The Cherokee Indian Reservation memorializes the fascinating and turbulent history of this Indian nation. Plan to take some time to see the museums, the Oconaluftee Indian Village and to take in a play, *Unto These Hills*, a historical drama about the Cherokees.

Of course you'll want to make a brief stop at Kill Devil Hills in the Outer Banks, where Orville and Wilbur Wright launched the first power-driven airplane. The Wright Brothers National memorial is nearby.

5 For active people who would like to take a break and watch sports, North Carolina comes close to being the country's basketball capital. See the professional Hornets in Charlotte, and great college games at Duke, the University of North Carolina and other colleges. Or, if auto racing is more to your taste, the NASCAR season begins in May at the Charlotte Motor Speedway and includes many major events.

West of Waynesville (named for Revolutionary war general "Mad" Anthony Wayne) on the Cape Fear River, is berthed the Battleship *North Carolina*. Nicknamed "The Showboat," it was considered the world's greatest sea weapon during World War II, earning 15 battle stars. Allow about 2 hours for a self-guided tour.

For further information about North Carolina, contact:

North Carolina Travel and Tourism Division
430 North Salisbury Street
Raleigh, NC 27611
☎ (919) 733-4171

WHAT PEOPLE LIKE ABOUT NORTH CAROLINA

Dependables

Centrics

Venturers

Dependables are not as carried away with the undeveloped and unspoiled character of North Carolina. They like having some development on the behalf of tourists! They say, give me a nice hotel and some entertaining things to see, and show me some interesting shops. They join all the other travelers in admiring North Carolina's varied and beautiful scenery.

In fact, *centrics* mention the mountains and the beaches about equally. Both areas delight in natural beauty, plenty of things to do and places to visit. Fishing and golf earn the most mentions from *centrics*, and sightseers seem intrigued with quaint villages like Ocracoke that emit a sense of timelessness. They describe their time in North Carolina as peaceful, quiet and relaxing. Of course this serenity is a direct result of the care taken by residents not to overdevelop or seem "touristy." Here are some thoughts about North Carolina from centrics:

The *venturers* are more active than the other groups, and seem to prefer the North Carolina seashore to the mountains. Camping, swimming, surfing, biking and sea kayaking join golf and fishing on the activities list. It wouldn't be the Carolinas if good restaurants weren't mentioned. *Venturers* also interest themselves in North Carolina's history, which includes the first British colony at Roanoke, relationships with the Cherokee Indian tribe and the Wright brothers' experiments with flight. These travelers also cover more ground when they sightsee, exploring undeveloped, isolated islands, hitting quaint little towns as well as exploring the museums, theatre and other amenities of modern Charlotte, one of the south's major cities. Here's what venturers tell us:

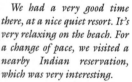

We had a very good time there, at a nice quiet resort. It's very relaxing on the beach. For a change of pace, we visited a nearby Indian reservation, which was very interesting.
**Homemaker,
Indianapolis, IN**

The Outer Banks is heaven on earth. You relax, look at the water and soak in the natural feel of the place. Pretty soon the day is over, and you wonder where it's gone. The local people are friendly. You just feel comfortable.
**Female office worker,
Garner, NC**

The people are friendly. How nice to find an uncrowded vacation spot on the seashore. From one end of the island to the other, you can surf and fish with almost no one around. It's a nice place to spend time with your kid.
**Male chemical worker,
Gold Hill, NC**

There were diverse activities—something fun for every age group.
31-year-old female sales rep,
Washington, PA

I have been so impressed with the Biltmore Estate. I've been twice now, and they have done such a wonderful job restoring and extending the scope of this remarkable mansion and grounds. It's worth a trip to North Carolina just for that.
Teacher, 35, Martin, TN

I like the Outer Banks because there is so little commercialization. Picture the natural beauty of wild horses roaming beautiful beaches and dolphins that swim in the same ocean water as humans. Unbelievable.
**Engineer, 33,
Hummelstown, PA**

WHAT PEOPLE LIKE ABOUT NORTH CAROLINA

Dependables

It was easy to get there and easy to get the things you need to have a good time. You don't want to struggle on a vacation! The scenery is stunning, and the shops entertained me, too.

Female office worker, Washington, D.C.

Centrics

The mountains are majestic. It's clean. You feel peaceful. The people are friendly and the food and shopping are good. Prices are reasonable, too!

Salesman, St. Louis, MO

The mountains are special. So is life there. The people live life at the right pace.

23-year-old salesman/ student, Holt, MI

We had a very relaxing vacation at Nag's Head in very picturesque surroundings. Played a little golf, ate some good seafood, enjoyed the local people.

Educator, 34, Wichita, KS

Venturers

We spent our last vacation there. It's unspoiled and beautiful. We admired the dunes the ferry out to the island was fun and the people are wonderful. Also visited the Orville and Wilbur Wright Museum for a little history.

Retired female, Iselin, NJ

I lived there for three years and really miss the beach life and laid back atmosphere.

Self-employed female, 46 Aliquippa, PA

It's got beautiful natural scenery and it's quiet and uncrowded. There are no traffic problems and you never get a sense of a tourist trap. Good weather, good golf, good food— it's terrific.

Male government employee Jacksonville, NC

Those clever North Carolinians have learned to attract visitors without overwhelming them with commercial overdevelopment. Why not investigate its mountains and islands and beaches soon?

Massachusetts

#17 RATING: ★★★

Centrics	Venturers	Dependables
7	6	7

The Pilgrims and Indians celebrated the first Thanksgiving in 1621.
Nineteen people were hanged and one crushed in the Salem witch trials.
Massachusetts has produced four U.S presidents.
Harvard University is the oldest university in the nation.
Webster Lake's official name is Lake Chargoggagoggmanchauggagogychaubunagugnamaug.

Massachusetts presents a unique and interesting profile in my surveys.

1. All personality types like the same things about Massachusetts. It's difficult to find any meaningful differences in what they say about the state or the specific areas that they like.

2. The places they mention most are located along the East coast, primarily limited to Boston, Cape Cod, and the islands of Martha's Vineyard and Nantucket. Very few other cities or areas ever get referenced. The picturesque north shore, the middle portion of the state, the western half and the quaint, historic towns located a short distance inland seem to get ignored.

3. The overall ratings by the three personality types are also very similar—each gives it between a 6 and 7.

4. One comment comes up most: the state is seen as *relaxing*, a characteristic that appeals to people who choose this extraordinarily historic part of the original colonies.

Massachusetts does not create the sense of energy, activity and excitement that characterize most of the western states. Rather, those who like it talk about how relaxed and calm they feel when they visit. There's plenty to do, but no sense of urgency to do it. Just set your own pace and get rid of all feelings of obligations and responsibilities. Cape Cod and Nantucket especially contribute to this blending of heart and soul. Visitors talk about a sense of isolation, their unspoiled qualities, a very natural kind of beauty, and the very friendly local people who don't push you or hurry you along. When they talk about Boston, you can feel the sense of respect and reverence that people have for its contribution to the beginnings of the nation. The charm of the city and the rich and varied kinds of food a traveler can get also receive many favorable comments.

Musical Theater

Berkshires

Skiing

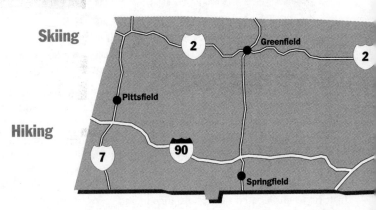

Hiking

Camping

Museums/Galleries

Bicycling

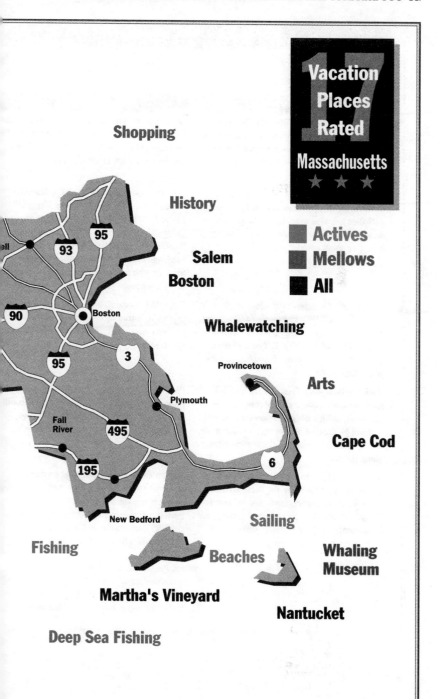

WHAT TO DO IN MASSACHUSETTS

Actives	Mellows
1 Vigorous travelers will find most of their action at the Massachusetts shore. One of the most popular activities is deep-sea fishing for tuna and marlin. Charter a boat at almost any seaside center.	Allow two or three hours for a tour of the New England Aquarium on Boston's waterfront. It's an excellent facility for observation, shows and hands-on fun in the tide pools.
2 Massachusetts offers winter skiing in the Berkshires, at several locations. All outdoor activities are also available in the mountains, and you can camp or choose from a variety of hotels or small country inns.	Boston began as, and remains, a fine commercial city. Enjoy shopping the elegant stores in Copley Place, then push on to Quincy Market (pronounced Kwinzee by the locals) where the stalls and shops in several buildings offer eclectic merchandise and food. Search for bargains at Filene's Basement downtown.
3 Bunker Hill Monument in Boston satisfies those who want both sightseeing and vigorous exercise. It memorializes a famous Revolutionary War battle with a 221-foot obelisk. You are welcome to climb the spiral staircase to the top!	Cape Cod is quaint, picturesque, artistic and often patronized by celebrities. Songs and stories celebrate its ambience. Can you ask for more?
4 Walk the three-mile Freedom Trail. In summer, there are ranger-guided tours on the half-hour, but it's easy to follow on your own. You will be amazed at how much of our early history manifests itself at the several sites along the way.	Old Sturbridge Village is a 200-acre recreation of a New England rural village. You will see a living museum with many buildings, exhibits and people pursuing their lives as they did in colonial days.
5 Nantucket Island and Martha's Vineyard are accessible by boat or by air. These islands were originally supply points and refuges for the shipping trade. The historical atmosphere is still there, and both islands offer varied recreation and wildlife refuges.	Boston and nearby cities offer so many rewarding activities and historical sightseeing that it is impossible to list them all. Here's a partial list: Harvard University (Cambridge), the *USS Constitution* in Charlestown Navy Yard, Faneuil Hall (Boston), the Old North Church (Boston), Minuteman National Historical Park (Concord), and Salem, site of Nathaniel Hawthorne's birth and of the infamous 17th century witch trials. Paul Revere took his famous ride through this territory.

For further information about Massachusetts, contact:
Massachusetts Office of Travel and Tourism
100 Cambridge Street, 13th Floor
Boston, MA 02202
☎ (617) 727-3201

WHAT PEOPLE LIKE ABOUT MASSACHUSETTS

Dependables

Dependables offer similar views to the *centrics* and *venturers.*

I like Cape Cod, Mass., especially Dennisport. It's got nice weather, the ocean, and excellent restaurants. And, it has a leisurely, casual atmosphere.
40-year-old middle level female executive, Solvay, NY

Boston, Mass has so much. It's friendly, clean, and there's lots to do. It's historical too.
Housewife, 26, Akron, OH

I like the Boston area, and most of New England, including New Hampshire, Vermont and Maine. There's a variety of activities and sights available to see and do. And you can do it at your own pace.
46-year-old military officer, Annandale, VA

The Mohawk Trail in Massachusetts is nice. There's lots of room to move about, and it's very historic.
Female executive, 45, Worcester, MA

Centrics

Notice the similarities in how each personality type describes their experiences. *Centrics:*

Give me Cape Cod. It's within three hours of where I live, you're on the water, and it's just totally relaxing when you're there.
40-year-old, male senior executive, Rocky Hill, CT

Martha's Vineyard, Mass has what I want. It's very safe and has great beaches. In off season, it's very quiet. And it has NO fast food!
Single, 41, senior female executive, Loveland, CO

My favorite place is Rockport, Mass. I like its quiet and relaxed air, and just the special quality of the area.
Retired male, Cornwall, NY

Cape Cod and Falmouth, Mass. are both my favorites. You have accessibility to other sites. You've got the ocean and things to see and do. It has quaintness, history, and things just seem to be happening. You have Boston nearby, and Hyannisport, and Woods Hole.
44-year-old female teacher, Nelsonville, OH

Venturers

Venturers, who typically jump into almost everything imaginable when they vacation, also seem to slow down when they arrive in Massachusetts.

Martha's Vineyard has a great atmosphere. It's relaxing, has great golf and beautiful scenery. It's just a good combination of things.
50-year-old entrepreneur, Los Gatos, CA

I like both Boston and Cape Cod. They have history, quaintness, quietness, and beauty.
Male bus company owner, 50, Fountain Valley, CA

Nantucket, Mass is what I choose. It has beauty, historical significance, the ocean, and pleasant weather. There's good food and it's a great place to run.
Senior female executive, 43, McLean, VA

I like Boston and the whole northeast coast area. It has historical significance, a difference in climate throughout the year, and excellent food. Also the prices are reasonable.
30-year-old female administrative assistant, Smyrna, GA

These comments demonstrate the relaxed state of mind that Massachusetts seems to impart quickly to its visitors. The pressures and feelings of stress that they bring with them vanish in the unhurried towns and cities of its eastern shores. If you have that need to unwind in a hurry, then Massachusetts may be the place you should seek. But after you've spent a couple of days doing nothing, then venture into other parts of the state. Almost indescribable scenery awaits you at every turn in the road. Surprisingly, no one spontaneously mentioned the fall colors. They can be as spectacular in Massachusetts as elsewhere in New England.

Washington, D.C.

#18 RATING: ★★★

Centrics	Venturers	Dependables
7	8	7

The cornerstone of the Capitol was laid by mason George Washington.

House Speaker Joe Cannon's recipe for bean soup has been on the Capitol menu since 1907.

Rises in temperature in the Washington Monument cause moisture to condense and "rain" falls inside.

In 1835, President Andrew Jackson paid off the national debt the first and only time in U.S. history.

The FBI Bldg. exhibits range from espionage devices to gangster weapons.

Visitors to the District of Columbia agree that a trip to our capitol is among those things that every American should do in their lifetime. They come away with the feeling that Washington D.C. not only belongs to the nation, but to each citizen individually, and there is no other place that speaks to us in that unique American voice.

When they talk about their trip to the District, travelers universally emphasize the historical significance of the city and its surroundings. They feel that they are indeed walking in the footsteps of the founding fathers, from Washington and Jefferson to Lincoln and FDR, and those who died in battle, from the Civil War to Vietnam. The imposing size and scale of the public buildings—the Senate and the House, the Treasury, the Supreme Court, the FBI building, the Lincoln and Jefferson monuments, and the Smithsonian complex—add to the sense of wonder and appreciation for this extraordinary place that houses and displays our history.

Because this is a special place for all Americans, there are fewer differences among *centrics, venturers* and *dependables* in how they describe their trips. Across the personality scale, visitors are about equal in remembering how easy it is to get around the city, especially citing the clean, safe metro system. They agree in equal numbers about the quality and extent of the museums and exhibits. Many pairs of shoes are worn out touring the Smithsonian complex without scratching the surface, and there is always something new to see. Admission to most attractions is free or nominal, another very attractive feature for all.

Dining/Shopping (Georgetown)

The White House

Arlington National Cemetery

Historic Buildings

Kennedy Center (Music/Theater)

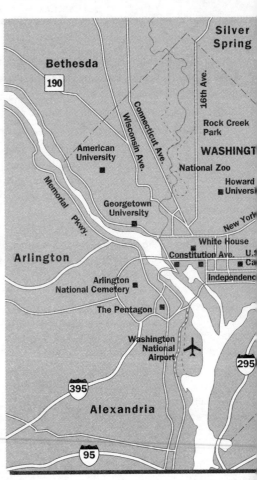

Tours of Monuments

Williamsburg (History)

National Zoo

**Hiking
(VA Mountains)**

Actives
Mellows
All

**George Washington
National Forest**

Shenandoah National Park

Smithsonian Museums

**Watersports
(Potomac and Chesapeake Bay)**

Side trips to Monticello and Mt. Vernon

WHAT TO DO IN WASHINGTON D.C.

Actives	Mellows
1 Climb all the stairs to the Washington Monument to get a panoramic view of the District. Warning: this is not for the faint-hearted or the physically unfit.	Spend a day at Williamsburg, a famous recreation of colonial America that is worth seeing. There are tours from the District, or you can drive.
2 Take side trips out of the district to the homes of Thomas Jefferson (Monticello) and George Washington (Mt. Vernon). Beautiful houses, they convey a sense of history and create feelings of reverence in most people.	Arlington National Cemetery is the final resting place for many American heroes, and is reachable via the metro. The eternal flame at the gravesite of John Kennedy is especially moving.
3 For an interesting look at one of our military services, call in advance to arrange a tour of the naval academy at Annapolis, Maryland.	In December or January, the District stages a Pageant of Peace. Call the National Park Service, ☎ *(202) 619-7222.*
4 If you need a break from sightseeing, investigate watersports on the Potomac or nearby Chesapeake Bay.	For a change of pace, there are plenty of spectator sports in the area. Take in a college basketball game at Georgetown University, a baseball game in the new Camden Yard in Baltimore or watch the Washington Redskins play football in the winter.
5 Do some hiking in the Virginia mountains, right next door. George Washington National Forest or Shenandoah National Park are two good choices.	Everyone will enjoy a performance at the Kennedy Center on the Potomac, one of the country's most beautiful venues for theater and music.

For further information about Washington, D.C., contact

Washington D.C. Convention & Visitors Association:
1212 New York Avenue NW
Washington, D.C. 20005
☎ (202) 789-7000

WHAT PEOPLE LIKE ABOUT WASHINGTON D.C.

Dependables

Centrics

Venturers

Following are some comments about Washington D.C. from *centrics*:

All the Smithsonian museums are great, but the Air and Space Museum is particularly impressive. I had just been to Kitty Hawk (where the Wright brothers launched their first flight), so it was even more meaningful to me.

**Self-employed male,
Concord, NH**

Our son goes to Georgetown, so we've spent some time in that area of the District. We like the architecture, the restaurants and shops, and the overall ambience. It's very civilized.

**Legal secretary,
Lexington, KY**

I really enjoyed all the typical tourist activities. Touring all the government agencies was very interesting, and I especially liked the mint. You get a good feeling for a change about government in action. The political atmosphere is exciting.

**Insurance risk manager,
Birmingham, AL**

Those leaning toward the *venturer* side offer these comments;

Getting around the city is easy. The metro rail system is clean and convenient to use. I enjoy the historic and informative sites, the fun hotels, the great food and the wonderful bookstores.

**Self-employed female,
Minneapolis, MN**

Nowhere else can the amount of historical sites be found. There are so many activities for me and my family, and there is always something new—and new people in town!

**Financial Manager,
Fort Mill, S.C.**

It's a beautiful city and there is so much to see! Everything is available for free, or for a small fee. All the people we met were helpful and friendly.

**Homemaker, 52,
Browntown, WI**

It's a clean, exciting, well-organized city. It's educational and historic. The historical significance is important to me. The whole area is very scenic and it's within driving distance. There is a lot to do when you get there.

**Manager, manufacturing,
Livonia, MI**

WHAT PEOPLE LIKE ABOUT WASHINGTON D.C.

Dependables	**Centrics**	**Venturers**

The city is filled with hundreds of places to visit. The weather is temperate in the spring and summer. I particularly enjoy the lovely sailing trips on Chesapeake Bay.

Female teacher, 34, Tucson, AZ

The architecture and general atmosphere is very different than we're used to at home. I think D.C. is unique partly because of all those buildings on a massive scale. I like visiting all the government agencies.

Banker, Los Angeles, CA

In addition to the great hotels, restaurants and cultural opportunities, there is all our history. Watching Congress in session is much better than a textbook.

Female attorney, Green Bay, WI

Clearly, Washington D.C. will continue to be a magnet for American visitors who enjoy exploring their history, and perhaps also for international travelers who want a "feel" for what the United States is all about.

New Hampshire

#19 RATING: ★★★

Centrics	Venturers	Dependables
7	6	6

In 1962 New Hampshire began the first state lottery since 1894.

Franconia's granite Old Man of the Mountain is 48 ft. from chin to forehead.

From Mt. Washington's summit, you can see the Atlantic and five states.

New Hampshire's 13 mile coastline is the shortest of the Atlantic states.

The nation's first regular stage run was from Portsmouth to Boston.

I enjoy doing consumer research because, as long as I've been conducting studies, the results still sometimes surprise me. New Hampshire is a revelation on several levels. First, that this small New England state makes the top 25 vacation destinations. Second, that it tends to be popular with *venturers,* who come to the state in large numbers and are the most enthusiastic in their comments. Last, that both residents and visitors are so entertainingly iconoclastic! A man from Massachusetts, when asked why he liked New Hampshire, fixed me with a stern gaze and announced, "Live Free or Die!" Very independent sorts, these New Englanders.

Next door, Vermont has its Green Mountains and New Hampshire boasts the White Mountains, which give the state its nickname of the Granite State. *Venturer* and *centric* tourists love New Hampshire largely because of this dramatic mountain scenery and the variety of activities offered. It doesn't hurt that the residents are friendly, but distinctively "New Hampshire" in their independence and points of view, as reported by people I interviewed.

Millions of years ago when the glaciers moved through the area, they created the wild, rugged passes and notches in the White Mountains that give New Hampshire some of its character. The wild terrain apparently discourages *dependables* from visiting these parts of the state. Rather, they come to the more accessible areas of New Hampshire and pursue less strenuous activities. They say that the slower pace of life in small towns creates a comfortable, relaxed feeling that sends them home refreshed.

Skiing

Mountain Biki

Galleries/Museums

White Mountains

Hiking

Rock Climbing

Franconia Notch

Flume Waterfalls

**Profile Lake
Scenery**

**Dartmouth College
(Hanover)**

Manchester

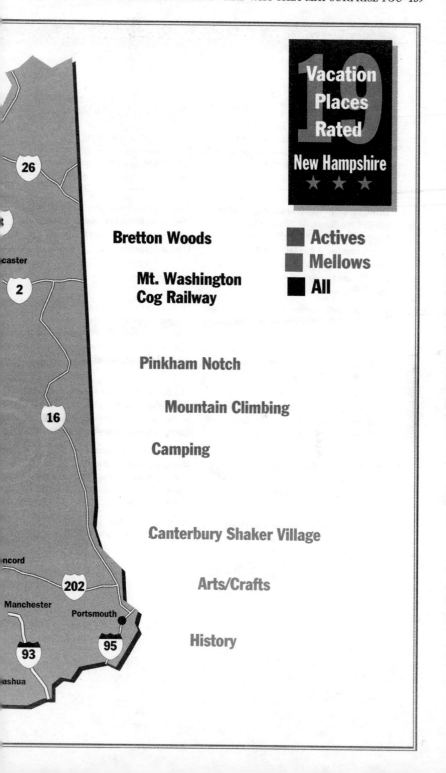

WHAT TO DO IN NEW HAMPSHIRE

Actives	**Mellows**

1 Bretton Woods has historical significance, lots of recreational facilities and the Mt. Washington Cog Railway that climbs the highest peak in the Northeast. Well worth a stop!

Canterbury Shaker Village is a restored Shaker religious community where you can take a good look at a simple, distinctive lifestyle. Traditional crafts are demonstrated, and there are several special events during the year.

2 At the southern end of Franconia Notch you will find the Flume, an 800 foot long chasm featuring a series of waterfalls, pools and rock formation. A bus takes visitors to the parking lot, then it's a two-mile walk to the gorge to see the natural sights and two covered bridges.

A famous New Hampshire landmark is the Old Man of the Mountains and Great Stone Face, made of naturally formed ledges above Profile Lake in Franconia Notch. Impressive!

3 The Lost River In Kinsman Notch will test your energy as well as it winds through glacier-formed caves and potholes. You see the sights using boardwalks, bridges and ladders, eventually reaching a remarkable rock formation called the Guillotine.

Dartmouth College, the northernmost Ivy League campus is located in Hanover. Highlights of the campus are the Baker Memorial Library, Hood Museum of Art and the Hopkins Center for Creative and Performing Arts.

4 The White Mountains are home to some of the best skiing and hiking in the country. The most daring hikers should try the Great Gulf Wilderness, accessible only on foot.

The Currier Gallery of Art in Manchester is worth a visit for its Italian Renaissance architecture and its collection of furniture emphasizing New Hampshire-made pieces.

5 Expert skiers will be challenged by the sheer west walls in the Pinkham Notch Scenic Area. Skiers rate this slope as the most difficult in the state, so strap your skis on carefully.

America has a Stonehenge of its own, and New Hampshire's got it. Near North Salem you can see stone structures that are the oldest megalithic site on this continent, possibly 4000 years old.

For further information about New Hampshire, contact:

New Hampshire Office of Travel and Tourism
P.O. Box 856
Concord, NH 03302
☎ (603) 271-2343

WHAT PEOPLE LIKE ABOUT NEW HAMPSHIRE

Dependables

Centrics

Venturers

Although the 10-point scale doesn't reflect it, *dependables* visit New Hampshire in fewer numbers, so the comments offered are also fewer and reflect the slower pace of this group:

Centrics, and especially *venturers*, enthuse about their experiences in the state. They can indulge their sense of adventure, their love of the outdoors and their desire for physical activity to whatever extent they wish. Here are some comments from *centrics*:

As we already know, *venturers* seek out vacation destinations that offer lots of activity, remain relatively uncrowded and appear different or unique in some way. New Hampshire fills the bill. *Venturers* like the winter skiing in the White Mountains and the rugged hiking trails and camp sites in the summer. This group also comments on New Hampshire's historical associations as the bedrock of American politics since colonial times. As we mentioned above, residents of New Hampshire project its unique personality—tough, proud and independent, and welcoming to those visitors who appreciate those qualities. Here's how some *venturers* describe their experiences:

It's a good place to go for us because we usually don't have a lot of time and it's easy to get there. The scenery is great and the pace is very different from the city, so we can really relax.
Female, copywriter, New York, NY

The life-style in New Hampshire is so very appealing. There are no big city problems, and the pace of life is slow and sensible. There is a lot to do and the scenery is fantastic. There are lakes, mountains, seashore all within reach.
Male loan officer, Durham, NC

There's a lot of great hiking in the mountains. Different degrees of difficulty, so everyone can enjoy themselves. You don't run into swarms of people, so it's very relaxing. Really, I fell in love with the mountains there.
Female office worker, Washington D.C.

I would describe the scenery as natural and pristine. It's also near to my home.
Laborer, 27, Charlestown, MA

We like to camp on our vacations, and do a lot of outdoor activities, especially hiking. We enjoyed New Hampshire more than any other place. Maybe it's the weather. Maybe it's the people.
Homemaker, 38, Cambridge, MA

We stayed in an area centrally located to the White Mountains and other parts of New England. Campgrounds in New Hampshire are great. They have good RV access and it's an inexpensive vacation with the family.
Attorney, 60, Canton, NY

WHAT PEOPLE LIKE ABOUT NEW HAMPSHIRE

Dependables

I toured a lot of the U.S. right after my college gradua-tion, and New Hampshire re-ally stands out in my memory because of the unique scenery and friendly attitude of the people.

Real estate salesman, Santa Ana, CA

Centrics

The Balsams up in Dixville Notch is a great resort where you can play hard any time of year or be as pampered as you like. The scenery is great, and the hotel is great.

Manufacturers rep, male, Albany, NY

It's close to home, which I like because I never have enough time. At the same time, I'm able to feel like I'm really get-ting away, because it's so natu-ral and beautiful and clean.

Journalist, Brookline, MA

Venturers

I got such a kick out of t people. They are nice ar friendly and sort of no-no sense types. They have minds their own, but a sense of h mor, too.

Factory foreman, Racine, W

The skiing is as good as an where in the country, and I from great ski country myse Good accommodations and n too expensive.

Male graduate stude Plymouth, V

There is a lot of exciteme in New Hampshire when presidential primary is he We went to ski, but enjoyed frenetic atmosphere that visiting politicians produc By the way, it's one of the f unspoiled recreation areas l

Female salesperson, Rehoboth Beach, I

If you are a *centric* or *venturer* person, or someone who needs a change of pace, discovering New Ha shire will probably prove worthwhile and fun for you.

Miami/ Southern Florida

#20 RATING: ★★★

Centrics	Venturers	Dependables
7	7	7

In 1763, the English returned captured Cuba to Spain and received Florida in trade.

Alligator stomachs contain everything from pickle jars to golf balls.

Almost half of Miami's population is Hispanic.

Ninety-six percent of Biscayne Park's acreage is underwater.

Miami is the world's largest cruise port.

Ponce de Leon failed to find the fountain of youth in Florida, nor did anyone ever find fabulous treasures in the swamps. However, Southern Florida has an attraction that impresses almost every tourist who's visited the area—the Florida Keys. In the "old days," the resorts of Miami Beach were the magnets that brought thousands of people to the area. But, my American Traveler Survey indicates that the Keys are the first choice of most visitors. Today's vacationers seek a casual and relaxed ambience, which happens to suit the life-style of the Keys very well.

Like Hawaii, this is as close as we get to the warm, tropical climate, palm trees, sun 'n fun beaches that many travelers dream of. And, it's only a skip and a hop to various Caribbean islands, which adds to the romantic, exotic atmosphere. Recent visitors tell me they find a definite flavor of the Caribbean in both Miami and the Keys, reflected in the food, the entertainment and the languages you hear spoken around you.

The comparative few who select Miami enjoy its weather and beaches, the shopping and the food and the amenities of city life. If your cruise ship embarks from the Port of Miami, Ft. Lauderdale and other South Florida cities (and many do), you may well take the opportunity to explore these communities before you leave. *Centrics* and *dependables* make up much of the cruise population and thus spend some time in the South Florida area. A few people also vacation a short way up the coast where the more upscale communities of Palm Beach and Boca Raton, longtime enclaves of wealthy society, house some of the most expensive golf clubs in the U.S.

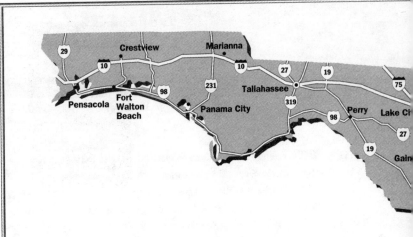

Crestview
Marianna
Pensacola
Fort
Walton
Beach
Panama City
Tallahassee
Perry
Lake Ci
Gain

Clearwater
St Petersburg

Shopping   Sara

Golf

Tennis

**Everglades
National Par**

History

Beaches

Scenery

N
W   E
S

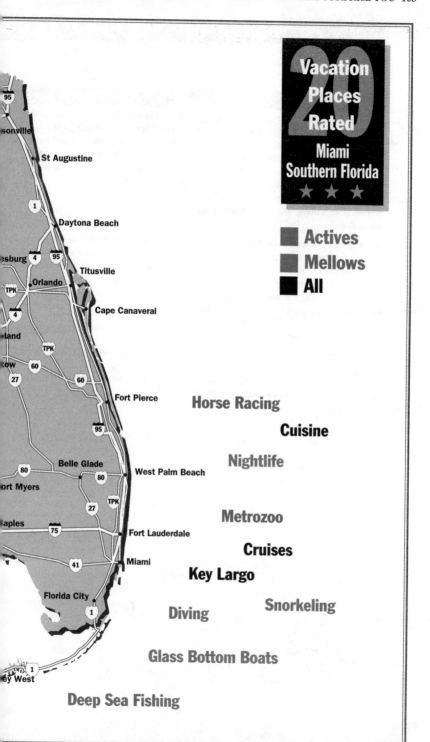

WHAT TO DO IN MIAMI/SOUTHERN FLORIDA

Actives | Mellows

1 Everglades National Park is unique among the country's treasures. A slow-moving river winds its way through a labyrinth of swamp, mangrove waterways and salt prairies. It is a true tropical wilderness whose flora and fauna are increasingly endangered. Recreation opportunities include boating, fishing and wilderness tours, and the sightseeing is unparalleled.

Want to take a chance with some disposable income? Several horse racing tracks offer the opportunity to test your luck and knowledge of the racing form. Check with Hialeah, Calder or Gulfstream Park to see when they're running.

2 Surrounded by water, Florida offers lots of scope for recreational boating. South Florida's marinas are impressively equipped, and there are many boat ramps. You can go out on your own, or hire someone to take you. Either way, keep an eye out for water fowl and especially for the endangered manatee that swim the coastal waterways.

To learn about Key West, take the Conch Train Tour through the old and new parts of the island. You can listen to narration about its history and points of interest, like Hemingway's house and Old Town, as you chug along.

3 You'll need to board a seaplane to access Dry Tortugas National Park from Key West. It's a perfect day or two for active sightseers who can view many varieties of migratory birds and sea turtles. Swim, snorkel and explore other aspects of these islands.

The Metrozoo in Miami is a fine example of a cageless zoo, where the animals roam in settings designed to imitate their natural habitats. Kids love it.

4 In Key Largo, visit John Pennekamp Coral Reef State Park. Snorkelers and scuba divers will want to see the "Christ of the Deep," a bronze statue only occasionally visible from boats.

For a taste of luxury, take a look at Palm Beach. Window shop the exclusive stores along Worth Avenue, then visit the Henry Morrison Flagler Museum, an opulent mansion built by Palm Beach's railroad magnate founder. You'll see beautiful and opulent furnishings and artifacts, and items of historical interest as well.

5 A different kind of activity is available in Miami Beach, where nightspots abound. You can see street entertainment in the Art Deco district, enjoy lavish extravaganzas at the large hotels and have a lot of fun in between the extremes as well. The Caribbean flavor of some places is particularly lively.

Finally, here's a brief list of things to see and do in Miami: the Ancient Spanish Monastery in North Miami Beach, Biscayne National Park Boat Tours, Miami Seaquarium, Miccosukee Indian Village and Airboat Tours, dine on stone crabs and Cuban cuisine.

For further information about Southern Florida, contact:

Florida Division of Tourism
126 West Van Buren Street
Tallahassee, FL 32399-2000
☎ (904) 487-1462

WHAT PEOPLE LIKE ABOUT MIAMI/SOUTHERN FLORIDA

Dependables

Dependables certainly visit South Florida, but don't express themselves as extensively as the other personalities. Here are a few words from *dependables*:

It's close to home, but far from the rat race. I can get in a lot of golf and my wife enjoys sightseeing and shopping.
Insurance executive, Nashville, TN

The ocean water is nice and warm, and there are a lot of interesting things to see, like the Everglades and Cypress Gardens.
Homemaker,35, Alexandria, VA

Centrics

The Keys attract a large variety of people and personalities. *Centrics* lie on the beaches, bathe in the warm ocean, play a little golf or tennis and generally relax. *Venturers* get in the water, go snorkeling and scuba diving, and take boats out to other islands. A lot of *centrics* and *venturers* say they enjoy the nightlife, so their days don't end with the magnificent sunsets. Here are some comments from *centrics*:

I can definitely get into the pace of life down there. The weather in winter is so beautiful. It's still quiet and non-touristy in many areas, the scenery is great and there are lots of restaurants with good, inexpensive food.
You can't beat the deep-sea fishing off this coast, no way!
45-year-old disabled male, Jacksonville, FL

Key West has such a peaceful atmosphere, balmy breezes, the ocean lapping practically at your door, the whole thing. It's not that expensive.
Salesman, 29, Atlanta, GA

It has sunny weather, nice clean beaches, good golf and tennis and a good selection of restaurants.
Female Supervisor, Tulsa, OK

Venturers

From those who like a little more action and are willing to follow where their curiosity leads them, the following are comments from *venturers*:

It's really fun to drive out to Key West over the causeway. Once there, it's the weather, the beaches, diving by the reefs and the nightlife. They make you feel a part of the community.
Self employed male, 31, Chicago, IL

I saw the most beautiful sunsets in Key Largo. It is a beautiful, scenic, atmospheric kind of place—a partying kind of place, as well!
Female supervisor, Hollywood, FL

There is a laid-back atmosphere, with no pressure. It's just what you want when you get away on vacation. People are nice without overwhelming you.
Consultant, 49, Westchester, NY

WHAT PEOPLE LIKE ABOUT
MIAMI/SOUTHERN FLORIDA

Dependables

Centrics

I hope I don't sound elitist, but Little Palm Island is a very upscale, private resort where I experienced total relaxation.

Office manager, law firm, Tallahassee, FL

If you live on the East Coast and you like to go away in the winter, then you go to Florida. My parents went to Miami for years, and now we do too, although we spend most of out time in the Keys. The weather is unbeatable .

Stockbroker, 39, Boston, MA

Venturers

There is a lot more to do down there than lie on the beach—although the beach is nice! We saw interesting flora and wildlife, both in zoos and in the wild. Culture, art and good seafood. You can do nothing or you can do everything.

Male CPA, Medford, OR

New Mexico

#21 RATING: ★★★

Centrics	Venturers	Dependables
7	9	6

In 1901, cowboy Jim White discovered "a hole in the ground," Carlsbad Caverns.

Santa Fe is the oldest capital city in the U.S.

Visitors often sprawl out at Four Corners so they can say they slept in four states at once.

Pueblo Bonito was the first condo—housing 1500 in 800 rooms.

The first atomic bomb was exploded at Trinity Site in 1945.

New Mexico attracts a more venturesome population who choose the northern part of the state as their favorite area. Surprisingly, Albuquerque and points south are only infrequently mentioned, even though Albuquerque is the largest city and is home to interesting shops and museums. Visitors tell me that they find the exotic ambience of Indian and Spanish cultures, combined with the lingering romance of the old west, to be unique.

Centrics also like northern New Mexico, and they particularly appreciate what Santa Fe offers: a charming plaza in the center of the oldest capital city in the United States, with a park surrounded by chic stores that display the Santa Fe "style" and expensive galleries featuring native American and western art. On one side, Indians from nearby pueblos sell authentic artwork, jewelry and crafts, with their wares spread out on blankets. It reminds you of nineteenth century photographs. A block or so away is the end of the old Santa Fe Trail, the route of many cattle drives, and the street still bears that name. Taos, an hour's drive north, has a similar picturesque plaza, worthwhile museums and one of the most photographed Native American dwelling places, Taos Pueblo.

Aztec Ruins

Bandelier National Monument

Hiking

Navajo Tribal Museum (Window Rock)

Pueblo Reservation

Zuni Reservation

Dining

Gila Cliff Dwellings

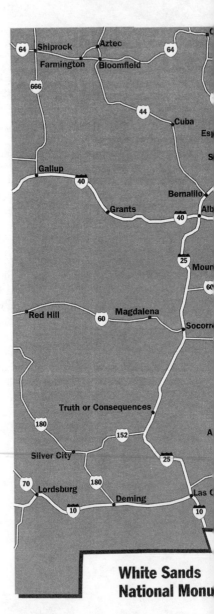

White Sands National Monu

Capulin Mountain National Monument

Taos Skiing/Hang-gliding

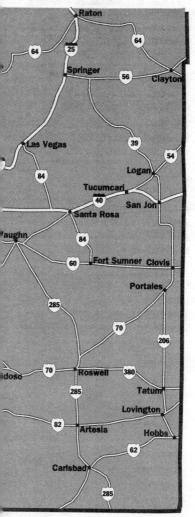

21 Vacation Places Rated

New Mexico
★ ★ ★

Santa Fe

■ **Actives**
■ **Mellows**
■ **All**

Arts/History

Los Alamos

Albuquerque Balloon Festival

Museums

Art Galleries

Lava Beds Carrizozo

Carlsbad Caverns

Rio Grande River Rafting

WHAT TO DO IN NEW MEXICO

Actives	Mellows
1 Reserve well in advance, but don't miss the balloon festival in Albuquerque in the fall. See New Mexico from above!	For a taste of recent history, drive out to Los Alamos, site of the Manhattan Project during World War II. Be sure to include the museum.
2 Ski Taos in the winter, or try hang-gliding in the summer in the Albuquerque area.	Arrange to see ceremonial dances at one or two of the larger pueblos.
3 Hike through Bandelier National Monument to explore the Anasazi ruins (the ancestors of the present Pueblo people).	Enjoy New Mexico-style cuisine, from gourmet to budget, guaranteed different from the Mexican food you're accustomed to.
4 Billy the Kid's notorious career began with the Lincoln County Wars in the southern part of the state. Those interested in the Old West might enjoy retracing his adventures with the help of the state tourist office or a knowledgeable travel agent.	Take your camera to White Sands National Monument near Las Cruces in the southern part of the state for some dramatic pictures of a remarkable area.
5 Arrange a tour to visit one of the distant ancient Indian sites like Chaco Canyon— partly by air! There are several tour companies operating out of Albuquerque or Santa Fe.	Experience the Santa Fe Opera in its remarkable outdoor venue in the hills just outside town. Even nonmusic lovers rave about this, so arrange for tickets early.

For further information about New Mexico, contact:

New Mexico Department of Tourism
491 Old Santa Fe Trail
Santa Fe, NM
☎ (505) 827-7400

WHAT PEOPLE LIKE ABOUT NEW MEXICO

Dependables

New Mexico attracts fewer *dependables* than *centrics* or *venturers*. Travelers from this group report that they enjoy the beautiful scenery and the abundant Indian lore:

When we drove through New Mexico, it reminded us of all the old western movies. There is a real sense of wide open spaces. You can almost see Indians on horseback on the mountain ridges, waiting to swoop down on the wagon train!
Accountant, 52, Atlanta, GA

Centrics

Centrics also like the fact that many celebrities have established homes around Santa Fe. As a consequence, real estate has become a bit pricey, but hotels are still reasonable for visitors. The possibility of bumping into a movie star in one of the area's great restaurants is exciting. *Centrics* tell us:

It has great food, great hotels, great shopping, beautiful scenery and lots of history. I've read about a lot of famous people who have bought homes there, and it's fun to know they like the same kind of place.
31-year-old homemaker, Glendale, CA

Venturers

The area around Santa Fe supports a rich variety of artists and artisans in all mediums, with much of the art manifesting Native American and Spanish influences. *Venturer* personalities enjoy the arts and cultural activities found here, and they also emphasize the good skiing in Northern New Mexico. The high road to Taos, or the alternate, beautiful route along the Rio Grande gets them to relatively uncrowded ski areas and more of the old west in the Taos area. Many fans of New Mexico, *venturers* in particular, talk about the special quality of light throughout the state, and the spirituality that seems to pervade their New Mexico experiences. Within a short driving distance of Albuquerque, Santa Fe or Taos, several pueblos offer native ceremonial dances. Archaeological sites of the ancient ones, the Anasazi, can be explored.

Following, *venturers* offer their own words:

Santa Fe lives in incredible natural beauty. It has that unique light and that spiritual and artistic setting. I find the history and the combination of cultures irresistible, and everyone is so friendly.
49-year-old female educator, Lancaster, PA

WHAT PEOPLE LIKE ABOUT NEW MEXICO

Dependables

Centrics

Venturers

Here are the 'purple mountain majesties' from the song. What beautiful places, open spaces, clear skies!

Mother of two, Fislers, IN

Driving through those wide open spaces is a very special experience. The history of the Southwest is all here. The museums are excellent. There is a big variety of things to do and see here.

Communications technician, Norman, OK

There is plenty to do for children and adults—lots of recreational facilities, and I think it's educational because of the history.

Male, mechanic, Monahans, TX

Although it's become more 'touristy' in recent years, the cultural and environmental surroundings are superb. It's very cultural, has a wonderful dry climate, and an open, friendly atmosphere. It's not ordinary. I hate Disney World.

Female artist, Buffalo, NY

I enjoy the Spanish culture, the hot summer weather and the sparse population. The scenery is very interesting. The high desert mountains and valleys are very different from ours.

53-year-old office worker, Anchorage, AK

You are surrounded by history. See the churches and museums. Explore the culture. The skiing is awesome. You can visit any time of year and never be bored.

29-year-old service manager Houston, TX

It's uncrowded, with a variety of cultures to explore. I like to ski there. The mountains are great. So is the climate.

Self-employed male Middlesex, NJ

The variety is amazing. If you drive the high road to Taos you see one kind of thing—old Spanish towns and the special crafts that are practiced there. Then the low road along the Rio Grande is beautiful in another way.

Medical researcher El Paso, TX

New Mexico may not attract the large numbers of travelers that visit Orlando, for example, but those who love New Mexico are dedicated to its unique and special qualities.

Utah

#22 RATING: ★ ★ ★

Centrics	Venturers	Dependables
9	9	5

Great Salt Lake is the largest salt lake in North America.
Rainbow Bridge is the highest and largest natural arch.
Moab is called "the mountain bike capital of the universe."
A pin dropped at one end of the Mormon Tabernacle can be heard 175 ft. away at the other end.
Utah is the world center of genealogical research.

First, as you can see by the degree of interest figures, *centrics* and *venturers* like Utah a lot, but not *dependables*. It follows the pattern of several other western states in providing beautiful, rugged scenery in its national parks and dynamic, active recreational opportunities. Utah invites you to be outdoors. This is not the place for theme parks or nightlife. Rather, you can camp, ski, hike and fish amidst the many natural splendors of the southwest. *Dependable* travelers, however, typically prefer more sedate vacations with warmer weather and in more familiar surroundings.

Three important qualities contribute to Utah's popularity among the people I surveyed. They talk about superlative winter skiing, spectacular and well-run national parks and a wholesome quality that pervades the atmosphere. Seventy-seven percent of the state's population belongs to the Church of Latter Day Saints. The church's influence runs deep and wide in Utah, accounting in part for the healthy attitude and feeling of serenity mentioned by so many.

Utah has five national parks, seven national forests and six national monuments. That's enough scenery for the most dedicated fan of natural beauty, and much of it is incomparable. Travelers find it hard to find the words to describe the wonders of Bryce Canyon and Zion National Parks, with their fantastic formations and other-worldly colors. *Centrics* enjoy the scenery and the outdoor activities in the parks, nature walks guided by rangers and exploring Native American ruins scattered throughout the state.

**Golden Spike
Historical Site**

Great Salt Lake

**Bonneville
Salt Flats**

Hunting

Mountain Biking

Rock Climbing

Fishing

**Bryce Canyon
National Park**

Hiking

**Zion
National Park**

22
Vacation
Places
Rated

Utah

★ ★ ★

Actives
Mellows
All

Skiing

Temple Square
History/Museums

Roosevelt
Vernal 40
Duchesne
491
elper
Price
191
70
Green River
Crescent Jct.
24
Moab
Hanksville
191
Monticello
95
Blanding
191

Dinosaur
National
Monument

Shopping

Arts

River Rafting

Canoeing

Lake Powell

Natural Bridges
National Monument

Rainbow Bridge

WHAT TO DO IN UTAH

Actives

Mellows

1 Utah provides some of the best hunting and fishing in the West. The marshes of the Great Salt Lake harbor many wildfowl, also deer and elk.

The beautiful Mormon Temple in Salt Lake City is closed to non-Mormons, but you can tour other parts of Temple Square. If you're there during the holidays, take in the Christmas Lights Festival.

2 At Dinosaur National Monument you can indulge an interest in prehistoric geology and some good recreation. It contains a large concentration of fossilized dinosaur bones, good hiking trails and river trips.

American history buffs will want to visit Golden Spike National Historic Site, where Union Pacific and Central Pacific rails met in 1869 to form the first transcontinental railroad. A visitor center is open daily.

3 Raft the mighty Colorado! Moab, Utah is the starting point for lots of white-water and canoe trips. Moab has historical associations, too. Butch Cassidy's gang was familiar with it, and Zane Grey made it the scene of many novels about the Old West.

There is more history in Salt Lake City, whose residents are proud of their heritage, and celebrate it all year long. A week of festivities culminates in a big parade and special activities on Pioneer Day in Salt Lake in July.

4 Rainbow Bridge National Monument near the Arizona border is the largest natural bridge in the world, and well worth the 13 mile hike to get there. It can also be reached by boat and a short hike. Rainbow Bridge is considered a sacred place by the Navaho.

Visit Lagoon Amusement Park in Farmington with the family. It's a re-created frontier settlement, with exhibits, entertainment, a wild animal farm, and a water park called Lagoona Beach.

5 Skiers, have you been paying attention? Pack up your gear and make reservations at Alta, Park City, Brighton, Snowbird, Solitude, Sundance or Brian Head. Have a great time!

For further information about Utah, contact:

Utah Travel Council
Council Hall/Capitol Hill
Salt Lake City, UT 84114
☎ (801) 538-1030

WHAT PEOPLE LIKE ABOUT UTAH

Dependables

As I indicated, *dependables* do not visit Utah as often as others, and they do not seem to appreciate its beauty and ambience as much as others. Those who like it value the scenery in the parks and the history of the state, encompassing the Mormon settlement and the legacies of the Old West and American Indians. Many also say they have friends and family there to visit. But, they offer more muted comments.

It's a very nice family vacation. Bryce and Zion are remarkably beautiful. You can feel safe and secure anywhere you travel in the state.
Family of four, Grand Island, NE

I had done some reading about the Mormons settling Utah, and found it interesting, so I was glad to have a chance to see what I could in Salt Lake around the Temple area.
Male, freelance graphics, Nampa, ID

Centrics

Centrics and others will also be interested in Utah's developing film industry. Movie makers find the state hospitable to their efforts, and appreciate the wonderful scenery as a backdrop. Robert Redford's Sundance Institute, which offers workshops and small festivals, has for several years established itself as an industry outpost with a Utah personality.

Here are some comments from *centrics:*

It's always hard to explain why you like something. I guess it's the southwest culture. The mountain and desert scenery, and the Native American ruins all contribute to that.
Female educator, Maynard, MA

The national parks, Bryce in particular, are well run and set up to be accessible. Our motel was right outside the entrance so it was easy to get to everything with the family.
Male, mid-level manager, Cary, NC

Venturers

If I was a skier, I'd head for Utah next winter. I have never heard such enthusiasm or seen so many exclamation points when travelers—especially *venturers*—talk or write about skiing in Utah. These active persons also take advantage of other recreational opportunities, such as hiking, fly-fishing, biking, horseback riding and rock climbing. But it is the skiers who wax rhapsodic about their favorite sport. Alta, Park City, Snowbird, Sundance and some others provide a good variety of ski areas, with consistently excellent weather conditions. I also hear from Utah visitors that the people they meet—residents and other tourists—are not just friendly and gracious, but are "good" people, too. Listen to the *venturers:*

There is great skiing at Park City. You can get to lots of varied ski areas close by. The town is quaint and picturesque, with excellent shopping. The accommodations are good, plentiful and varied.
Homemaker, 32, Haworth, NJ

Great skiing! They have good snow and the snowfall is predictable and consistent. The weather is good and it's easy to get around. The surroundings are just beautiful.
Female college professor, Little Rock, AR

WHAT PEOPLE LIKE ABOUT UTAH

Dependables

Centrics

Venturers

I've been there to ski a couple of times with people from the office—it has really good snow.
Accounts receivable clerk, female, Costa Mesa, CA

I thought Salt Lake City was beautiful. Everything is so clean and white and orderly. The people you meet are very kind.
Engineer, 40, Oklahoma City, OK

It's quiet and calming o Lake Powell. There are n phones and there's no rush t get anywhere.
Self-employed male Ogden, U

We enjoyed Bryce and Zion very much. Everyone was friendly and helpful. The children got to horseback ride, which they had never done, and the scenery was really great.
Male computer consultant, Iowa City, IA

I travel on my motorcycle to Moab. Getting there is half the fun! You get a really close look at the great scenery.
Male, computer technician, Colorado Springs, CO

The best skiing ever, ever!
Saleswoman, 46 Littleton, CC

Lake Powell! Desert + water + freedom + scenery = a great trip!
Self-employed female, Salt Lake City, UT

We went to Salt Lake in Fe ruary. We did a lot of things—skiing, hiking and horseba riding. The people are nice. W like the area because it's clea there's no smoking, etc. I wou say I found it spiritual cleansing.
Female project manager, 2 Los Angeles, C

It's no wonder that filmmakers seek out Utah more and more. It's beautiful, puts out the welcome and remains relatively uncrowded. If you lean to the centric or venturer side of the personality scale, yo love it as well.

Tennessee

#23 RATING: ★ ★ ★

Centrics	Venturers	Dependables
6	5	6

Tennessee claims the greatest variety of birds in the U.S.

The earthquake of 1811 created Reelfoot Lake.

Oak Ridge manufactured the bomb that was dropped on Hiroshima.

Cumberland Caverns was once a saltpeter mine.

Memphis is known as the birthplace of the blues.

Come on down and see Tennessee, y'all! The folks here will entertain you, feed you good southern cooking and let you relax in their beautiful Smoky Mountains, if that's what you've a mind to do. Sorry, but it's hard not to fall into the Tennessee manner of speaking when I review the enthusiastic comments from the travelers who choose that state as their favorite vacation spot.

Tennessee's tourists establish a solid *centric* base, tilting slightly to the *dependable* side, but with enough *venturers* to commend it to that group. It's especially interesting to see how neatly the extremes divide Tennessee. *Venturers* single out the scenic mountains and the recreation found there. Those who lean to the *dependable* side never quit talking about the entertainment offered in Nashville and other parts of the state.

Nashville, home of the country music industry, has seen its fortunes rise and fall over the years But, it never falls too low. Country music and its stars will always have a faithful audience, and they will often "cross over" to enjoy extended popularity with other pop music lovers. The Grand Ol' Opry is its showcase, and a visit to Nashville gives you an opportunity to take in a performance.

Actives
Mellows
All

Opryland

Riverboat Rides

Nashvil

Cumberland Caverns Park

Opryland Amusement Park

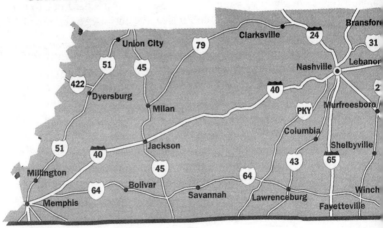

Bransfor
Clarksville
24
31
Union City
79
51
45
Nashville
Lebanor
422
Dyersburg
40
2
Milan
PKY
Murfreesboro
Columbia
Shelbyville
51
40
Jackson
Millington
45
43
65
64
Bolivar
64
Winch
Memphis
Savannah
Lawrenceburg
Fayetteville

Graceland   **Museums**   **Chattanoo Aquarium**

Shiloh Military Park

Fishing

Vacation Places Rated 23 Tennessee
★ ★ ★

The Hermitage

The Parthenon

Music Row

Oak Ridge (History)

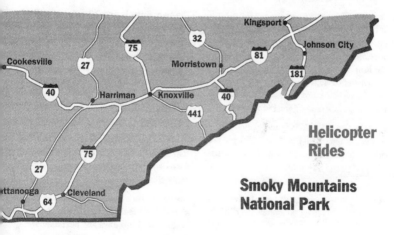

Helicopter Rides

Smoky Mountains National Park

Dollywood

Rock City Gardens

Lookout Mountain

Hiking

Camping

WHAT TO DO IN TENNESSEE

Actives

Mellows

1 Be as active as you like at Rock City Gardens near Chattanooga. At the least, you must walk the 4000 foot long Enchanted Trail that leads through tunnels and over bridges to the summit, where you will be treated to a panoramic view of seven states.

If you like aquariums, Chattanooga has a fairly new one, the first to feature entirely freshwater fish. The city has recently redeveloped its riverfront area, and it's pleasant to stroll around before or after your visit to the aquarium.

2 In addition to its beauty and scenic vistas, Great Smoky Mountains National Park boasts more variations of plant life than most places in the country. If you have an interest in botany, or appreciate variety and beauty of flora (especially trees), ask the park rangers for good sites to explore.

If Nashville means country music, Memphis means the blues. Stay for a few days in this extraordinary city on the Mississippi to hear some of the best jazz and blues musicians in the world. Remember, Memphis is the city that launched the "king," Elvis Presley.

3 Visit Oak Ridge—it's sightseeing for the active mind and body. The entire city was built during World War II for research and development resulting in the manufacture of the first atomic bomb. Be sure to tour the American Museum of Science and Energy. Two Tennessee Valley Authority sites near Oak Ridge also welcome interested visitors.

The Hermitage is only 12 miles from Nashville's center, but it feels a lot farther away in time and distance. Many consider Andrew Jackson's home to be a highlight of their trip. Its excellent restoration and interesting family history are well presented, educational and enjoyable.

4 View the Great Smokies from the air. Rainbow Helicopter Mountain Flights will take you for a ride while the pilot discusses the area's history and points of interest.

Also in Nashville, the Country Music Hall of Fame is an outstanding example of a museum that specializes in a particular genre. Well designed, informative, and even worth a second visit.

5 Visit Opryland amusement park. Roller coasters like the Wabash Cannonball offer thrills.

You can relive a famous battle of the Civil War at Shiloh National Military Park. The bloody battle lasted two days and cost almost 24,000 lives. There is a Visitor Center and a well-marked 10-mile tour route. Pre-Columbian Indian mounds are also found in the park.

For further information about Tennessee, contact:

Tennessee Department of Tourist Development
P.O. Box 23170
Nashville, TN 37202
☎ (615) 741-2158

WHAT PEOPLE LIKE ABOUT TENNESSEE

Dependables

The Volunteer State has a lot of history. It got its nickname during the war of 1812 and is second only to Virginia in Civil War battles fought on its terrain. These and more recent developments like the Tennessee Valley Authority and Oak Ridge provide *dependable* tourists with lots of the significant sightseeing that they like. They also say that, as country music fans, they enjoy the "country" atmosphere and appreciate the fact that Tennessee is easy to get to from other parts of the country.

Hurray for Dollywood! We hit every theme park in the state, I think. The grownups liked Graceland the best. You can't beat Tennessee for a family vacation. Love the music, and it's pretty, too!
**Beautician, 33,
Jefferson, MO**

It's quiet and peaceful in the mountains. You feel like you are really getting away from the rat race for awhile. The cabin we had was comfortable and not expensive.
**Operations manager,
Atlanta, GA**

Centrics

Centric visitors also praise Opryland, the theme park that surrounds the Opry, for its homespun shows, rides and other attractions. If you can't get enough of the music, choose from many clubs in Nashville (or almost any Tennessee city) to listen and two-step the night away. Entertainment holds much of the interest for *centrics*, but quite a few also visit the mountain areas near Knoxville at the eastern end of the state for a different kind of experience. Here's how they describe it:

The Smokies around Gatlinburg have spectacular fall colors and clean, crisp air. You're surrounded by unspoiled nature, away from dense population, yet near cities. We love the southern hospitality and the low crime rate. Country and mountain music sounds authentic there.
**Military man, 47,
St. Cloud, MN**

There's a lot to do in Nashville, especially during the summer months. We were there for Fan Fair Week in June. Opryland is great fun!
**Female vending company
employee, Dundee, MI**

Venturers

A much larger percentage of *venturers* pick recreation areas in the mountains in preference to Tennessee's city life. They like country music a lot, but they like to enjoy it in a more quiet and relaxing atmosphere, surrounded by beautiful mountain scenery, with a variety of recreational options. Camping is very popular in the Great Smoky Mountains National Park, where visitors can also enjoy fishing, boating, swimming and hiking nature trails. As usual, whether it's city or country, *venturers* who like Tennessee say it's because it offers many and diverse activities, historical sites and great entertainment. It provides an opportunity, as one man put it, "to be doing something all the time."

We like to camp, and Cades Cove is such a beautiful place. It is really nice to be surrounded by natural beauty in the mountains, and share your environment with the wildlife.
**Homemaker, 23,
Grand Rapids, MI**

I love the chalets, the hot tubs, the fires at night in the quiet, peaceful Smokies, near Gatlinburg.
**Nuclear medical technician,
42, Louisville, KY**

WHAT PEOPLE LIKE ABOUT TENNESSEE

Dependables

We really enjoyed our trip to Nashville. We went to the Opry, spent a day at Opryland, saw the Country Hall of Fame—it's great—and took a couple of city tours. Nashville has some beautiful homes. I've always wanted to take that trip and I'm glad we did.

Secretary, Baton Rouge, LA

Visiting Great Smoky National Park was great. You can do nothing and come home rested and relaxed.

Male administrator, Fairhope, AL

We took the kids to many historical sites. Civil War battlefields, the Hermitage, good museums—they were all great. My grandfather worked at Oak Ridge for awhile, so I was interested in seeing it.

Male professor, 40, New Canaan, CT

Centrics

From Memphis to Nashville we had only good times. Amusement parks, fine hotels and restaurants, all kinds of music and night life. Even Graceland was much more interesting than we expected.

Female bookkeeper, 28, San Francisco, CA

We thought Tennessee had a big variety of things to do, so everyone found something they really liked. The mountain scenery is beautiful, the music is fun, and we bought a lot of souvenirs—maybe too many!

Homemaker, Pittsburg, PA

We have always loved country music, so it was a treat for us to go to the Opry and tour Nashville.

Consultant, Tampa, FL

I just love the friendly atmosphere. We went to Nashville for the music, then drove down to look at Chattanooga, which is a lovely city on the river. The scenery is different from home, and so is the food—we ate very well, chicken and biscuits and that kind of thing.

Farming family, Amarillo, TX

Venturers

Had a great time in Nashville. Loved the music, night clubs, sightseeing. It's a stimulating city.

Male graduate student, New York City, N

The abundance and variety of activities is great, ranging from hiking in the Great Smokies to local arts and crafts to children's activities, shopping dining and amusement parks.

35-year-old homemaker, Canfield, O

So, what will it be for you? Up a lazy river to Chattanooga, a beautiful campsite in the Smokies or a paced country music experience in Nashville? Since so many different people from my American Travel Survey like Tennessee, there's a good chance that you'll like it too.

Wisconsin

#24 RATING: ★★★

Centrics	Venturers	Dependables
6	6	6

Wisconsin leads the nation in dairy product production.
Pioneer WI was so sparsely settled, Justice of the Peace Pat Kelly used trees as "witnesses."
The state has over 14,000 lakes—Winnebago is the largest.
Harley Davidson assembles its engines in Milwaukee.
Wisconsin has the world's oldest continuously operating radio station—WHA Madison.

Surprises happen frequently when I conduct research, and Wisconsin is one of them. At number 24, it beat out quite a few other destinations that seem more likely. Plenty of people in the north central area of the country know about Wisconsin. They relax at its lakes and forests and enjoy the amenities of cities like Milwaukee, Madison and Racine.

Wisconsin is Great Lakes country and the only destination in the Midwest to break into the top 25. Lake Superior to the north and Lake Michigan to the east provide huge expanses of water where vacationers play, in boats or on the shore. Lakes and rivers abound in the interior as well, and the abundant rainfall creates heavily forested areas that are not only beautiful, but full of game.

Everyone agrees that Wisconsin's lake-and-forest scenery offers a prime example of what the north-central states are like (somewhat like Vermont in the New England area). The natural environment and the people who live there also manifest a definite individual personality that visitors describe as down-to-earth, hard working and outdoor-oriented. Milwaukee was once known as the German Athens, and the entire state still manifests its European roots. Much of the population descends from the waves of immigrants who settled there from Germany and Scandinavia, and its foods and festivals celebrate its heritage.

Those who like to combine city life with outdoor recreation say that a trip to Milwaukee fits the bill. With a population of about one million, this city on Lake Michigan offers many cultural and sightseeing opportunities.

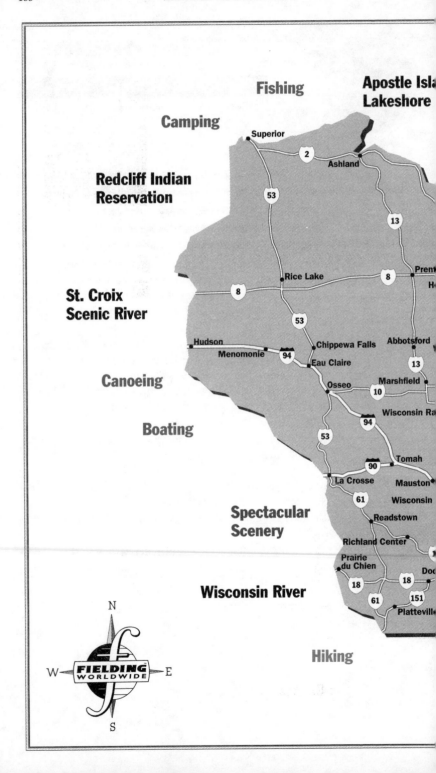

WHAT TO DO IN WISCONSIN

Actives

1 Explore Apostle Islands National Lakeshore (Lake Superior). Created by movement of glaciers in the Ice Age, the islands contain rose-colored cliffs and wild formations and caves. Hike, camp, fish. Take a nature-oriented sightseeing tour if you wish.

2 Green Bay may be the quintessential Wisconsin city and is of great interest to those who want a real feel for the area. It has a fascinating history, is a paper and cheese producer, shipping center, home to the Green Bay Packers football team, offers water and snow sports and you'll enjoy the National Railroad Museum, an excellent national treasure.

3 For more of the region's wildlife, visit St. Croix National Scenic Riverway. Camping and accommodations are primitive, but you'll be able to capture the feeling of the trappers and loggers who made a living along this still pristine water route. Canoeing and boating are popular.

4 The scenic dells of the winding Wisconsin River are the state's premier natural attraction. In winter you ski cross-country or downhill; in summer enjoy fishing, hiking, natural phenomena and many shows and attractions. You can spend a lot of time in the Wisconsin Dells.

5 Are you a competitive fisherman? More than one of our travelers mentioned the Salmon-a-Rama in Racine. It draws 300,000 contestants each year. And even if don't win, this small city jutting into Lake Michigan merits a visit.

Mellows

For a real taste of Wisconsin, take in the Lumberjack World Championships in Hayward, late July. This is a serious industry, but they can have a lot of fun with it, and who could resist a Lumberjack Championship?

And here's an interesting stop: the Circus World Museum in Baraboo, the original winter quarters of the Ringling Bros. Circus. The museum re-creates the history of the American circus and there are actual performances in the summer.

Old World Wisconsin in Eagle is an outdoor (of course!) museum which features miniature villages and structures from Wisconsin's many immigrant groups. It takes four to six hours to walk the whole museum, so wear comfortable shoes.

Lake Geneva is one of the better known resorts in the north central states. Summer and winter sports are plentiful, there are remains of a Potawatomi village at one end of the lake and there is even a greyhound racing facility.

One of Wisconsin's more famous residents was the architect Frank Lloyd Wright, who chose Spring Green as the site of his home and school. Although not designed by Wright, be sure to see The House on the Rock, an extraordinary multilevel complex 450 feet above the Wyoming Valley. Its marvels are too numerous to list.

For further information about Wisconsin, contact:

Wisconsin Division of Tourism
Box 7606
Madison, WI 53707
☎ (608) 266-2161

WHAT PEOPLE LIKE ABOUT WISCONSIN

Dependables

Dependable personalities typically visit Wisconsin more often from nearby states than is true for others. They like the feeling of familiarity, of knowing what to expect from people in the north and central United States. For them it's an easy to drive, with many choices of accommodations at reasonable cost. As in many other situations, *dependables* are less expressive about why they choose Wisconsin. But, beneath the quiet tone of their remarks lies a real affection for this truly remarkable playground.

It's peaceful and relaxing. There is good hunting and fishing. It's back to nature and the simple life, but you can easily get to a large city for the conveniences you need.
Female salesperson, Milwaukee, WI

For several years we've rented an inexpensive cabin on the lake for a week or two. It's not far from home, it's very pretty and there is plenty to do. Actually, it will be a perfect retirement area for us someday.
Engineer, 50, Davenport, IA

Centrics

Centrics feel comfortable in Wisconsin. They find enough activity to keep them busy, yet they fit into the slower pace of life that they frequently mention. If they travel from other parts of the country, they say that just seeing a couple of the Great Lakes is an impressive experience that immediately washes away most of their troubles.

I didn't expect the Great Lakes to take my breath away! In the southwest, Lake Superior would be an ocean—we don't have bodies of water like that. The landscape is different, too. It's very green and forestlike. very refreshing to travel through.
Female cosmetics executive, Phoenix, AZ

At the same resort we had all of these things with a cabin on the lake: tennis, volleyball, beach, swimming pool, fishing, game room and playground for the kids. Never a dull moment!
Dentist, 27, Winfield, IL

When I want to get away, I go to my hunting cabin with my hunting pals to hunt deer. Being in the woods is great.
Male, sales manager, West Bend, WI

Venturers

Venturers take advantage of outdoor activities, especially watersports. Serious fishermen report landing salmon and trout up to 30 pounds in size on the Great Lakes. Although they like to be active, that doesn't mean that venturers don't also appreciate the slower, simpler pace of life and tranquillity that Wisconsin offers.

We have a second home there and friends nearby. When we spend time there, I feel a sense of freedom. I can express myself physically, mentally and emotionally.
Retired male, Milton, WI

I have been there often, and particularly like to experience real weather in each of the four seasons! The woods and water are different each time, and all different from my home environment.
Sales rep, Tempe, AZ

It's scenic, there's no fast food, and there are lots of outdoor activities. We like the watersports, biking, hiking, nature walks, good shopping and the relaxing environment.
Self employed male, 31, Tinley Park, IL

WHAT PEOPLE LIKE ABOUT WISCONSIN

Dependables

Centrics

We drive up a couple of times each year to Lake Michigan for a few days of R and R. It's nice to relax by the lake, and also sometimes to go into Milwaukee for theater or whatever.

**Optometrist,
Indianapolis, IN**

We found so much to do. I remember arts and crafts, the symphony, hiking, boating, fish boils, unique natural geography, sandy beach, shores with cliffs, historical inns, quiet places, small towns within minutes' drive of each other. We ate at a restaurant where goats eat grass off the thatched roofs.

**Self-employed female,
Branson, MO**

Venturers

The Wisconsin Dells are a very beautiful and different kind of scenery. We enjoyed our car trip through the state very much indeed.

Homemaker, Rapid City, SD

I happened to go to Madison on business in the winter, and was invited to go on a snowmobile outing, which was great fun. I'd like to go back and spend more time.

Sales rep, 29, Salem, OR

American travelers tell me that Wisconsin is a lot more than cheese and beer. It's a wonderful combination of the Great Lakes geography and the spirit of our heartland. It's worth a visit if you want a more relaxed and quiet kind of a vacation.

New York City

#25 RATING: ★★★

Centrics	Venturers	Dependables
6	8	7

The world's first speed limit law was passed in NYC in 1652.

Washington Square was once a potter's field where trees were used for hangings.

Approximately 2.6 million New Yorkers were born in another country.

The Verrazano is the world's largest suspension bridge.

The Statue of Liberty was shipped to NYC in 214 packing crates.

Because of its size and the importance it places on tourism, I've listed New York City as a separate destination, rather than classifying it with the rest of New York state. How different it is. It appeals primarily to specific personality types, even more surprising, its most enthusiastic visitors are women.

This town belongs to *venturers*, as judged by the higher rating they give and the richness of their descriptions. They feel captivated by the energy of the city that never sleeps. They want to get involved and experience, firsthand, as many of its treasures as possible. The diversity and number of activities from which to choose almost overwhelm them because no other place offers such rich variety. The words they use in the American Traveler Survey to paint a picture of New York reflect their emotions and sense of personal excitement. They describe it as being alive, exciting, entertaining, different from any other place they know about, scenic, never dull or boring, cultural, cosmopolitan and a great place to do people-watching. Unlike so many other destinations where a few points of interest get mentioned frequently by most travelers, the names of a variety of places and events flow from the tongues of *venturers* as they tick off what makes the city so great. Broadway theater, opera at the Met, symphony concerts in Carnegie Hall, the Guggenheim Museum and the Museum of Modern Art, the many things to do in Central Park, the quaintness of Greenwich Village, the sophistication of Park Avenue and Fifth Avenue, the SoHo district, the beauty of the upper east side, the New York Stock Exchange, the Statue of Liberty, some of the great restaurants of the world, and just the ambience of the city all capture their imagination. No other place comes close in this richness and diversity, they believe.

Helicopter Tour

Roller Skating

Horseback Riding

Ice Skating

Bicycling

Dining

Nightlife

Manhattan

Central Park

Broadway

Park Av.

F. D. Roosevelt Drive

12

42nd

23rd

Sightseeing

Ferry to Statue of Liberty

N.Y.U.

Ellis Island

Canal

Ellis Is.

Statue of Liberty

Brooklyn Bridge

Broo

N

W   E

S

FIELDING
WORLDWIDE

Bronx Zoo

Actives
Mellows
All

Shopping

Museums

Galleries   **Parades**

Skyline Views

Walking Tours

People Watching

Brooklyn Bridge

WHAT TO DO IN NEW YORK CITY

Actives	Mellows
1 New York City's ethnic neighborhoods come alive when you walk through them. For exciting food, shopping and general interest, see Chinatown, Little Italy, and Atlantic Avenue's Middle Eastern enclave.	Ellis Island in New York Harbor was the point of entry for millions of immigrants until the 1920s. A tour of the museum and the Wall of Honor is a moving experience, especially for those whose family arrived here through that portal.
2 Get out of Manhattan for a look at the other boroughs. Brooklyn has beautiful botanical gardens and Coney Island; Queens features Shea Stadium, site of many big-time sporting events; take a ferry ride to Staten Island; the Bronx has a good zoo and Yankee Stadium, too.	United Nations headquarters is scenically situated on the East River. Each building is beautiful and distinctive. Try to time your visit when the General Assembly is in session, starting in September.
3 To fully appreciate the size, density and man-made topography of the city, be adventurous and take a helicopter tour.	Manhattan means museums. Get your fill of art and culture at the Guggenheim, American Museum of Natural History, the Cloisters, the Museum of Modern Art, the Metropolitan Museum (partial list). It is usually essential to purchase tickets in advance for special shows.
4 Central Park is a popular site for biking and horseback riding for natives and visitors alike. Get your exercise, enjoy the beauty of the park and stop for lunch at Tavern on the Green (make reservations in advance).	Some special events that are worthwhile if you're in town at the right time are: the St. Patrick's Day Parade, the Macy's Thanksgiving Day Parade, Chinese New Year, New Year's at Times Square, Greenwich Village Jazz Festival, Tree Lighting Ceremony and Christmas Carols at Rockefeller Center, Festa Italiana and Fourth of July Fireworks.
5 Like the nightlife? No city can match New York's Broadway (and off-Broadway) for legitimate theatre to suit every taste. And the same is true for nightspots. Choose from little pubs and cocktail lounges or dance clubs and full-blown lavish nightclubs.	Stroll down Fifth Avenue from 60th Street to Rockefeller Center. You'll pass some of the most expensive real estate in the city (like the Trump Tower), elegant shops, upscale hotels and lots of tony places to dine. Rockefeller Center, a model of urban planning, houses Radio City Music Hall, NBC Studios, office shops and restaurants. In the winter months ice skaters put on a show for free.

For further information about New York City, contact:

New York Convention And Visitors Bureau
2 Columbus Circle
New York, NY 10019
☎ (212) 397-8222

WHAT PEOPLE LIKE ABOUT NEW YORK CITY

Dependables

Centrics

Venturers

Very few *dependables* select New York City as their favorite place—it generally does not fit their personality. They tend to be even more reserved in their comments. Even more striking is the degree to which they notice differences between New York City and where they live.

Not as many *centrics* like New York City, and their comments are much more subdued. When they come, they visit more as observers than participants. They express their amazement about a place that is so different from any other city they know. Often, they are not very specific in naming the places that capture their interest. Instead, they talk about cultural places, without indicating which are of greatest interest. They tend not to become as involved as *venturers* in all that the city has to offer. Note the more restrained tone of the *centrics* who choose New York City as their favorite place and the fact that they generally use fewer words to describe what they like.

Listen to their sense of excitement, and how many places of interest each visitor mentions, when *venturers* describe their favorite city.

It's very un-Minnesotan. It's cosmopolitan with limitless things to do. The food is great and it's easy to get around. It has varied nationalities.

Female, mid-level executive, 44, Glencoe, MN

I have family nearby and there's lots to do there. You've got the museums, shows, etc. And you've got the surrounding area with beaches, parks, hiking and historical areas.

Female technical writer, 42, Longmont, CO

New York City just seems to wake me up when I go there. Its got so much. I like the theater, its restaurants and its variety of ambience. I go around and try to see and do so much. I like Central Park, the upper east side, Greenwich Village, SoHo, Chinatown and Little Italy. I just love its different kinds of people.

46-year-old senior female executive, Minneapolis, MN

New York City has what I want—shopping, plays and food.

Female lawyer, 43, Kingsport, TN

There's a wide variety of sites to visit, like the galleries, restaurants, shopping and the theater.

Male physician, 55, Houston, TX

It has so many places of interest, like the Statue of Liberty, Wall Street and the New York Stock Exchange, F.A.O. Schwartz (toy store) and just great shopping in general. I try to get to as much of it as possible when I visit.

40-year-old female elementary teacher, New Roads, LA

WHAT PEOPLE LIKE ABOUT NEW YORK CITY

Dependables

It has museums and histori-cal sights. There is a variety of entertainment to choose from, you don't have to travel far to get to the ocean.
36-year-old male custodian, Ogden UT

I like the theater, museums, dining and the hotels.
40-year-old woman director of a teaching program, Los Angeles, CA

I had never visited New York before last June. Even though I wouldn't want to live there, I love what a short visit offers in scenic and cultural events.
Female CPA, 48, Des Moines, IA

It's so different from Mem-phis. You could sit and watch the people forever. Their way of life is so different, there's very little trees or grass.
Female entrepreneur, 35, Covington, TN

Centrics

You've got art museums, theatrical arts, shopping malls, historical sites, educational fa-cilities and great dining at the restaurants.
Female real estate broker, 43, Honolulu, HI

My family lives there and I like to go there for the food, en-tertainment and the muse-ums.
Housewife, 48, Austin, TX

Venturers

New York has the marathon the arts (such as concerts, mu seums and plays), and real hi tory. It's so different from m home, Montana. I think t people are interesting too.
Female teacher, 5 Missoula, M

New York City is so alive. has lots of people and things do, places to go to and things see.
Female middle level manage 32, Houston, T

New York City has such large selection of things to d like the theater, shopping an restaurants. It's a city of e: citement.
Male buyer for a departme store, 41, Myrtle Beach, S

In summary, if your personality fits the *venturer*, and you are a woman, you have the greatest likeliho that you'll love New York City. It has many charms for those who want excitement and a sense of exp encing something different from where they live. No other place in the world packs so much culture diversity into such a compact space.

RATINGS OF OTHER U.S. PLACES

Because a destination didn't make it into the top 25 doesn't mean it has very little to offer travelers. It only indicates that *fewer* people chose it as one of their *favorite* places. But those who like it can be just as rhapsodic in their praise as the many persons who gave perfect "10" scores to many of the top spots.

From your point of view, three-star states and destinations offer a broad diversity of activities. You don't need to worry about finding enough interesting things to do. But the two-star and one-star states need second thoughts. They can be fabulous, but only for somewhat more limited numbers of people. Make certain you're one of them and that you've planned out your itinerary quite thoroughly before you leave. I personally love the Dakotas (part of my childhood was spent there)—the hard-working and honest people, the majestic open plains, fabulous farm style cooking and interesting local events that accent cultural differences. But, that's not for everyone, obviously, because the Dakotas don't rank very high on the Satisfaction Index.

Armed with new information, you now have a better chance of planning that dream vacation by selecting the right place and knowing what you want to do when you get there.

One thing to remember: U.S. destinations generally do a very good job in sending their visitors home happy and satisfied. The majority of other places in the world have a tough time catching up. The likelihood of having a bad vacation when you wander around almost any part of our 50 states is low. Most of your choices will probably be pretty good, providing you put some thought and planning into it.

The listing of the additional U.S. places includes the addresses and telephone numbers of the visitor information bureaus so that you can write for more information. The relative satisfaction ratings given by *venturers, centrics* and *dependables* are included to help you determine the degree to which each place would suit your personality.

RATINGS OF OTHER U.S. LOCATIONS				
Rank	Location	Rating	Centrics	Venturers	Dependables
#26	TEXAS	★★★	6	7	6
#27	VIRGINIA	★★★	6	6	6
#28	MICHIGAN	★★★	6	6	5
#29	MINNESOTA	★★★	6	6	7
#30	IDAHO	★★★	6	8	4
#31	MISSOURI	★★★	6	3	8
#32	SOUTH DAKOTA	★★	5	4	7
#33	LOUISIANA	★★	5	6	7
#34	NEW JERSEY	★★	4	3	4
#35	PENNSYLVANIA	★★	5	4	5
#36	RHODE ISLAND	★★	4	5	3
#37	WEST VIRGINIA	★★	4	5	1
#38	ARKANSAS	★★	4	4	4
#39	CONNECTICUT	★★	4	5	2
#40	GEORGIA	★★	4	4	4
#41	ILLINOIS	★★	4	4	5
#42	KENTUCKY	★★	4	4	5
#43	MARYLAND	★★	4	5	3
#44	ALABAMA	★★	3	3	3
#45	DELAWARE	★	3	3	2
#46	MISSISSIPPI	★	3	3	1
#47	OHIO	★	3	3	3
#48	NEBRASKA	★	3	2	2
#49	INDIANA	★	3	2	2
#50	IOWA	★	2	2	3
#51	OKLAHOMA	★	2	1	2
#52	NORTH DAKOTA	★	2	2	1
#53	KANSAS	★	1	1	1

Location	Where to Write for Information
TEXAS	Tourism Division, Texas Department of Commerce, P.O. Box 12728, Austin, TX 78711, ☎ (512) 462-9191
VIRGINIA	Department of Economic Development, Tourism Development Group, 901 East Byrd Street, Richmond, VA 23219, ☎ (804) 786-2051
MICHIGAN	Michigan Travel Bureau, Department of Commerce, P.O. Box 30226, Lansing, MI 48909, ☎ (517) 373-0670
MINNESOTA	Department of Trade & Economic Development, Office of Tourism, 375 Jackson 250 Skyway, St. Paul, MN 55101, ☎ (800) 657-3700

Location	Where to Write for Information
IDAHO	Idaho Department of Commerce, P.O. Box 83720, Boise, ID 83720, ☎ (208) 334-2470
MISSOURI	Missouri Division of Tourism, Truman Building, P.O. Box 1055, Jefferson City, MO 65102, ☎ (800) 877-1234
SOUTH DAKOTA	South Dakota Department of Tourism, Capitol Lake Plaza, 711 Wells Avenue, Pierre, SD 57501, ☎ (605) 773-3301
LOUISIANA	Louisiana Office of Tourism, P.O. Box 94291, Baton Rouge, LA 70804, ☎ (504) 342-8100
NEW JERSEY	Atlantic City Convention & Visitors Bureau, 2314 Pacific Avenue, Atlantic City, NJ 08401, ☎ (800) 537-7397
PENNSYLVANIA	Travel Marketing Bureau, Department of Commerce, Forum Building, Harrisburg, PA 17120, ☎ (800) 847-4872
RHODE ISLAND	Rhode Island Office of Tourism, 7 Jackson Walkway, Providence, RI 02903, ☎ (800) 556-2484
WEST VIRGINIA	West Virginia Division of Tourism and Parks, 2101 Washington Street, East, Charleston, WV 25305, ☎ (800) 225-5982
ARKANSAS	Arkansas Department of State Parks and Tourism, One Capitol Mall, Little Rock, AR 72201, ☎ (800) 643-8383 or (800) 628-8725
CONNECTICUT	Connecticut Office of Tourism, 865 Brook Street, Rocky Hill, CT 06067, ☎ (800) 282-4355
GEORGIA	Georgia Department of Industry, Trade and Tourism, 285 Peachtree Center Avenue, Atlanta, GA 30301, ☎ (800) 847-4842
ILLINOIS	Illinois Bureau of Tourism, James R. Thompson, 100 W. Randolph #3-40, Chicago, IL 60601, ☎ (800) 223-0121
KENTUCKY	Kentucky Tourism Cabinet, Capital Plaza Tower, 24nd Floor, 500 Mero Street, Frankfort, KY 40601, ☎ (800) 225-8746
MARYLAND	Maryland Office Tourism Development, 217 East Redwood Street, Baltimore, MD 21202, ☎ (800) 453-1036
ALABAMA	Alabama Bureau of Tourism and Travel, 401 Adams Ave, Suite. 126, Montgomery, Al 36104, ☎ (800) 252-2262
DELAWARE	Delaware Tourism Office, 99 Kings Highway, P.O. Box 1401, Dover, DE 19903, ☎ (800) 441-8846
MISSISSIPPI	Mississippi Tourism Division, P.O. Box 849, Jackson, MS 39205, ☎ (800) 927-6378
OHIO	Ohio Division of Travel & Tourism, 77 South High Street, 29th Floor, P.O. Box 1001, Columbus, OH 43266-0101, ☎ (800) 282-5393
NEBRASKA	Nebraska Division of Travel & Tourism, 301 Centennial Mall South, P.O. Box 94666, Lincoln, NE 68509, ☎ (800) 228-4307
INDIANA	Indiana Division of Tourism, One North Capitol #700, Indianapolis, IN 46204, ☎ (800) 289-6646
IOWA	Iowa Tourism Office, 200 East Grand Avenue, Des Moines, IA 50309, ☎ (800) 345-4692
OKLAHOMA	Oklahoma Tourism & Recreation Department, 505 Will Rogers Building, Oklahoma City, OK 73105, ☎ (800) 652-6552

Location	Where to Write for Information
NORTH DAKOTA	North Dakota State Parks & Tourism Office, Liberty Memorial Building, 600 East Boulevard, Bismarck, ND 58505, ☎ (800) 437-2077
KANSAS	Kansas Department of Travel & Tourism, 700 SW. Harrison Street, Suite 1300, Topeka, KS 66603-3712, ☎ (800) 252-6727

THE TOP 25 INTERNATIONAL DESTINATIONS: MORE SURPRISES

I was surprised, and I bet you will be, too, when I looked at the list of international destinations that provide the highest levels of satisfaction. Some well known places receive relatively low scores and other smaller spots do very well.

Many international destinations attract more *venturers* than *centrics* and *dependables*. Considering what you now know about these personality types, it makes sense. Many of the places listed are far from home, involving more time and expense. Residents of many speak a foreign language, and that intimidates the more timid traveler. Sometimes it's just a question of not knowing much about a particular place, and what it offers. However, as you review the comments and the quotes from visitors, I think you'll begin to agree with me that few things in life can equal the excitement of planning and setting off on a vacation to a foreign land.

As in the case of U.S. spots, any place that gets at least three stars, which all of these do, will probably send you home satisfied. It offers enough things to do, the people are likely to be very friendly, the food is good, and your entire experience will be quite enjoyable. As you read the following descriptions, remember that longer distances and language barriers make international travel a little different than domestic vacations. You might want to plan your itinerary more carefully, for example, by allowing yourself more flexibility with time and transportation.

One of the truisms of travel is that our world is shrinking quickly. Transportation and communications technologies open up leisure destinations that we never thought about a few years ago. Enjoy reading about the top 25 international destinations that follow, and see how each might fit into your own interests and personality.

Ireland

#1 RATING: ★★★★★+

Centrics	Venturers	Dependables
10+	10	10+

Dublin suffers from severe truck congestion.

Ireland has one of Europe's fastest growing economies.

Rural Ireland has the EU's lowest crime rate.

Ireland has the EU's lowest per capita consumption of alcohol.

From 1845-1855, one million people died in the famine.

We're number one! The Irish should shout that boast at the finish of one of their beloved rugby or soccer games. If that isn't possible, they can be proud to be number one in the hearts of American travelers.

Sometimes it's hard to figure out why any one destination becomes popular. I know this much: thousands of conversations with travelers have taught me that beautiful scenery and interesting, friendly native people are the two items that tourists mention most often. No one who has visited Ireland can doubt that in those two areas, it reigns supreme. Poets don't call Old Eire the Emerald Isle for no reason. It is surrounded by water, which reflects its unique kelly green meadows and valleys like a jewel. This isn't sissy scenery, either. Ireland's rocky coast matches up well with the most rugged shoreline, and the surrounding seas can buffet coastal areas with wild waves. My goodness, the Irish! What a wonderful bunch these Celts are, funny and wild, admirers of good horses and pretty women, happy to see you, and happy to have you buy them a drink!

So many Americans descend from Irish stock that a trip to the Ould Sod becomes for many a search, or a confirmation, of their heritage. *Centrics, venturers* and *dependables* alike share this feeling of returning home to their roots. Once they arrive, they find a great variety of attractions, sightseeing and recreation to keep them busy. "The troubles" in Northern Ireland, or Ulster, prevent it from being as popular as the larger Republic of Ireland in the south, but tourist business should improve as the truce endures.

Scenery

Horse-drawn Caravans

Museums

Shannon River Cruise

North Atlantic Ocean

Golf

Fishing

Hiking

Ring of Kerry Drive

Creeslough

Letterk

Doneg

Ardara

Donega

Donegal Bay

Leitrim

Sligo

Bangor
Erris

Ballina   Sligo

Lough
Conn   Charlestown

Carrick on
Shannon

Mayo

Castlebar

Roscommon

Westport   Claremorris

Roscommon   Lon

Lough
Mask

Tuam

Lou
Ree

Clifden

Lough
Corrib

Galway

Athlon

Galway

Ennistimon

Lough
Derg

Ros

Ennis   Clare

Nenagh

Kilkee

Limerick

Limerick

Ti

Cal

Tralee

Kerry

Mallow

Fermoy

Kilarney

Cork

Youg

Kenmare

Cork

Macroom

Bantry

N
W — **FIELDING** WORLDWIDE — E
S

North Channel

NORTHERN IRELAND (U.K.)

Vacation Places Rated Ireland
★★★★★+

Actives
Mellows
All

Monaghan
Monaghan
van   Dundalk
ugh   Liouth
eelin   Drogheda
Meath
. Navan
ullingar   • Trim
ore   Dublin
Naas .
Kildare
Laoise
Wicklow
Wicklow
rrow   • Carlow   Arklow
Carlow
Kilkenny
enny
Wexford
Wexford
terford   Rosslare

Dublin

Horseback Riding

Irish Sea

Exploring Castles

Historical Sights

Quaint Pubs

Bed and Breakfasts

Fox Hunts

**Shopping
(Crystal, Porcelain, Sweaters)**

Saint Georges Channel

WHAT TO DO IN IRELAND

Actives	Mellows
1 You haven't really gone fishing until you've done it in Ireland. One suggestion: take a look at magnificent Ashford Castle (now a hotel), and fish for salmon in uncrowded streams nearby. Other sites and other fish abound, and all the settings are beautiful.	Yes, it seems a little "touristy," but see Blarney Castle, and kiss the stone anyway. Who knows? Maybe the legends are true, and you'll receive the gift of gab.
2 Here's a unique adventure: tour the Irish countryside in a horse-drawn caravan that sleeps four and is equipped for housekeeping. You'll be briefed on care of the horse, then left on your own. Call Slattery's Travel Agency in Tralee, County Kerry, for information.	Be sure to drive the Ring of Kerry, a 100-mile circle of meadows, mountains, moors, and beaches and coastal views. When people talk about "beautiful scenery," this is what they mean.
3 Charter a cabin cruiser and explore Ireland via the clean, clear Shannon River, tying up at a different village each night. The boats are safe and easy to handle—you'll get instructions.	In Dublin, you'll want to tour tradition-steeped Trinity College. Don't miss the library which houses the original *Book of Kells*, one of the most famous illuminated manuscripts.
4 Belfast Castle invites you to climb Cave Hill and admire its architectural features. Enjoy walks and picnics, and visit the Heritage Centre that interprets local geology, wildlife and folklore.	Ireland exports Waterford crystal and Belleek porcelain, both justifiably famous. Ask about facility tours (Waterford in the Republic of Ireland, Belleek in Ulster).
5 Golfers won't have to neglect their game here—it's a popular sport throughout the British Isles. Ask your travel agent or club pro about courses in both the north and south.	I can't close without reminding you that Ireland is a land where myth and legend live side-by-side with everyday life. To get a feel for it, visit the Muckross House Folk Museum in Killarney or Siamsa, the National Folk Theatre in Tralee.

For further information, contact:

Irish Tourist Board
757 3rd Avenue
New York, NY 10017
☎ (212) 481-0800

WHAT PEOPLE LIKE ABOUT IRELAND

Dependables

Dependables, who typically don't like to travel far from home, fly to Ireland in great numbers and they like this destination even more than the other two personality types. Many are Irish-Americans who have family or friends to visit; others feel comfortable with the Irish temperament, and are relieved to communicate in English. They enthuse about the scenery—in fact every single person mentions the beauty of the country—and the word "charm" comes up often. The Irish life-style has enough interesting quirks to be different, but familiar enough to put *dependables* at ease. Outside of the big cities (Belfast in the north, Dublin and Cork in the south), Ireland is rural country, and people tell me that traveling through the green countryside is tranquil and relaxing. Read on for comments from *dependables*.

Oh, the beauty of the land is breathtaking. The people are so friendly, which makes me proud since my family roots are there. The prices are reasonable too.

Female government employee, 59, Des Moines, IA

I enjoyed experiencing the customs and life-style in Ireland. The scenery is just beautiful.

30-year-old woman administrator, Prairie Village, KS

Centrics

Irish history and sightseeing appeal to *centrics*. You will see them all over the island, exploring old castles, having drinks in a village pub, shopping for crystal or fishermen's sweaters, watching a breeder exercise his fine horses against a background of white fences and green hills. They want to explore Dublin and soak up the atmosphere of Ireland's religious, artistic and literary history that is found at Trinity College, The National Theatre and even the pubs that played host to the likes of Oscar Wilde, Shaw, Joyce, Beckett and Brendan Behan. Following are comments from *centrics*.

We were able to drive through the entire country. It was nice to go at our pace and relax with the people, who are down to earth and friendly. The food was good and there was no McDonalds on every corner. It's just a beautiful country.

51-year-old female administrator, Lockport, IL

We visited relatives and toured the countryside. We really enjoyed learning more about the history and culture of Ireland. We bought some wonderful gifts, too.

Male graduate student, 47, Bellevue, WA

Venturers

"Where there are Irish there's loving and fighting. And when we stop either, it's Ireland no more!" What *venturer* could resist that spirit in the quote from Rudyard Kipling? *Venturers* share the zest for life of the Irish people and identify with their vitality and energy. For them, Ireland becomes an adventure. They don't just look at the countryside from the window of a tour bus, they enjoy the scenery as they jog or walk through it. Some go to Ireland for a fishing holiday and report that the salmon fishing is unbeatable. Those who ride will find great mounts and plenty of company, since the Irish are great lovers of horses. Of course, Irish history is turbulent and exciting enough to involve any *venturer* in seeking out the sights that reflect it. Here are some comments from *venturers*:

Ireland is great horse country, for races, fox hunts, whatever. We hit the sights pretty hard: castles, ocean, quaint pubs, wonderful shopping. Everything is accessible, and the atmosphere is relaxing. I loved the people.

Senior corporate executive, 63, Palm Beach, FL

We had a particularly good time at Sandy Cove. It has good jogging and walking areas, quite good food and beautiful scenery.

Female teacher, 52, Richmond, VA

WHAT PEOPLE LIKE ABOUT IRELAND

Dependables	Centrics	Venturers
What's not to like? It's colorful, relaxing, charming and unspoiled. **Social worker, 59, Brookhaven, MS**	*Ireland is known for its beauty, simplicity, great golf, friendly people and wonderful accommodations. It didn't disappoint in any way.* **Senior vice president, male, 56, Fountain Hills, AZ**	*I like the green, the people, the energy, the food, the water, the adventure.* **Female stage manager, 38, Bozeman, MT**
It was easy to travel there. Transportation is good, we could speak English. We have family roots in Ireland, and really enjoyed the historical places and beautiful scenery. It's not too expensive. **Attorney, male, 35, Monroeville, PA**	*We met so many wonderful people, all courteous, helpful and friendly. It has easy to get around Dublin—easy to get around the whole country really, by car, train or bicycle.* **Female field supervisor, 23, Washington D.C.**	*Irish history and Irish literature are extremely significant.* **Male illustrator, 60, Boston, MA**
We enjoyed the beautiful scenery, and appreciated the slow pace. I was impressed with both the natural and historic sights. People are very friendly. **Female department manager, 33, Wheaton, IL**	*We had a wonderful time discovering what Ireland is all about. It has an old-fashioned feel, but never stuffy. Fascinating history, beauty, nature, wonderful B&Bs and homes, friendly proprietors—it has everything. Dublin is a great city.* **Teacher, 34, Lake Orion, MI**	*The people were very friendly, the countryside was beautiful and the food was so much better than expected! The cost of the trip was very reasonable.* **Female office manager, 32, New York, NY**
It was a great vacation at a reasonable price. The sightseeing is wonderful. We went to castles, lakes and rivers, pubs and lots of historic sites. It's a clean country with immense natural beauty. We ate and drank well too. **Retired fireman, 58, San Diego, CA**		

I hope I've conveyed an impression of a country steeped in beauty, laughter and legend, because that' the experience of travelers who have been to Ireland. It's hard to write or talk about Ireland without falling into a Gaelic lilt—that's how infectious the Irish spirit is, and that's what makes it number one.

English Countryside and Scotland

#2 RATING: ★★★★★

Centrics	Venturers	Dependables
10+	10	10

Marriage is in decline in the U.K.

More newspapers are sold in the UK than anywhere else in Europe.

Fort William boasts the highest mountain in Britain.

Coventry is the home of Jaguar cars and the Lady Godiva legend.

The Scottish Highlands are less populated today than in the 18th century.

As more than one person in my American Traveler Survey said with a smile, "Hooray for the English!" They all had the time of their lives in the British Isles, and the character of the Brit is a big part of the reason why this destination hits number two on the chart. Lack of a language problem facilitates communication between traveler and host, so the kindness, politeness and sense of humor of the British come through.

American travelers feel at home there for other reasons. No matter that we're a melting pot; we inherit our literary heritage, legal system, ethics and social customs directly from our English mother country and traditional ally. Many choose England or Scotland as a favorite destination because they have family there, or because their ancestors originated there. "Roots" are a powerful attraction for a lot of us.

Britain occupies such a small amount of land surface compared to nations in North America, and American travelers are pleased that they can cover so much of it in one visit. From the gently rolling hills of the Cotswolds, to the majestic topography of the Lake District and Scotland, to the mysterious, misty mountains of Wales, the countryside reveals so much diversity of beauty it can leave you speechless. History and historic sites (of which there are too many to mention) are even more important than scenic beauty to most people I interviewed, except for *dependables*.

Tourists find out quickly that Scotland and Wales, although part of Great Britain, consider themselves fiercely independent countries—in fact Wales still uses its own hard-to-pronounce language, side by side with English. Each manifests a different kind of charm and personality to its guests. But everyone agrees on one constant: the people they meet are polite, friendly and helpful, and it's a pleasure to become acquainted with them. This seems especially true of the Scots, particularly as seen by *venturers* and *centrics* who take advantage of the common language to involve themselves more with the natives.

Camping

Hunting

Fishing

Canoeing

Stornoway

Skye   Inver

SCOT

Mull

North Atlantic Ocean

Islay   Gl
                        Arra
North
Channel

Antiques
Cornwall

Lochness

NORTHERN IRELAND
Belfast

Lively Pubs

ISLE OF M

Irish Se

IRELAND

Anglese
Cae

Scenic Countryside

Hot Air
Ballooning

Carn

Tinturn Abbey

Horseback Riding

N

FIELDING
WORLDWIDE
W   E

S

Tru

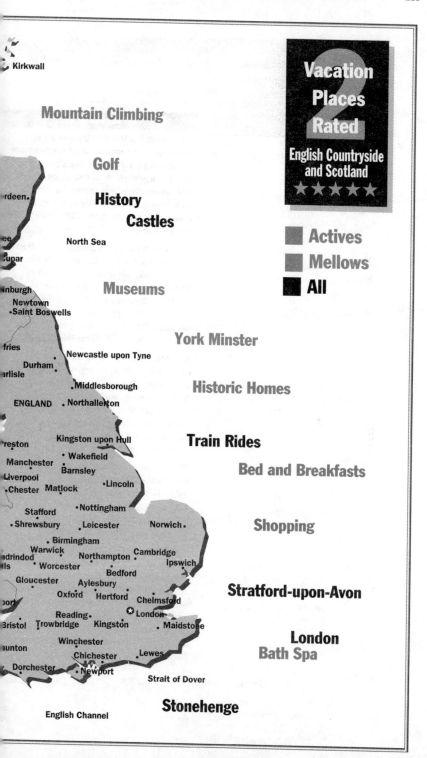

Vacation Places Rated

English Countryside and Scotland
★★★★★

■ Actives
■ Mellows
■ All

Mountain Climbing

Golf

History

Castles

North Sea

Kirkwall

rdeen.

ee

'upar

nburgh
Newtown
•Saint Boswells

fries

Durham

arlisle

Newcastle upon Tyne

•Middlesborough

ENGLAND   • Northallerton

Museums

York Minster

Historic Homes

'reston

Manchester

Liverpool

•Chester   Matlock

Kingston upon Hull

• Wakefield

Barnsley

•Lincoln

Train Rides

Bed and Breakfasts

Stafford

•Shrewsbury

•Nottingham

•Leicester

Norwich•

Shopping

•Birmingham

Warwick

adrindod

ells

•Worcester

Gloucester

ork

Northampton   Cambridge

Bedford

Aylesbury

Oxford   •Hertford

Ipswich

Chelmsford

Reading.

3ristol   Trowbridge

Winchester

aunton

Chichester

Dorchester   • Newport

Kingston

•London

•Maidstone

Stratford-upon-Avon

London
Bath Spa

Lewes

Strait of Dover

Stonehenge

English Channel

WHAT TO DO IN
THE ENGLISH COUNRTYSIDE AND SCOTLAND

Actives	Mellows

1   Wales is a bit off the beaten track, so an excursion there qualifies as an adventure. For picturesque beauty stay overnight in Portmeirion, and bring your camera with you. Or plan to take a one-week mountain skills course in Capel Curig, and try your luck on the local hills.

Stonehenge is a tourist attraction for very good reason. It's amazing to speculate on how a primitive people raised those stones, and why; you'll hear plenty of discussion. A definite "atmosphere" will impress you as you walk around the circle. Stay in nearby Salisbury and take a look at the 13th century cathedral there.

2   Some of the most spectacular scenery in England can be seen on horseback. Find a lovely inn in the Lake District and arrange half-day trips to your pleasure.

Of course you should include Stratford-Upon-Avon on your itinerary! Spend a little time at Ann Hathaway's thatched cottage with its English garden, and attend a performance of one of the Bard's masterpieces in the town where he (Shakespeare) flourished. Visit the Old Globe Theater. You don't often get more than one chance to do these things.

3   The Country House Hotel in Berkshire will accommodate you for a weekend that includes hot-air ballooning as well as lovely walks in lovely lanes.

Bath sometimes bills itself as the most beautiful city in England. No argument! Try to see it in spring, when proud residents deck homes and public areas with flowers. The Romans built Bath as a spa, and much of the original work can still be seen. "Take the cure" at the spa, if you dare. The water is not to everyone's taste.

4   For outdoor activities, Scotland will please you. Play a wild round of golf, fish the Highland streams, camp and canoe through Loch Ness, arrange a shooting weekend and even ski (although most ski facilities are not up to those in the U.S.).

Find historical, religious and architectural significance at the romantic ruins of Tintern Abbey, in Wales near the English border. This 12th century church and home of monks inspired Wordsworth, and its beauty and spiritual ambience will inspire you today.

5   Personally, I think Cornwall in the West Country is the most exciting part of England. The rocks are rugged, the ocean is wild, the weather is extreme and the ambience is steeped in myth—think of smugglers and King Arthur legends. Lots to see, lots to do, and even some nice (comparatively warm) resort areas.

York Minster is the north's answer to Westminster Abbey, and is actually England's largest medieval church. Take special note of the famous Rose Window. Yorkshire offers much interesting sightseeing outside of York. Here are England's famous moorlands and dales, lots of Roman ruins and Norman churches, and it's on the direct route to Bronte country. Remember *Wuthering Heights*?

For further information, contact:

British Tourist Authority
40 West 57th Street
New York, NY
☎ (212) 581-4700

WHAT PEOPLE LIKE ABOUT
THE ENGLISH COUNTRYSIDE AND SCOTLAND

Dependables

Dependables echo other groups in their dedication to seeing the sights and identifying a common cultural heritage with Britain. From the way they describe their trips, I sense that more *dependables* see the countryside with an escorted tour, in order to maximize comfort and have the advantage of a guide who talks knowledgeably about the region. They remember castles and gardens, museums and historic homes, varied and interesting shopping, good restaurants and pubs. Here is a place where asking directions is no problem, where places they've studied in school come alive, where natural beauty abounds and where they feel at home. Here is what they say:

We took a very nice personal trip to England and Scotland. We stayed mostly in B&Bs and encountered very polite people everywhere. Beautiful scenery, history and culture, also, very peaceful and safe.
**Male teacher, 35,
Westchester, PA**

It has history, great age, nice people, and beautiful countryside. How well the people keep it!
**Illustrator, 53,
Laguna Beach, CA**

Centrics

Writers and artists have long celebrated the beauty of the country landscape, and *centrics* are eager to see it for themselves. They comment favorably on the ease of travel within Britain that enables them to see so many sights in a short time. The trains run on time here, and there is good service from King Arthur country in the West, to Portsmouth where Lord Nelson's ship is berthed and to Bronte country in the north and up to Sir Walter Scott country in the Highlands. It's difficult to avoid a literary or historical confrontation almost anyplace you go! When they have their fill of sightseeing, *centrics* like to discover nice B & B's in quaint villages, stroll around, shop, or have a quiet drink with the locals in a pub that might date to Queen Anne's reign. Here are some comments from *centrics*:

The countryside outside of London is extremely beautiful. It's clear that the people are proud of their history, and they go out of their way to show it.
**Retired male, 77,
Hinsdale, IL**

I waited a long time to visit England, but it was worth it. My ancestral roots are there. The countryside, the climate and the people all appeal to me.
Retired male, Hicksville, NY

Venturers

Venturers have discovered Scotland. Like explorers before them, after touring England, they ask, "What next?" Craggy Scotland offers history, castles, romance, antiques and magnificent scenery from the lowlands to the Hebrides Islands. *Active venturers* can play golf where the sport was born, and on much wilder courses than they're accustomed to in the U.S. Even the pros tell me that 18 holes at St. Andrews is a far cry from the manicured greens at their hometown country clubs. Outdoor activities are popular throughout the countryside in England, Wales and Scotland and many a single malt whisky from a Highlands distillery is downed after a day on the river or the golf course. Following are some thoughts and memories from *venturers*:

It has so much! Historical sights, beautiful scenery, literary significance, religious significance, art and academic interests. And, oh, the English!
**College professor,
Fresno, CA**

The people are wonderful, it's easy to get around, all the sights are beautiful and historic. The place is a never-ending adventure of the mind and spirit.
**Male journalist, 40,
Sacramento, CA**

WHAT PEOPLE LIKE ABOUT THE ENGLISH COUNTRYSIDE AND SCOTLAND

Dependables

Centrics

Venturers

Dependables	Centrics	Venturers
People are friendly to us Yanks. I think they are still grateful for our help in World War II. **Homemaker, 74, Prescott, AZ**	*I've been to all the British Isles, and can always find something new and interesting to do or see. I'm definitely an anglophile!* **Law firm librarian, female, New York, NY**	*We like looking at historical sites that we've read about. The familiarity, yet difference, of the country when compared to the U.S. is interesting to us. The ease of communication allows more meaningful interactions between people.* **Female college professor, 47, Tucson, AZ**
Scotland seems untouched and unspoiled. I had heard little about it before I went and expected nothing. Was very surprised at beautiful scenery, friendly people, and how clean it was. **Female, retail sales, Mequon, WI**	*In Branscombe (England), we stayed at a four-star inn situated in a simple, but beautiful region. They treated us royally and fed us great food. Romantic is the word for it.* **Female, 57, senior manager, White Plains, NY**	*In Scotland, we enjoyed the golf, certainly. Even more important are the people and their sense of humor.* **Self-employed male, Smithfield, NC**
	Went on a bird-shooting holiday in Scotland. It was wonderful, and very well organized. **Female professor, 52, Amity, OR**	*There are lots of opportunities for nice walks that end up in a pub!* **Teacher, 43, Hubbardsville, NY**
	We were enchanted with the beauty of the landscape, the historic associations, literary interest, architecture and art. There are lots of interesting driving tour possibilities, wonderful hotels and inns, fine dining, theater and places that seem familiar. **Education administrator, 50, Randolph, NJ**	*The Highlands are awesome!* **Retired male, Tampa, FL**
		In England and Scotland, the fact that we share a common language helps to know people. They are consistently friendly and helpful. The countryside is charming and the train service is excellent. **Administrator, Bonaire, GA**

British Columbia

#3 RATING: ★★★★★

Centrics	Venturers	Dependables
10	10	10+

British Columbia is larger than CA, OR and WA combined.
Whistler Mountain has the highest accessible vertical drop in North America.
Vancouver's OmniMax Theater is the world's most technologically advanced.
Gastown is named for the man who opened Vancouver's first saloon.
The Vancouver Sea Festival includes a bathtub race.

You've probably heard the saying in the real estate business that success lies in "location, location, location." The popularity of British Columbia as a vacation destination owes much to that same idea. Its geography and topography bless it with a splendid physical setting on Canada's west coast. Surrounded by water and mountains, it also enjoys a mild climate that makes it more inviting than the colder interior or east coast areas of Canada. While it's most accessible to the west coast of the United States, it attracts visitors from all areas who find it easily accessible by air or car. Americans find it very comfortable to visit British Columbia (especially *dependables*) because there are no border or customs hassles, no language problems, yet they are still in a foreign country.

Travelers to British Columbia most often focus their discussion on Victoria, the island capital, and Vancouver, which many consider the most beautiful city in North America. Everyone says that this is a "veddy British" outpost in Canada, and Anglophiles will appreciate the ambience and culture—civilized, but not stuffy. *Venturers,* and many *centrics,* will enjoy diversifying their trip with excursions into the interior. Places like Whistler Mountain and Emerald Lake lure more adventurous travelers for recreation and breathtaking vistas of lakes and snow-capped mountains.

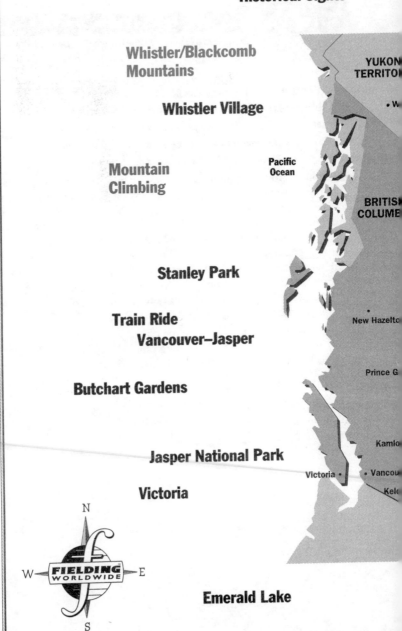

Historical Sights

Whistler/Blackcomb
Mountains

Whistler Village

Mountain
Climbing

Pacific
Ocean

YUKON
TERRITO

• W

BRITIS
COLUME

Stanley Park

Train Ride
Vancouver–Jasper

New Hazelto

Prince G

Butchart Gardens

Kamlo

Jasper National Park

Victoria •   • Vancou

Victoria

Kelo

Emerald Lake

Vacation Places Rated

British Columbia

★ ★ ★ ★ ★

Actives

Mellows

All

Museums/Arts

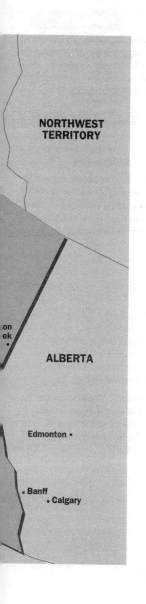

NORTHWEST TERRITORY

ALBERTA

Edmonton •

• Banff

• Calgary

Hiking

Skiing

Fishing

Boating

Mount Revelstoke National Park

Dining

Shopping

Swimming

WHAT TO DO IN BRITISH COLUMBIA

Actives	Mellows
1 On a winter vacation, sportsmen will want to try the skiing at the Whistler/Blackcomb Mountain ski areas, right next door to each other, not far from Vancouver. Facilities are quite good, and there's that breathtaking backdrop!	For a relaxing way to tour the high desert and mountains of interior British Columbia, take the train from Vancouver to Kamloops and all the way to Jasper. Experience the magnificent scenery with no effort at all.
2 Another ski area to try is Mount Revelstoke National Park, which also provides guided tours, hiking, swimming, boating and fishing, farther northeast of Vancouver.	If you have to choose just one stop in Vancouver, make it Stanley Park. It's justifiably famous for its views of the city and waterways and its many attractions.
3 Ready for a real adventure that will put human pettiness into perspective? Pack your woolies for a climb up one of the slow-moving glaciers that form the Rockies on the border of British Columbia and Alberta. Athabasca Glacier in the Columbia Icefield descends almost to Jasper. Check with authorities at Jasper National Park.	Here are some other Vancouver sights that will grab your interest: Chinatown (include the Sun Yat-Sen Classical Chinese Garden), historical Gastown and the noted Museum of Anthropology at the University of British Columbia.
4 A good friend wants me to be sure you know about the Natural History Museum in Victoria, which she rates a "don't miss." It is indeed an outstanding museum and a visit will give you a more "up close and personal" feel for the development of this region of the world.	Vancouver Island, where Victoria holds sway over the province, lies across the water from Seattle and Vancouver and is easily reached by air, but take the ferry—it's more fun. Victoria is the English picture-postcard town travelers talk about. First stop could be Butchart Gardens which flames with color from thousands of flowers.
5 Sample some of the area's great restaurants and don't count the calories! Here are a few suggestions in Victoria: the Chanticleer Restaurant for Continental cuisine, and the Harbour House for seafood and the Inner Harbour ambience. In Vancouver, try the Cloud Nine revolving restaurant atop the Sheraton, Hy's Mansion for steaks, or Bridges on Granville Island for seafood and views of the marina.	Other popular sights in Victoria are the old Parliament Building, the Empress Hotel (where high tea is a tradition) and the federal astrophysical observatory. Shop and dine along the Inner Harbor.

For more information, contact:

Greater Vancouver Convention & Visitors Bureau
Suite 210, Waterfront Centre
200 Burrard Street
Vancouver, British Columbia V6C 3L6 Canada
☎ (604) 682-2222

WHAT PEOPLE LIKE ABOUT BRITISH COLUMBIA

Dependables

Dependables say that British Columbia is a wonderful vacation choice. They can visit a foreign country, see architecture, gardens and customs that are different, but not so different that they feel uncomfortable. *Dependables* like to sightsee, and there is plenty of that, from the harbors, shops and other city delights of Victoria and Vancouver to the forests, mountains, rivers and lakes nearby. British Columbia offers lots of options. For example, at Mt. Whistler, *venturers* can ski and hike while *dependables* stroll around the alpinelike Whistler Village, shop and sip a cup of tea or glass of wine in the afternoon. Several travelers mention that the exchange rate is usually in their favor, which can only add to the pleasure of their Canadian getaway. *Dependables* share some thoughts, following:

I enjoyed the English atmosphere in Victoria. The whole area is like a picture postcard, and I'm amazed at how clean it is. The gardens are almost as spectacular as the natural scenery—it's like the gardeners have to live up to the natural environment.
Female librarian, 60, Harper's Ferry, WVA

It's peaceful, uncrowded, picturesque, easy to get to. Different from the east coast. What more could you want?
Homemaker, 41, Brooklyn, NY

Centrics

Centrics find opportunities for an absolutely super vacation in British Columbia. Travelers I interviewed sound as if they are describing a picture-book scene of distinctive architecture, flowers everywhere, little congestion and above all, it's "very, very, very clean." Clearly, residents realize what a treasure they have in this beautiful region, and how important it is to keep it appealing to the tourist trade. Everyone remembers the ferry ride to Victoria, and the wonderful sights to see in this "English" city, surrounded by water and filled with flowers. In Vancouver, *centrics* especially love Stanley Park with its gardens, native Indian totems, views of the city, and the 9 'o clock gun. Imagine a day of sightseeing, shopping and sophisticated dining, concluding with a view of the sun setting over this magnificent city and harbor. Then go to bed truly contented and happy. *Centrics* tell me:

People told us for years that we should take a trip to western Canada. I'm sorry we waited so long! Even though it's so close to the United States, the culture is different and the people are wonderful. Victoria is so charming. I'm sure we'll go back because there's a lot to see.
Female proofreader, 40, Albuquerque, NM

Love the clean, clear air over an absolutely beautiful city (Victoria). There's also watersports and boating that we enjoy. People are friendly.
Office worker, 50, San Jose, CA

Venturers

That clean environment and the variety of activities attract lots of *venturers* to British Columbia. They appreciate the amenities of Vancouver and the quaintness of Victoria, especially hopping on and off boats and floatplanes and other sorts of transportation that are required to see everything. It's a striking scene to see the boats and seaplanes sharing the same busy waters in the harbor. The more venturous can fly one of these out to Mt. Whistler or across the Columbia River to Emerald Lake. Along the way, *actives* can fish B.C.'s streams, hike or walk trails and villages and ski mountain slopes surrounded by some of the most spectacular, unspoiled grandeur anywhere in the world. That's what *venturers* report, and here are some of their comments:

We all loved our vacation in British Columbia. The drive from Vancouver to Emerald Lake is so beautiful, it's almost unbelievable. Lots of outdoor recreation around the lake, and the hotel was excellent, in a rustic style that we like.
Word processing manager, 40, Reno, NV

Rivers Inlet in BC (a fishing resort) is beautiful and remote. It's just what I wanted.
59-year-old retired male, Bellingham, WA

WHAT PEOPLE LIKE ABOUT BRITISH COLUMBIA

Dependables

The weather's nice there, it doesn't get too hot. I found it relaxing, with lots of sights available if I want to see them.
Retired male, 66, Omaha, NE

I particularly enjoyed the time on boats in the harbor, and going back and forth to Victoria. You get different views and perspectives from the water.
Male attorney, 44, Minneapolis, MN

What stands out most in my memory are the parks and harbor areas of Vancouver and Victoria. They seem to be well planned and peaceful, yet there is a lot to catch your attention. The plants are just beautiful— the whole area is just beautiful.
College student, 20, Portland, OR

Centrics

Its a very interesting place to go. Also, it's not congested, so you can see the sights without fighting a million other people. It's clean and well-kept, a nice change!
Banker, male, 48, Los Angeles, CA

Vancouver proves that all big cities are not alike. It's gorgeous and sophisticated.
Homemaker, 39, Tarrytown, NY

Vancouver and the surrounding areas probably have the most scenic beauty of any place I've been. There is a good mix of cultural and outdoor activities. The people have a good sense of their local history.
Female property manager, 43, Alameda, CA

Venturers

When we went in July, the weather was cool and pleasant. I remember how clean it was, and flowers everywhere. Nice people, too.
Salesman, 52, Louisville, KY

British Columbia is clean, beautiful and a good value for your dollar.
Professor, 47, Newcastle, WY

What beautiful waterfronts in Vancouver and Victoria both. Lots of flowers, an elegant, old world atmosphere among newer multicultural points of interest. I recommend seeing the British Parliament building, the Indian museum and the Empress Hotel.
Female software engineer, Raleigh, NC

Costa Rica

#4 RATING: ★★★★★

Centrics	Venturers	Dependables
10	10	1

Costa Rica was once entirely forested; now less than 17 percent.
The national army was abolished in 1949.
Costa Rica is the least violent Central American country.
There are only about 5000 indigenous Indians.
The Jungle Train railroad has been revived for tourists.

No, it's not a misprint. Travelers really do rank little Costa Rica at number four on the international list, and it is largely *venturers* who put it there. You may not even be sure where Costa Rica is situated. From Mexico, climb down several Central American countries to the southeast. If you hit Panama, you've gone too far!

Costa Rica provides a very good example of something I discussed earlier in the book. Venturers discovered it not long ago and *active centrics* follow in their wake. Before long the rest of the traveling public will hear about this unique vacation destination and want to see it for themselves. That explains the low *dependable* score above. It takes time for word of mouth to reach them, and for them to be sure there is a tourist infrastructure to support their needs. Therefore, there's no time like the present to take a trip to Costa Rica, before the rest of the world catches on to its charm.

The people I interviewed tell me that it's fantastically beautiful in the way that only tropical countries can be. You will find the people are warm and friendly, with no bias against Americans or Europeans. If you like cultural events, look for theaters and museums in San Jose, the capital and a large, bustling city. But, the real reasons that people visit Costa Rica lie in the tremendous bio-diversity of the country and the conscious efforts of the people and government to practice sound conservation. Tourists who want to experience the tropics in the most natural way head for Costa Rica. It offers varied habitats, active volcanoes, distinctive flora and fauna, and two seasons (wet and dry). You can count on a good time either way, as long you prepare for rain May through December.

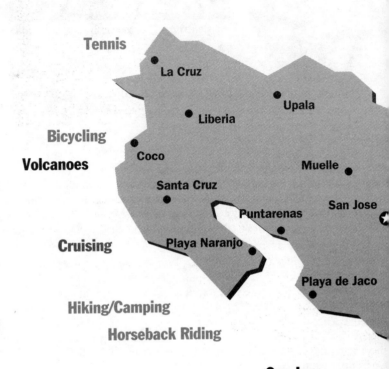

Tennis

La Cruz

Upala

Liberia

Bicycling

Volcanoes

Coco

Muelle

Santa Cruz

San Jose

Puntarenas

Cruising

Playa Naranjo

Playa de Jaco

Hiking/Camping

Horseback Riding

San Jose

Museums/Arts

Off-road Adventures

Serpentarium

Fishing

N

W — E

S

FIELDING
WORLDWIDE

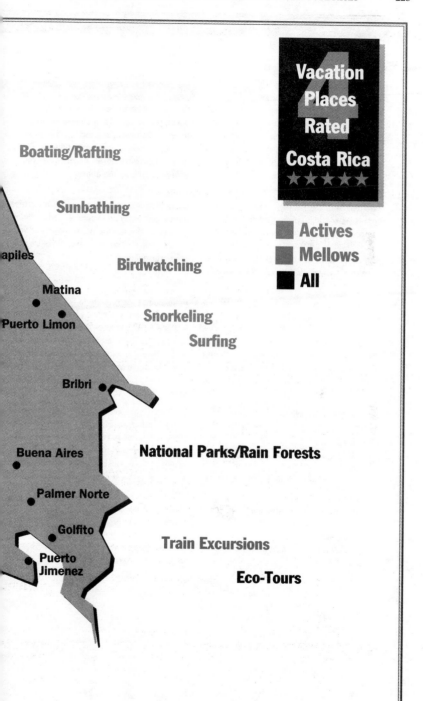

WHAT TO DO IN COSTA RICA

Actives	Mellows
1 Oddly enough, you can reach the top of an active volcano by public bus—or, you can hike, horseback ride or take a jeep. Costa Rica is home to 10 volcanoes, three of which are active. In addition to studying the volcano, you can enjoy great views of the country and two oceans.	Choose a color for your beach sand: white, black, yellow, red? Then choose an area of interest: driftwood, sea turtles, fish, polished stones, monkeys? Your sunbathing on Costa Rica's uncrowded, lovely beaches can be enhanced with all the above.
2 Bicycling is a major sport here. Do plan on some bike touring, but be sure to provide yourself with liquids and a mask (in case you're stuck in city traffic), depending on your route. In December, you can watch the "Vuelta a Costa Rica," an international 12-day event.	Costa Rica is a cruise stop, and many cruise passengers enjoy an excursion across the country on the electric narrow-gauge train. It's a scenic and fun ride, even if you're not off a cruise ship.
3 Costa Rica has set aside a whopping 12 percent of its land for national parks, and another 15 percent is protected. Take a multi-day eco-tour (you can get as "rough" as you like) to see the wildlife. Monkeys, coatimundis, peccaries, armadillos and hundreds of fantastic birds will entertain and educate you.	People don't really come to Costa Rica for culture and art, but while you are in San Jose it would be silly to miss the very good National Museum (especially for pre-Columbian art), the Entomology Museum (the only insect museum in Central America), or a play or musical performance at the National Theater.
4 You can take a watery tour in regions where no land routes exist. It's a fantastic ride along passages sometimes as narrow as 100 feet and hemmed in by jungle. You will see incredible, wild sights juxtaposed with quiet fishing and farming villages. This is a photographic must.	You can't avoid seeing a lot of animals outside the urban areas, but possibly the only place to see native reptiles is the Serpentarium in San Jose. Perhaps you prefer to meet deadly pythons, bushmasters, fer-de-lances and frogs in this venue, rather than the jungle!
5 Go fishing. Play tennis at your hotel. Surf long, consistent waves at several beaches. Go snorkeling at coral reefs. Arrange a trip to a research station. The possibilities are all exciting and endless.	Flowering trees and shrubs show off the most in February and March. Orchids are particularly spectacular, and you can buy starter plants produced at one of the research stations to take home.

For further information, contact:

Costa Rican National Tourist Bureau
1101 Brickel Avenue
BIV Tower, Suite 801
Miami, FL 33131
☎ (305) 358-2150

WHAT PEOPLE LIKE ABOUT COSTA RICA

Dependables

Dependables haven't found the way to San Jose yet. At least, not the one in Costa Rica. Hopefully, *dependables* who read the above description will realize that they don't have to use four-wheel drive vehicles or speak fluent Spanish to enjoy Costa Rica, and I can offer some comments from them in the next edition.

Centrics

Costa Rica's tropical beauty and opportunities for learning and enrichment also draw many *centrics*. More and more travelers express curiosity and concern about environmental issues, and they say that this is the place to follow their interests. It doesn't hurt that the beaches are lovely, the atmosphere is peaceful, and the people exhibit a remarkable gentleness and sweetness. Those who want a taste of city life will find it in San Jose, and because the country is small, they can take day trips (or longer excursions) using San Jose as a convenient base. Several people mention that eco-tours are extremely popular, and a knowledgable guide with a minivan is easily furnished by one of many companies. *Centric* visitors to Costa Rica also like the fact that the country is stable and they can feel safe from violence or other crime while there. Following are some quotes from *centrics*:

We stayed at the Mariposa Resort. It's an isolated hotel in a natural, undeveloped area. It offered great food and service in a beautiful tropical environment.

Male management consultant, 49, Dubuque, IA

Venturers

I can't emphasize enough how unusual it is to find a modern country as aware of its ecology and the need to preserve it as Costa Rica is. It leads the world in developing conservation programs in an organized and scientific manner. That explains why *venturers* like it so much. They can explore rainforests and mountains, oceans and interior ruins without running into swarms of tour groups or fast food restaurants. They can camp on the beach, or take excursions using a nice hotel as their base. Or, they can choose one of the wilderness lodges, located away from cities in interesting areas, that are more rustic, but not uncomfortable. They can fish the rivers and lakes, snorkel on tropical reefs and even go whitewater rafting on rivers surrounded by dense tropical trees and plants. Most of all, *venturers* like the sense of discovery Costa Rica offers, the feeling of being a "stranger in a strange land." At this point in time, Costa Rica attracts proportionally more *venturers* than many destinations. Here's what they have to say:

Costa Rica offers incredible bio-diversity in an exotic foreign country. It's very stable politically and doesn't even have an army. I enjoyed great birding and hiking there. I hope it never changes.

Senior corporate officer, female, 42, Kilauea, HI

WHAT PEOPLE LIKE ABOUT COSTA RICA

Dependables

Centrics

Venturers

It's not overdeveloped yet, and I hope it won't be. I enjoyed great bird-watching and nature experiences. The people are very friendly.
Self-employed female, 44, Murray, KY

The geography is fantastic. You can look into a live volcano! There are lots of great beaches, good fishing, interesting history, great people, good food and lots of photo opportunities.
Male teacher, 52, New Braunfels, TX

Costa Rica was a wonderful and inexpensive vacation. Even with my weak Spanish, there was no trouble going anywhere or getting what I needed.
Salesman, 41, Redding, CA

It's not overdeveloped, except for San Jose, which is a modern, sophisticated city. It's wonderful to visit such a beautiful place with so few tourists.
Male government employee, 33, Tallahassee, FL

I enjoyed the cultural differences from home. The natural environment is beautiful and amazingly diversified. The people are gentle and sweet, and I wish my parents would come here.
College student, 22, Berkeley, CA

It was perfect for me. I think a vacation spot should be very different from home. Vacations should be for learning.
Female college professor, 50, Sacramento, CA

There's no hype. It's just beautiful and natural and not commercialized. It's clean and safe and they like Americans. You see a lot more Americans and Europeans here than in other countries in Central America.
Male professor, 47, Cary, NC

I thought the climate was great. Also, I found it very affordable, especially during the "border" season. I enjoyed side trips into the jungle, the rainforests and the ruins. The food was good and the people are friendly and helpful.
Woman supervisor, 50, San Pedro, CA

Australia

#5 RATING: ★★★★★

Centrics	Venturers	Dependables
10	10+	10

Australia is the world's sixth largest country.
In 2000, Sydney will host the Millennium Olympics.
Aborigines make up less than one percent of the population.
Great Barrier Reef stretches 1240 miles, has 1500 species of fish.
The Northwest offers pearl fishing.

Australia must be something special, mate. You'll be 13 hours in the air from the West Coast before your plane sets down in Sydney, and Americans don't usually have a lot of patience for long plane trips. Yet Australia ranks way up there as a favorite destination. Why? Because the friendliest, most hospitable, most spirited people in the world live there, or that's how it seems to people who tell me about Australia. Although it's not around the corner, like British Columbia and Bermuda, it's an English-speaking country with traditions and customs that are different enough to intrigue, yet are similar enough to make Americans feel at home. Its perfect rating scores show that it appeals to all personality types.

Australia deserves its reputation as a wild and rugged place with a population to match. It's a huge and largely desolate country that demanded tough people to tame it—and much of it remains untamed! This gives Australia and its inhabitants an exciting quality, very much like the "Old West" in the United States, and accounts for its appeal to active, adventurous travelers.

Since it takes awhile to get there, most travelers take their time when touring Australia, and what amazing scenery and wildlife they see along the way. If you are a *venturer*, (and *venturers* love everything about Australia), you'll want to investigate the Outback, the Opal Mines, Ayers Rock, maybe Tasmania. *Dependables* can live the good life in Sydney or Melbourne, augmented with day trips to see interesting sights and remarkable animals. *Centrics* will want to fit in as many stops as possible to get a good feel for what this amazing continent has to offer.

Arafura Se

Pubs

Darwi

Wyndham

Indian Ocean

Cricket   Derby

NORTHE
TERRITO

Sailing

Hiking   WESTERN AUSTRALIA

Alice Sp

Ayers Rock

Watersports   Geraldton

SOU
AUSTR

Perth   Kalgoorlie

Perth

Indian Oce

Kakadu National Park   Albany

Ayers Rock

Arts/Gardens

The Outback

Exotic Wildlife/Birds

Opal Mines

N

FIELDING
WORLDWIDE

W   E

S

WHAT TO DO IN AUSTRALIA

Actives	Mellows
1 Go as far north as you can go in Australia, to Kakadu National Park, site of some ancient human art and a huge variety of animals and birds. In fact, beware of crocodiles, especially if you take one of many Kakadu adventure tours.	Where to begin in Sydney? See the famous Opera House (love it or hate it), the magnificent harbor, the world-class hotels, the Royal Botanic Gardens, the Sydney Aquarium, etc.
2 Due south from Kakadu is Ayers Rock, a geologic and spiritual wonder, rising over 1000 feet in the air. Aboriginal people have lived in the area for 10,000 years, and the Rock carries historical significance beyond its size and beauty.	Also in Sydney, don't fail to explore The Rocks, the area at the base of the Harbour Bridge. The old alleys, stone walls, pubs and houses have a rowdy history, now developed into a quaint, appealing tourist area complete with atmosphere, interesting shopping and restaurants.
3 Great Barrier Reef gets lots of votes as the most beautiful place on earth, a mass of living coral more than 1400 miles long. Go to Queensland with your diving gear, and see one of the wonders of the world for yourself. It's good for snorkelers, too.	Join the Australians for cricket madness in January (remember, it's summer there). Championship matches take place in Sydney, Brisbane, Melbourne, Adelaide and Perth.
4 The Outback, or interior of Australia, is reached by car or a 4-wheel drive vehicle from Sydney. You'll see desert, operating opal mines and deserted gold and copper mines, a great wildlife park and hundreds of sights you'll never forget.	Get up close and personal with Australia's odd animals at Lone Pine Koala Sanctuary near Brisbane. You can get your picture taken with koalas and kangaroos and take a boat tour of the park where you might also see emus, platypuses, dingoes and Tasmanian devils.
5 Finally, for your last stop in Australia, visit Perth on the southwest coast, far away from normal tourist activity. It's a relaxed, casual city with a great climate and has become a mecca for watersportsmen of all kinds.	Melbourne was the capitol city of Australia for a while, and still retains the dignity and traditionalism that makes it ultra-modern Sydney's opposite number. You'll see beautiful Victorian buildings, magnificent gardens and enjoy the ethnic delights of Australia's most multicultural city.

For further information, contact:

Australian Tourist Commission
2121 Avenue of the Stars, Suite 1200
Los Angeles, CA 90067
☎ (310) 552-1988

WHAT PEOPLE LIKE ABOUT AUSTRALIA

Dependables

Australians make you feel at home. That's one of the things *dependables* appreciate about the land down under. The friendliness of the people seems to impress everyone. The language is the same—well, almost—and they go out of their way to help you when you make tour arrangements, seek recreation opportunities, or make reservations for hotels, restaurants or sightseeing excursions. *Dependables* mention the cities more often than the other personalities, but they also want to see the sights of the country. Fortunately, Australia has a good tourist infrastructure that launches more timid travelers on many kinds of excursions for local color and excitement. *Dependables* offer these comments:

We took a four-week tour. We met friendly people and saw outstandingly beautiful scenery. I was very interested in the history and evolving culture of the country. I saw graffiti only once—there are just no negatives.

Retired female, 73, Ironwood, MI

Sydney is a beautiful city with so much to do. The people are friendly and speak English. By Los Angeles standards, it's uncrowded.

Retired male, 60, Temple City, CA

Centrics

Centrics may not want to go as far as trekking through the bush, but they find plenty of things to do and see. Legacies of the past reside in sacred aborigine places like Ayers Rock in the Northern Territories; Alice Springs, where Neville Shute set his famous novel *A Town Like Alice*; lovely Holy Trinity Church in Sydney, commandeered by the military in colonial times; and sheep stations in the interior on which much of Australia's economy rests. *Centrics* are good sightseers, and they want to see it all. They also want to sail in the harbor, scuba dive in coral reefs, eat wonderful food in Melbourne's multicultural restaurants and gape at platypuses, wallabies, cassowaries and Tasmanian devils. Read the comments from *centrics*:

We rented a car and traveled all over. The countryside is beautiful, with exotic birds that are especially interesting. People are very courteous, but they have a challenging way of driving! The population is sparse, the women are beautiful. Most of all, I have wonderful relatives there.

Civil engineer, 35, Stanwood, WA

There is a nice combination of city and rural atmospheres. There's a lot to do and no language problem.

Female office worker, 36, Santa Clara, CA

Venturers

In life, and especially at play, *venturers* seek the unique experience, the offbeat situation, the undiscovered place and the physically challenging. Where better to pursue these things than in Australia, which is essentially earth's last frontier—not very different from our American frontier, and requiring the same dynamic people to tame it. "Adventure!" insisted one excited traveler, just back from his trip. Like others, he saw kangaroos and koalas, deserts and rainforests, sheep farmers, aboriginal peoples and sophisticated hoteliers. But, he also climbed mountains and snorkeled at the Great Barrier Reef. He'll never see anything like it again. Comments I received from *venturers* include:

In the Australian Outback we saw a totally different lifestyle. People live underground! We "noodled" in the opal mine area. There is such a sense of freedom in being able to drive, camp, tour wherever and whenever you want. I actually can't decide whether Australia or the art galleries in Paris is my favorite.

Retired female, 65, Santa Rosa Beach, FL

It's exotic and completely different from home. The animals, birds, trees, plants, scenery, nature, people and climate are unique in our experience. Totally absorbing!

Self-employed female, 51, Pharr, TX

WHAT PEOPLE LIKE ABOUT AUSTRALIA

Dependables

I have developed a broad spectrum of close friends over an extended period of time in South Australia. It's always worth going back to.
Retired CEO, 67, Carmel Valley, CA

It has everything—water, mountains, desert, city lights. It's great sightseeing, some of the best you can get!
25-year-old restaurant employee, Pfafftown, NC

I like the beautiful land and seascapes, and especially enjoyed Sydney. We acclimated easily because of the lack of a language barrier. Once you get there, the prices are reasonable for most things.
Salesman, 35, Essex, CT

Centrics

We saw lots of different flora and fauna. The rain forest is fantastic. Outside the city, Australia's like a different planet—but with very nice people!
47-year-old physician, Denver, CO

Lizard Island is private, uncrowded and unspoiled. The service was elegant. We enjoyed it immensely.
Male CPA, 60, St. Louis, MO

I only spent two days in Sydney and am anxious to return. The city was modern, clean and there is too much to do and see in a short time. I loved the Opera House! The people are extremely friendly.
Female student, 18, West Upton, MA

Venturers

What a diversification of scenery, activities and culture! Beaches, mountains, deserts and rain forests are all reachable in one vacation.
Male administrator, 44, Exton, PA

I love learning and experiencing new things. I also write and photograph, so exotic travel found in Australia really lends itself to those activities.
Female writer, 47, Tamuning, GU

Tasmania is a small, remote island state, very quaint, very hospitable. The countryside is beautiful and the people are wonderful! I love it!
47-year-old government employee, Casa Grande, AZ

So, get your scuba gear together, learn the lyrics to "Waltzing Mathilda" and set off for "the wonder down under" and enjoy the vacation of a lifetime. Fair dinkum!

Bermuda

#6 RATING: ★★★★★

Centrics	Venturers	Dependables
10	10	10

With 21 sq. miles, Bermuda is about the size of Manhattan.

The botanical gardens sprawl over 36 acres.

Devil's Hole is a natural aquarium made by a collapsed cave.

Gibb's Hill Lighthouse (362 ft. tall) is made entirely of cast iron.

Bermuda was first inhabited by English settlers shipwrecked offshore.

Sometimes even the most daring and venturesome traveler gets tired of "pushing the envelope" and just needs to rest and relax. Out in the Atlantic, Bermuda lies shimmering like a jewel, waiting to soothe and rejuvenate the tired traveler. All three personality types unite in their praise of the island's friendly, casual atmosphere, warm air and water, good food and service. Judging from the individuals I spoke with, the entire Northeast part of the country must vacation in Bermuda! At least three-quarters of the people in my survey find Bermuda convenient to visit because of the short airplane trip from anywhere on the east coast. Conversely, few people west of the Mississippi choose Bermuda.

Two things particularly strike me as I review what people feel about Bermuda. First, *centrics, venturers* and *dependables* alike all emphasize how clean the island appears, how clear the water, how pure the air. In fact, "clean" often elicits more mentions than "beautiful scenery" or "good climate." I'm not sure what this says about our own living areas, or about other vacation destinations, but it certainly demonstrates that tourists notice and appreciate a well-kept spot. Second, many people I spoke with comment on the good, even elegant service, they receive in Bermuda. The fact that service is mentioned by all three personality types indicates how nice it is to feel pampered and cared for when you want to relax. Perhaps we can all thank the British influence, with its tradition of fine service and visitor hospitality.

November to March is "the season" for tourist travel to Bermuda. It lies roughly parallel to the Carolinas, but ocean currents keep it warmer in the winter. The temperature hovers around 70 degrees, and your hosts plan many special events for those months. So certain are they of perfect weather during the season that discounts and specials are offered when the thermometer falls below 68 degrees. But don't worry. Bermuda maintains its universal popularity all year long. The beaches are just as beautiful in July, and the people are just as happy to welcome you.

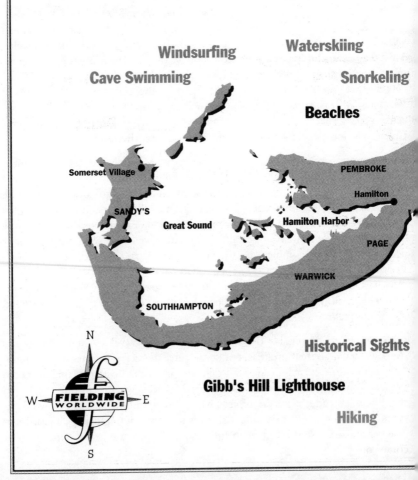

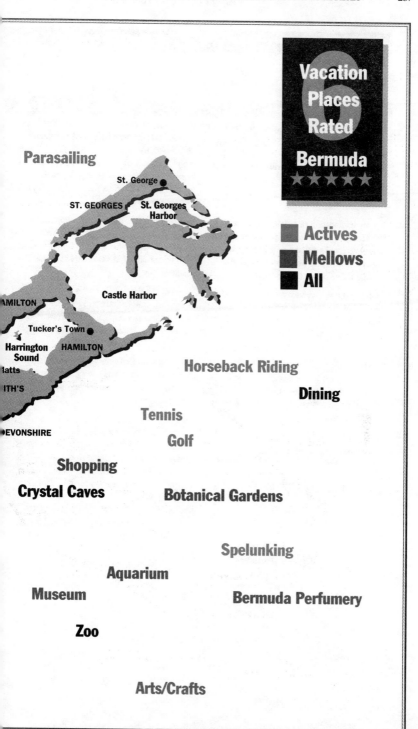

WHAT TO DO IN BERMUDA

Actives	Mellows
1 Charter a fishing boat and angle for over 650 species of fish. Enjoy your catch, and watch for endangered species such as marine turtles, porpoises, whales, corals and sea fans.	Of course, an ocean-based tourist destination should have an aquarium, and Bermuda's Aquarium, Museum and Zoo does not disappoint. Learn about the local marine life and watch the feedings of the seals and zoo animals. This is a good stop for children if you've brought them along.
2 For an exhilarating ride, launch yourself from the deck of a boat and parasail over the blue-green waters. There are several locations to choose from. Other popular watersports include water skiing and snorkeling.	Tropical weather produces spectacular flowers and foliage. Get a good look at the Botanical Gardens. Guided tours are offered every Friday, but check at your hotel for recent updates.
3 Tennis and golf involve many visitors and residents, and the facilities are excellent and beautiful.	Shop til you drop. Bermuda is a duty-free port and offers a wide variety of merchandise and prices from all over the world. Don't miss the locally-made items, especially pottery, blown glass and pictures by local artists.
4 Explore down under Bermuda, which has a huge concentration of limestone caves. Casual or dedicated spelunkers enjoy walking silent miles of remarkable colors, stalactites and stalagmites.	The Bermuda Perfumery produces scents from flowers that blossom on the grounds. Take a free guided tour for an unusual learning experience.
5 Take a nature walk around Spittal Pond, Bermuda's largest reserve. This is excellent territory for bird-watching and pristine scenery. A rocky ledge also houses a mysterious bronze plaque and a huge carved checkerboard. How did they get there?	Want to try some spectator sports with an English flavor? (Remember, this was a British possession for a very long time.) Cricket really heats up in the summer time, bridge players gather in January for an annual regional tournament, soccer fans can see matches September to April, equestrian events and parades take place all year long.

For further information, contact:

Bermuda Department of Tourism
U.S. Sales Office
310 Madison Avenue, Suite 201
New York, NY 10017
☎ (800) 223-6106

WHAT PEOPLE LIKE ABOUT BERMUDA

Dependables

Centrics

Venturers

As one woman simply says, "It's heaven on earth." That's what *dependables* think about Bermuda, and why not? It's gorgeous, it's comfortably warm, people speak English and make visitors welcome. You can choose from a variety of activities, go sightseeing in a relaxed and safe manner, or just lie on the beach in front of an elegant or quaint hotel. Since most can get there in less than two hours from the east coast, it's an easy and quick trip.

Centrics tell me how much they like the variety of accommodations on the island. It offers a choice of traditional hotels, large or small, cottage colonies which are very typically Bermudian-style, housekeeping apartments, and guest houses (like our B&Bs). You can explore the island with minimal trouble. Public transportation is easy to figure out. If you've got a little more energy, rent a bicycle or a moped, and tour the island under your own power. *Centrics* who responded to the American Traveler Survey satisfied lots of sensuous pleasures in romantic Bermuda, but the one they stress the most is eating! Quality and variety of food and restaurants come in very high on the rating scale. Here are some of their memories:

Even *venturers* need to recharge their batteries at times, and many come to Bermuda to do just that. The ocean, the golf courses and the jogging and hiking paths offer unlimited opportunity for activity. They can indulge their curious natures by learning about the history and culture of this semitropical paradise and, like *centrics*, they can experiment with new and exciting foods of excellent quality. But, from what they tell me, their visit to Bermuda remains a vision of tranquillity, relaxation and a hiatus from life's hectic pace. Here's what *venturers* say:

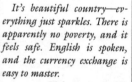

It's beautiful country—everything just sparkles. There is apparently no poverty, and it feels safe. English is spoken, and the currency exchange is easy to master.

Male attorney, 42, Garden City, NY

It's a great place to relax. First, it's unbelievably beautiful. Once you're there, you appreciate how quiet, clean and friendly the atmosphere is. It's a short flight from New York, and you can't beat the dining experiences.

Female administrator, 31, North Haven, CT

One year I went to Hawaii and the next year to Bermuda. There was no comparison, Bermuda was much better. It has all the things you want to do—good beaches and clear, warm water, sailing, scuba diving, fishing, golf and tennis. It was clean, clean, clean and I didn't see any evidence of poverty. The people are friendly and helpful and really seem to like tourists.

Entrepreneur, 57, Yorba Linda, CA

WHAT PEOPLE LIKE ABOUT BERMUDA

Dependables

Everything you could want is taken care of—all the amenities are there. Our stay was pleasure-filled. They make it easy for you to enjoy yourself.
Self-employed female, 51, Center Harbor, NH

It's warm and beautiful, and a nice short plane ride from home. Beaches are gorgeous.
Homemaker, 39, Durham, NC

It's clean, clean, clean!
Retired woman, 63, West Warwick, RI

It was a cruise destination for us, and we wish we had more time there. The atmosphere is casual, perfect for unwinding. I played a great golf course. Of course, the physical setting is magnificent.
CEO, 60, Secaucus, NJ

Centrics

Bermuda is clean, the people are friendly, and the beaches are wonderful. The climate is perfect. The food is really excellent.
Saleswoman, 51, Waterbury, CT

It's a perfect rest and relaxation atmosphere. Warm weather, sandy beaches, a beautiful, picturesque setting. One hotel nicer than the next.
Male paralegal, 29, Reston, VA

You can sightsee the whole island in a short time. It's peaceful, lovely and casual.
Self-employed male, 55, West Monroe, LA

Tourism is second only to banking in revenues for Bermuda, and it shows in the service. It's clean, beautiful, there's lots to do and there are no hassles.
Senior financial executive, 37, Kansas City, MO

Venturers

It's a magnificent setting, and fun to explore. They have great public transportation and a lot of historic sights to see. The food is wonderful. There are many options for sports—golf, snorkeling, whatever—excitement or quiet, whatever you like.
39 year old female teacher, Tampa, FL

The people are wonderfully friendly. We saw no poverty and understand there is little crime or violence. The beaches and countryside are beautiful, and I enjoyed the duty-free shopping.
Woman CPA, 36, Houston, TX

People are friendly, the island is clean and pretty, the weather is good. It was the first trip my wife and I took together, and we have many very special memories.
Firefighter, 47, Philadelphia, PA

We really relaxed, but it's nice that there are so many different things to do. Loved seeing the island on mopeds, loved the shopping and the beaches. The restaurants are very good and varied.
Homemaker, 39, Durham, NH

British royalty and aristocracy historically favor Bermuda as a getaway, and Mark Twain called it the "right country for a jaded man to loaf in." Now you know why so many American travelers agree. Next time you want to get away, relax and enjoy some sun and fun, investigate this island jewel, so close to home.

New Zealand

#7 RATING: ★★★★★

Centrics	Venturers	Dependables
10	10	5

Bungee jumping originated in New Zealand.
Greenpeace's sunken Rainbow Warrior is a popular diving site.
New Zealand is one of the most pollution-free countries in the world.
Yachts are a major status symbol.
Kiwi birds are flightless, shy, nocturnal and omnivorous.

I would certainly be intrigued by a country that wants the world to know it is "clean, green and nuclear free." New Zealand wants to clarify something else: New Zealand is not Australia! Although the two countries link up in several ways—their "upside down" location, their Anglo-Scots-Irish settlers, and their codependent economies—their histories and their geographical differences result in very different personalities displayed to travelers. New Zealand is small and green, with no large metropolises. Australia is mostly a huge desert with several cities over one million in population. After all, 1300 miles of ocean separate New Zealand from Australia. You wouldn't expect New York City to be much like Wichita, Kansas.

You'll notice that *centrics* and *venturers* give New Zealand a perfect 10 score. *Dependables* rate it much lower. Since the Kiwis take very good care of all their tourists, perhaps the reason lies in the fact that the activities travelers talk about most often are outdoor activities. Travelers often mention that New Zealand is great for backpacking and mountain or rock climbing, activities that *dependables* seldom pursue. More active and curious travelers also appreciate the variety of scenery—North Island is very different from South Island—and the lack of crowds and obvious commercial development. New Zealanders lead the world in caring for the land and conserving its remarkable natural resources, qualities that *centrics*, and especially *venturers*, heartily approve. All three personality types unite in praising the New Zealand people. Like Australians, they are unpretentious, warm and welcoming to visitors who make the long trip across the Pacific.

Three K
Isl

Volcanoes

Auckland

Glowworm Grotto

Spelunking

Maori Art   Tasman Sea

Wine Tasting

Hiking

Camping   Colli

                              South
                              Island

Skiing   Hokiti

Heli-skiing
                         Westland   Ca

                                         Chris
Glacier Flights   Haast Mt. Cook
                              Ashburton

                              Timaru
Sheep Shearing   Milford Sound
                    Queenstown   Wanaka
Bungee Jumping   Cromwell   Oamaru
                              Alexandra
                    Te Anau
                              Otago
                         Southland   Dunedin

                              Balclutha
                    Foveaux Strait, Invercargill

N   Oban

W—FIELDING—E   Stewart Island
  WORLDWIDE

S   The Snares

Vacation Places Rated 7

New Zealand

★★★★★

Actives
Mellows
All

Bay of Islands

Diving/Snorkeling

Great Barrier Island

Coromandel Peninsula

Auckland

Thames

Bay of Plenty

Tauranga
Hamilton

Waitomo Caves
Rotorua

Whakatane

Taupo

Auckland
Gisborne

Beaches

ew Plymouth
Stratford
aranaki

Hawke's Bay

Napier
Wellington

Wanganui Hastings

Hawke Bay

Thermal Pools

Shopping

Palmerston North

Masterton

ook
trait

Wellington
cton
enheim

Pubs/Nightlife

History

Scenic Tours

ura

Fishing

Pacific Ocean

Whitewater Rafting

Whalewatching

Mt. Cook National Park

Mountain Climbing

Christchurch

Tennis

Golf

WHAT TO DO IN NEW ZEALAND

Actives	Mellows
1 The Southern Alps exist for those travelers with an affinity for mountains. Ski in the summer, hike and camp in the winter, and enjoy the magnificent views.	To see geysers and bathe in thermal pools, visit Rotorua on North Island. Whakarewarewa Thermal Reserve is the most popular and is also home to a Maori cultural center displaying arts and crafts and offering performances.
2 Fish for trout and salmon, or troll the ocean for bigger game. What's especially nice about New Zealand fishing is the solitude. It's a wonderful sport and you can angle without a crowd.	New Zealanders know a great vacation secret. The Coromandel Peninsula on North Island, east of Auckland, is the favorite leisure spot for residents. Nice beaches, an assortment of accommodations, Maori and mining history and some lovely scenery are the attractions.
3 Lots of companies will indulge your passion for white-water rafting. The Shotover River is known to be a challenge.	Ambitious vintners are developing a nice wine industry near Auckland. Most welcome visitors for tastings, and it's a lovely way to see a bit of the country.
4 Good skiers always seek the next level, which might be heli-skiing in the Southern Alps. It's expensive, but the ultimate thrill might be a ski plane trip to the top of the Tasman glacier, and the ensuing ski trip down.	New Zealand is part of the Pacific's "Ring of Fire," a circle of volcanic and seismic activity that includes our own Pacific Coast. The city of Auckland sits on many extinct volcanoes. Its charms include the Aotea Centre, a first-class theatre built at the behest of New Zealand's famous opera diva, Kiri te Kanewa.
5 Watch the whales, plus a supporting cast of dolphins, penguins, fur seals and sea birds. Whaling for profit was a very big deal in New Zealand; now the Kiwis make a profit from taking interested tourists on observation boats from Christchurch.	Can you imagine planning a vacation stop to see a bunch of insects? Do it anyway! The caves at Waitomo are home to the Glow Worm Grotto where thousands of the insects emit a spooky greenish light that attracts their food, and many tourists as well.

For further information, contact:

New Zealand Tourist Department
501 Santa Monica Boulevard, No.300
Santa Monica, CA 90401
☎ (800) 388-5494

WHAT PEOPLE LIKE ABOUT NEW ZEALAND

Dependables

Dependables don't appreciate New Zealand to the same degree, as I mentioned above, but maybe they'll discover it soon. The traditional, family-oriented personality of the people should appeal to *dependables*, as well as the lack of a language barrier, the scenic beauty and the city amenities of the relatively populous North Island. Following are a couple of comments from the few *dependables* who enjoy New Zealand.

Centrics

The variety of New Zealand's terrain, especially the Alps of South Island, impresses *centrics* immensely. Temperature extremes also contribute to the differences in appearance of the land and the kinds of attractions available. New Zealand residents are largely more traditional in their outlook than their Australian cousins, and a little gentler, a characteristic that *centrics* especially like. Those who take an interest in the history of places they visit find much to admire in the relationship of the newer settlers to the native Maori population, who influence New Zealand culture much more than is true for the aborigines in Australia. *Centrics* who study the people and their customs say that this ambience combines with a beautiful country and a good exchange rate to create the perfect vacation. They also say:

Venturers

As one *venturer* says, the trouble with New Zealand is trying to find time to fit in all the possible activities. Tourist attractions and recreation emphasize the outdoors, from the alpine-like southern Alps to the balmy, subtropical northern tip of North Island. So, *venturers* can camp and hike (with or without backpacks), enjoy the fishing (very popular with those I interviewed), climbing and sailing and skiing in the winter. Here's a surprise: If the calm and sensible New Zealanders have a national sport, it's bungee-jumping! No one I know admits to participating in this form of Kiwi craziness, but there are several spots in the Queenstown area where thousands of people take the plunge. From the *venturers* come most of the comments acknowledging the conservation efforts of New Zealanders to ensure that their country's beauty and economy will endure. Here are some other thoughts from *venturers*:

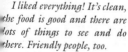

I liked everything! It's clean, the food is good and there are lots of things to see and do there. Friendly people, too.

Self-employed male, 63, Hudson, FL

It's like seeing the whole world in one country, because of the varied geography. The people are varied, too, and very friendly. They seem to have few racial problems and appear very harmonious with each other.

Self-employed female, 36, Jenkintown, PA

I enjoyed the people and the scenery, especially South Island. There are a lot of natural wonders to see and I always found being near the ocean. I found the traveling easy and convenient.

Retired male, 70, Hendersonville, NC

WHAT PEOPLE LIKE ABOUT NEW ZEALAND

Dependables

Centrics

Venturers

Dependables	Centrics	Venturers
Their Alps are something to see! **Retired male, Roanoke Rapids, NC**	*It's a very beautiful place, with friendly people and wonderful food, especially the fresh fruits and vegetables. It offers safety, variety and lots of family oriented lodgings and restaurants.* **Retired female, 65, Long Beach, CA**	*It reminds me of Alaska in many ways, except for the variation in climate. It's a very versatile land and underdeveloped.* **37-year-old engineer, Anaheim, CA**
Beautiful country, very hospitable. It's surprisingly inexpensive, after the airfare. **Marketing manager, 49, Oakland, CA**	*The scenery was beautiful, it was uncrowded, the people were nice and it was fun.* **30-year-old female scientist, Perkasie, PA**	*We enjoyed the slow pace and the laid-back atmosphere. We got to see and do a lot of interesting things, but never felt pressured or rushed.* **CFO, male, 47, Denver, CO**
	You just feel good about being there. **Retired female, 63, Denver, CO**	*We came a long way, but it was worth it. It is so different than the states. Even bigger cities like Auckland feel very different to us. Such beauty, and such nice people!* **Government employee, 50, Flagstaff, AZ**
	We took a tour of Australia and New Zealand. If I could go again, I'd spend all my time in New Zealand, which is much prettier in my opinion. The thermal springs area is very interesting, and there's a Maori Cultural Center there. **Male teacher, 42, Puyallup, WA**	*The climate is varied, and so are the sights and recreation. Pollution is minimal. The people are friendly and down to earth. Distances within the country are short, and yet There is so much to do.* **Retired professional female 62, Spruce Head, MI**

If you'd like a vacation with "kinder, gentler" people and so much to see and do that you wish you h more time, New Zealand may be your choice.

Switzerland

#8 RATING: ★★★★★

Centrics	Venturers	Dependables
10	10	7

Grand St. Bernard Pass gave its name to the famous dogs.

Davos at 5062 ft. is the highest town in Europe.

Gruyeres has a cheesemaking musuem.

Fribourg has more than 200 historic buildings.

Gstaad attracts celebrities like Roger Moore, Sophia Loren.

Switzerland apparently does everything right. In fact, it ties with Australia as the number one choice for *venturers* in my American Traveler study. The question is not what people like about it—they like everything—but why don't *dependables* like it as well as others? Perhaps a perusal of this destination will encourage them to take another look at this remarkable little country in the heart of Europe. Since the Swiss have avoided war in their country for over 700 years, the countryside, towns and villages, and the many tangible monuments to their heritage remain impressively intact. It has a higher density of castles, forts and historic churches than any country in Europe.

Banish the image you may have of a yodeling Swiss mountaineer wearing lederhosen and suspenders. The Swiss and their country have come a long way. Travelers who designate Switzerland as a favorite vacation choice do so because of memories of beautiful valleys filled with charming villages framed by the breathtaking Alps. They appreciate the way the Swiss bid tourists welcome, the efficiency and comfort of the services, lodgings and delicious food and drink. Think of Switzerland as a country with beautiful natural resources and fine opportunities for recreation, but bear in mind also that the Swiss are a sophisticated, well-educated people who have made their country a significant factor in world trade and finance. More than one recent visitor to Switzerland commented to me that they found their hosts intelligent, educated, honorable and excellent company, as well as friendly and helpful. Interestingly, I notice that among people in my survey who like Switzerland, more tend to have professional occupations and slightly higher incomes and education.

Switzerland can't help but be cosmopolitan. Thanks to its location in the center of Europe, it borrows customs, language and cuisine from several bordering nations and cultures. Within very short distances, you will experience the French Swiss, the German Swiss, the Italian Swiss and the Romansch Swiss, all charming and at bottom, all distinctly Swiss. Food and wine in each area reflect the differences.

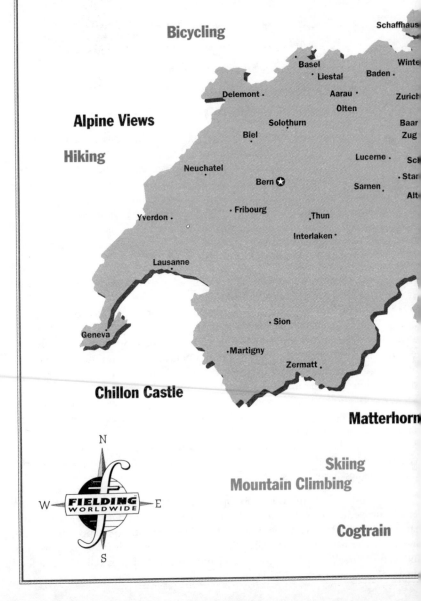

Motorscooter Touring

Bicycling

Schaffhaus

Basel   Winte
• Liestal   Baden •

Delemont •   Aarau •   Zurich
                  Olten

Alpine Views   Solothurn   Baar
              Biel   Zug

Hiking
                           Lucerne •   Sc
         Neuchatel
                  Bern ⭐   • Star
                      Sarnen •
                                  Alt

         • Fribourg
Yverdon •   • Thun

              Interlaken •

   Lausanne

Geneva   • Sion

        • Martigny
              Zermatt •

Chillon Castle

                              Matterhorn

         N

              Skiing
    Mountain Climbing

W ◄ **FIELDING** ► E
    WORLDWIDE
                      Cogtrain

         S

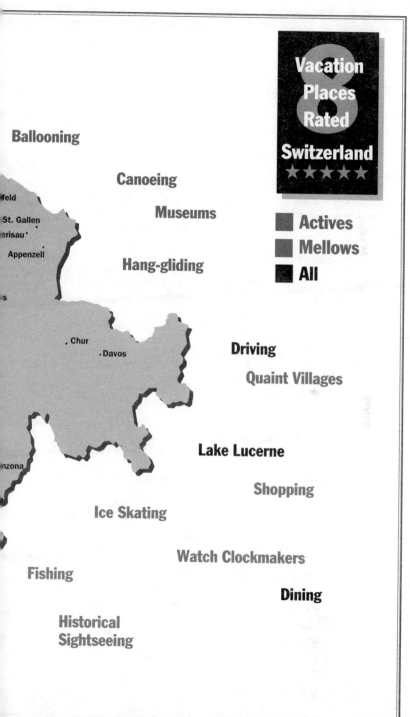

WHAT TO DO IN SWITZERLAND

Actives	Mellows

1 If you're a skier, strap them on at Zermatt (for the highest glacier skiing), Gstaad (to ski with the international jet-set), St. Moritz and St. Cergue. Switzerland also offers fine ice skating, hockey and curling.

If it's castles you like, you can't do better than Chillon Castle on the shore of Lake Geneva in Montreux. It's like a trip back to the 11th century.

2 The Matterhorn dominates the scenery near Zermatt, and there are plenty of other peaks nearby. Talk to guides about mountain climbing, or make the trip by cog train for spectacular vistas.

Switzerland has a well-earned reputation for clock and watch making. In Geneva, the Musée de l'Horlogerie et de l'Emaillerie celebrates the history of the trade, displaying countless fine examples.

3 Motorscooters are a popular way to see the sights in and around the cities and towns. They are easily rentable. Just brush up on the traffic laws, and don't attempt to climb glaciers on them!

It's hard to choose just one area for scenery, but you can't go wrong in the Bernese Oberland, land of countless valleys, towering granite walls and waterfalls. This is where Alpine legends originate.

4 A good place for active sightseeing is Interlaken in the Romansh area. Confident drivers will enjoy the Alpine views on the way from Geneva or Montreux. Once there, take the funicular up the Harder Kulm, visit the ibex preserve, see innumerable castles and experience one more of Switzerland's varied cultures.

Berne, the capital of Switzerland, is a unique and beautiful medieval city. Note the historic clock tower, dine in an ancient building overlooking the River Aare and enjoy many other sights.

5 Try this adventure for a real thrill: rent a bike at one of the cities in the Alps. Coast down the mountain through the beautiful valleys and head toward a city where you can leave the bike and move on to your next destination! Check with tourist information for details. Cities all over Switzerland offer this opportunity.

One of the most popular tourist destinations in Europe is Lake Lucerne, which mirrors mountain scenery and medieval town walls in its clear water. You can stay in Lucerne, or take a day trip from Zurich if time is short.

For further information, contact:

Swiss National Tourist Office
608 Fifth Avenue
New York, NY 10020
☎ (212) 757-5944

WHAT PEOPLE LIKE ABOUT SWITZERLAND

Dependables

Dependables are uniformly delighted with the quality of service they receive while in Switzerland. Here they travel through beautiful mountain scenery, peacefully, with no fear of crime even in the larger cities. They find it easy to get from place to place, since train travel is efficient, clean and comfortable. Everyone they meet is friendly, open and honest. Here's what they have to say:

My only experience so far is Lucerne and the drive to and from that area. It definitely left me wanting to see more. I love the cleanliness, the mountain landscapes and the wonderfully polite and honest people.

Male corporate vice-president, 37, Miami, FL

Centrics

Centrics enthuse about Switzerland for all the reasons above, with somewhat less emphasis on sports and recreation. They seem interested in Switzerland's history, and their sightseeing includes old castles and other venues where historical dramas played out. They say that it's easy to locate good shopping areas, and offer special praise for hotels and restaurants. After all, Switzerland sets the training standards for the hotel industry, and its kitchens (although less well-known) are easily the equal of many-starred places in France. Because the Swiss know how to treat tourists, *centrics* feel comfortable here, and can return home relaxed and serene. Here are some quotes from *centrics*:

What do I like—everything! The beauty, the historic sites, the cleanliness, the music, the food, the people, the beautiful water of Lake Lucerne, the Alps. One always feels safe, and everything and everyone has such CHARM!

Teacher/artist, female, 50, Fort Worth, TX

Venturers

True to their nature, *venturers* particularly appreciate this exposure to a variety of people and cultures. As they travel through Switzerland, they can enjoy sophisticated cities like Zurich or quaint mountain villages like Wengen where there are no cars and no "glitz," just unspoiled beauty. They will hear several languages and enjoy consistently excellent and varied cuisines and local wines. They will hit the slopes for some of the best skiing in the world. Thanks to the Alps, skiing dominates the winter sports scene, but actives also praise Switzerland's hiking trails and boating activities on its many lakes. Active *venturers* are the first to applaud the fact that Switzerland leads all industrialized nations in environmental enforcement. You can swim in its lakes and rivers and eat the fresh fish you catch without fear. For those who have the time to venture further, Switzerland is a great jumping-off point to see many other European countries. The following are quotes from *venturers*:

The scenery is so beautiful, and the country is so clean. We loved eating there. Some of the dishes are so very unique. Best of all is the quality of living we observed, and the genuineness of the people.

56-year-old physician, Redlands, CA

WHAT PEOPLE LIKE ABOUT SWITZERLAND

Dependables

I like everything. The people, food, sights, the slow pace. Everything!
Homemaker, 32, Atco, NJ

I love mountains, water and flowers. I like the food, the people and the cleanliness of the country.
Retired female, 60, Morris, MN

Its beauty lies in the topography of the countryside. The people are friendly and offer excellent service. We enjoyed seeing lovely vineyards, old castles and quaint hotels.
55-year-old homemaker, Salem, OR

Centrics

Zermatt is breathtakingly beautiful. Plus, I saw it on my honeymoon trip.
Female administrator, 40, Fort Thomas, KY

Summer or winter, it's beautiful. I like the jazz festival in summer, and the nearby skiing in winter (in Montreaux).
Government employee, 44, Bettendorf, IA

This is beautiful, old Europe to me.
75-year-old male, Green Valley, AZ

Berne is a beautiful, energetic city, with great shopping, good food and very helpful and friendly people.
Female writer, 38, Boise, ID

I thought the hiking was fabulous. Train travel is so convenient that car rental is unnecessary. Also, the Swiss people are very accommodating to tourists.
67-year-old female CPA, Highland Park, NJ

Venturers

The varied cultures and languages are interesting. It's a very clean country, and it offers efficient services, very hospitable people and great natural beauty.
Attorney, 41, St. Louis, MO

I lived there for a year, and always want to go back. No cars, no locks, great skiing and great food!
Female graduate student, 26, Milwaukee, WI

Fantastic scenery to walk and hike through. The trails are well marked. Accommodations are consistently good, and there is good help and information for tourists.
Female college professor, 55, West Bethesda, MD

If you want a taste of Europe and only have time to see one country, Switzerland is the one that will make you feel that you've experienced the best that the Continent has to offer.

Israel

#9 RATING: ★★★★★

Centrics	Venturers	Dependables
10	10	7

Elat and The Dead Sea have been developed as beach resorts.
Thousands of Russian Jews have emigrated to Israel since 1989.
In size, Israel is slightly smaller than Massachusetts.
Some Israelis shun material wealth, live in communes.
The state owns 90 percent of land, controls 20 percent of industries.

Israel draws American visitors for somewhat different reasons than other places. It's not for the fabulous scenery (thought it has that) or the interesting people (and it certainly has that) or the chance to relax on sunny beaches (yes, it has those, too). People primarily come to Israel for reasons of significant historical, spiritual or ethnic identity, which make their trips as much a pilgrimage as a vacation. All three personality types emphasize these qualities when they talk about Israel, although *dependables* are less likely to choose it than *centrics* or *venturers*.

When you think of Israel, does it simply conjure thoughts of a few square miles of constantly disputed desert? Think again. This tiny country offers so much diversity of experience that it boggles the mind. Travelers tell me of sun-drenched Mediterranean beaches adjacent to chic health spas. They relate how much fun they had in the modern "with it" city of Tel Aviv with its shops and nightlife. Everyone visits a kibbutz and comes away with a new view of communal agricultural life. Most impressive is the sense of awe respondents convey when describing the ancient wonders and monuments they see in Jerusalem, and throughout the countryside. This is the land that is home to the history of three great religious traditions; the evidence of Moses and the Maccabees, Jesus and his disciples, Mohammed and Suleiman the Magnificent lies all around you. Whether your interest is historical, religious or archaeological, you won't go home disappointed.

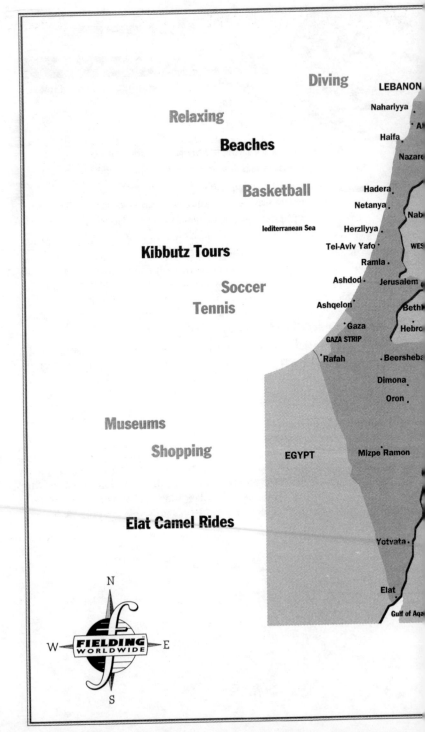

AN
HTS

of Galilee

SYRIA

Sea

ORDAN

Watersports

Vacation
Places
Rated
Israel
★★★★★

Actives
Mellows
All

**Archaeological
Sites**

Walking Tours

Dome of the Rock

Hot Springs

Biblical Sites
Masada Fortress

Historical Sightseeing

Observatory/Aquarium

WHAT TO DO IN ISRAEL

Actives	Mellows
1 You can join an archaeological dig, or just observe one. Write the Department of Antiquities and Museums, P.O.B. 586, Jerusalem for information. Perhaps you'll be on hand for the next major discovery.	Local inhabitants have been soaking in the hot springs of Tiberius or the Dead Sea region from ancient times to the present. The health spas offer medical advice and recreation as well.
2 Kibbutz life requires a certain kind of person—it's not for everyone. Many of these communal settlements are large and thriving, but the original settlers are true pioneers. Visit a couple before you leave.	Highlights of Jerusalem: Walk along the ramparts of the Old City in Jerusalem to see famous Jewish sites like the Western Wall where you'll observe prayers offered all day, and sometimes a Bar Mitzvah service, Temple Mount excavations and historic synagogues. Also in the Old City, don't miss the Dome of the Rock, whose splendor dazzles the eye. Christians will want to follow the Stations of the Cross along the Via Dolorosa and the Church of the Holy Sepulchre.
3 Bring or rent diving gear for a fantastic experience at Elat on the Red Sea. The fish and the coral reefs are something to remember forever. Negotiate for a camel ride in Elat, too.	Highlights of Tel Aviv: Tour Old Jaffa for a feel of ancient Israel, including the Museum of Antiquities of Tel Aviv-Jaffa. Oddly enough, this is also the nightclub capital of Israel, so save some energy for music and dance. Shoppers are entranced with the variety of local and international goods for sale in this ultra-modern commercial city. Enjoy expensive boutiques and outdoor markets, but remember that most places will be closed Saturdays.
4 The story of Masada has been told so often that it has assumed myth status. You can see the actual mountain fortress near the Dead Sea.	If you don't dive, you can see undersea wonders at Elat's underwater Observatory/Aquarium, one of four in the world. The water is crystal clear, so you can easily study colorful fish and coral.
5 Want to know the best way to get to know the communities of Israel? Take a walking tour in each city. You'll be able to chat with the people, investigate little alleys and get close-ups of the way life is lead there while you get your exercise.	Relax in Haifa in Galilee, arguably Israel's prettiest city, and one where Arab and Jewish life intertwines most agreeably. Lie on the beach and compliment yourself on your choice of a vacation in Israel.

For further information, contact:

Israel Government Tourist Office
350 Fifth Avenue
New York, NY 10001
☎ (800) 596-1199 or (212) 560-0600

WHAT PEOPLE LIKE ABOUT ISRAEL

Dependables

Dependable travelers to Israel are fewer and have less to say. Like the others, they feel a great sense of spiritual identification and renewal when they tour the ancient sites, both historical and Biblical. They find the country beautiful and different, the weather agreeable and the amenities acceptable. Here are a couple of remarks from *dependable* tourists:

When you take a sightseeing tour, you feel that this place has been here since the beginning of time. It has great meaning for me.

Religious administrator, male, 55, Clifton, NJ

It was a wonderful place to go with our children, to expose them to the history and a different way of life. We enjoyed visiting relatives there, and the country is quite beautiful.

Homemaker 40, St. Louis, MO

Centrics

Based on results of the American Traveler survey, there is little difference among the personality types in where people go and what they do in Israel. *Centrics* perhaps emphasize the historical sites and educational qualities of their trip a bit more than do *venturers*, but the difference is negligible. Although they may have paid a visit to the beach resort area around Elat and Tiberius, their comments really center around sightseeing in this ancient, yet modern country. Here are some comments from *centrics*:

It was so different from anywhere I've ever been. There's tons of interesting history—a great mix of history, culture and 'fun stuff.' Different customs, different attitudes of the people. I loved it!

Saleswoman, 35, Columbus OH

It was hard to believe that I walked in the land where Jesus walked. Hotels and food were adequate, but it's the feeling of Biblical history that overwhelms you.

Minister, 55, Wellington, TX

Venturers

Many *venturers* make the trip to Israel because of ethnic ties, to discover or rediscover their roots. More people in this group also express admiration for the way the Israelis have created an ultramodern nation in the desert in a very short time, and for the ongoing attempts to incorporate all ethnic and religious groups. As one man put it, "After all, Israelis can be Jewish, Christian, Moslem, Arab, African or European." *Venturers* are also more likely to seek some active recreation, especially watersports in Tiberius on the Sea of Galilee or skin diving near Elat on the Red Sea. In the area of sports, Israel takes after its European side, and you can watch (and maybe get into) games of tennis, soccer and basketball. Listen to what some *venturers* say:

We happened to be there during the Maccabee Games, which was a lot of fun. Israelis are very competitive and the games are well run and well attended.

CFO, male, 47, Cleveland, OH

The amount of history and the variety of things to see are amazing. The Bible comes alive in Israel.

Male attorney, 61, Evergreen Park, IL

WHAT PEOPLE LIKE ABOUT ISRAEL

Dependables	**Centrics**	**Venturers**
	The vitality of the country and the people is amazing. They make the country what it is! **Senior corporate executive, 56, Chattanooga, TN**	*The combination of scenic travel and the historical and cultural qualities is hard to beat.* **Teacher, 36, Narberth, PA**
	I have visited often because my daughter lives there. I like it so much that I intend to live there myself some day. **Retired female, 64, Brooklyn, NY**	*Diving in the Red Sea, driving in the desert—that's what I remember most.* **47-year-old dentist, Amherst, NH**
	It's loaded with historical and archaeological sites. The finds are tremendous and there are always new excavations going on. **Military male, 56, Madison, WI**	*Each day was an adventure!* **Female teacher, 59, Staten Island, NY**
		I felt that being there taught me more about my culture and history than I could learn any other way. It's very beautiful. **Artist/engraver, female, 37, Baltimore, MD**

So much of our own political and religious history and culture connects us to Israel and the Israelis. You might want to see it all come alive for yourself one day soon.

London

#10 RATING: ★★★★

Centrics	Venturers	Dependables
9	10	10

The Thames flows past 3000 acres of wharves.

Fanatics from all over rant at Speaker's Corner in Hyde Park.

The best way to see London is atop a double-decker bus.

Madame Tussaud's Chamber of Horrors guarantees nightmares.

Most popular tour is "In the Footsteps of Sherlock Holmes."

Samuel Johnson really said it best, and one of the people I interviewed paraphrased him: "Whoever is tired of London is tired of living." One of the world's great cities for hundreds of years, London shows us how to survive invasions, fires, plagues and modern warfare and yet maintain its dignity and historical significance. Americans especially feel a cultural connection to the English and enjoy the ability to communicate in the same language. The importance of the city is indicated by the fact that I included it as a specific destination, distinct from the rest of the English countryside. As you will see, everyone loves it—*venturers, centrics* and *dependables.*

People who like London especially enjoy city life, and London offers everything they could wish for. Travelers most often mention the city's centuries of traditions and the heritage of its exciting past. The variety and quality of plays and other theatrical performances draw much praise, and you can even take your choice of tours designed specifically around theatre-going. The beauty of the city is represented by its architecture and its site on the River Thames. *Venturers* emphasize the diversity of activities and talk about the energy of the city. *Centrics* and *dependables* highlight sightseeing opportunities and great shopping. The shopping on every level is superb, from Harrods and Bond Street to the stalls in Portobello Road and Covent Garden. Don't forget your charge cards!

London provides spectacle and entertainment outside of the theatres, too. The Royals have taken a drubbing lately, but they still maintain for England a sense of history and charisma. Tourists still gather in large numbers to watch the changing of the guard, and to tour the palaces—Buckingham in the city and Hampton Court and Windsor Castle just outside. Most museums are excellent, but the British Museum in Bloomsbury has no peer in size and quality of its exhibits.

Shopping

Westminster Abbey

Nightlife

Tea

Theater
Music

Hyde Park

Tower of London

Barge Expeditions

St. Paul's Cathedral

Chelsea

Vacation Places Rated 10

London
★ ★ ★ ★

Actives
Mellows
All

llesborough
llerton
n upon Hull
eld
•Lincoln
ttingham
Norwich •
rthampton   Cambridge
Bedford   Ipswich
ord
ONDON ⭐
Kingston   Maidstone
ster
Lewes
Newport

WHAT TO DO IN LONDON

Actives	Mellows

1 In urban centers where less outdoor recreation is available, active people find that walking satisfies the need for action. Here are some neighborhoods of particular interest: "The city" is the financial hub, Soho and Chelsea are Greenwich Village-like areas, Whitehall contains the prime minister's residence and other government buildings, the Docklands on the Thames is self explanatory.

Westminster Abbey and St. Paul's Cathedral are the two churches to visit. Famous architect Christopher Wren designed St. Paul's. Both serve as final resting places for England's political and literary elite, and both have a reverential quality about them that must be experienced.

2 The Thames provides even more. You'll get a different perspective of London by boat (either hired with crew or self-piloted). At low tide you can scavenge the shore for long ago deposited treasures. Coins, marine artifacts and other relics are still found. The Port Authority will advise you on where and when to dig.

Shop at Harrods by all means, but don't neglect other areas: Portobello Road for antiques on Saturdays, Fulham, Chelsea, and Notting Hill Gate for moderate pocketbooks, Beauchamp Place and Bond Street for the wealthy. Regent and Oxford Streets provide many items that tourists want. Be sure to stop at "Marks and Sparks" (Marks and Spencer) department stores for better prices on wool sweaters.

3 Kew Gardens is also the Royal Botanical Gardens. A short trip will bring you to an oasis of thousands of plants and trees separated by rolling lawns and paths. The British are great gardeners, and this is their showplace.

Hotels in London run the gamut of price and atmosphere. Have tea, or just pay a brief visit to some of the more interesting, such as the Ritz (very posh), the Savoy (traditional), Brown's (smaller and cozy), Claridge's or the Royal Garden.

4 You'll need some energy to see the Tower of London. This is actually a fortress on the river with several buildings, the oldest dating to the 12th century. Henry VIII's second wife, the beautiful Anne Boleyn, was beheaded here. Many historical characters and events passed through the Tower, and the atmosphere lingers on. You'll also want to see the Crown Jewels displayed here.

Hyde Park, near the center of the city, is famous for its Speakers' Corner where debaters and orators hold forth on any subject, at any time. The park is lovely, too.

5 Arrange a week-long barge expedition through London and on the Thames. It's wonderful fun and you'll have great experiences to tell your friends about. Call Another Britain in London for information, or ask your travel agent for help.

The British Museum is king, but I would hate to miss any of the others. Try the Victoria and Albert, the National Gallery, the Tate Gallery, and some of the specialty museums you'll find in your guidebook.

For further information, contact:

British Tourist Authority
40 West 57th St.
New York, NY 10019
☎ (212) 986-2200

WHAT PEOPLE LIKE ABOUT LONDON

Dependables

Now that you're familiar with the three personality types, it should surprise no one that London is also a favorite of *dependables*. If they're going to travel internationally, they like places that they know a lot about, where English is spoken and where familiar amenities surround them. Like *centrics*, *dependables* are eager sightseers and London's user-friendly transportation system makes it easy. Or, they can choose from many good guided tours. Evenings find them at one of the many fine restaurants (the food is quite good in London, but can be inexpensive) or at the theatre. They return home satisfied with the feeling that they have experienced an entertaining and cultural vacation to tell their friends about. The following are comments from *dependables*:

We were busy all the time, because there is so much to see and do: wonderful theatre, shops, fine restaurants and historic places. It's easy to get to the countryside.

**Female professor, 46,
Ann Arbor, Mi**

We have family there, so a visit gives us a feeling of 'roots.' London is an exciting, cosmopolitan city, with great theatre, restaurants and sights.

**Male banker, 39,
Arlington, IL**

Centrics

Most of us have studied English history at school, watched movies or plays about its kings and queens and read English writers from Dickens and Eliot to Agatha Christie. But *centrics* are especially eager to see all of the places in London they've carried for years in their imaginations. Excellent public transportation facilitates sightseeing around London, and they praise the underground and the bus systems. They also find Londoners easy, friendly and willing to help or advise at all times, so it's really a pleasure to explore the city. *Centrics* offer the following comments:

Historical and cultural considerations are most important to me. There is a great deal to see and do in London. It's easy to get around in the city and the people are nice and helpful.

**Female attorney, 33,
Los Angeles, CA**

I like being able to see history. The variety of theatre is such a pleasure. It has a great transportation system and great shopping. There is no language problem. Also, I feel safe there.

**Salesman, 60,
Birmingham, AL**

Venturers

When *venturers* visit urban areas on vacation, they concentrate on diverse activities and getting to know people rather than just seeking active recreation. They tell me that London is a "great walking city," with lots of unique shops and restaurants that can't be discovered from a bus, along with interesting street activity, especially in ethnic areas. The city appeals as a convenient "jumping off" base for excursions to the nearby countryside. Read on to hear from *venturers*.

We loved the nightlife, the restaurants and all the activities for families. There is so much history. We appreciated the weather (yes!) and the friendliness of the people. Driving on the left presented quite a challenge!

**Marketing manager, male,
42, Brooklyn, NY**

What a great capitol, the seat of an empire. It was a feast of fascinating aspects.

**Male attorney, 55,
Atlanta, GA**

WHAT PEOPLE LIKE ABOUT LONDON

Dependables

We think London has a very different 'look' from American cities. We spent time just wandering around admiring the old buildings, parks and gardens.

Homemaker 35, Annapolis, MD

What I remember most vividly are the castles—especially Windsor—and the museums—especially the British Museum. I liked the homes of famous people. We stuffed ourselves at high tea every day!

Female college student, 20, San Francisco, CA

Centrics

I remember how easy it was to get around the city. There are unlimited tourist opportunities and excellent food and service. Hotels are cozy and comfortable.

Retired male, 65, Bradenton Beach, FL

There is plenty of history to explore, and a variety of entertainment with an elegant touch.

Office supervisor, female, 24, Grover, MO

It's a very interesting combination of an ancient city with a very modern attitude. The cultural opportunities are unparalleled. I have never seen anything like the British Museum and can't wait to go back. The weather was good, too.

Female teacher, 50, Davenport, IA

Venturers

It's a wonderful walking city. It has everything—you name it.

Senior corporate executive, 59, Marietta, GA

There are so many different things to see, and even though English is spoken, it feels very different from the U.S.

37-year-old homemaker, Salisbury, NC

I like speaking English because I feel I'm really understanding the people. The places to visit in London are unending, and we also used London as a base for day trips. I liked the food and admired the transportation system.

Senior Vice President, 59, Montgomery, AL

If you're a city person, you must see London. It's easy to get there and it offers experiences and an ambience that is unique. Pack a "brolly" (English slang for umbrella) and have fun!

Austria

#11 RATING: ★★★★

Centrics	Venturers	Dependables
9	9	3

Austria is smaller than the state of Maine.
Hitler was born in the Austrian town of Braunau.
Grossglockner is the highest mountain (12,454 ft.).
More than 279 species of birds are found in Austria.
Brewed coffee originated in Vienna.

Although Austria's history and language parallel Germany's and Switzerland's in many ways, it establishes its own identity and an appeal to tourists in two areas: culture and winter sports. Austrians know how to live the good life, which they generously share with visitors. You'll find that the people you meet are warm, welcoming and cheerful as they go about their daily activities. Austrians also demonstrate their pleasure in life through cultural activities, especially music. It's so much a part of the national heritage that they insisted that the concert hall in Vienna would be one of the first buildings to be rebuilt after the war.

As you'll notice, *dependables* have yet to discover the delightful Austrian personality their fellow travelers like so much. They may feel intimidated by a different language, or may not have a good idea of what Austria is all about. Time could change all that.

Imagine for a moment a typical vacation day in Vienna or Salzburg. You wake to a delicious breakfast, with plenty of time for a walk around the historic square where your hotel is located. You'll probably want to stop for a midmorning coffee and pastry "mit schlag" (heavy whipped cream). Working Austrians often eat a big meal at this time of day, but you don't have time for that. Take a boat tour on the river, visit any one of the splendid museums, have a wonderful dinner followed by a concert of magnificent music that is so much a part of Austrian life. In the countryside, you will vary this routine with visits to quaint villages and old castles and rolling valley meadows filled with flowers. In winter, sportsmen spend much of the daytime on the slopes and reward themselves later with hot drinks, convivial company and perhaps with some musical entertainment as well.

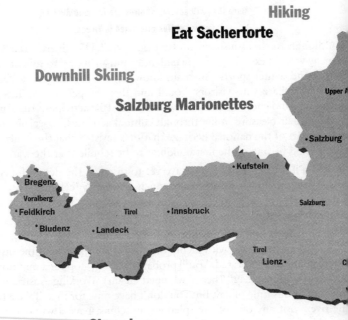

Castles

Hiking

Eat Sachertorte

Downhill Skiing

Salzburg Marionettes

Upper A

• Salzburg

• Kufstein

Bregenz

Voralberg

• Feldkirch   Tirol   • Innsbruck   Salzburg

• Bludenz   • Landeck

Tirol

Lienz •

Shopping

Eat Regional Cuisine

Cable Car to Monchsberg

Vacation
Places
Rated
11

Austria
★★★★

Actives
Mellows
All

Vienna Concerts

Lipizzaner Stallions
(Vienna)

• Gmund

• Krems

Lower Austria   ✪ Vienna

Steyr   • Baden

Wiener Neustadt •   Eisenstadt

• Eisenerz
• Bruck

Styria   Burgenland

• Graz

Klagenfurt

Hofburg (Vienna)

Picturesque Villages

Kitzbuhel

Cross-country Skiing

Boating on the Danube

WHAT TO DO IN AUSTRIA

Actives	Mellows
1 The main ski season is New Year's to Easter, but there is lots of activity immediately before and after. Take your choice of downhill or cross-country, expensive chic resorts, or small casual ones.	Architecture and history buffs will want to tour the Hofburg. It's a self-contained city within Vienna that was the winter home of the Imperial Family, and contains palaces, museums, libraries and many royal treasures.
2 Investigate boating on the Danube. All kinds are available, from hovercraft to putt-putts. Sail over to Budapest and take a quick walking (or shopping) tour of the Hungarian capital.	Take in a performance of the Salzburg Marionette Theater, the most famous of its kind and technologically very advanced.
3 Get out of the cities for a while and sample regional attitudes and cuisine. Several places near Innsbruck would qualify: Philippine Welser or Wildermann are two restaurants with fine reputations.	Austria hosts many festivals that celebrate its love of art and music. The Salzburg Festival in July and August is the most famous. But if you miss that, try the Vienna Festival or the Schubert Festival earlier in the summer
4 You'll notice a lot of German guests at beautiful Kitzbuhel, since Munich is so near. Skiing is the main recreation, but try other attractions on your own or via a guided tour, like the wildlife park, the copper mine at Jochberg and the nearby glass factory.	The all-white Lipizzaner stallions put on a show for you at the Spanish Riding School in Vienna, and it's usually standing room only. This showcase for the horses and horsemanship has visited the U.S., but it's worth seeing on its home grounds.
5 Hike (or ride the cable car) up the Monchsberg above Salzburg. Rewards are many: great scenery, castles, tours of giant ice caves and a large salt mine.	You will never forget hearing an opera or symphony in Vienna or Salzburg. The venues are historic and magnificent, the music feels different here. Be sure to arrange tickets well in advance to avoid disappointment.

For further information, contact:

Austrian National Tourist Office
500 Fifth Avenue, Suite 2009-22
New York, NY 10110
☎ (212) 944-6880

WHAT PEOPLE LIKE ABOUT AUSTRIA

Dependables

Centrics

Venturers

It appears from the 10-point scale that *dependables* have little interest in Austria. This personality type is less willing to travel far from home. When he or she does, the visit will more likely be to the top five or six international destinations that are more familiar and where English is spoken. Those who like Austria seem to come more often in the summer for the sightseeing or for a specific cultural event. *Dependable* skiers might enjoy their schussing in a foreign country, if they would only venture forth to a new place. Here are a few of their comments:

Centrics very much admire what they describe as the civilized life-style of Austrians. It's easy to get there and price ranges for lodgings and food exist to suit every budget. One can afford to enjoy cultural events such as concerts, theatrical performances and museum exhibitions. Sightseeing opportunities abound for *centrics* who can concentrate on historical sites of a region that has seen it all for centuries—science, art, history and music all have left their marks. Or, they can soak up the beauty of the countryside. People talk mostly about the splendid snowcapped mountains, how picturesque they find the towns and villages and the quality of shopping and dining at almost every stop. Don't try to count calories in Austria! Here are some quotes from *centrics*:

One *venturer* sums up Austria as "interesting, hospitable and fun." Here they find enough outlets of all kinds to satisfy their lively, curious natures and need for physical activity. Most recreation centers around winter sports, especially downhill skiing, but cross-country skiing also has made gains in popularity recently. In summer, *venturers* can stretch their legs on miles of walking or hiking trails, with interesting and beautiful things to see along the way. Austria's lakes and rivers offer wonderful opportunities for boating, both for recreation and sightseeing. Any *venturer* will enjoy getting into the hearts and minds of the Austrians by experiencing their food and wine, their music and the conversations in the coffee houses. That's a lot more fun than reading Sigmund Freud, who practically founded modern psychiatry while practicing in his native Vienna! Listen to some words from *venturers*:

Austria is romantic, full of history, music and fabulous castles on the river. There are incredible amounts of things to see and do.
Homemaker, 38, Napierville, IL

In Vienna, I can easily walk to participate in cultural events and see a lot of history. It's such a pleasure to visit a beautiful, clean, attractively landscaped city with a real sense of European tradition.
Homemaker, 55, Topeka, KS

The landscape is breathtaking and unspoiled. The local people are quite friendly everywhere. The culture is charming and the food is wonderful. Winter skiing is superb and hiking in the summer is lovely.
Homemaker, 40, Wyomissing, PA

The cleanliness and beauty of the country really impressed me.
38-year-old self-employed woman, West Milford, NJ

What a nice place to be for a couple of weeks! It's so neat and clean, with very friendly people.
Female office worker, 55, Scottsdale, AZ

Austria is very European, romantic and exciting.
Female office worker, 48, Honolulu, HI

WHAT PEOPLE LIKE ABOUT AUSTRIA

Dependables

Austria just has everything—friendly people, excellent food, historic sites to visit, beautiful countryside to see, great cities and very good prices, too.

Female writer, 43,
Portland, OR

Centrics

We were fortunate to be there at Christmas time. It was very festive, very beautiful and clean. We had a wonderful holiday.

Female author, 59,
Tempe, AZ

I can't imagine any other city (Salzburg) that can offer the same combination of beauty, hospitality and cultural events. The music is fantastic—everyone is musical.

Self-employed male, 45,
Cleveland, OH

We usually fly into Zurich, then take a private car to Bregenz, where we stay with family. We go in the winter because the skiing is very good, and we like the people very much. They have a wonderful attitude.

Homemaker, 43,
Lake Forest, IL

Venturers

It has such beautiful mountains and lakes. I think the climate is great and makes it a good European sports headquarters. In Zell am See you can ski in July!

Female, sales, 30,
Jamaica, NY

I especially enjoyed the cultural activities in Vienna, the concerts and the opera. Also remember fondly winetasting in Grienzig, and Donau boat trips.

Self-employed male, 62,
Merrimack, NH

Austria celebrates the quintessential Christmas, rich in tradition and the unusual. I had the most moving experience in Salzburg, standing in the cemetery one cold night, listening to the alpenhorns play Christmas hymns, with everything lit by candlelight. Unforgettable!

Female research director, 58,
Los Angeles, CA

The skiing was just wonderful. We really had great food and accommodations, and enjoyed the climate and atmosphere—meaning both the weather and the people.

College professor, 62,
Princeton Junction, NJ

Listen to a Mozart opera, boat on the Danube to Budapest, savor a slice of sinful Sachertorte in your historic hotel, ski down a gorgeous mountain on perfect snow—this is what travelers remember about Austria. Sounds pretty good, doesn't it?

U.S. Virgin Islands

#12 RATING: ★★★★

Centrics	Venturers	Dependables
9	9	9

The islands were discovered by Columbus in 1493.

U.S. citizenship was granted to natives in 1932.

St. John has a large population of wild donkeys.

Chickens, pigs, cows and goats have the right of way on roads.

Atlantis submarine plunges 150 ft. so nondivers can see underwater life.

It's easy to list the reasons that attract travelers to the three U.S. Virgin Islands. Their tropical beauty, a warm and balmy climate, clean clear ocean waters, and the fact they are a U.S. possession—all these combine to entice Americans to these Caribbean isles for rest, relaxation and recreation at reasonable prices.

The three islands share some characteristics, while at the same time displaying their individuality. Denmark owned the islands prior to 1917, and you'll see many Danish legacies, notably place names and architecture. Airlines and cruise ships make it easy to get there, and visitors enjoy the slower, casual pace of life that is common in the Caribbean. Sometimes so many cruise ships pull into St. Thomas' principal harbor that they can't all fit, and passengers must be "shuttled" in by small boat. St. Thomas is the most developed of the three and, not surprisingly, *dependables* like it the most for its good shopping and amenities for tourists. St. John draws a higher number of *venturers*, who appreciate its unspoiled, protected environment. The people I interviewed mention St. Croix the least often of the three. In spite of St. Croix's interesting terrain (a combination of rain forest and desert), and interesting historical sites, fewer travelers in my survey single it out.

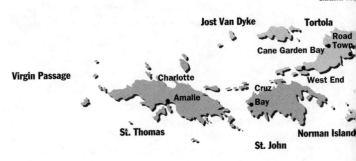

Tennis/Golf

Great Beaches   Atlantic Ocean

Guana Is

Jost Van Dyke   **Tortola**
                                                 Road
                                    Cane Garden Bay ● Town
Virgin Passage
                  Charlotte   **West End**
                        ● Amalie   Cruz
                                          ● Bay
St. Thomas   **Norman Island**
                                  St. John

Windsurfing

Coral Worl

Whim Greathouse

Caribbean Sea

Snorkeling/Diving

Shopping

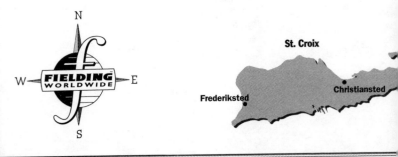

St. Croix

W ─── E   Christiansted

Frederiksted

Anegada

The Settlement

Vacation Places Rated 12

U.S. Virgin Islands

★ ★ ★ ★

■ **Actives**

■ **Mellows**

■ **All**

Virgin Gorda

Camano

Buck Island Reef

Spanish Town

Ginger Island

Cooper Island

Island

Reef Bay Estate

Cinnamon Bay Campgrounds

Botanical Gardens

Museums

Crafts

Cruising

Danish Architecture

WHAT TO DO IN THE U.S. VIRGIN ISLANDS

Actives	Mellows
1 Those who disdain conventional hotel accommodations should spend a few days at Cinnamon Bay Campgrounds on St. John. You may use their cottages and tents, or reserve bare ground for your own equipment. The beaches here are spectacular, and you can participate in lots of sporting activities and nature walks.	To see Danish architecture at its best on St. Croix, explore Fort Christiansvaern, the Scalehouse, Government House, and especially, the Danish Customs House. The best example on St. Thomas is Government House in Charlotte Amalie.
2 In Coral Bay, St. John, the original settlement, ask about hiking to Reef Bay Estate. You'll have great scenery on the way and be rewarded by a bit of history when you finish up at the remains of an old steam-driven sugar mill, now almost buried by jungle.	Children and adults love Coral World in Charlotte Amalie, an aquarium with an underwater viewing room that is unique—especially if you're not a snorkeler or scuba diver.
3 Snorkelers and scuba divers gear up to swim the underwater trail between St. Croix and offshore Buck Island. Buck Island Reef is a national monument and well preserved for your enjoyment.	A word about shopping: perfumes and liquors are the touted best buys here, but be sure to check your hometown prices before you buy in the islands. Items made in the Virgin Islands (some great jewelry and textiles) are duty free. Check for dates of the Arts Alive Festival, held several times a year on St. Thomas, for art and handcrafts.
4 Fishing is popular and easy to arrange through your hotel. Serious fishermen will be challenged by the USVI Blue Marlin Tournament in August where record catches of this huge, feisty fish have been recorded.	The islands were very different in the 18th Century, and you can sample the life-style of a sugar plantation at Whim Greathouse on St. Croix. The complex, beautifully restored, includes a small museum, a working sugar mill and the estate house filled with antiques and surrounded by a moat.
5 The newest watersport in the Caribbean is windsurfing, and the U.S. Virgin Islands can launch your board off St. Thomas or St. Croix.	Enjoy strolling through St. George Village Botanical Garden on St. Croix for a close up of the island's astonishing flora. The past lingers in ruins of a greathouse and a special historic garden of plants known to the earliest settlers, the Arawaks.

For further information, contact:

Virgin Islands Division of Tourism
1270 Avenue of the Americas
New York, NY 10020
☎ (212) 332-2222

WHAT PEOPLE LIKE ABOUT THE U.S. VIRGIN ISLANDS

Dependables

Many *dependables* first view the U.S. Virgin Islands (probably St. Thomas) from the deck of a cruise ship, which is not very different from the early explorers who took their bearings from St. Thomas's three main mountains. Whether they arrive by ship or by plane, they like the islands because they offer warm weather and a relaxing atmosphere in an exotic, yet familiar environment. St. Thomas, St. John and St. Croix are American possessions with nice hotels, people who speak English and where tourists can spend American dollars. They are ideal places for *dependables* to sample a different lifestyle with no cares or worries. Here is what some of them say about their trips:

We took a cruise to St. Thomas, which was beautiful, warm and relaxing. It didn't seem too 'touristy' when we were there. The water is clear and beautiful and Charlotte Amalie is a very nice city.

Homemaker, 33, Houston, TX

You have a nice feeling of isolation, yet it's close. There is a lot of unspoiled natural beauty to enjoy on all the islands. No one bothers you, and the snorkeling is great.

Teacher's assistant, 33, Bolton, CT

Centrics

When talking to people about their favorite places, I hear the following phrase over and over again: "There is a great deal to see and do there." *Centrics* especially find this true in the U.S. Virgin Islands. Every kind of watersport is available, and the warm, translucent ocean waters are particularly conducive to swimming, snorkeling and scuba diving. Almost every hotel of any size offers tennis, and golfers can play on all three islands, but the Robert Trent Jones course on St. Croix is the star. Each island offers interesting and beautiful scenery and lovely soft-sand beaches to lie on. *Centrics*, and others, better bring their checkbooks, because shopping is a favorite occupation at St. Thomas' duty-free port. With no currency exchange problems, they tell me it's easy to spend. Comments from *centrics* follow.

Caneel Bay on St. John ranks among the best in the Caribbean for geographical interest and beaches. Constant flights from JFK make it easy. It's a great vacation value. We have been seven or eight times, with and without the kids, and it's always great.

Senior corporate executive, 52, Westport, CT

It was a very relaxing vacation. They had great shopping, great beaches, great water sports, good food and wonderful, warm weather that we needed.

Woman teacher, 47, Marlboro, NJ

Venturers

History in this part of the world has its racy side. As *venturers* sail between the islands, they can imagine themselves plying the same waters as infamous pirates of old, who have left reminders like sunken ships, hotel names (Bluebeard's Castle, Blackbeard's Castle) and museum exhibits to be viewed by today's visitors. Interesting history always appeals to *venturers*, who are sure to seek out the unusual or unknown. They really appreciate lots of activity, so the wide variety of sporting activities meets their needs. Since they most like to stray from the beaten paths, St. John is the island they prefer. The United States created its 29th national park on St. John and this very pristine, undeveloped area appeals greatly to *venturers'* psychology. Here are some of their comments:

It doesn't take long to get there, and it's so wonderful when you do. It's clean, friendly, very unpopulated and romantic. There are many things to do and to see, interesting day trips, diving, sailing, windsurfing and great food.

Self-employed female, 26, Elmhurst, IL

I was there some years ago (St. John), and it was wild, beautiful and virtually untouched by commerce, and no gambling.

Saleswoman, 52, Jefferson City, MO

WHAT PEOPLE LIKE ABOUT THE U.S. VIRGIN ISLANDS

Dependables

The islands are beautiful, quiet and peaceful, with wonderful weather, For me, the main pleasure is snorkeling, snorkeling and more snorkeling.

Senior executive, male, 38, Sandy, UT

The cruise was paid for and all arrangements were made up front, so once the trip began we were able to enjoy the islands without worrying about anything. We enjoyed the sightseeing, the atmosphere and speaking English.

Male department manager, 35, Coppell, TX

Centrics

The whole trip seemed to be summed up in sunsets, snorkeling and piña coladas.

Senior executive, male, 64, Croton on Hudson, NY

Everything was great, the sun, sand, clear water and the privacy.

Male construction foreman, 36, Gautier, MS

The scenery is beautiful, especially the mountains on St. Thomas. It's relaxing because of the nice warm weather, and the quiet, simple elegance. The people are nice and the watersports are excellent.

Female accountant, 32, Bethesda, MD

Venturers

It's an absolutely beautiful part of the world, especially if you are wanting peace and quiet.

Self-employed female, 45, Holland, MI

It offers seclusion plus civilization. I love the clean, clear water, the nice people, great food, beaches and wonderful weather.

Dog trainer, 39, Greenbrae, CA

I have family there and plan to build a home and retire there myself. I enjoy the historical significance of the island, the climate and scuba diving. The people are friendly and I like that they are not all white and don't all speak English.

Clergywoman, 43, Vernon Rockville, CT

It's interesting, isn't it, how very different personalities choose to enjoy the same place? The vacations the U.S. Virgin Islands make a lot of people happy. Take the chance to visit them soon.

Germany

#13 RATING: ★★★★

Centrics	Venturers	Dependables
9	8	7

Heidelberg has the world's largest wine barrel (58,000 gallons).
Dusseldorf is Germany's center of haute couture.
There are more than 220 nightclubs in the heart of Berlin.
Cologne's cathedral is the largest Gothic building in the world.
Frankfurt has the busiest airport in Europe.

One of the people I interviewed sums up his favorite vacation spot in Germany by commenting, "It's the culture and historical environments that are significant when you visit a European country." No question this is true for many Americans. They travel to Europe to experience something different in the way of lifestyle, yet seeking landmarks that are familiar to them through a study of history, literature or family heritage. Germany fits this description like a glove. It's a sightseer's paradise that can be easily explored independently or with a guided tour. Visitors can race from town to town on the autobahn or cruise leisurely along the Rhine, with every bend exposing a view of charming villages or medieval castles. In the cultural centers of Munich and Berlin, people enthuse about the wonderful music from German composers, and the art and architecture that still is very impressive, in spite of destruction from two world wars. Images of German people created by the movies and other popular media can mislead. Travelers say the people they meet are warm and cheerful and happy to welcome Americans to their country.

How Germany heals its split personality makes travel there even more compelling to those with an interest in military and political history. The Berlin wall is no more, and this opens up both great possibilities and old wounds. Most of the tourist travel remains centered in the west, but there are many attractions in the eastern sector that are worth seeing. More than one tourist comments that they are watching carefully how the reunification progresses, and what it means to people who like to travel in the area.

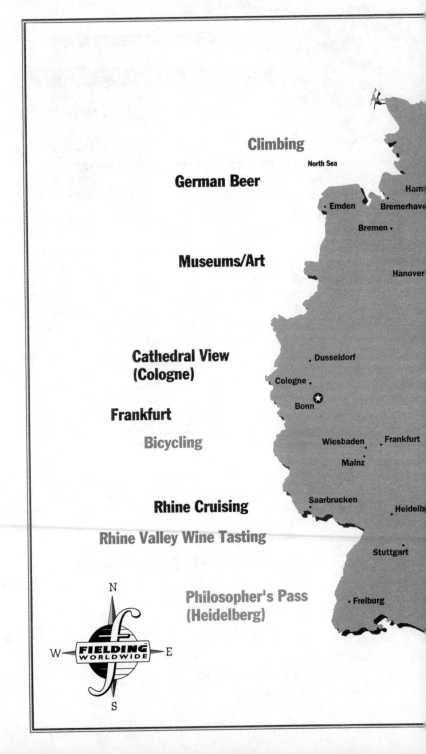

WHAT TO DO IN GERMANY

Actives	Mellows

1 You really must take a Rhine cruise and plan to stop and explore interesting sites along the way. Some of these are: Rhine Valley vineyards, Marskburg Castle, the old cities of Remagen, Sinzig and Koblenz and the Lorelei Rock. From Cologne (on the Rhine), drive up the Moselle Valley and sample its light white wines at the many small outdoor cafes.

Berlin offers so much that I can only make a few suggestions: the 18th century Brandenburg Gate was intended to be the triumphal arch into Berlin; Checkpoint Charlie Museum will sum up the many attempted escapes from East Berlin; Schloss Charlottenburg, whose gardens, royal tombs and architectural delights recall another era; Olymipiastadion, built for the 1936 Olympic Games; and the Museum Center in Dahlem, which houses several state museums of excellent quality.

2 If you fly, you will probably land in Frankfurt. Take some time to explore this bustling trading center, which dates back to prehistoric times. It has many excellent museums and art attractions.

Try to celebrate Oktoberfest in Bavaria (late September through October). It's a lot more fun than the pale imitations in the U.S., and you'll taste your fill of German food and beer.

3 The medieval university town of Heidelberg is a stunning city that will delight those who are fans of *The Student Prince*. Climb to Philosopher's Pass on the bank opposite the city for a great view of the town, the castle and the Neckar River.

In the east, the lovely city of Dresden was once called "Florence on the Elbe." After you admire the exquisite art and architecture, you can arrange to tour Meissen, Europe's oldest porcelain factory that produces its valuable "white gold."

4 One of the most famous landmarks in Europe is the splendid cathedral in Cologne, which survived allied bombing to stand out among the ruins. Active visitors can climb the 500 steps to the top of the spire for a view of this old city on the Rhine.

Perhaps you will recall some of the stories and legends that arose from this area as you travel along the Black Forest High Road, a most scenic part of Germany. Recharge your batteries at beautiful Lake Constance at the end of the road.

5 Munich is a wonderful city, filled with art and music and museums for your pleasure. If you headquarter here for a few days, you can take some fascinating day trips in the Bavarian countryside, such as to Garmische-Partenkirchen, which is famous for its painted murals, its folk festivals and its churches. Also see the three famous castles built by poor, mad King Ludwig II, and visit Oberammergau, which not only presents the Passion Play every 10 years, but offers a health spa and winter sports as well.

Rothenburg is a picture-perfect, much photographed town with cobbled streets, walls and towers and wonderful wood carvings. It has looked the same for hundreds of years, and is only one of the many romantic sights along the Romantic Road in the south, begun as a trade and transport link between fortresses in the Middle Ages.

For further information, contact:

German National Tourist Office
122 East 42nd Street, 52nd Floor
New York, NY 10168
☎ (212) 661-7200

WHAT PEOPLE LIKE ABOUT GERMANY

Dependables

As they usually do, *dependables* appreciate traveling in a country where their needs will be met as they see and do interesting things. In Germany, they see beautiful scenery, explore cities and villages with an old world flavor and magnificent old buildings, enjoy good food and drink, and can communicate fairly well since many Germans speak English. The transportation system is easy to understand, hotels are good and people are friendly and helpful. Thus, all the ingredients that *dependables* look for in a leisure trip come together nicely in Germany. Here are some of their comments:

Centrics

As is sometimes the case, *venturers*, *centrics* and *dependables* exhibit few differences in their degree of interest in this destination. *Centrics* emphasize Germany's historic significance somewhat more than its scenic beauty, and they uniformly praise its food, wine and beer. German food has received a "bad rap" in the U.S. for being heavy and bland, but German cuisine in its native land is delicious and innovative. The Rhine and Moselle Valleys produce white wines that compare favorably with those of any country. Any aficionado will tell you that nothing compares anywhere to German draft beer in a Biergarten, especially during Oktoberfest. An excellent train system makes it easy to get around the country without a car and German people extend a warm, efficient and gracious hospitality to visitors. Comments from *centrics* include.

Venturers

Venturers like being in a foreign country and some enjoy the opportunity to speak the little bit of German they learned in school or at home. Getting close to other life-styles and customs is fun for this group, and this is what they talk about in Germany, much more than sports and recreation. From sophisticated Berlin in the north to Munich and the Black Forest in the south, Germany presents many faces of its landscape and culture to the ambitious sightseer. Mountains and forests, small towns and villages, lakes and riverways provide food for the eye while Germany's plethora of ancient castles, churches, concert halls and museums do the same for the soul. *Venturers* reflect some of this in their comments.

I enjoy the contrast with a different culture and language, yet in a modern urban environment with safety, convenience and comforts.

**Male attorney, 55,
Richardson, TX**

Germany is a great country with very pleasant people. The historic sights were most interesting, especially cathedrals, castles and manor houses. We had very good food, and the traveling was easy.

**Retired female, 74,
Pensacola, FL**

I have enjoyed good music, wonderful historical sights and other cultural activities. I am fortunate to have friends there, and like to practice my German. The train transport is very good, and Germany is central to other interesting European countries.

**Female professor, 58,
University Park, MD**

Germany is clean, well organized, and offers good food, beer and wine. It's very scenic, has good museums, helpful people and the trains are on time.

**Male physician, 41,
San Diego, CA**

I felt like I stepped back in time at Rothenburg ob der Tauber. It was quaint, charming and historically significant.

**Retired female,
Charlotte, NC**

In Garmische the people are very friendly, and the topography is gorgeous. They gave us excellent food and wine and a wide variety of activities. It's remote from major cities, which felt good to us.

**Self-employed man, 61,
Lake Forest, IL**

WHAT PEOPLE LIKE ABOUT GERMANY

Dependables

I am interested in the culture and the people because my ancestors are from southern Germany.

Female accountant, 57, Benton, AR

I love the old world charm of castles and quaint villages contrasted with recent history, like World War II. You can see so many different places from history and literature that you have studied all of your life.

Retired female, 63, Greeley, CO

Centrics

I was a career soldier and retired for a while in Germany. I like the countryside, the food and beer, and of course I speak the language well.

Military man, 68, Kailua, HI

Munich has wonderful, quaint, old world charm. Much of Germany now is like the United States was in the 50s and 60s.

Retired male, 71, San Diego, CA

Oberdorf was quiet, small and friendly. The surrounding country is very pretty, the food is great, and there is excellent attention to detail.

Management consultant, 39, Bolingbrook, IL

Venturers

I have family in Berlin, and always find it a very exciting city. I enjoy watching the changes in the country since the wall came down.

Consultant, male, 50, Marietta, GA

I still enjoy it after three visits. The sense of history is awesome. We like to camp, and find the campgrounds clean and reasonable.

Female teacher, 52, Corvallis, OR

The people were terrific and were very helpful to my husband and me during our honeymoon. Kronweiler was nice, quiet, unspoiled and not 'touristy.'

Female engineer, 30, Arbutus, MD

Germany really does offer an incredible variety of natural attractions, historical sites and cultural activities. You may have heard the legend of Lorelei, who lured sailors on the Rhine with her song, only to crash their ships against the rocks. That old myth is long discredited, but the lure of Germany is still very strong

Rome

#14 RATING: ★★★★

Centrics	Venturers	Dependables
8	8	10

The Basilica of St. Peter took over 100 years to complete.

To reduce pollution, cars are allowed on Roman streets only every other day.

It took Michelangelo 2 1/2 years to paint the Sistine Chapel ceiling.

Romans dine late (1-3 p.m. for lunch; after 9 p.m. for dinner.)

A low voltage electric shock system keeps pigeons off the Trevi Fountain.

Rome stands alone in many areas. An ancient city (founded 2000 years B.C. by some reckonings), it served as the hub of a great empire for hundreds of years. Those visual reminders still remain to create a sense of excitement and awe among its visitors. Travelers also remark that Rome's ambience and personality are unique and not matched anywhere else in the world. A woman from Idaho calls it, without question, "the most beautiful city in the world."

You'll notice from the degree of interest scores that *dependables* give Rome the highest score, the only non-English speaking destination to receive a top rating from them. As you'll read later, Italy as a whole receives high scores from *dependables*. Clearly, people feel very comfortable here. Tour companies usually include Rome in itineraries of the great cities of Europe, and *dependables* are most likely to travel with an escorted tour. Vatican City, the city within a city in Rome, gives all American Catholics an extra incentive to visit the Eternal City (it's also a fascinating stop for tourists of any religious background).

Perhaps nowhere else in Europe do art, history and myth combine to such an extent. People tell me that seeing and touching legacies from the time of the Caesars and St. Paul evokes tremendous emotion. Others remember most vividly the magnificent churches and religious art. Almost everyone who visits Rome comes home carrying a couple of extra pounds, raving about the food and restaurants.

Etruscan Ruins

Ostia Antica Ruins

Bolzano

Sondrio•

Pordenone•

•Aosta

Milan   Verona•   Venice•

Vercelli•

•Alessandria   Parma

Cuneo•   •Genoa   •Bologna

Florence
                                              Pesar
•Pisa   •

Mac
Perugia•

Elba   •Grosseto

Collisseum   ROMI

VATICAN
CITY

Vatican City   Tyrrhenian Sea

Roman Forum

Basilica of St. Peter
                    Excursion to Tivoli

                              Circus Maximu

N

W — **FIELDING** WORLDWIDE — E

S

Caligula's Palace

Vacation Places Rated 14

Rome
★ ★ ★ ★

Actives
Mellows
All

Sistine Chapel
Delicious Food

Boat Tour on Tiber

Michelangelo's Pieta

Historical Sites

Adriatic Sea

Walk to Seven Hills

Shopping

Campobasso
Benevento   Bari
les
Salerno   Matera   Brindisi
Lecce

Strait of
Otranto   **Museums/Art**

Golfo di
Taranto   **Pantheon**

.Cosenza   **Trevi Fountain**

Catanzaro.

Ionian Sea

.Reggio di Calabria   **The Spanish Steps**

Nightlife

WHAT TO DO IN ROME

Actives	Mellows

1 The story goes that Rome was founded by Romulus on a special site of seven hills near the Tiber. You can get a different view of Rome from the top of each of the seven hills, and a good look at interesting neighborhoods if you walk. Don't try to do them all in one day!

The Roman Colosseum evokes the spirit of the emperors who built it and the gladiators who fought there 2000 years ago. It's an incredibly impressive monument, both in technology and emotional impact. The Pantheon, which has survived almost whole, is another ancient wonder with the same feeling. These, the viaduct system and ancient roads are all "must see" stops on your itinerary.

2 The city was actually founded on the Palatine Hill, and it was the center of the ancient city. There is plenty left of the Roman Forum for you to see, several temples dedicated to various gods, Caligula's palace and the Circus Maximus, which could accommodate 300,000 at chariot races.

Put Vatican City at the top of your list, but try to visit at the least crowded times because it's deservedly popular. For the full treatment, make advance reservations for a guided tour. There are enough worthwhile sights in Vatican City to fill a day. Don't miss the Basilica of St. Peter (where you can see Michelangelo's *Pietà*), the Sistine Chapel (also courtesy of Signore Buonarotti), and the "Raphael Rooms" that contain some of that Renaissance artist's most famous works.

3 Take a somewhat offbeat walk through the small Jewish quarter, a lively neighborhood with an eastern-style synagogue, considered the oldest Jewish community in the west.

Italy is famous for fashion design and precious Mediterranean antiques. The best shopping area for both includes the streets at the foot of the Spanish Steps—the Steps are a sightseeing must on their own. You'll see plenty of famous names (Armani, Fendi, Valentino), exquisite jewelry and antiques.

4 If you are fortunate enough to be in Rome during Holy Week, you can join the Good Friday procession of the cross, and experience in person the Pope's blessing to the city and the world at Easter.

In what other place can you dine while overlooking an entire city and thousands of years of history? Have a delicious breakfast or lunch at the top of the Forum Hotel (across from the Roman forum of course) as you scan the panorama of ancient ruins below.

5 Hop on one of the tour boats that take you down the Tiber from the center of Rome to the old port area of Ostia Antica. Abandoned now, memories of ancient international trade and dockside life linger in its ruins.

Do you want to return to Rome? Toss some spare change into the famous Trevi Fountain at the foot of the Quirinal Hill, and it's guaranteed. The fountain is spectacular and there are several lovely churches nearby.

For further information, contact:
Italian Government Travel Office
630 Fifth Avenue, Suite 1565
New York, NY 10111
☎ (212) 245-4822

WHAT PEOPLE LIKE ABOUT ROME

Dependables

Centrics

Venturers

Since *dependables* evidence so much interest in Rome, let's talk first about what they like. In their eyes, Rome is a very beautiful place. It appears very different from U.S. cities, with a grandeur of architecture and an overwhelming amount of public art and statuary. Romans are modern and sophisticated, but they share the well-known Italian qualities of warmth and enthusiasm that are so appealing. *Dependables* return home with memories of Rome and its culture, warm hospitality and outstanding food. Here are some of their comments:

Both Rome and London seem like home, in spite of their differences. We have friends in Rome and feel a familiarity and comfort level with the environment. This is a beautiful city with a fascinating past, and the food is wonderful.
Senior corporate executive, male, 59, Silver Spring, MD

I very much enjoyed the historic and religious art, the churches and of course, the food.
Female CPA, 52, Virginia Beach, VA

There is so much interesting sightseeing that it can't be done in one trip. The people are friendly and outgoing, even though you don't speak their language.
Marketing manager, male, Los Angeles, CA

Centrics also find Rome a city of beauty, full of sights to see and wonderful Italian food to eat. They seem to conquer the language barrier more easily, and they like finding their way around town on their own. More *centrics* mention good weather when they visit Rome, and they find time to enjoy the city's many discos and night spots after touring its historic and artistic sights. Movies and books create the image of Rome for many *centrics*—remember *Roman Holiday* and *Three Coins in the Fountain?*—and no one is disappointed when they see it for themselves. The following are comments from *centrics*:

I'm very interested in historic. sites. People are friendly. Bus and train transportation are easy to understand and it's relatively safe to walk around the city.
Female government employee, 52, Crystal lake, IL

All the historical aspects are great. We had good weather, found the local people friendly and enjoyed some super nightlife. Italian is a relatively easy language to learn.
30-year-old military female, Newport News, VA

Things to see are never ending. You almost overdose on beautiful sights and romantic ambience.
Self-employed female, 38, Racine, WI

Let's count some of the ways that Rome appeals to *venturers*: the familiar mythology of gods, goddesses and wonders of the ancient world; a history of great rulers and lawgivers and definitive military endeavors; a population that speaks a romantic and mellifluous foreign tongue and has different customs; the seat of one of the world's great and powerful religions existing as a separate nation, and lots of walking and exploring up and down the seven hills. With all this and more, how can they not have a wonderful vacation in Rome? Here are comments from some *venturers*:

It's the most beautiful city in the world. You can walk forever, and still not discover everything Rome has to offer. Art, history, museums, restaurants, the energy and vitality of the city—everything is marvelous.
Professional female, 43, Coeur D'Alene, ID

It's a wonderful place to headquarter a trip to Italy. The city itself is great, and you can easily get to the surrounding countryside.
Retired male, 66, Oklahoma City, OK

Vatican City is just remarkable. It contains so many treasures and magnificent art—not to mention the religious significance—that alone is worth a trip to Italy.
Retired female teacher, 59, Seattle, WA

WHAT PEOPLE LIKE ABOUT ROME

Dependables

It's alive with culture and history.
Self-employed male, 63, Doylestown, PA

The weather was beautiful, the people were nice, and the city is very beautiful and romantic. The food is great at sidewalk cafes or expensive restaurants. I can't wait to return.
Homemaker, 41, Hollywood, FL

Centrics

The climate was warm, the people were friendly and we saw a great deal of historical art. Rome is a fantastic city for food and restaurants.
Banker, 48, New York, NY

Venturers

Rome has everything—wonderful people, wonderful history, wonderful churches to see, wonderful art everywhere you turn and wonderful food.
Restaurateur, 35, Cherry Hills, NJ

Fortunately for all of us who love to travel, many great cities lie waiting to be discovered. Rome might well be at the very top of the list, especially if the combination of a fabulous ancient and vital modern civilization appeals to you.

France

#15 RATING: ★★★★

Centrics	Venturers	Dependables
8	10	6

Five million people trek to Lourdes each year seeking miracle cures.
The sun shines 300 days a year on the French Riviera.
The strongest tides in Europe churn into the bay of Mont-Saint-Michel.
The Grand Canyon of Verdon is the best of its kind in Europe.
The French lead the world in high speed train technology.

If you and I have learned to appreciate wine, we can thank France. If we've elevated our taste, we owe the French our gratitude. If we take pride in being "cultured" or well-mannered, we know that the French have defined those terms for us. Much of the art we love, you guessed it, flows from the brushes of French artists. You would expect, then, that France would attract many Americans, especially *venturers*. They love anything that has a French mystique about it. The following discussion concentrates on travelers' reactions to all areas of France outside of Paris, which deserves its own description in this chapter.

"Everything ends this way in France...everything is a pretext for a good dinner," said Jean Anouilh. Travelers agree. Almost everyone places fine food and restaurants at the top of their list when they recall their trips through France, regardless of personality types. The French countryside draws praise for its special beauty, with visitors singling out the Loire Valley and the South of France in particular. History abounds, beginning with the famous caves of the Dordogne, where prehistoric man has left significant records, to royal castles, churches and abbeys, and the battlefields of Normandy. Paris dominates the museum scene, but art lovers can visit many fine smaller museums and galleries, especially in the south, where impressionists found the light and the faces that inspired them.

Just a word about the French: they have earned a reputation for arrogance and impatience, but the people I interviewed say these qualities disappear when you leave Paris. In spite of the language barrier, French men and women are proud of their country and like to show it off in a friendly and helpful manner.

Paris

Eiffel Tower

English Channel

Amiens

Rouen

Mont St. Michel
(Brittany)

Caen

Saint-Lô   Evreaux·   Paris

Versailles

St-Brieuc·   Chartres

Shopping

·Quimper   ·Rennes   ·Laval   ·Le Mans

Vannes   Blois

Tours

Normandy   Nantes   Angers   Bour

Chateaur

La Roche-sur-Yon   ·Poitiers

History   ·Niort

Museums   La Rochelle   Limoges

Angouleme

Provence   Perigueux·   Tu

Burgundy Vineyards   Bordeaux   Cahors

Food/Wine   Agen·

Montaubân

Mont-de-Marsan   Toulous

Bay of Biscay

Pau·   ·Tarbes   Carcas

Horseback Riding   Foix

N

W ─ FIELDING WORLDWIDE ─ E

S

Notre-Dame

Champs-Elysees

Bicycling

Hiking

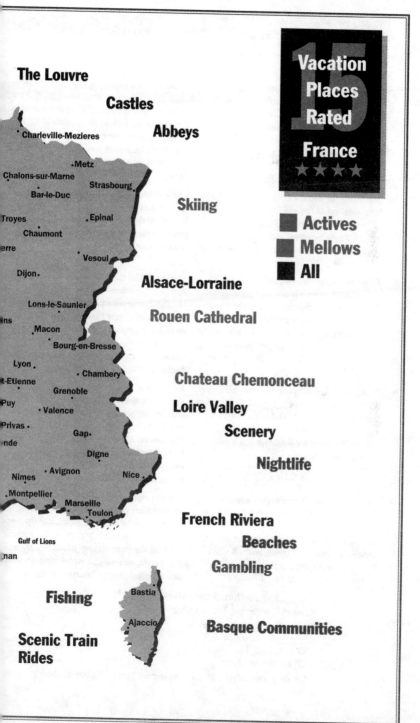

The Louvre

Castles

Abbeys

· Charleville-Mezieres

·Metz

Chalons-sur-Marne

Strasbourg.

Bar-le-Duc

Troyes

. Epinal

Chaumont

erre

· Vesoul

Dijon.

Lons-le-Saunier

.

ins

.Macon

Bourg-en-Bresse

Lyon .

· Chambery

t-Etienne

Grenoble

Puy

· Valence

Privas .

Gap.

nde

Digne

Nimes · Avignon   Nice .

.Montpellier

Marseille

Toulon

Gulf of Lions

nan

Fishing

Bastia

Ajaccio

Scenic Train
Rides

Vacation Places Rated France ★★★★

Actives
Mellows
All

Skiing

Alsace-Lorraine

Rouen Cathedral

Chateau Chemonceau

Loire Valley

Scenery

Nightlife

French Riviera

Beaches

Gambling

Basque Communities

WHAT TO DO IN FRANCE

Actives	Mellows
1 You'll get your exercise exploring Mont St. Michel in Brittany, the famous and stunning abbey that is one of western civilization's great achievements. Wear comfortable shoes for going up and downhill.	At Rouen on the Seine, Joan of Arc was condemned to burn alive. The church of St. Joan stands on the market square in her honor, and the Cathedral of Rouen, on a more grandiose level, is a perfect example of French Gothic.
2 What did your daddy do in the war? Maybe he landed at one of the beaches in Normandy at one of the most famous episodes of military history. Those beaches, code named Omaha, Utah, Gold, Juno and Sword hold many powerful memories.	Chateau Chenonceau on the Loire seems to rise up out of the water like a fairy tale castle. It's one of the most beautiful in Europe and has a fascinating past. Of course, this is one of many castles in France.
3 All French communities celebrate two festivals: Bastille Day (July 14) with parades and fireworks the evening before, and the summer solstice on June 21, with dancing and music well into the night. Both festivals invite you to be a part of the fun with local residents.	You might find the French Riviera expensive and overdeveloped—or you might find it absolutely marvelous. This is the sun 'n fun part of France, very Mediterranean in atmosphere and cuisine, and very liberal in beach attire (nude beaches). Cannes hosts the world's most famous film festival in May.
4 Perhaps you'd like to help with the picking in a Burgundian vineyard in the fall. Contact the Comité Interprofessional des Vins de Bourgogne to find out how to go about it, or ask your travel agent for help. You can sample their wares while you're at it.	Spend some time in Alsace-Lorraine on the German border. France changes its visage once again, presenting you with pink-stoned renaissance architecture, flowers and great cleanliness, attributes influenced by its Teutonic neighbors. The food and wine also borrow from Germany and are absolutely delicious, served with French flair.
5 They don't extend the warmest welcome in France, but the Basque communities on the border with Spain are fascinating. The Basques have retained their own traditions, dances, clothing and foods, and will share them. In the province of Bordeaux, travel inland from Biarritz to find them.	You can also gamble in French style. Large casinos have operated on the Riviera and the Atlantic coastal cities for years, and the fever is spreading. If this is your pleasure, remember that the more elegant rooms impose a dress code, and the atmosphere is more quiet and dignified than in American casinos.

For further information, contact:
French Government Tourist Office
610 Fifth Avenue, Suite 222
New York, NY 10020
☎ (212) 767-1125
☎ 1-900-990-0040 *
* Note: phone calls cost 50 cents per minute, a surprising burden the French put tourists.

WHAT PEOPLE LIKE ABOUT FRANCE

Dependables

Dependables who choose France return home also very pleased with their vacations. They eat wonderful French food, tour historic sites they know about from school, and see original art masterpieces previously experienced only in coffee table books. They appreciate the variation from their usual trips and probably find the language barrier and the French people more fun and less intimidating than they thought. Here's what some *dependables* have to say:

Everything was wonderful—the atmosphere, food, people, prices, scenic views, mountains, Orangina, Reims—everything, especially the Pyrenees.

Female student, 19, Poughkeepsie, NY

I really enjoyed seeing a different culture, especially the historical sightseeing and the food.

Homemaker, 40, Kansas City, MO

Centrics

A small hotel, a small museum, a slower pace in a smaller town, not-so-small castles on the Loire—these are a few of *centrics'* favorite things. Away from the bustle of Paris are never ending sights that help them define France. Most popular is the south of France, which adds sunny beaches and a casual but sophisticated atmosphere to the attractions mentioned above. Many future French tourists have been prompted to visit this area by the Peter Mayles book and public television series *A Year in Provence.* Several painters from the Impressionist school also celebrated life in Provence, Van Gogh being the outstanding example. *Centrics* tell me things like:

The country is very beautiful, both urban and rural areas. The French Riviera especially has great weather, beaches, restaurants, accommodations and wonderful 'joie de vivre!'

Self-employed male, 65, Long Beach, NY

I enjoyed the combination of great art and natural beauty. The aesthetics are wonderful. The atmosphere is low key, the food is terrific, and it gave me a chance to speak French.

Executive vice-president, 43, female, Haddonfield, NJ

Venturers

Venturers show more interest in France than others, perhaps because they enjoy the diversity of landscape and sightseeing and have less trepidation about foreign languages. In fact, those who have even slight familiarity with the language say they enjoy the challenge of speaking French, even if they stumble over words a lot. From the Normandy beaches to the wine country of Bordeaux and Champagne, from German-influenced Alsace to the sunny Mediterranean ambience of Provence and the Riviera, France provides an immense diversity for peripatetic *venturers.* Each area displays a very different aspect to the eye, distinct cooking styles and regional variations of the French character—all grist to the mill of intellectually curious *venturers* with adventurous palates. In the following quotes, *venturers* speak out:

The south of France is so very beautiful. We went to school there and have great memories. I have taken all of my children there and I hope to share it with all of my grandchildren as well.

Retired female, 58, Boca Raton, FL

I love the climate, the ambience and the food. We took a bike tour and saw wonderful scenery and experienced a great sense of history.

Senior corporate executive 37, Syracuse, NY

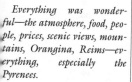

WHAT PEOPLE LIKE ABOUT FRANCE

Dependables

Lourdes really gives a feeling of peace and spirituality.
Minister, 55, Dallas, TX

I am lucky to speak the language, so my pleasure is increased by communication. I love the food, the diversity of geography and the pace of life.
Self-employed female, 43, St. Paul, MN

Centrics

I was surprised at the regional differences between Normandy, the Loire Valley and other areas.
Self-employed female, 59, St. Louis, MO

Basque country was really wonderful. There was a wonderful harbor, interesting Basque tradition, clothing, food, culture, family ties and architecture. The people's friendliness was very pleasant.
Female rehab specialist, 50, Oviedo, FL

Venturers

I love the culture, the customs of daily life, the people, food and art. I prefer the "backwoods" to major cities.
Female teacher, 55, Van Nuys, CA

It's both interesting and fun. Beauty, history, variety, art and great food are all there for you.
Budget analyst, female, 48, San Jose, CA

We walked hundreds of kilometers on rural trails throughout France. We ate well, met the locals and encountered no Americans. That is a delight in itself.
50-year-old homemaker, Santa Fe, NM

Alors, mes amis, come and visit La Belle France. It's not just icing on the cake—it's the whole meal from hors d'oeuvre to petits fours. You'll be glad you went.

Cayman Islands

#16 RATING: ★★★★

Centrics	Venturers	Dependables
8	10	7

Tourists have cards/letters postmarked from Hell, near West Bay.

The islands get their name from the Carib word for crocodile.

North Sound is the largest area of inland mangrove in the Caribbean.

The North Wall of Cayman Brac drops from 60 to 14,000 ft.

The deepest known Caribbean point is Cayman Trench (24,724 ft.)

In the old days, people came for turtles. Then they came to relax in the warm Caribbean sunshine. Now they arrive to dive in the incredibly clear waters that surround the three Caymans. A fortunate few might come to arrange a tax shelter, or come on some other financial business, since banking is the number one industry, followed by tourism.

Tourists make the three Caymans come alive, so they are well looked after. If there is crime or pollution or poverty, visitors say they don't see it. They commend the various types of accommodations throughout the islands, all comfortable, clean, and luxurious, if desired. If you've made the trip to relax or get away from a cold winter, no one will prevent you from soaking up the sun all day. If you'd like a little more action, the warm waters around the Caymans provide watersports galore. Since *venturers* favor this destination, and they tend to be active types, you can assume the Caymans hold a special incentive for them. It's scuba diving!

A quick note about atmosphere: The Cayman Islands are British owned, but you will find them more casual and American in feeling. Unlike most other Caribbean locales, the Caymans don't offer lush tropical scenery. They are built largely on coral and seashell, and their wonders are largely under the sea—hence the diving mania. But, there are a couple of beaches that compare with any in the world for beauty and comfort.

Actives
Mellows
All

Scooter Tours

Hiking

Museums

Nature Walk

Beaches

Relaxing

Bird Watching

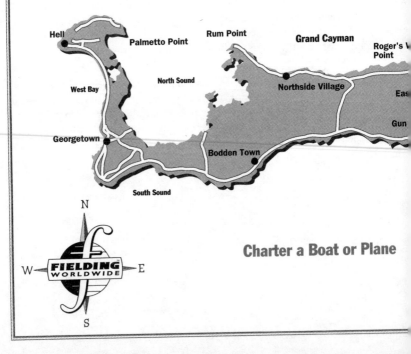

Hell

Palmetto Point

Rum Point

Grand Cayman

Roger's W
Point

West Bay

North Sound

Northside Village

Eas

Georgetown

Gun

Bodden Town

South Sound

N

W — FIELDING WORLDWIDE — E

S

Charter a Boat or Plane

Turtle Watching

Booby Point

Stake Bay Point

North East Point

Cayman Brac

Crawl Bay

Little Cayman

Bloody Bay Point

West End Point

Blossom Village

Scuba Diving

Shopping

Snorkeling

Sailing

Windsurfing

Fishing

WHAT TO DO IN THE CAYMAN ISLANDS

Actives	Mellows
1 You'll probably want to explore all three islands, so check into some different ways to travel among them. Charter boats and small planes are two possibilities.	Bird fanciers will want to observe the Cayman Brac parrot, a protected species with markings unique to the Caymans. Cayman Brac is one of two smaller islands north of Grand Cayman.
2 Grand Cayman is flat, so even novices have an easy time handling hired motor scooters for getting quickly around the island.	Join the locals in celebrating Pirate's Week at the end of October. Parades, costumes and music are part of the festive goings-on, and it's become so popular you'll need to reserve well in advance.
3 If scuba diving is your thing (and it might be before you leave), consider staying at one of the inns whose main focus is diving. They are usually smaller, often owner-managed and they care about what you care about—fantastic undersea gardens, fish and other sea life.	Turtle hunting attracted attention to the Caymans, but it almost wiped out these magnificent reptiles. Don't miss a chance to observe several varieties, and join your voice with others to support their preservation. Ask at your hotel or at a tourist information site for help.
4 Scuba diving is the king of sports here, but don't pass up the fishing. You'll relax and have great sport setting out from any of the three islands.	If you want to visit a museum on your vacation, The Cayman Islands National Museum on George Town's waterfront is waiting for you. It's simple, but the nice building and displays will give you a good "feel" for the Caymans.
5 As I noted, the Caymans don't offer a lot of active sightseeing away from the water, but walkers and hikers will find good nature walks. Again, ask locally for the best trails, and take plenty of water, as it gets warmer as you go inland.	Enjoy shopping by all means, but do a little research first. "Duty-free" doesn't mean that everything is a bargain, but the jewelry and perfume shops are very tempting.

For further information, contact:

Cayman Islands Department of Tourism
420 Lexington Avenue #2733
New York, NY 10170
☎ (212) 682-5582

WHAT PEOPLE LIKE ABOUT THE CAYMAN ISLANDS

Dependables

Dependables don't offer much help in understanding the appeal of the Caymans. Since they tend to be less active, expertise in scuba diving holds less appeal for them. If they head for the Caribbean on vacation, they are more likely to choose an island better known for scenic beauty, sightseeing and perhaps gambling. *Dependables* who do come to the Caymans have a good time, and they emphasize the weather, the unspoiled, clean appearance, and the lack of crime and poverty. Here are a couple of quotes from *dependables*:

Centrics

Think about this scenario. You live in the midwest or the eastern United States. It's a cold winter, and you commute to a very stressful or boring job every day. Your kids have runny noses. Somewhere in the sun, not too far away, lies a place with beautiful, clean beaches, interesting ambience and nice people to answer questions and bring you what you need. All your cares disappear for a week or so. The Cayman Islands make this dream come true for *centrics*. Many other islands can offer this escape, but the Caymans do it their way, with understated, but upscale hotels and facilities, British hospitality and American attitudes. This is not one of the places with a great deal to see and do. Rather, it's a place to let a weary traveler unwind, be lazy or enjoy some water activities where the ocean is warm, blue and clear. That's what *centrics* tell me, and here are a few quotes from them:

Venturers

You can probably anticipate what *venturers* like about the Caymans. They describe the joys of diving and snorkeling enthusiastically, singling out the local divemasters for special praise. The fantastic plants and ocean life so clearly visible in the clear blue waters entice them below the surface and over again. Sailing and windsurfing are popular on top of the water. Like some other islands in the Caribbean, the Caymans have learned the dangers to their environment from overcrowding and pollution, and they are making sincere attempts to protect native flora and fauna. *Venturers* like that, too. Here's what they say:

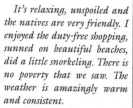

It's relaxing, unspoiled and the natives are very friendly. I enjoyed the duty-free shopping, sunned on beautiful beaches, did a little snorkeling. There is no poverty that we saw. The weather is amazingly warm and consistent.

Part-time legal assistant, female, 24, Portland, ME

It's nice, it's different, and it's not too far away.

Homemaker, 34, Knoxville, TN

There are several great beaches there. The water is so blue, the environment feels so clean, and we felt safe, too. It's easy to get around the island, and the Hyatt is really a wonderful resort. It's absolutely a no-pressure vacation.

Female paralegal, 24, New York, NY

I like the relaxed, low-key atmosphere. There's not much to do except enjoy the beach and snorkel. With great weather and pleasant people, you have to relax.

Female teacher, 56, Shrewsbury, MA

That is just great scuba diving! The beaches are beautiful, the weather is perfect. I like the option of staying in a condo rather than a hotel, and I like the friendly people and the interesting food.

Female department manager, 39, Alameda, CA

The Sunset House facilities and staff are excellent. The divemasters are knowledgeable and friendly and the diving is outstanding.

Self-employed male, 38, Madison, WI

WHAT PEOPLE LIKE ABOUT THE CAYMAN ISLANDS

Dependables

Centrics

Venturers

Dependables	Centrics	Venturers
	What stands out is the weather, the cleanliness and the upscale environment. **Senior corporate executive, 47, Shrewsbury, PA**	*I really feel like I got away from everything and experienced something different. It's a friendly, relaxing place and the watersports are great.* **Senior executive, male, 35, Tucker, GA**
	It's a most beautiful island. **Female accountant, 24, Livingston, NJ**	*Superior diving!* **Marketing manager, 31, Monroe, CT**
	The water is fantastic! Prices are reasonable, and it's not too far away. People are nice to you everywhere. I'll certainly travel there more often, once I find a job! **Female office worker, 35, Houston, TX**	*I enjoy seeing animals in their natural habitat. To swim with the turtles and watch all kinds of birds was a great experience. I hope to return.* **Librarian, 39, Midland, TX**

The people I interviewed indicate the Caymans are Caribbean Islands with a difference. If you're interested in diving, this is certainly the place. If not, visit the Cayman Islands as a delightful cure for the winter blues.

Aruba

#17 RATING: ★★★★

Centrics	Venturers	Dependables
8	6	10+

Aruba is 72 sq. miles and shaped like an arrowhead.
Yamanota Hill at 617 ft. is the highest peak.
Boulders at Casibau and Ayo have been carved into weird shapes by wind.
Boca Ruins is popular for dune sliding.
Aruba's landscape looks more like the moon's surface than tropical.

Everybody talks about the weather in Aruba, and apparently it's not a boring subject. I have never seen so many compliments from travelers concerning climatic conditions, but they all rave about the warm, consistently perfect conditions. Actually, Aruba is a very interesting spot. The winds that blow are desertlike rather than tropical, and the island that greets you is a rocky, cactus-studded terrain that some people consider very beautiful. The winds blow in one direction only, which results in the unusually-shaped divi-divi trees that are one of Aruba's trademarks. Many influences shape its atmosphere: the Dutch who own it, the African heritage of its native people and the Latin touch from nearby South America.

One of the reasons *dependables* like it so much is that Aruba has committed itself to the tourist trade, with excellent results. Accommodations are varied and comfortable, service is good and the people are happy to help you enjoy yourself. Because of the Dutch influence, this is a slightly more reserved society than on some other islands. Your hosts prefer you to observe some decorum, which mostly means to dress appropriately downtown and in nice restaurants. In return they extend a very nice welcome and share their island with a very individual charm and ability.

Beaches

Arasji

Malmok   Druif

Boca Cura

Bon Bini Festivals

Palm Beach   Noord

Bushribana

Nightlife

Gambling

Oranjestad

Santa Cruz

Jazz Festivals

Balashi

Fort Zoutman

Dune Sliding

Great Food

Vacation Places Rated

Aruba

★★★★

Actives
Mellows
All

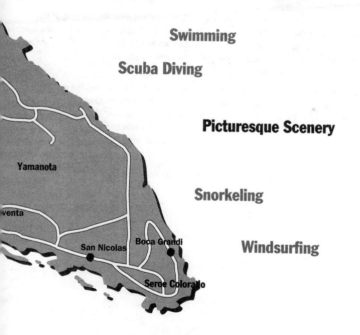

Tennis

Shopping

Swimming

Scuba Diving

Picturesque Scenery

Yamanota

Snorkeling

venta

San Nicolas   Boca Grandi

Windsurfing

Seroe Colorado

WHAT TO DO IN ARUBA

Actives	Mellows
1 Scuba dive at stunning reefs or shipwrecked boats. Many hotels hold classes for novices in the pool, so don't hesitate to experience the translucent warm waters of the Caribbean, and explore the sights beneath.	Attend one of the regular Tuesday evening parties called the "Bon Bini Festival" at Fort Zoutman in Oranjestad. For a small admission fee, you can mix with other guests and locals, sample drinks and browse local crafts.
2 Windsurfing is a fast growing sport because of the constant trade winds and its fans like several locations on Aruba. June is a big month for races 'round the island, and you'll find it exciting to join in or watch.	Oranjestad grew up around Fort Zoutman, which the Dutch built to protect its interests on Aruba. The fort is worth a tour, housing many museum-type exhibits of the island's history.
3 Jazz in June? Arubans like festivals, and this one in Oranjestad is great fun for music lovers. Jazz at this festival will have a special Aruban sizzle.	Walk around the waterfront in Oranjestad and soak up the atmosphere. Look at what's being traded from the boats, enjoy people watching and a snack or two.
4 Speaking of sizzle, don't pass up the chance to experiment with the varied cuisine of Aruba. Classic French, Dutch specialties, Spanish paella and Aruban style seafood are all favorites. Don't forget to dress up a little.	Gambling and nightlife are part of this island's package. Visit a couple of the upscale casinos and be sure to attend one of the extravagant shows.
5 Let your hair down and go dune-sliding at Boca Prins—it's a desert, remember? Wear jeans, tennis shoes and long sleeves.	Drive over to San Nicolas, the second town on Aruba. It's on the southern end of the island, so you'll see some of the picturesque terrain. San Nicolas was once "the place to live" on Aruba, but now is a quiet contrast to the developed tourist areas.

For further information, contact:

Aruba Tourism Authority
2344 Salzedo Street
Miami, FL 33134
☎ (305) 567-2720

WHAT PEOPLE LIKE ABOUT ARUBA

Dependables

If you've just finished reading about the Cayman Islands, Aruba's neighbor in the Caribbean, you'll see how different these islands can be from one another. *Dependables* choose Aruba much more often than the Caymans because it offers very different and more varied options. Here on Aruba, you can do nothing at all in very comfortable surroundings, participate in watersports, play tennis, gamble in several casinos, attend a lavish show at one of the big hotels, or shop, and so on, ad infinitum. *Dependables* always enjoy entertainment and gaming activities (as in Las Vegas) and are consistent here. Although it can't be described as totally English-speaking, it's not hard to communicate if you're patient. Why wouldn't you be patient? They tell me you start to relax as soon as you unpack and hit the beach. Your whole vacation will be quiet and tranquil if that's the way you want it. Read on for comments from *dependables*, the personality types who like it the most:

Aruba had been recommended to us by friends, and we like it very much. The weather is marvelous, the people are extremely nice, and the island is very clean and safe.
Female office worker, 36, Neptune City, NJ

Centrics

Centrics enjoy the Caribbean very much, and Aruba is no exception. It's casual and relaxing, yet exciting and glamorous. It's close to home, but foreign and "different." Come with a significant other for a romantic getaway or bring the whole family to enjoy the activities at one of the all-inclusive resorts. It's fun to anticipate a night on the town at one of the casinos or an evening dancing to a combination of Latin/Caribbean rhythms. Whatever you do, people tell me, you will feel safe and comfortable, and have fond memories of your vacation. *Centrics* say:

We didn't realize the people would be so capable and so nice. What a great climate they have! We enjoyed the shopping and nightlife, and the choice to be active or to relax.
Female health care professional, 30, Lansdale, PA

Venturers

Aurba's more limited range of sports activities and its heavier commercial development are not what *venturers* want. Too many big hotels and cruise ship tourists do not excite them when on vacation. Still, their degree of interest score is quite respectable, which means this island has enough going for it to hang on to its more active and venturesome visitors. They pursue water sports like diving, snorkeling, and fishing at which Caribbean islands excel, and they enjoy the distinctive mixed culture of Aruba, which manifests itself in music, manners and food. Here are some quotes from *venturers*:

We had some wonderful dinners in Oranjestad—imagine Indonesian rijstaffel one night and spicy local seafood the next. It's my favorite Caribbean island so far. I think it draws a more adult crowd than some of them.
Homemaker, 41, San Antonio, TX

WHAT PEOPLE LIKE ABOUT ARUBA

Dependables

We liked just about everything, The weather is perfect, the beaches are beautiful, and you can stay at a hotel or condo, both good. We enjoyed the restaurants.

> Retired male, 67,
> Chicago, IL

The beaches and swimming are first rate!
CFO, male, 49, Hamden, CT

It's a very interesting area, and not too commercialized. We had a good time.

> Homemaker, 44,
> Wheeling, WVA

We bought a timeshare there and each year we see the same people and have made good friends. It's a wonderful place to spend leisure time, with unbelievable weather.
Retired male 60, Bristol, PA

Centrics

The accommodations are very good, and I like the all-inclusive price packages. Everything is simplified. Aruba is an interesting place with a nice slow pace.

> Retired male, 68,
> Harrisburg, IL

Aruba's a nice clean island, real relaxing.
35-year-old female office worker, Hurst, TX

There is a surprising amount of things to do, especially around the water. We like the life-style, the Dutch influence on the architecture and the food. It's nice to have a choice of entertainment at night, too. Some very professional shows!

> Female researcher, 50,
> Prairie Village, KS

Venturers

I enjoyed diving and windsurfing, sports I cannot do easily at home. The climate in winter is like heaven for us midwesterners, the hotels are good and there is a lot to do.

> Union official, Shaker
> Heights, OH

Aruba has a very distinctive and different look that we find stunning. The water is clear and beautiful, the people offer very good service, and it feels like an adventure to go there.
Manufacturing executive, 55, Raleigh, NC

Aruba does sound fun and fascinating, doesn't it?

Scandinavia

#18 RATING: ★★★★

Centrics	Venturers	Dependables
8	9	10+

Gerranger is the most spectacular of the fjords.

Finland is the only country in Europe that has paid off its war debt.

In Finnish Lapland, reindeer outnumber people.

Kronberg Castle supposedly inspired Shakespeare's "Hamlet."

North Cape is 1300 miles from the North Pole.

Considering the high scores from both *venturers* and *dependables*, you may wonder why Scandinavia doesn't climb higher on the Top 25 list. Travelers find this group of countries in Northern Europe remarkably beautiful and exciting, and it's almost unfair to lump them together as we often must. Let me make one thing clear right away: Shakespeare misled us when he wrote about the "Melancholy Dane." In spite of long, cold winters, residents of Denmark and Norway are outgoing and cheerful with a terrific sense of humor. Swedes and Finns are more dignified and shy, respectively, but always gracious and pleasant to visitors.

It's not unfair to say that ice and water rule these countries, and that Scandinavians in turn rule the waters. Glaciers create the magnificent scenery of the fjords, the constant gentle rains produce unbelievable springtime beauty and Scandinavian economies have been linked to the seas since their time began. A high proportion of residents own boats for pleasure or commerce, and pictures of major cities will almost always include a water scene. Most churches in fishing regions still have a scale model boat hanging from the ceiling, not far from the pulpit, for when pastors blessed fishermen and their families prior to their sailings. Cruise ships now ply Scandinavian waters to show off the natural beauty of the rugged coastline to its best advantage. Cruising is a very popular mode of travel (as I discuss elsewhere in the book), especially for *dependables*.

Scandinavia probably has more influence on our lives than we think. Let me throw out some expressions, and you'll see how familiar things Scandinavian are. "Land of the Midnight Sun." "Danish modern." "Taking a sauna." "Nobel Prize." "Hans Christian Andersen's fairy tales." "Lapland and reindeer." "Vikings." "Smorgasbord," and so on. Quite a few people tell me they have relatives to visit, or their ancestry is Scandinavian, which heightens the pleasure of their visit even more.

Midnight Sun

Castles
Scenery

Skiing

Swedish Glassblowers
Viking Museum

● Mos

Norwegian Sea

Shopping

Osters

Watersports

● Trondheim

Fishing

NORWAY

● Gudvangen

Boat Trip to Fjords   ● Bergen

● Oslo
⭐

Kronberg Castle

● Stavanger

Legoland

Goteb

Skegerrak

Nightwatchman Tour

DENMARK Copenhag
⭐

Ferry to Copenhagen

Arctic Ocean

Lakslev

Santa Claus Village

Reindeer Safaris

Kelloselka

runa

Rovaniemi

Golf

Taivalkoski

DEN

Oulu

lea

FINLAND

Snowmobiling

Hatuvaara

Vaasa

Imatra

Medievel Towns

Tampere

Brewery Tours

Turku   Helsinki

f Bothnia

Hiking

osala

Stockholm

Bicycling

Tivoli Gardens (Copenhagen)

altic Sea

Little Mermaid

Harbor Cruises

Nightlife

Vacation Places Rated

18

Scandinavia
★★★★

Actives
Mellows
All

WHAT TO DO IN SCANDINAVIA

Actives	Mellows
1 Even if you are not on a cruise, arrange a boat trip to see some of Norway's fjord country by sea. All the scenery is thrilling, but for an extra sense of danger, navigate the narrow passage of Stokksund, where horns sound to signal oncoming traffic.	Shakespeare students will want to visit Kronborg Castle in Denmark, which the Bard used as a setting for *Hamlet*, making it one of the world's most famous castles.
2 Not far out of Copenhagen, you can take the ferry to a little Swedish island with a beach, bike rentals and picnic lunches for sale. Ride round the island and relax over lunch, but do pick a dry, pleasant day.	Copenhagen's Tivoli Gardens is an enchanting combination of gardens, music, childrens' amusements and very expensive restaurants. Food is expensive, as is the theme park, but it's great to walk through, and you can often come upon a free band concert.
3 Believe it or not, golf is taking Finland by storm. There are more than 70 courses in the country, one of which is just below the Arctic Circle. You can play the first nine in Finland and finish in Sweden!	The Vikings were arguably the greatest seamen of all time. Recapture their daring spirit by visiting the Viking Ship Museum near Oslo, where Thor Heyerdahl's raft *Kon-Tiki* is also on display. In Stockholm, take an afternoon cruise around the harbor, where there are lots of historic and attractive things to see.
4 If you should find yourself in Ribe on the wild Jutland peninsula, you can join the night watchman's tour. Beginning at 10 PM, he will lead you through the streets of this old town, calling out the hour and revealing some of the history as he goes. This is a unique opportunity to see into the windows and the soul of a Danish city.	The area between Kalmar and Vaxjo in Sweden bears the romantic title of "The Kingdom of Glass." You'll see glassblowers at work at Orrefors and Kosta, creating some of the most elegant and valuable glassware in the world. You can buy factory seconds at a fraction of U.S. prices.
5 Remember that all Scandinavian countries are water-oriented and its people love the outdoor life. There is almost nowhere that you can't find skiing, fishing, hiking, bicycling and boating for every activity level. Enjoy!	Denmark's Jutland peninsula houses a very different kind of creativity: Legoland, a miniature world built entirely of plastic Lego blocks. It's part amusement park and part museum, and a real salute to the ingenuity and whimsical nature of the Danes.

For further information, contact:

Scandinavian Tourist Board
655 Third Avenue
New York, NY 10017
☎ (212) 949-2333

WHAT PEOPLE LIKE ABOUT SCANDINAVIA

Dependables

As I mentioned, *dependables* traditionally enjoy cruising and it's one of the best ways to tour Scandinavia and the North Cape. Probably only Alaska comes close to the cool, wild scenery that geography and climate have created in these northern countries. The transportation systems within all countries make it easy to travel from one major city to another and to explore the inland areas. *Dependables* find that many Scandinavians speak English and are sociable and friendly to their American visitors. Here are some comments from *dependables*:

I have been coming to Denmark for years, to see relatives and because I love it. The people are absolutely wonderful. They are funny and sociable, and anxious to help you. Copenhagen is a beautiful and sophisticated European city, with outstanding restaurants.
Male writer, 45,
New York City, NY

It's actually very much like home. That's the atmosphere they establish. We were treated very well and enjoyed the beautiful countryside.
Male lab technician, 31,
Jamestown, NY

Centrics

Centrics echo others in their admiration for the way Scandinavia looks. From Norway's spectacular fjords to Finland's lakes and forests, the natural beauty is pristine and breathtaking. Cities and towns are civilized, picturesque and clean. Tourists see no poverty, no homelessness and no graffiti in these socialized nations, whose people pay high taxes to maintain their life-styles and protected environment. *Centrics* like the museums in Oslo, the bridges and canals of Stockholm, the pastel buildings and incomprehensible Finnish language in Helsinki and the Little Mermaid in the harbor in wonderful Copenhagen. Here are a few quotes from *centrics*:

I love the beautiful scenery all through Scandinavia. The history of the area is very interesting, and they have developed a culture I admire. The people are consistently friendly and accommodating to tourists.
Retired male 60,
Longmont, CO

Norway's scenery is breathtaking. We found it easy traveling throughout the country, meeting very friendly people. Everything is clean, there is minimal hassle with customs, the food is great. I'd come back!
Senior engineer, male, 52,
Reading, MA

Venturers

A couple of *venturers* used the word "adventure" in describing their vacation in Scandinavia. They can travel past the Arctic Circle to the farthest north, see the sun shine at midnight, become acquainted with the Laplanders, a distinctly different culture within Scandinavia. All Scandinavian countries offer plenty of opportunity for outdoor sports, especially cross country skiing, hiking, fishing and anything to do with boats. The cities provide museums, theatre, art, and all the comforts that a weary *venturer* could want as a change from his or her adventures! Following are some of their comments.

In Finland, where we go gets us away from all the traffic and commercial development. There is nobody to tell you what you should be doing, just the tranquil beauty of the lake and forest.
Male teacher, 39,
Storrs Mansfield, CT

What terrific people! The food and scenery are both great and I enjoy the skiing of the cross-country variety.
Retired female, 62,
Grants Pass, OR

WHAT PEOPLE LIKE ABOUT SCANDINAVIA

Dependables	**Centrics**	**Venturers**

Dependables	Centrics	Venturers
Norway is especially beautiful in the spring. The sightseeing is lovely, the people are friendly. It seems that development is well controlled. **70-year-old retired male, Miami, FL**	*Summer is a great time to visit Sweden. The countryside is just beautiful that time of year.* **Male CPA, 63, Altadena, CA**	*I like the archipelago of Stockholm, where the Swedes go to escape. There is no commercial development.* **Woman teacher, 47, Newtown Square, PA**
People are hospitable and friendly, and there is a feeling of safety. Everything is very beautiful. Even the cities are surrounded by water, and everything looks clean and prosperous. **Homemaker, 61, Indianapolis, IN**	*Traveling around Scandinavia was easy to do and gave us a variety of scenic options, charming urban and rural settings. There are a lot of interesting activities and things to do.* **Retired female, 72, Guilford, CT**	*The Scandinavian countries are different from anywhere else in Europe. They have the most beautiful scenery, the most interesting history and culture, the nicest people with the best attitude and the most charming cities, without being "cute" or "touristy."* **General partner, male, 54, Phoenix, AZ**

Some places are so unusual and offer such unique experiences that it's hard to describe in print. It sounds like Scandinavia works a special magic that must be experienced in person.

Ontario

#19 RATING: ★★★★

Centrics	Venturers	Dependables
8	8	7

Ontario is the most Americanized of the Canadian provinces.

The UN dubbed Toronto the world's most multi-cultural city.

The Bata Shoe Museum (Toronto)has the moon boots worn by Buzz Aldrin.

Sumptuous lobster suppers are a Prince Edward Island tradition.

In winter, thousands of Ottawans skate to work on frozen Rideau Canal.

Travelers select Ontario as one of three Canadian destinations to finish in the top 25 (British Columbia and Quebec are the others). This is quite a tribute to our northern neighbor, whose vacation destinations have in common a clean, attractive appearance and a feeling that you'll be safe regardless of where you wander. Those issues come up often when travelers list what's important, and Toronto makes many Americans wish that our cities could be as inviting to visitors. You know the feeling when you visit a place that is dirty and run down, or one where you fear for your safety when you walk the streets.

The people who choose Ontario generally divide between those who like the principal city of Toronto and those who choose its more rural recreation areas. Next door to Toronto, Niagara Falls, the longtime "honeymoon city" remains a popular place for all vacationers.

Toronto, Canada's largest city, is a hub for both commerce and culture in Canada. While it reflects the British heritage of its mother country, it also claims almost the greatest ethnic diversity of any city in North America, counting in its population large communities of Italians, Asians, East Indians, Greeks, Portuguese, Ukrainians, Germans and native Americans. Visitors say that Toronto has all the excitement of a large, multicultural city, the charm and hospitality of English tradition and the architectural diversity and immaculate appearance that rival any city in North America. American visitors feel especially entertained by Toronto's underground city, an entire network of stores, restaurants, offices and other businesses linked by subway stops. It's possible to avoid bad weather by staying below-ground for days!

Ontario covers many square miles and allows active travelers to find many opportunities for recreation, especially on its lakes and rivers. Those who seek solitude enjoy the tranquillity of Ontario's unspoiled wilderness areas where wide open spaces and natural beauty refresh and renew tired urban souls. Although all three personality types indicate a solid interest in Ontario, its visitors consist of largely *centrics*, with those who like Toronto leaning to the dependable side. Those who travel farther afield, to the countryside are *venturers*.

Polar Bear Express

Fishing

Backpacking

Cross-country Skiing

London

Storybook Gardens

CN Tower

Hockey Hall of Fame

Nightlife

Wonderland

Hudson Bay

MANITOBA

Fort Seven

Big Trout Lake

ONTARIO

Kenora

Thunder Bay

Sault Ste. M

Lake Superior

Lake Michigan

Vacation Places Rated

Ontario

★ ★ ★ ★

Actives

Mellows

All

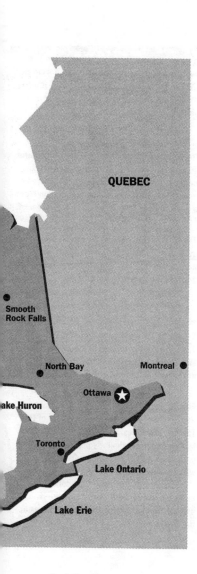

QUEBEC

Smooth Rock Falls

North Bay   Montreal ●

Ottawa ☆

ake Huron

Toronto

Lake Ontario

Lake Erie

Hiking

Algonquin Provincia Park

Shopping

Museums

Canoeing

Harbourfront

Niagara Falls

Cable Cars

MetroZoo

Helicopter Rides

WHAT TO DO IN ONTARIO

Actives	Mellows
1 Niagara Falls is best viewed from the Ontario side, and there are some venturesome viewing methods for daring travelers. You can take an incline railway, a helicopter ride or an aerocar (cable car) that is guaranteed to make you dizzy.	To orient yourself in Toronto, scan it from the CN Tower that dominates the skyline. It's one of the tallest structures in the world and provides an incomparable view of the city.
2 Algonquin Provincial Park is a wildlife sanctuary at the headwaters of five major rivers. Near the highway, the park is well-developed, but the farther regions are dedicated to hikers and canoers and there are no motor vehicles allowed.	Harbourfront on Lake Ontario near downtown Toronto is a complex of cultural and crafts centers, restaurants and shops that is a mecca for sightseers and shoppers. You'll get a good feel for Toronto's role as a major port.
3 Railroads still connect many communities in Canada, and are important to commercial interests. For an interesting day trip, take the Polar Bear Express from Cochrane (a mining and lumbering center) to Moosonee, where the Hudson Bay Company established a trading post in the 17th century.	The Hockey Hall of Fame is a must-see for even casual fans of the sport. It's an excellent museum of its kind, and of course, hockey is part of Canada's national culture.
4 You can fish for bass in the same waters as Franklin Delano Roosevelt at the North Channel of Lake Huron. Or, hire an Ojibwa guide to take you to the watersheds north of Geraldton for a more rugged experience.	Especially for children in Toronto: The Metro Zoo is one of the largest in the world, and Wonderland, Canada's major theme park is not far out of the city.
5 Algonquin National Park is the place for a myriad of outdoor recreation, notably canoeing. It also provides backpacking trails, wildlife observation and cross-country skiing, so it's a great place to visit any time of year.	Finally, a change of pace from Toronto: London is a lovely city situated on a fork of the Thames River (yes, we're still in Canada). Residents are particularly proud of their parks and gardens, and if you're traveling with children, Storybook Gardens is a small theme park just for them. Visit some of the many museums, take a cruise on the river, and see one of the theatrical productions at the Grand Theatre.

For further information, contact:

Ontario Travel
Eaton Centre
220 Yonge Street
Toronto, Ontario M5B 2H1 Canada
☎ (800) 668-2746

WHAT PEOPLE LIKE ABOUT ONTARIO

Centric-Dependables

Ontario is a good place for family vacations, whether you go for urban culture in Toronto, rustic luxury at a lakeside resort or parking your RV at a park campsite. Everyone speaks English, transportation is easy, and the people I spoke to say they perceive less crime in Ontario's cities than in the U.S. *Centric-dependables* particularly enjoy the wide variety of things to do in Toronto: museums, universities, the parliament buildings and other distinctive edifices, the zoo, Chinatown, wonderful restaurants and shops, and even theme parks that invite visitors to explore and be entertained. Read some of the comments from *centric-dependables*.

In Toronto, there are always a lot of things to do for the entire family, by day or by night. It's never boring and we always do something different.
Human resource manager, male, 38, Canton, NY

I particularly enjoy visiting Toronto for the nightlife and the shopping.
35-year-old female government employee, Detroit, MI

There is good winter skiing in Kempenfeldt Bay, and it's very pretty, too. The town nearby always seems to have a lot of good local crafts .
Male banker, 55, St. Paul, MN

Toronto is cosmopolitan, metropolitan, diversified, friendly and safe, and reasonably priced.
Sales rep, male, Marietta, GA

Centric-Venturers

Ontario is a large province, offering a lot of options for vacationers. *Centric-venturers* may well spend a day or two in Toronto or Niagara Falls, then head for one of the national parks or conservation areas to fish, hike, water ski or just enjoy nature. In fact, you can take Yonge Street from downtown Toronto 1142 miles across southern Ontario to the Manitoba border, and see all the characteristics that make Ontario special: farmland, lake country, mining districts and fur trapping country. The *Guinness Book of Records* says Yonge Street is the longest in the world, and they'll get no argument here. Read the following comments from *centric venturers* for their feelings.

Red Lake, Ontario equals peace and tranquillity. It's the closest thing to heaven that I've found. You get the impression that you are standing in a place where no one else has ever stood.
Self employed male, 26, Traer, IA

We rented a nice cottage within easy reach of several lakes. I enjoyed water-skiing, swimming and power boating, beautiful trees, beautiful scenery.
Female controller, 40, Indianapolis, IN

The communities in the south are like little bits of England with a North American feel - they even have English names, Stratford and Blenheim, and so forth. It's very charming.
Female department administrator, 39, Madison, WI

Cleanliness, culture and climate, that's Canada, and that's Ontario!
AIDS Educator, male, 34, South Charleston, WVA

Canada is really a good neighbor to provide us with so many diversified vacation spots. Next time you need a change, head north for Ontario and discover its urban and wilderness pleasures.

Greece

Residents of Mykonos believe pelicans bring good luck.
Corfu has more than 4 million olive trees.
Hippocrates lived and taught at Kos.
Bouzouki revelers pay a hefty price for broken plates.
Sunset at Oia is one of the most romantic anywhere.

Once upon a very long time ago, gods and goddesses took an active role in the world of humans, interfering in their lives, deciding the course of wars, occasionally granting a favor and even mating with humans to produce demigods like Hercules. It all happened in Greece, which produced not only this fantastic and well-loved mythology, but became the birthplace of all western civilization. "…nothing moves in this world which is not Greek in its origin," said Sir Henry James Main of Cambridge.

Most of today's travelers don't go there to study Homer or Socrates, but the monuments to its glorious past add to Greece's strong appeal and popularity. The people I interviewed speak warmly of the weather, hot in the summer and mild in the winter, with lovely springs and falls. "It sure beats Omaha in February," is one man's opinion. You can see by the degree of interest scores that Greece is a favorite destination for *venturers* and *centrics* who like to explore the many beautiful islands that flank the mainland, and who find cruising around the Aegean stimulating to the mind and relaxing to the body. If you haven't been to Greece, here are three images to pique your interest: 1) white-on-white buildings profiled against stark mountains, blue sky and water, 2) magnificent architecture and statues recalling Greece's ancient glory days, 3) sipping strong Greek coffee or a glass of retsina after a Mediterranean meal at a cafe overlooking the sea and ships on Santorini.

It's idyllic.

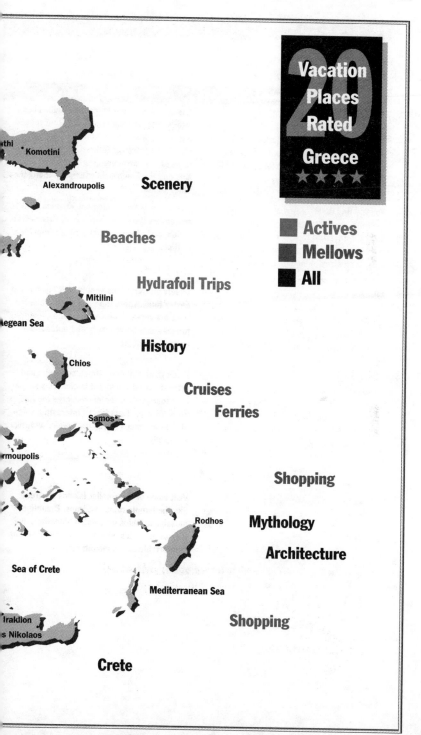

WHAT TO DO IN GREECE

S

Actives	Mellows
1 If you are based in Athens, take a day trip by hydrofoil to Sounion for fabulous scenery and the Temple of Poseidon. Another choice is a shorter trip to Eleusis, among whose awesome ruins the ancient mysteries were celebrated for thousands of years.	The complex on the Acropolis reaches back into legend, and undergoes constant rebuilding. This is where the goddess Athena won the right to be patron of Athens. You must see the ruins of the Parthenon, the Theater of Dionysius and the Erechtheum Temple, among the other sights.
2 You will find dining a real adventure in all but the most sophisticated restaurants. Accompany the chef into the kitchen to choose your own seafood and watch it prepared. Be daring—even strange looking items are delicious.	The National Archaeological Museum in Athens covers the entire expanse of Greek civilization, and offers special exhibits from time to time.
3 Visit the Oracle at Delphi, as did many of the ancient Greeks, for incomprehensible answers to your questions, or for a spiritual experience unlike any other. Some like to climb the hill to view the plain below by moonlight.	Observant Christians should visit Mykonos at Easter time, where the services and celebrations are spectacular performances, featuring processions, firecrackers and outdoor services at midnight.
4 Minoan civilization really began in Crete, to which Athens paid tribute for many years. Legend has it that the incident of Theseus' slaying of the Minotaur at the Palace of Knossos broke Crete's control, but earthquakes and fires probably contributed also. Take the ferry for maximum pleasure, or fly to see the ruins and the excellent Archaeological Museum.	If you want authentic Greek souvenirs and artwork, avoid the street hucksters and ask your tour guide or hotel concierge for suggestions. Athens offers lots of interesting shopping experiences for crafts, jewelry and rugs especially.
5 Epidauros hosts a world famous drama festival each summer. Join 50,000 other theater buffs or historians for Greek drama at its purest.	Visit some of the smaller islands for treats like the temple ruins at Samos, Byzantine mosaics at Chios or isolated hideaways like Kassos and Tilos, still primitive but providing comfortable accommodations.

For further information, contact:

National Tourist Organization of Greece
645 Fifth Avenue
New York, NY 10022
☎ (212) 421-5777

WHAT PEOPLE LIKE ABOUT GREECE

Dependables

Centrics

Venturers

Considering its familiar history and the availability of cruises, it seems strange that *dependables* do not visit Greece. The few that I could find enjoyed their vacation very much, as the following quote will tell you:

Centrics like Greece for all of the above reasons. The fact that it can be inexpensive compared to other European destinations adds to its attractions. Whether they cruised or tried local hotels and restaurants, visitors tell me that they were pleased with the price-value ratio.

Sightseers find an overwhelming amount to see and do on the mainland and the islands, and if your interest lies in ancient history, you're in heaven—or Mt. Olympus. Greek people are warm and friendly, say *centrics*, and the modern culture is still exotic enough to charm strangers, along with the warm weather and beautiful islands. Read on for comments from *centrics:*

Venturers seem to take a quick look at Athens, then head for the hills or the water. Where there are mountains and islands, there are, respectively, hiking and watersports. *Venturers* take breaks from sightseeing by scuba diving, fishing and exploratory walks in the hills. The pace of modern life slows down outside of Athens, and traveling through this beautiful land with its many reminders of ancient and mysterious civilizations puts life into another dimension for a few sunny days, at least. Read on for some comments from *venturers.*

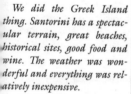

We did the Greek Island thing. Santorini has a spectacular terrain, great beaches, historical sites, good food and wine. The weather was wonderful and everything was relatively inexpensive.
Mid-level manager, male, 29, San Francisco, CA

The Mediterranean area around Greece has the most excellent climate, and a relaxing, low key atmosphere. We enjoyed swimming and very good food. People are friendly—many speak English—and the exchange rate is favorable.
Male physician, 58, Amherst, MA

I love cruising everywhere, because it's no hassle, no packing. Cruising the Greek Islands was a fabulous vacation. The islands are beautiful and mysterious, and everyone is charming and friendly.
Part-time office worker, 39, Cincinnati, OH

I love the hot weather in the summertime and the sound of a foreign language. Greece holds thrilling historical impact. The preparation (reading materials, etc.) was wonderful in itself.
Homemaker, 57, Lake Oswego, OR

The simplicity of life there is so appealing, the beauty and the history behind it, the people who live there. I could live there!
Female accountant, 39, Laguna Niguel, CA

WHAT PEOPLE LIKE ABOUT GREECE

Dependables

Centrics

I like ruins and ancient history. Visiting Santorini, Rhodes and Crete was a very special experience. Access to all these places is easy and comfortable. Most important was the peacefulness of the islands.
Saleswoman, 34, Haverstraw, NY

Greece is so exciting, historically and artistically.
Female graduate student, Princeton, NJ

Mykonos was unforgettable: the whitewashed buildings against the blue sky and water. We enjoyed the nice beaches, good food and relaxing atmosphere.
Male government employee, 35, Bensalem, PA

Venturers

Perissa Beach is clean and perfect for outdoor activities. It has a healthy atmosphere, excellent for exercise and is very relaxing.
29-year-old free-lance journalist, female, New York, NY

I enjoyed the remoteness of some of the rural islands, typically reached only by boat. Everywhere we went we met friendly people and had great food. All of Greece, even Athens, has a special mystique.
Senior executive, male, 41, Duluth, GA

Mykonos is pretty, exotic and not terribly expensive, yet cosmopolitan. I like that it's a "walking" as opposed to automobile atmosphere.
Male attorney, 44, Kenner, LA

The glory that was Greece is still there for you to discover, and present day Greece clearly offers its own special attractions as well.

Italy

#21 RATING: ★★★★

Centrics	Venturers	Dependables
8	10	7

The word "university" was invented in Bologna.

Florence is known as the "Athens of Italy" for its art collections.

The Leaning Tower of Pisa leans 17 ft. off the perpendicular.

Italians eat pizza with knives and forks.

Venice has 400 bridges spanning its 114 canals.

Boot-shaped Italy enjoys a fortuitous combination of ambience and attractions that entices travelers to its sunny shores. As you travel from north to south, the country unrolls a variety of landscapes, climates, customs and cuisines that provide warm and lovely memories for visitors. Italians are not only friendly, they are animated and they draw people in to whatever little drama is being played. Few countries enjoy a richer historical background, and few can boast its wealth of art, architecture and music. When I talk with people about Italy, I also get the idea that they eat and drink their way through its varied regions. Only France rivals Italy in the number of mentions about delicious meals and good wines.

To those fortunate tourists who have time to visit several parts of the country, Italy presents a nice combination of cities, small towns and mountains in the alpine region rolling gently out to sunny beaches on the Italian Riviera. It appears that people spend more of their time in the area north of Rome. Florence and Venice garner the most comments as city destinations, and are also used as bases from which to explore the surrounding countryside. The Italian Riviera bordering France draws a few votes, as does the Amalfi Coast south of Naples. Florence claims the title of the cradle of the Renaissance, and anyone who has seen its magnificent museums and public art won't argue. Venice, which was an independent kingdom for many years, weaves its own unique spell as tourists float from one beautiful site to another along its famous canals.

Milan

Skiing

Shopping

Florence

Leaning Tower of Pisa

Ligurian Sea

Art/Museums

Olive Groves

Boat Trips to Islands

Bolzano

Sondrio

Trento

Porden

•Aosta Varese Bergamo Tre
                Vicenza
         Milan Verona Vicenza Venice
Vercelli

Turin
       Alessandria Parma Ferrara
  Asti

Cuneo Savona Genoa Modena Bologna

Imperia
                    SAN MARI
                Florence
         • Pisa

                         Perug

Elba Grosseto

         T
       Viterbo

Corsica
(FRANCE)

                    VATICA
                    CITY

                    Tyrrhenian S

•Sassari

       Nuor   Rome
                 Naple
Oristano

                 Vatican Ci
Cagliari

Pompeii   Tra

Tuscany   Strait of Sicily

N

W FIELDING E
   WORLDWIDE

S

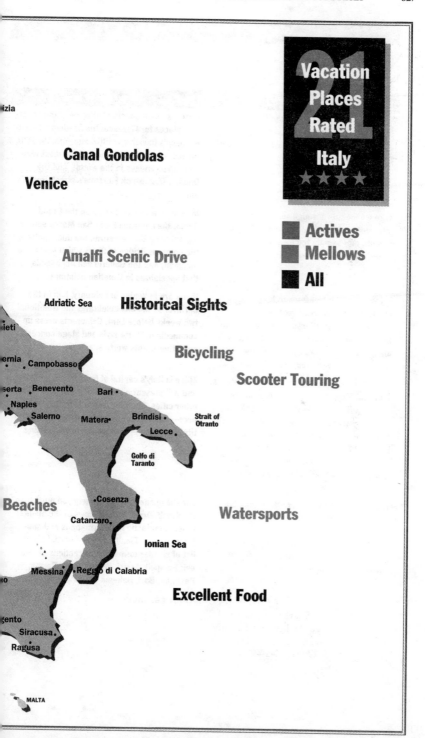

WHAT TO DO IN ITALY

Actives	Mellows
1 For winter sports, head for the Alps or the Dolomites. The skiing is great and the prices are somewhat less, by comparison, than other European ski areas.	Here's a quick checklist of some of the 'must-see' places for Florence: the Academia (Michelangelo's David), the Uffizi Museum, the Pitti Palace, Ponte Vecchio (one of the most photographed bridges in the world), and the Duomo, from which Florence's streets radiate.
2 Take a wine tour through some of Italy's premier vineyards south of Florence. Sip your Chianti, and sample the food, at San Casciano, Siena and thereabouts.	In Venice: a vaporetto ride on the Grand Canal, the immense Plaza San Marco spreading out from the cathedral, the ducal palace, the dolorous Bridge of Sighs which leads to a dungeon, and the Gallerie dell Accademia that specializes in Venetian paintings.
3 If you want to travel through Italy in an unusual way, ask about renting a motorscooter or taking a bicycle tour. You should be in reasonably good shape for the latter, but many organized tours accompany the cyclists with a van for when your legs give out.	If you are in Venice in February, join in the Carnival as the city celebrates the traditional two weeks before Lent. Celebrants dress up commedia dell'arte style and stage concerts and other events worth sharing.
4 Travelers in our survey did not visit southern Italy and Sicily as often as Rome and Northern Italy. However, I encourage people who want a total experience of this country to visit the more rural south, where they'll see the beautiful Bay of Naples, sun-drenched olive and citrus groves, and enjoy heartier Mediterranean cuisine than is found farther north. It's usually less crowded, as well.	Milan is Italy's capital of finance and industry, and will present a more modern visage than other cities. Shop for Italian high fashions here—don't count on bargains, but the quantity and range of choices are overwhelming.
5 You also might like to get off the mainland and take a boat to one or more of Italy's nearby islands. Sardinia and Corsica, Elba and Capri each offer historical significance, natural beauty or special charm that will enrich your experience.	For sheer, spectacular scenery you must take the Amalfi Drive, with its views of the Mediterranean, fantastic rock formations and subtropical flora. Finally, here's a partial checklist of smaller towns with attractions of interest: Pompeii, Assisi, Verona, Pisa, Parma, Positano, Bari, Bologna (and many more).

For further information, contact:

Italian Government Travel Office
630 Fifth Avenue, Suite 1565
New York, NY 10111
☎ (212) 245-4822

WHAT PEOPLE LIKE ABOUT ITALY

Dependables

Dependables are more typical Italian tourists. They enjoy seeing famous art and architecture and historical sites. It's easy to arrange transportation to see the country by car or train, and there are many choices of accommodations, from elegant hotels to seaside resorts to small pensiones. Providers of all kinds of group tours exist for travelers who enjoy having the details handled by someone else, or who have special interests such as food and wine, or archaeology. *Dependables* also demonstrate their enthusiasm in their comments.

This is a wonderful country to visit with its delightful people, terrific food, historic sights, and lovely countryside. I enjoyed speaking Italian and drinking Italian wines.
Female department manager, 48, Washington, D.C.

Italy was the seat of the Renaissance and is the most interesting and stimulating of places.
Self-employed female, 44, Lyle, MN

Centrics

It's hard not to sound repetitive, but all the personality types, *centrics* included, visit Italy for similar reasons. They study its ancient history, the importance of the Renaissance, and its involvement in Europe's wars. They also enjoy Italian personalities and Italian foods and wines. Several speak about family ties in Italy, familiarity with the language and about the feeling of discovering their roots. As they move in and out of the larger metropolises, *centrics* talk a lot about interesting local color, the charm of the countryside and the attractive life-styles they want to experience more intimately. There is nothing as satisfying as telling a friend at home, "In Italy, they do it this way..." Read on for comments from *centrics.*

I love the culture of Tuscany, the grandeur of the countryside and Florence, and also the people and the wine! It's also easy to visit other interesting areas of Italy from there.
Male investor, 756, Geneva, IL

The Amalfi Coast has so much charm, it's almost illegal. We stayed in a wonderful hotel, enjoyed the mountain scenery, great Mediterranean restaurants and delicious wine and cheese.
Self-employed male, 65, Ft. Lauderdale, FL

Venturers

Italy attracts all personality types but *venturers* like it most. They appreciate its bountiful scenery and especially enjoy interacting with their Italian hosts at every stop they make. Think of the pleasures that go with skiing the Italian Alps, walking through Florence to enjoy its art and history, spending a few days in the country to appreciate the relaxing life-style of quiet villages, and sampling the foods and wines that vary by each region through which you travel. Visitors do not come to Italy primarily for its recreational sport, but active *venturers* can ski, enjoy water sports in the breathtaking lake district (unfortunately, they should inquire about pollution levels), and tour parts of Italy by bicycle whenever they desire. You can catch the enthusiasm of *venturers* from their comments:

All of Italy is beautiful, but Venice has a distinctive culture and lots of artistic events that interest me. It's also very romantic, with so much to see and do. I need to find a permanent companion to go with!
Male physician, 60, Lake Forest, CA

We took the Orient Express into Venice, and the whole experience was romantic and exciting. It's a beautiful city with great food.
Male attorney, 44, Davie, FL

WHAT PEOPLE LIKE ABOUT ITALY

Dependables

A tour of Italy offers everything a traveler could want. There wasn't much I didn't like!

Desktop publishing specialist, New York, NY

Capri is romantic, gorgeous and alive!

Female attorney, 38, Los Altos Hills, CA

I especially loved Assisi. Everything is connected to St. Francis. The Italians in this area are wonderful and so are the food and scenery.

60-year-old senior corporate executive, Fort Wayne, IN

Centrics

The people know how to live and enjoy life in Italy. We should learn from them.

Male accountant, 68, Wayne, NJ

Venice is like stepping back in time. I enjoyed the unhurried pace and the beauty all around. That trip fulfilled a dream, my lifelong attraction to the city.

Senior corporate executive, female, 44, Flushing, NY

We love the great food and warm people in Northern Italy. It was easy to get to, and there is lots to see and do, We did some hiking and enjoyed the wonderful variety of small towns and big cities.

Self-employed female, 41, Chicago, IL

Venturers

Florence is the soul of Italy. and you must always visit the soul of a country.

Self employed female, 38, San Antonio, TX

Venice has unusual historic sites and an atmosphere of adventure. It invites you to do things, to come alive!

Male attorney, 45, Arlington, VA

Tuscany is a wonderful combination of quaintness on the one hand and cosmopolitan cities on the other. Florence, with all it has to offer, is small enough to do a lot of walking, therefore it's easy to get to know. You can find everything you ever wanted on a trip when you visit Italy.

Female supervisor, 35, New York, NY

Samuel Johnson, that famous Englishman of letters, seems to have an opinion about everything, and Boswell quotes him about Italy: "A man who has not been in Italy is always conscious of an inferiority. Don't let that happen to you. Plan a trip soon to experience that magical combination of attractions and culture that make Italy a great vacation destination.

Paris

#22 RATING: ★★★★

Centrics	Venturers	Dependables
8	9	7

The Eiffel Tower is 984 ft. tall with a 69 ft. TV antenna on top.

Sacre Coeur at Montmarte has one of the world's largest ringable bells.

Chateau de Vincennes is the only fortified castle in Paris.

Louis XIV's jealousy over Vaux Le Vicomte led to Versailles' construction.

The bodies of Voltaire and Rousseau are in the Pantheon's crypt.

Ahh, Paris, the City of Light. Paris, the moveable feast, Paris when it sizzles. Travelers surely love Paris. Lots of people visit it and afterwards they talk about it in terms used for no other city. It's romantic and it's beautiful, with magnificent architecture. Its food and restaurants are superb, its museums are incomparable. The historical sights overwhelm you. About the Parisians, there remains some doubt. Many visitors find them delightful (probably those who speak French), but one professional woman remarked that she liked "everything, except the French."

Our three personality types echo each other about what they like. Food and restaurants receive the most frequent mentions. The beauty of the city and its historical significance come next, followed by the number and quality of museums, sightseeing in general, and Paris' romantic ambience. Although it's a large, sophisticated, international city, most visitors find a special corner of Paris that they love and remember. It could be a sidewalk cafe, flower stalls on the Left Bank of the Seine, a boulangerie with wonderful bread to be munched at a nearby park, a street of shops that other tourists haven't found, a wonderful little hotel—all these contribute to the Paris experience.

The Louvre

Galleries

· Charleville-Mezieres

·Metz

Strasbourg·

Tennis

royes   · Epinal

Chaumont

· Vesoul

Dijon·

Lons-le-Saunier

·Macon

· Bourg-en-Bresse

Lyon·   · Chambery

·Etienne

Grenoble

· Valence

nde

Nice·

Montpellier   Marseille
Toulon

Gulf of Lions

nan

22 Vacation Places Rated

Paris

★★★★

■ **Actives**
■ **Mellows**
■ **All**

People Watching

Sidewalk Cafes

Bois de Boulogne

Arc de Triomph

Tuileries
Fashion Shows

Palace of Versailles

Left Bank

Jogging

Nightlife

WHAT TO DO IN PARIS

Actives	Mellows
1 Two of the most famous monuments in Paris encourage active travelers to climb to the top for fabulous views of the city. The Eiffel Tower on the Left Bank and the Arc de Triomph on the Right Bank provide camera buffs with great shots, and each has an interesting history as well.	Everyone plans to sample the famous museums of Paris, and so they should. Just a word of advice about the larger ones, like the Louvre: don't try to "do" the whole place in one day. It's overwhelming, and you won't appreciate what you see. Obtain a current guide to the exhibits, then plan 2-4 hour visits at one time, depending on your interest level.
2 The French are especially fond of tennis and bicycling. If you time your visit for late May and early June, try for a seat at the French Open at Roland Garros Stadium. One man actually listed Roland Garros as one of his favorite things in Paris. The famous Tour de France bicycle race ends on the Champs-Elysees in July, with lots of festivities.	Get away from traffic and tour buses in the Tuileries, near Place de la Concorde. The pace slows down here, and you'll want to admire the gardens, watch children sail their boats, and have a snack at one of the cafes. There are a couple of smaller museums to look at, also.
3 The Left Bank is traditionally the more intellectual, 'counter-culture' part of Paris. You'll enjoy strolling through the famous Latin Quarter which houses medieval university buildings of the Sorbonne, wonderful old churches, plus jazz clubs and other night spots for night owls.	If you can possibly wangle a ticket to a Paris couture show, don't let anything stop you. This a unique performance that no one even mildly interested in fashion should miss.
4 At the western end of Paris is a wonderful refuge from the hectic mid-city life called the Bois de Boulogne. Stroll the woods and parks, jog up and down the alleyways, and find lots of attractions for children, if you have any with you.	At Place de la Bastille, pay tribute to the storming of the old prison in 1790 that ignited the Revolution. If you happen to be there on July 14, join the crowds who dance and celebrate the occasion each year. For a different experience, attend a performance of the opera at the Bastille Opera House in a very modern building that contrasts sharply with most of the architecture tourists see.
5 Just outside Paris is the Palace of Versailles, erected by Louis XIV, the Sun King, to his greater glory. It is almost too popular, but it's also too amazing too miss. Try to time your visit at the least crowded hours.	As with museums, there are an abundance of fine churches to be seen in Paris. The most famous are Notre Dame on the Isle de la Cite in the Seine, and Sacre Coeur in Montmartre. The village of Montmartre itself has a bohemian, artistic heritage that you'll enjoy.

For further information, contact:

French Government Tourist Office
610 Fifth Avenue, Suite 222
New York, NY 10020
☎ (212) 767-1125

WHAT PEOPLE LIKE ABOUT PARIS

Dependables

Centrics

Venturers

Dependables like touring the sights of Paris, very often with a group of other tourists. They've heard all their lives about the Revolution, Napoleon, the Eiffel Tower and the Louvre, and find it thrilling to see history come to life for them. Interestingly, *dependables* actually compliment the people of Paris more than the other personalities.

Night spots and shopping in Paris create vivid memories among *centrics* when they recall their vacations. After all, how can one return home without seeing a show and purchasing at least a small item of Parisian couture? This group talks less about the beauty of the city, and more about its ambience, culture, the excitement, and the romance and charm of the surroundings. The people of Paris earn less praise from *centrics* than we have seen in other destinations, but it's certainly no hindrance to them as they explore the sights, sounds and tastes of the city. Read on for comments from *centrics*:

Venturers love Paris! It has all the diversity they could ever want: a very foreign culture with a language that sounds exotic to the ear, paintings and artwork that attract and please your eyes, cuisine that quickens your taste buds, and perfumes of Frenchwomen that surround your nostrils. You can discover Paris best by walking its neighborhoods, which suits *venturers'* need for activity and enables them to get closer to Paris' culture. Here are comments from *venturers*:

Our trip to Paris reminded me of the 50s. We walked a lot and took public transportation and felt very safe everywhere. The old architecture contributes to the atmosphere of the city.
Homemaker, 53, Suffolk, VA

The excitement and atmosphere of the city is so stimulating. I loved seeing in person things that I had always heard about, or only seen in pictures.
Male teacher, 29, White Plains, NY

There is no place like this city—it's unique. I love walking the different districts. There is a wide choice of hotels and restaurants, wonderful museums and public art, and charming parks.
Homemaker, 70, Mill Valley, CA

Paris is endlessly beautiful and interesting. It is truly 'a moveable feast.' We felt that people were helpful—if you are polite, they are polite in turn.
Male teacher, 57, Bronx, NY

Paris is the quintessential European city, beautiful and cultural It's world class!
Female attorney, 28, Palo Alto, CA

An awful lot of European cultural history is socked away in all the museums in Paris.
Military male, 31, Sumter, SC

It's historically exciting, very romantic, different, enchanting, full of terrific museums, and two wonderful churches, Notre Dame and Sacre Coeuer.
Female office worker 36, Columbus, OH

I found it more pleasurable than Italy, that was my previous favorite. The standards are higher and doing business is more "up front".
Retired male, 62, Novato, CA

It's the most scenic city in the world. Just watching the people and the customs is fascinating.
58-year-old male in government, Ocean City, MD

WHAT PEOPLE LIKE ABOUT PARIS

Dependables

I was so impressed with the beautiful hotels and restaurants.

Homemaker, 33, St. Louis, MO

There are so many things to see and do in this very beautiful city. It has wonderful hotels and restaurants, and many sights to see. I was surprised that most people seem to speak English.

Retired female, 51, Atlanta, GA

Centrics

Sometimes you hesitate to approach someone (a Parisian) in a shop, or ask a question, because they seem so dismissive and uninterested. You just learn to ignore it and not let it spoil anything, because everything else is wonderful.

Executive vice president, female, 44, River Edge, NJ

I was a French major and visiting there gives me a chance to practice. It's a beautiful city, full of history and culture. I became engaged to my husband there, so it's very romantic for me.

Underwriter, 40, Bartlett, IL

Venturers

Everything is an art to the Parisians.

Homemaker, 40, Riverside, CA

It sounds as if you haven't lived unless you've seen Paris. If you don't make the trip, you will miss an outstandingly beautiful city, possibly the greatest cultural experience in Europe, and a very good time as well.

Spain

#23 RATING: ★★★

Centrics	Venturers	Dependables
8	9	6

Alcazar in Segovia looks like a fairy tale castle.

Bullfighting's popularity is in decline.

The tomb of Columbus is housed in Seville's Cathedral.

Andalusia is famous for its cold soup, gazpacho.

Granada has a large gypsy population.

The 1992 Olympic Games reintroduced the world to Barcelona and the rest of Spain. Plenty of people didn't need the reminder—they know that Spain offers a great vacation destination, full of history, exciting big cities and beautiful scenery, sunny weather and interesting food and drink. Travelers to Spain also reveal one other important advantage: it's a much more economical vacation than those in most European countries.

Spain's presence in the world has been somewhat muted in the 20th century (with the notable exception of the Civil War), but its illustrious past comes to life for tourists. While the rest of the world struggled through the dark Middle Ages, Spain's literary, scientific and artistic light shone brightly thanks to the unique combination of Spanish, Moorish and Jewish influences. Spain led all nations in exploration of the New World, and her empire and influence remained strong until this century. Wonderful art, architecture and other memorabilia remain throughout the country to recall these golden days for visitors. Those who want to relax on a warm, sunny beach can take their choice on several coasts (the Costa del Sol is often mentioned by the people I interviewed), or hop a boat across the Gulf of Valencia to Ibiza or Majorca.

Altimera Caves

Horseback Riding

Golf

Museums

Galleries

Windmills near Toledo

Nightlife

Monastery of Montserrat

Running of Bulls

Bullfighting

mplona

ANDORRA

. Huesca   Gerona

goza   .Lleida
        Barcelona .
   Tarragona .   **Boating**

.Teruel   Balearic
               Sea   Minorca
a
Castellon .   Palma Majorca
de la Plana
               Balearic
Valencia`   Islands   **Majorca**
cete   Iviza
          Formentera   **Zoo**
Alicante .
a .   Mediterranean Sea

Flamenco Dancing

                                  Casinos

   The Prado

        Alhambra Palace

Beaches

     Gardens

23
Vacation
Places
Rated
Spain
★ ★ ★

Actives
Mellows
All

WHAT TO DO IN SPAIN

Actives	Mellows
1 Do the Hemingway thing and take in a bull-fight—it's part of the culture. Try to pick a top matador for the best experience. The season runs from March to October.	The Prado in Madrid is one of the foremost museums in the world, where you'll see paintings from the great Spanish artists like El Greco, Velasquez, and Goya in addition to works of Italian and Flemish masters. For contrast, take a ride to the Museo Picasso in Buitrago to inspect works of a modern Spaniard.
2 The Fiesta of San Fermin in July kick-starts by the running of the bulls in Pamplona. You can run, too, although tourists are discouraged because of the potential danger. Pamplona has some nice hotels and restaurants to sample if you need to beat a retreat.	Like bullfighting, flamenco is also part of Spanish culture, and very entertaining to watch. There are good clubs in both Madrid and Barcelona. Your hotel should be able to refer you to the best place.
3 The Spanish have a weakness for horses, and you can see part of the country on horseback yourself. Call the Parador Nacional de Gredos in Madrid, or ask your travel agent.	The Moors dominated the south of Spain for hundreds of years, and Granada houses the highlight of Muslim architecture, the Alhambra Palace. The Generalife Gardens alone are worth the visit, and the palace will move you most at sunset, but evokes great emotion any time.
4 Visit the island of Majorca. Take a ferry or steamer from Barcelona, and spend a couple of days on this recently upgraded island. Play golf, see a medieval jousting contest, and take the spooky boat ride on an underground lake at the Caves of Drach.	Barcelona offers many attractions. It's an important commercial port city trying to join the modern world while holding on to a thriving artistic and cultural life. Choose from many museums, a good zoo and aquarium, three nearby casinos.
5 Santander on Spain's northern coast is a cultural and museum center that is closest to the famous Altamira Caves, site of extensive prehistoric art. To see the paintings, you must apply months in advance, but it's a must-see if you have any interest in all.	About 30 miles from Barcelona is the famous Monastery of Montserrat, offering magnificent views and surrounded by strangely-formed mountains—yet another face that Spain can show.

For further information, contact:
The Spanish National Tourist Office
665 Fifth Avenue
New York, NY 10022
☎ (212) 759-8822

WHAT PEOPLE LIKE ABOUT SPAIN

Dependables

Centrics

Venturers

Spain continues to encourage tourist travel and has made efforts to control petty crime and hold down costs, which is appreciated by *dependables*. Another interesting effort is the parador system. The government has renovated castles and other historical buildings to serve as hotels and inns at a reasonable cost. Size and cost vary, service is usually local and sometimes less than professional, but cheerful. Spain's sunny weather, reasonable prices and a good variety of activities are all important to *dependables*, who offer the following comments:

Centrics add their voices in praise of Spain's life-style and atmosphere. Museums and city life in Madrid and Barcelona, the grandeur of the Moorish influence in Seville and Granada, the sunny, lively Costa del Sol, the orange groves in Valencia, the windmills near Toledo where Cervantes imagined Don Quixote practicing his swordplay—all these and more provide *centrics* with the sightseeing pleasures that they enjoy. It's a novelty to finish lunch late, take a siesta, do some more touring, and plan to dine as late as 9:30 or 10 PM, as is the Spanish habit. Late dinners often lead to a taste for nightlife and *centrics* mention the flamenco clubs in Barcelona, discos in Madrid and the Costa del Sol, plus several casinos in the larger cities. Some comments from *centrics* follow.

Venturers lead the pack in visiting Spain, as is often the case in Europe. *Centrics* are not far behind, and *dependables* are just beginning to find this Mediterranean country quite comfortable and entertaining. The variety of landscapes and cultures intrigue *venturers*, who could potentially ski the Pyrenees in the morning and loll in the sun on the Costa del Sol the same afternoon. *Venturers* like that the spirit of Spain is strong and distinctive. It comes not only from its proud past, but from its music and dance, especially flamenco, its lively food, the national drink of sherry, and the varied cultures (including Basque and Arabic) that are closely woven into Spain's through the centuries in many regions. Here are a few comments from *venturers*:

Spain is aesthetically and culturally beautiful. People are friendly the seafood is terrific and the accommodations are magnificent.

Retired female, 50, New York, NY

Tourists and natives mingle easily in Mijas. It's very quaint, with a gorgeous view of the Mediterranean.

Male supervisor, 49, Mead, CO

Spain has beautiful beaches and beautiful architecture. The food is delicious and most of the people are very friendly. I would call it a country of exciting nightlife and relaxing days.

Homemaker, 33, Pittsburgh, PA

What's important to me is that the people are warm and friendly, the culture is rich, especially in the southwest, and the whole country is very beautiful.

Male supervisor, 46, Redlands, CA

People make us feel very welcome throughout Spain. I understand the language and appreciate the culture. It's fun!

41-year-old male government employee, Rome, NY

I loved the beauty and serenity of the Alhambra. It looks like a place suspended in time, and I wish I could have spent more of my time there.

Female paralegal 41, Long Beach, NY

WHAT PEOPLE LIKE ABOUT SPAIN

Dependables	Centrics	Venturers
	I know a lot of local people and places throughout Spain. Thanks to relatives, I avoid the expense of hotels and am able to return there. It's really a nice country.	*The spirit of the country is very special. I was especially impressed with Barcelona as a pleasant urban environment.*
	Homemaker, 34, Valdosta, GA	**Self-employed male, 66, McLean, VA**
	The mixture of Spanish and Arabic culture in Malaga was fascinating. We had lovely accommodations, beautiful weather and enjoyed the seashore.	*What I remember most specifically are the women! Beautiful and vibrant! Also I enjoyed the nightclubs, the beach and the small racetrack outside of town. Finally, it's also very economical.*
	Female teacher, 60, Alexandria, IN	**Male accountant, 28, Circleville, OH**
		I loved everything in Marbella! The climate, the people, the sense of adventure. Everything feels different. It's affordable, too.
		Data processor, 37, Milford, MI

The Spanish poet Federico Garcia Lorca said, "In Spain, the dead are more alive than the dead of any other country in the world." I think that's one way of describing how important the past is to the present in this beautiful country that is waiting to be discovered by you.

Quebec

#24 RATING: ★★★

Centrics	Venturers	Dependables
7	8	5

Quebec is larger than Alaska and more than twice the size of Texas.
All city signs in Montreal are in French.
Montreal's French bread is considered the best on the continent.
The Citadel is the largest fort still guarded by troops in North America.
A whole underground city exists beneath Montreal.

There was a time when the French empire in North America stretched from Mexico to Canada, but the influence of France now concentrates in the Canadian province of Quebec. It may be a distant and lonely outpost of the mother country, but it is definitely and aggressively French! (Although a gastronome from Paris would shudder at the French Canadian habit of pouring maple syrup over anything edible). Visitors to Quebec who have an interest in genetics will observe the Gallic features (think Charles de Gaulle) on every other face they meet in the province, an indication of how well this community has stayed together and preserved its culture over the years.

Quebec is another destination favored by *venturers* and *centrics*, much less so by *dependables*. Those who choose it for a vacation head either for Quebec's main cities of Montreal and Quebec City, or to the outdoor recreation areas of the Laurentian Mountains and the Eastern Townships. The French and British fought for control of Canada in a battle on the Plain of Abraham near Quebec City that still has much historical significance (the British won, but the remaining French still maintain an identity with their homeland). Once a fortress, the old walled city of Quebec welcomes visitors through its gates to enjoy the cobbled walkways, quaint shops and wonderful French restaurants. In spring and summer, flower baskets hang from every lamppost in the city and every cafe spills out onto the sidewalk. Montreal is the bustling metropolis of this province, with rich traditions to go with its fine churches, universities and an underground city where people can live and carry out their business for days.

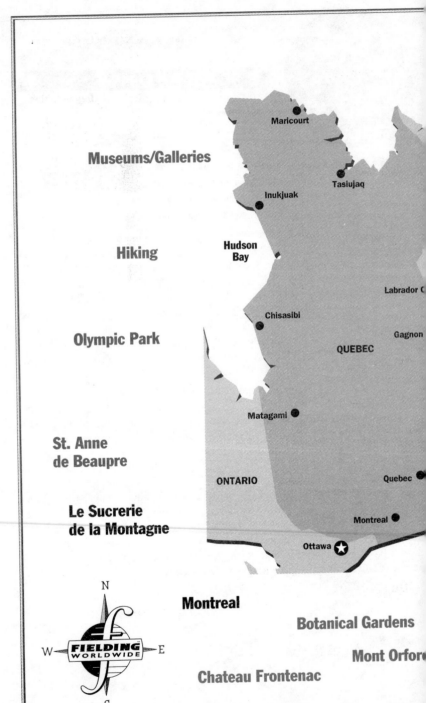

Museums/Galleries

Hiking

Olympic Park

St. Anne
de Beaupre

Le Sucrerie
de la Montagne

Maricourt

Tasiujaq

Inukjuak

Hudson
Bay

Labrador C

Chisasibi

Gagnon

QUEBEC

Matagami

ONTARIO

Quebec

Montreal

Ottawa

N

Montreal

Botanical Gardens

W FIELDING WORLDWIDE E

Mont Orfor

Chateau Frontenac

S

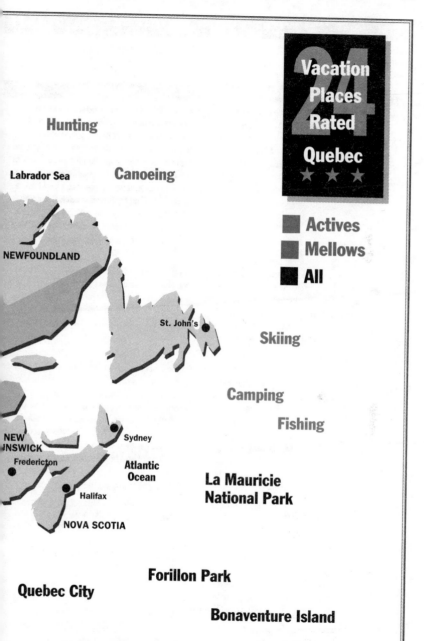

WHAT TO DO IN QUEBEC

Actives	Mellows
1 There are 20 alpine ski areas within easy reach of Montreal in the Laurentians, and cross country skiing is offered as well. These ancient mountains are dotted with large lakes and rivers, so lots of watersports are available.	Let me tell you about a very special experience you can have. In one of the Laurentian forests is a working maple syrup mill that hosts guests for meals and parties in the old French Canadian style. You'll have a beautiful drive to get there, learn all you ever want to know about making maple syrup and have a wonderful meal featuring French Canadian specialties, accompanied, of course, by syrup. Entertainment is provided by folk singers, and you are invited to join in. Ask about Le Sucrerie de la Montagne—it's terrific fun.
2 At La Mauricie National Park, you can camp, hike and fish in largely unspoiled wilderness. Much of the park is reachable only by canoe. Look for the mountain at the north end of Lake la Peche, the top half of which was sheared off by a glacier, exposing the solid rock interior.	High above the St. Lawrence River, the Chateau Frontenac dominates Quebec City. Now a luxury hotel, it's had several historical lives, and it's a fantastic experience just to stroll through its extravagant public areas and look at the view.
3 You can hunt and fish on the Gaspé Peninsula, but its main attractions are the wildlife species (especially birds) that are protected here. Forillon Park on Gaspé and Bonaventure Island off Perce are two places to observe. You may also like the fact that there is no community on the peninsula with much more than 5000 people.	Make a pilgrimage to Ste. Anne de Beaupre, a small village near Quebec City which is home to a magnificent cathedral and Catholic shrine, where thousands of people have been healed. Piles of crutches, canes and other appurtenances of the sick are piled in the church as evidence. The grandeur of the architecture and the legends about Ste. Anne make this an unforgettable experience whether or not you are a believer.
4 Music lovers who are looking for a different setting should investigate the Festival Orford in Mont Orford, one of the pretty towns east of Montreal. The festival takes place in August and is one of Canada's best known. Since Mont Orford is the summer home of the national youth orchestra, the city reverberates with all kinds of music all summer long.	Montreal's Museum of Fine Arts is Canada's oldest. Its collections include art from all over the world, and it is especially notable for its displays of Inuit and Amerind art.
5 To see all of Montreal, hike up Mont Royal, the symbol and namesake of the city (764 feet), and hope for a clear day.	Also in Montreal: explore the old city; visit Olympic Park, site of the 76 games, where the Expos play baseball today.

For further information, contact:

Tourisme Quebec
P.O. Box 979
Montreal, Quebec H3C 2W3, Canada
☎ (514) 873-2015

WHAT PEOPLE LIKE ABOUT QUEBEC

Dependables

I interviewed few *dependables* who like Quebec as much as *venturers* or *centrics*. They seem to prefer western Canada or Toronto to the charms of French Canada. Montreal and Quebec City are close enough, and certainly interesting enough, to entice more *dependables*. Perhaps Quebec should more often promote the quality of its accommodations, its great restaurants and the wonderful shopping that its cities offer. Following is a comment from one *dependable* who had a great time:

Centrics

Centrics are also drawn to Quebec by its European atmosphere and its interesting history. which tour guides will point out to you as you see the sights. Since Canada borders the U.S., curious *centrics* enjoy understanding the events and forces that shape present-day Quebec, its culture and its sometimes tumultuous politics. There is a distinct French Canadian personality that changes as you get away from the cities into the forest and lake regions where fishermen, trappers and farmers live close to the land of "Gentil Alouette." When *centrics* want to get away from the city, they can choose from many quiet hideaways in the Laurentian Mountains, or the Eastern Townships where many Canadians like to relax. *Centrics* comment:

Venturers

Venturers enjoy sampling the amenities of both Montreal and Quebec City, cities that bring Europe to North America. Make no mistake, mes amis, when you enter Quebec from the states or from other parts of Canada, you enter a different country, and this is lots of fun for *venturers*. The province has a special area named the Gaspé Peninsula that draws outdoor loving *venturers* when they tire of city life. The Gaspé is thought to be one of the oldest land masses in the world, and because of its semi-isolation by water, supports life forms that have long disappeared elsewhere. The economy of this area is based on fishing, and the natives augment this by trade and living off the land in the abundant forests. Few tourists find their way here, which makes it doubly desirable to curious and exploring *venturers*. Here are some quotes about Quebec from *venturers*:

I tend to like cities, and Montreal and Quebec City remain two of my favorites. They are so old world and picturesque, yet they are North American. The clothes and souvenirs I bought there are unique and give me a lot of pleasure.

Writer/homemaker, 50, Santa Fe, NM

I was impressed with the friendliness of everyone in French Canada. I traveled with a group of friends, which heightened the enjoyment of everything we saw and did.

Female student, 18, Frankfort, KY

It's a big province, with many, many things to do. It's also very clean, which is delightful. The people are nice, there's no noise from blaring car horns, and no crime that I could see.

49-year-old salesman, Essex Junction, VT

It's a very European environment. You don't have to speak French, but it helps. The food was reasonable in price and wonderful to eat!

Homemaker, 43, Clifton, VA

I love the charm of Quebec City and Montreal, and all the sights to see. There is terrific skiing near both cities.

Male corporate executive, 45, Pridescrossing, MA

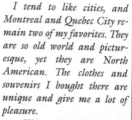

WHAT PEOPLE LIKE ABOUT QUEBEC

Dependables

Centrics

We had a nice fishing holiday in Quebec Province. The fact that everything is so French adds a little something extra.

Retired male, 59, Holland, MI

Venturers

The French Canadians are very friendly people. The countryside is beautiful and everywhere seems steeped in history and tradition.

Female accountant, 38, Houston, TX

The underground city in Montreal is fascinating from a cultural and engineering viewpoint. Outside of the cities in Quebec Province, the landscape reminds me of the forest primeval; it's so natural and unspoiled.

Retired female, 55, Los Angeles, CA

Like the people who are quoted above, Quebec has wormed its way into my affections, too—it's one of my personal favorites for its choice of landscape and activities, and its French Canadian flair. I have enjoyed it for both business and leisure trips. Try it for yourself, and especially sample French onion soup—thicker and tastier than anything you'll get in the U.S!

Tahiti

#25 RATING: ★★★

Centrics	Venturers	Dependables
7	8	4

Tahiti is 33 miles long, ringed by coral reefs and lagoons.
Le Truck buses are the best way to see the island and meet locals.
Tahiti was visited by Bounty captain William Bligh in 1788.
Teiaroa near Tahiti is a 10 island bird santuary.
Gauguin created his famous art in Tahiti between 1891–1901.

Several of the top 25 international destinations in my survey involve an island or island groups, so it's fitting that we end this section with Tahiti. It has all the features that people like about islands: sun, warm weather, beautiful beaches and watersports, but Tahiti's location in the South Pacific and its French Polynesian culture make it truly unique. Several islands, including Moorea and Bora Bora, comprise this French territory of which Tahiti is the largest and most well known.

The impressionist painter, Paul Gauguin, fled Paris and his family to paint on Tahiti, and one has only to look at his lush, sensual pictures to feel the pull of this island. It offers not only great scenic beauty, but a mixture of a simple and tranquil native life-style overlaid with the sophistication of its longtime French rulers. Remote destinations like Tahiti face the problem of being far away, and tourists are somewhat reluctant to spend so many hours just getting there. There's no question that life for tourists and residents is expensive. On the other hand, its location protects it from being overcommercialized and spoiled by too much traffic, which pleases the travelers who like its culture just the way it is.

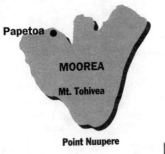

Golf

Gorgeous Beach

Snorkeling

Papetoa

MOOREA

Mt. Tohivea

PAPEETE

Faaa

Point Nuupere

Diving

Punaauia

Shopping

Relaxing

Papar.

Boating

Windsurfing

Gauguin Museum

Horseback Riding

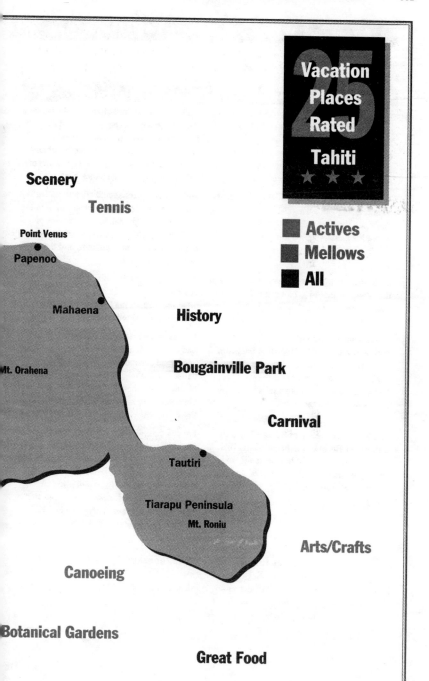

WHAT TO DO IN TAHITI

Actives	Mellows
1 Tahiti is wonderful, but get out to some of the other islands. All kinds of boat rentals (on your own, or with a captain and crew) are available out of Papeete. See Moorea, Bora Bora, Marlon Brando's private island and other spots you'll find on your own.	Walk around the marketplace in the center of Papeete on a main shopping day like Sunday. It's a gigantic farmers market filled with strange and exotic produce representing all the ethnic groups of the island. You can even get a hamburger in the snack bar!
2 These are volcanic islands, dotted with reefs, so snorkeling and scuba diving are popular. You'll see the best fish on the outer islands, where the human population has less effect.	Souvenir shoppers should stick to native crafts for the best value. Those with a fatter pocketbook might like to buy samples of Tahiti's native black pearls. Pearling is one of the mainstays of the economy, and the black pearls are distinctive.
3 Horseback riding is a good way to see some of the island, or just to get a change from water sports. Check into rentals in Papeete.	Bougainville Park is a nice oasis where you can relax in the shade of giant banyan trees after you inspect the two cannons off ships with historical significance.
4 Windsurfing in these islands is for experts only, who will enjoy their sport in the warm water and ocean breezes. However, too much coral in the shallow waters presents a problem for beginners and the equipment available is not always top-notch.	Thanks to the French and Chinese, it's hard to find a bad restaurant in Papeete. Try the various island cuisines separately and in combination: La Corbeille d'eau is French, Le Mandarin for Chinese, Le Baie d'Along for Vietnamese, Acajou and Waikiki for combinations.
5 Join in the celebration of Bastille Day (July 14), called Tiurai by the Polynesians. This holiday means carnival time in Tahiti, and you'll see lots of traditional sports, dancing and general 'carrying-on.'	For you culture starved travelers who like a museum or two wherever you vacation: The Botanical Gardens and Gauguin Museum are on the south coast of Tahiti. The museum needs a little sprucing up and owns no Gauguin originals. However it's a good source of information about the famous artist's time in Tahiti and displays other island artists worth seeing. The restaurant is good, too.

For further information, contact:

Tahiti Tourist Board
300 North Continental Boulevard, Suite 180
El Segundo, CA 90245
☎ (310) 414-8484

WHAT PEOPLE LIKE ABOUT TAHITI

Dependables

Only a few *dependables* make the trip across the Pacific to Tahiti. It doesn't have the amount of commercial development they typically expect and appreciate. But its warm weather and good accommodations, along with a successful Club Med operation attract some *dependables*. Perhaps it's just too far away. When high speed transport becomes commonplace, outlying areas like French Polynesia may increase their popularity with all personality types. One *dependable* woman who likes Tahiti describes her trip like this:

Centrics

More adventurous *centrics* come to Tahiti for the same reasons as *venturers*. It's a beautiful place that none of their friends have been before them. Perhaps they have read some of the famous writers who make Tahiti sound romantic and exciting and different—as indeed it is. *Centrics* who are history buffs want to see in person the land where the *Bounty* crew was marooned, where Gauguin painted, and which helped supply our own Hawaiian Islands with its original population. Papeete (the only real city in the islands) is not as pretty as some other island capitals, but it's lively and fun for *centrics* to explore before they head for the beach. Read on for some comments from *centrics*.

Venturers

Tahiti is a classic *venturer* destination. They like the wild beauty of these volcanic islands, the exotic culture, and the activities to be pursued in and around the ocean. Many famous *venturers* explored the South Pacific, including Tahiti and Moorea, beginning with Captain James Cook, and including Herman Melville, Somerset Maugham, Robert Louis Stevenson, Jack London, Thor Heyerdahl and Captain Bligh of the *H.M.S. Bounty*. Today's active visitors can swim and snorkel, race canoes and play tennis, squash and golf where some very well-known feet have walked. And, unlike so many places in the world, Tahiti casts a spell that these islands exist just for you. No crowds, no noise, and a feeling that you can escape with your loved one to a corner of the world where you'll be alone and unbothered by the press of modern civilization. Here are some comments from *venturers*:

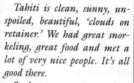

Tahiti is clean, sunny, unspoiled, beautiful, 'clouds on retainer.' We had great snorkeling, great food and met a lot of very nice people. It's all good there.

Senior corporate executive, Cupertino, CA

I think all volcanic islands have the most spectacular scenery, and Tahiti lives up to that. There are a lot of things to do, and except for a few areas of Papeete, it is relaxing and noncommercial.

Male financial executive, 60, Los Angeles, CA

The people are friendly. There is no begging or 'pushing' by anyone, and I love the peace and quiet. The food is great and the weather is divine. Clubs and resorts invite the locals to join in their evening fun. The people share their culture with you, and in turn are not exploited by the tourists.

Self-employed female, 40, New York, NY

WHAT PEOPLE LIKE ABOUT TAHITI

Dependables

Centrics

Venturers

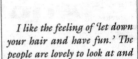

I like the sun, surf, sand, and the French food. It's clean and feels fairly safe.
Female sales consultant, 34, East Syracuse, NY

This is a low-key, friendly, 'nonplastic' environment. The scenery is unbelievably outstanding and you are allowed to have a good time in your own way.
Female office worker, 54, Mercer Island, WA

I like the feeling of 'let down your hair and have fun.' The people are lovely to look at and lovely to be around.
Female lab technician, 29, Cleveland, OH

It's a glorious place. People are friendly and accommodating. When you want to relax, this is the place.
Saleswoman, 34, East Syracuse, NY

Tahiti and the South Pacific have a really fascinating history, starting in prehistoric times to the present. It's very beautiful, the people are friendly to visitors, and it has more going for it than people realize.
Male teacher, 56, Boise, ID

It's very different from the Caribbean islands. The scenery is more dramatic, the French Polynesian culture is a treat, and the local food is wonderful.
Salesman, 39, San Francisco, CA

RATINGS FOR OTHER INTERNATIONAL PLACES: FROM GOOD TO NOT VERY GOOD

More international destinations get high ratings than is true for U.S. places—but only because there are so many of them. This statement points to the fact that quite a number of great places for vacations get left off of the list of the Top 25.

As before, this list rank-orders destinations and provides a star rating system, along with an indication (on a 10-point scale) as to the degree to which *venturers*, *centrics*, and *dependables* enjoy them. Also consistent with everything I've said up until now, three-star places generally will provide you with great vacations—lots to do for everyone in your travel group, particularly for the kinds of experiences that Americans like. Places with only two-star ratings should probably be reviewed carefully before you plan a visit. If a place receives only one star, it most likely will not offer the best vacation experiences for most travelers.

For the most part, you'll find that *venturers* appreciate these international destinations more than *dependables*, or even *centrics*. The inquisitive spirit of venturers leads them to explore the world farther from home than is true for other personality types.

RATINGS OF OTHER INTERNATIONAL LOCATIONS					
Rank	Location	Rating	Centrics	Venturers	Dependable
#26	HONG KONG	★★★	7	7	8
#27	INDONESIA	★★★	7	9	6
#28	JAPAN	★★★	7	5	2
#29	SINT MAARTEN	★★★	7	7	8
#30	THAILAND	★★★	7	10	10
#31	CZECH REPUBLIC	★★★	7	7	1
#32	CANCUN	★★★	7	6	6
#33	MANITOBA	★★★	6	2	1
#34	CABO SAN LUCAS	★★★	8	10	5
#35	BAHAMAS	★★★	6	10	5
#36	NEW BRUNSWICK	★★★	6	7	1
#37	BELGIUM/ NETHERLANDS	★★★	6	9	7
#38	PORTUGAL	★★★	6	8	7
#39	JAMAICA	★★	5	7	5
#40	SASKATCHEWAN	★★	5	4	1
#41	DOMINICAN REPUBLIC	★★	5	7	2
#42	HUNGARY	★★	5	4	1
#43	PUERTO RICO	★★	5	4	3
#44	BARBADOS	★★	7	6	5
#45	ACAPULCO	★★	5	6	7
#46	SINGAPORE	★★	4	6	3
#47	TURKEY	★★	4	7	6
#48	CHINA	★★	5	6	4
#49	RUSSIA	★★	4	7	6
#50	MEXICO CITY	★★	3	6	3

Location	Where to Write for Information
HONG KONG	Hong Kong Tourism Association, 590 5th Avenue, 5th Floor, New York, NY 10036, ☎ (212) 869-5008
INDONESIA	Indonesian Tourist Promotion Office, 3457 Wilshire Blvd., Suite 104, Los Angeles, CA 90010, ☎ (213) 387-8309
JAPAN	Japan National Tourism Organization, 630 5th Avenue, New York, NY 3210X ☎ (212) 757-5640
ST. MAARTEN	St. Maarten Tourism Office, 275 7th Avenue, 19th Floor, New York, NY 10001-6788, ☎ (212) 989-0000
THAILAND	Tourism Authority of Thailand, 5 World Trade Center, Room 3443, New York NY 10048, ☎ (212) 432-0433

Location	Where to Write for Information
CZECH REPUBLIC	Cedok Center European Tourism & Travel, 10 East 4th Street, Suite 3604, New York, NY 10016, ☎ (212) 689-9720
CANCUN	Mexican Government Tourism Office, 405 Park Avenue, Suite 1401, New York, NY 10022, ☎ (212) 755-7261
MANITOBA	155 Carlton Street, 7th Floor, Winnipeg, Manitoba R3C 3H8, ☎ (800) 665-0040
CABO SAN LUCAS	Mexican Government Tourism Office, 405 Park Avenue, Suite 1401, New York, NY 10022, ☎ (212) 755-7261
BAHAMAS	Bahamas Tourist Office, 150 E. 52nd Street, 28th Floor, North, New York, NY 10022, ☎ (212) 432-0433
NEW BRUNSWICK	Department of Economic Development of Tourism, P.O. Box 6000, Fredericton, New Brunswick E3B 5H1 Canada, ☎ (800) 561-0123
BELGIUM/ NETHERLANDS	Belgian Tourist Office, 78 3rd Avenue, New York, NY 10017, ☎ (212) 758-8130
PORTUGAL	Portuguese National Tourist Office, 590 5th Avenue, 4th Floor, New York, NY 10036, ☎ (212) 354-4403
JAMAICA	Jamaica Tourist Board, 3440 Wilshire Blvd., Suite 1207, Los Angeles, CA 90010, ☎ (213) 384-1123
SASKATCHEWAN	Saskatchewan Tourism, 500 1900 Albert Street, Regina, Saskatchewan S4P 4L9 Canada, ☎ (800) 667-7191
DOMINICAN REPUB- IC	Consulate General of the Dominican Republic:, Tourism Department, 1 Times Square, 11th Floor, New York, NY 10036, ☎ (212) 768-2481
HUNGARY	1 Parker Plaza/Ibusz Travel, 4th Floor, Fort Lee, NJ 070242, ☎ (201) 592-8585
PUERTO RICO	Puerto Rico Tourism Company, P.O. Box 025268, Department H, Miami, Florida 33102-5268, ☎ (800) 223-6530
BARBADOS	Barbados Tourism Authority, 800 2nd Avenue, 2nd Floor, New York, NY 10017, ☎ (800) 221-9831
ACAPULCO	Mexican Government Tourism Office, 405 Park Avenue, Suite 1401, New York, NY 10022, ☎ (212) 755-7261
SINGAPORE	Singapore Tourist Promotion Board, 8484 Wilshire Blvd., Suite 510, Beverly Hills, CA 90211, ☎ (213) 852-1901
TURKEY	Turkish Tourist Office, 821 U.N. Plaza, 4th Floor, New York, NY 10017, ☎ (212) 687-2194
CHINA	China National Tourist Office, 354 5th Avenue, Room 6413, Empire State Building, New York, NY 10108, ☎ (212) 760-9700
RUSSIA	Russian National Tourism Office, 800 3rd Avenue, Suite 3101, New York, NY 10022, ☎ (212) 758-1162
MEXICO CITY	Mexican Government Tourism Office, 405 Park Avenue, Suite 1401, New York, NY 10022, ☎ (212) 755-7261

VACATION PLACES THAT WILL GROW; GET THERE BEFORE OTHERS DO

Now that I've covered the places that provide the most satisfying vacation experiences, based on the ratings of people who have visited them, I'll give you insight into which destinations in the U.S., and the world, should grow during the next several years. Destinations wax and wane, like the ebb and flow of the tide, depending upon a lot of factors. For the most part, destinations grow when they are new, relatively uncrowded and still have a unique charm about them. They decline when they become too popular and uncontrolled development takes over, destroying everything that initially attracted people.

Other factors also influence their rise and fall in popularity. The Gulf War in 1991 pulled a lot of Americans away from travel to foreign countries because of fears about international terrorism. The recession further dampened travel demand as households had to cut back on expenses. As a result, people traveled less. When they did leave town, they went on shorter trips closer to home, stayed for fewer nights, and more frequently jumped into the family car rather than an airplane.

Now the psychology of the nation has changed. For too long, many people believe, they have cut back, scrimped, delayed buying things and put off taking a trip they really want. Talk to someone who hasn't taken a nice vacation in the past several years, and you're likely to hear a familiar refrain: "I'm not getting any younger, and who knows what tomorrow will bring. So I'm taking that trip I've been longing for while I still have my health and can travel, even if I think I can't afford it."

The result is a travel boom that is just beginning and will last several years. So, some of the places you're thinking about may have "no vacancy" signs if you don't get there soon. Expect prices to go up. The law of supply and demand has a nasty way of making itself felt in leisure travel also.

Trying out a new place for your next trip is kind of like going to a carnival. There are lots of things to do but do you want to go on the ferris wheel, the bumper cars, or the sky ride? Let's make sure you get a place that'll deliver—one that lives up to its promise of offering a rip-roaring good time.

This listing of the hot spots also comes from the American Traveler Survey (ATS) I conduct each year. I ask people about which places they have visited in the last three years, and which places they are thinking about visiting in the next three. By comparing the two, it's possible to determine which ones will increase in popularity and which ones could decline.

When you look at the list, you'll notice that it doesn't include many U.S. destinations. Vacationers now want to go farther from home. Demand has been building for vacations in Europe and other international spots because of the travel constraints I mentioned. Air fares are ridiculously low at present, allowing people to travel more often and for greater distances. But, not all destinations will follow the exact pattern listed here. Foreign travel is expensive now and many people will reconsider and go elsewhere. Advertising has a big impact. You may have selected a place you want to visit, but some very effective TV or magazine ads convince you to choose somewhere else. You can always get to that dream spot next year, you believe. Whatever happens, you can be certain that these places will grow, even if it's not at their maximum potential rates. People turn their travel interests into definitive travel plans at some point.

Forty-six destinations, out of the nearly 160 that I asked about in the American Traveler Survey, appear on this growth list—only nine in the U.S. and 37 foreign places. The rank ordering, based on growth potential, appears along with their satisfaction scores (the same scores for centrics that you've seen earlier). It's possible to determine not only which destinations will grow but also those that will send you home happier and more satisfied. Looking at the chart, you can determine if a place you were considering is likely to meet your expectations.

Most of the growth will occur because venturers want to go to these places. They ultimately set the travel patterns for others because what they make popular will ultimately convince the less venturesome that it must be good if the place is growing in the number of tourists it attracts.

When you examine the rankings, it's easy to see a few things:

1. Internationally, the highest growth potential exists in the Pacific area. The top three spots are occupied by Australia, New Zealand and Tahiti, in that order. Travelers now want to venture farther beyond their doorsteps, especially *venturers*. The growth of these places could be in the 15 percent to 20 percent range, if they develop their marketing and advertising plans properly. The only thing that can hold the Pacific region back is the cost of getting there. It's a long flight, especially from the middle or eastern parts of the country, and long flights cost a lot.

2. Beyond this conclusion, it's difficult to see a pattern. Countries in central, northern and southern Europe all appear, along with places in the UK, Asia, the Caribbean, Canada and Latin America. But no Mexican destination shows up in the top 30.

3. You need not worry about enjoying your trip to any of the U.S. growth places. Each has a very high satisfaction ratio, so you should have a very nice trip. But a few of the international destinations don't measure up as

well on the Satisfaction Index. If you decide to go to one of those places, be certain you know why you're going and what you plan to do while you're there. Otherwise, you could go home disappointed.

Let's take a look at how the destinations stack up, both in the U.S. and in other countries. I've used the same 10 point scale to give you a feeling for the potential of each place. Places that score between seven and 10 have strong growth potential. These destinations could see increases in tourists from the U.S. in the range of 12 to 20 percent each year for the next several years. Those places measuring between four and six on the index have moderate prospects for the future. Their growth could be in the five to 10 percent range. Those registering at 3 and below should experience only modest growth in the future, in the two percent to four percent range, unless they come up with superior advertising and promotional campaigns. What cannot be forgotten is that this list indicates the inherent ability of each place for growth. That potential is modified by the cost of travel, the difficulty of getting there (after you decide you'd like to go to some place, you may also realize you'd spend too much of your vacation time getting there and back), and effective advertising of a competing place that convinces you to go there first—you can always get to your dream spot next year. The following list rank-orders prospects down to those with the lowest potential.

FIGURE 4
THE DESTINATIONS THAT WILL GROW

Rank	Destination	Growth Potential (10 point scale)	Satisfaction Index (10 point scale)
DOMESTIC			
1	Alaska	10	10
2	Hawaii	8	10
3	Maine	2	10
4	Vermont	2	9
5	Colorado	1	10
6	Washington	1	9
7	Montana	1	9
8	Arizona	1	9
9	Las Vegas	1	9
INTERNATIONAL			
1	Australia	10	10
2	New Zealand	10	10
3	Tahiti	10	7
4	Scandinavia	10	8
5	Ireland	10	10
6	Greece	10	8
7	Costa Rica	10	10

FIGURE 4
THE DESTINATIONS THAT WILL GROW

Rank	Destination	Growth Potential (10 point scale)	Satisfaction Index (10 point scale)
8	Israel	9	10
9	Prince Edward Island	9	8
10	English countryside/Scotland	8	10
11	Cayman Islands	7	8
12	Japan	7	7
13	Spain	7	8
14	Portugal	6	6
15	China	6	4
16	Rome, Italy	6	8
16 tie	Italy, small villages	6	8
18	Hong Kong	6	7
18 tie	Singapore	6	4
20	Aruba	5	8
21	Bermuda	5	10
22	Paris, France	4	8
23	Germany	4	9
24	Switzerland	4	10
25	US Virgin Islands	4	9
26	London, England	3	9
26 tie	Austria	3	9
28	Cancun	2	7
28 tie	French countryside	2	8
30	Alberta, Canada	2	9
31	Belgium/Netherlands	2	6
32	British Columbia, Canada	2	10
33	Cabo San Lucas, Mexico	2	6
34	Acapulco, Mexico	1	5
34 tie	Mexico City	1	3
36	Saskatchewan, Canada	1	5

In the next list, the same international destinations are reordered to make you
choices a bit easier. It summarizes them according to those that deliver high sa
isfaction and have strong, moderate or modest growth potential, those that pro
vide moderate satisfaction (and varying growth prospects), and those that onl
deliver low levels of satisfaction to visitors (along with their growth prospects). B
making more informed choices, you can hopefully avoid some of your mistakes

the past in choosing the wrong places for your vacation. You want to maximize every trip away from home.

FIGURE 5
INTERNATIONAL GROWTH DESTINATIONS

(Categorized by Satisfaction Levels and Growth Potential)

High Satisfaction Destinations

Strong Growth Potential

1.	Australia
2.	New Zealand
3.	Scandinavia
4.	Ireland
5.	Greece
6.	Costa Rica
7.	Israel
8.	Prince Edward Island
9.	English Countryside and Scotland
10.	Cayman Islands
11.	Spain

Moderate Growth Potential

1.	Rome, Italy
2.	Other parts of Italy
3.	Aruba
4.	Ixtapa
5.	Bermuda
6.	Paris, France
7.	Germany
8.	Switzerland
9.	U.S. Virgin Islands

Modest Growth Potential

1.	Austria
2.	London, England
3.	France (other than Paris)
4.	Alberta
5.	British Columbia

Moderate Satisfaction Destinations

Strong Growth Potential

1.	Tahiti
2.	Japan

FIGURE 5
INTERNATIONAL GROWTH DESTINATIONS

Moderate Growth Potential

1.	Portugal
2.	Hong Kong

Modest Growth Potential

1.	Cancun
2.	Belgium, Netherlands
3.	Cabo San Lucas
4.	Acapulco
5.	Saskatchewan

Low Satisfaction Destinations

Strong Growth Potential

None.

Moderate Growth Potential

1.	China
2.	Singapore

Modest Growth Potential

1.	Mexico City

GETTING INTO CRUISING: WHY NOW

If you have never cruised before, do it now. If you have cruised and thought about doing it again, don't delay. Why? The time has never been better. More new and beautiful cruise ships have been launched in recent years than at any time in history, and the competition to get passengers is intense. Discounts are currently available that may not be given in the future, often up to 50 percent below full fares. As a result, you can get a very reasonably priced cruise on a brand new or nearly new ship. After about three years, demand for cruise space could grow at a rate faster than ships are being launched, resulting in rising cruise fares. More important, most cruise lines have plans in place to give away fewer cabins at discount prices. You could have trouble matching today's deals when that happens.

Selecting a cruise line is a bit like choosing a marriage partner. You're going to be together for a while, 24 hours a day, so you better choose well. My advice is to select the best cruise line and cruise ship you can possibly afford. Since almost all of your experience will be on board, enjoyment of your cabin, along with the quality of the cruise ship and the services provided, constitute the most important part of that vacation. The best cruise lines, and the best ships of those cruise lines, obviously offer the greatest likelihood of maximum enjoyment. With attractive cruise fares and deep discounts available even from high-end cruise lines, you can get strong value at every level of choice. It could truly be one of your most memorable vacations—ever.

In 1970, only 500,000 Americans had ever cruised. By 1988, that number had jumped to 3 million, a sixfold increase in less than two decades. But, everything moves quickly these days. In 1995, about 5 million Americans will have taken a cruise. That's more people than live in the states of Maine, New Hampshire, Vermont, Idaho and Montana combined. For the rest of the decade of the 90s, more *new* cruise passengers will take the plunge for their first trip each year than had ever cruised—prior to 1972.

If that many people are trying it, and so many prior cruisers keep coming back for more, it must be good. You better believe it is! The cruise experience has changed so much in the last decade that you can't compare it to anything you knew about cruising before. At one time it earned a well deserved stuffy, snobbish image. Its heritage comes from the British. The term for luxury service, "posh," refers to preferred cabins on cruise ships for the passage to India ("Portside Out, Starboard Home"). Trip itineraries were usually 10 to 21 days or longer. Devotees of cruising were older, generally wealthy, with lots of time on their hands, and decidedly snobbish. Passengers were usually required to eat the evening meal in formal wear, and most often with the same couple at their table night after night. Beyond dancing to big bands and shuffleboard, you didn't have a whole lot of entertainment choices on board.

In all of my surveys, until about four years ago, the cruise experience primarily appealed to the psychology of the *mellow dependable* types. *Venturers*, particularly the actives, wouldn't even consider cruising. Boring, slow moving, and deadly dull—a total waste of time, they believed.

No longer is any of the above true. Cruising can be swinging or sedate, shamelessly expensive or offering exceptionally good value. You can totally relax for a week or two, or party wildly until two in the morning. So much diversity exists in cruising you must consider it as an acceptable alternative to a more traditional vacation on land. That's why I've included it in this section of the book. I'll put some perspective on it so that you can decide whether you might want to take a cruise and, if you do, how to select the right cruise line and itinerary for your tastes and personality.

How Cruising Got To Be So Popular

You've seen the ads. Bright, perky Kathie Lee Gifford bounces across your TV screen singing and shouting about the wonders and excitement of a cruise on one of the "fun ships" of Carnival Cruise Lines. She's done that for just a little over a decade now. Behind that appealing ad lies a story about a revolution in marketing.

Carnival came on to the scene in 1973 with its first ship, the 906 passenger *Mardis Gras*, converted from the former *Empress of Canada*, an old ship that no "respectable" cruise line wanted to keep in service. Carnival's founder, entrepreneur Ted Arison, had an idea. He reasoned that he could attract a new generation of cruisers by creating a party atmosphere on board and focusing on the Caribbean (as his former partner, Knute Kloster was doing with Norwegian Cruise Line/ NCL). Arison also lowered the price for a cruise since his cruises were shorter than trans-Atlantic sailings. Putting more people on board and shortening the cruise length to seven (later to three and four) days also helped to keep cruise prices down. It worked like magic. New cruisers flocked to the relaunch of the ship as the *Mardi Gras*, and to every other vessel he has constructed since. Together with Kloster of NCL, Arison helped to start the current cruise boom, lowered the age profile from about 55 years to the current 46 years, and redefined how cruising should be positioned to the public. Carnival now is the largest line carrying about 25 percent of all passengers, and should stay that way at least through the end of this century.

The sitcom series, "Love Boat," also helped considerably. Each week for nine years (from 1977 to 1986, and syndicated after that), interesting people of varying ages and backgrounds sorted out their lives while enjoying a romantic cruise on board a Princess cruise ship. With all of this newfound interest, cruise lines responded by building new ships creating different on-board experiences (often called *theme cruises*). Quite a number of new cruise lines began service, most of these with the intent of capturing a new market segment that the owners believed had previously been overlooked.

Now you can choose from more than 160 cruise ships, varying in size from megaliners that carry 2500 passengers or more to smaller ships about a twentieth of that size. With itineraries that frequently vary with each sailing, you can literally select from hundreds of ports of call. The options of what to do when you're afloat also seem endless. Relax in your cabin and enjoy the calming effect of the open sea, or choose one that offers a party atmosphere; watch Broadway show productions (a different one almost every night from a very versatile group of actors, singers and dancers), listen to top jazz artists or dance to the big band sounds of Glenn Miller, Benny Goodman and others. You can also join groups that share common interests, such as lovers of mystery novels (you'll work with fellow passengers to solve "whodunits"), enjoy historic lecture series tied to places you visit, fulfill a lifelong dream and go for a Holy Land tour directed by a pastor steeped in knowledge of the area, or see the fall colors of New England from your cruise ship and from brief shore excursions. While on board, relax in your own private veranda deck chair, improve your golf swing at an indoor driving range or exercise in an ultramodern facility while you watch nearby islands pass by. With endless possibilities, if you choose right, you can't be bored. You could have the time of your life. Well over 90 percent of cruise passengers return home saying they had a marvelous time.

Ten Reasons Why You'll Love Cruising

Each year, I gather information (along with cruise industry expert, Murray Markin of Strategic Decisions, Inc.) from people who have cruised to learn how much they liked their experience, where they want to cruise next (if they have plans) and, very important, why they selected a cruise. What passengers say is revealing and can help you decide whether or not cruising should become part of your next vacation plans.

Figure 6 summarizes what passengers say are their top ten reasons for taking a cruise (based on the Cruise-Trak survey conducted with Mr. Markin). Interestingly, the reasons are the same for people who recently completed a cruise and those who did so three or four years ago and plan on taking another in the future. People who have cruised love it and, by and large, they want to do it again.

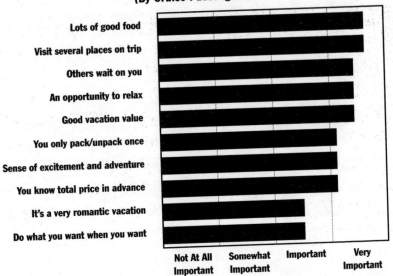

Figure 6
Reasons Given For Taking A Cruise
(By Cruise Passengers)

Lots of good food

Visit several places on trip

Others wait on you

An opportunity to relax

Good vacation value

You only pack/unpack once

Sense of excitement and adventure

You know total price in advance

It's a very romantic vacation

Do what you want when you want

| Not At All Important | Somewhat Important | Important | Very Important |

Let's take a look at the top ten reasons people give. Let me emphasize that each of these reasons, even the last one, scores high on the scale, indicating that cruising offers multiple advantages to most people who try it.

1. Lots of Good Food

People say that the chance to eat lots of great food is the most important reason they decided to take a cruise. You can expect to be dazzled by fabulous food six times a day: elaborate dinners, mid-morning and mid-afternoon snacks, midnight buffets. Culinary surprises reflecting great cuisines from around the world and desserts that rival anything you've ever tasted will surprise and delight you. Unless you choose the wrong cruise line, one that promotes its cheap price rather than its quality, you can expect great selections at all seatings. Or you can also dine in your stateroom on the more upscale lines. In fact, the food is so good and tempting that many people delay taking a cruise for fear of how much weight they'll gain. Don't put it off. Do your dieting before and after, and use the exercise room on board. But for once, enjoy yourself and just do it.

If you still want to follow a health oriented routine, cruise lines have changed in recent years and most now offer special meal selections for the health conscious. You can eat vegetarian, low sodium, low calorie and low fat meals during your entire trip that be tasty and attractively presented.

2. Visit Several Places on the Same Trip

Some noncruisers don't recognize that the ships stop at interesting ports. You will spend a few hours to a day or two in each of these places, either with time on your own or as part of a day tour (occasionally with overnight trips to the interior of a country). The interesting or historic places usually have optional shore excur sions that include a guide. Selection of an interesting itinerary is critically important because it adds so much diversity and memorability to a trip. In the next section, I'll provide some recommendations on which places you should think about visiting, whether you're a first timer or an experienced cruiser.

3. Others Will Wait On Me

Ah hah! Cruisers are more honest about themselves than landlubbers! They admit that they like the care and attention they get on a cruise, with the crew catering to almost their every whim. You'll remember from the third chapter ("Why Do You Want To Travel?") that only one out of twenty vacationers confesses that the chance to be waited on by others is an important motive for leisure travel. Let's face it. It simply feels good to have others do things for us, to regress a bit in life and forget about responsibilities, to enjoy the kind of pampering we probably have not experienced since childhood. You can match, or even exceed, this amount of personal care and attention you'll have on-board if you visit an expensive spa or resort, but you will also probably pay a lot more for that trip. Cruise lines pamper their guests and it feels good. They also do it at relatively reasonable prices.

4. An Opportunity to Relax

On board activities are not the same on all cruise lines, as we'll see in a moment. But you at least have lots of opportunity to relax whenever you feel like it. In a hectic and stressed out world, that alone can be sufficient motivation to take a cruise. Interestingly, the desire to just relax while on a cruise measures more strongly in people over 40 years of age. Are they winding down in life or feeling more of its stresses and strains? If you feel constantly under pressure in your daily life, cruising will get rid of these negative "vibes" almost from the moment you step on board.

5. Good Vacation Value

This confirms it. Cruisers, including those who have cruised in the past and future intenders, believe that cruising offers good value. It's true. You have your hotel room, meals and entertainment included in one price. With the discounting going on today, you can get super deals. The experience compares favorably, price-wise, with most land based vacations you might consider. If you don't believe me, sit down and write out all of the expenses you face each day on a conventional vacation: hotel, meals, rental cars and taxis, entertainment, tipping and various incidental items. Cruising may come out less expensive, overall. Excluding airfare, you can enjoy a very good cruise experience for about $200 a day, per person. But choose the right cruise line at that price (see the Loyalty Index ratings in this chapter).

6. You Only Have to Pack and Unpack Once

Tired of lugging your bags around when you travel, and having to pack and unpack so often? Admit it, it's a hassle. Having your own cabin to retreat to at the end of the day, or even for an afternoon nap, is an important advantage of being on a cruise ship. Once again, my data indicates that, as people age, they see this as a more important reason for taking a cruise.

7. Sense of Excitement and Adventure

I'll bet you never thought of a cruise as being exciting. Well, earlier I mentioned that *venturers* have now taken it up as willingly as *dependables*, even *active venturers*. There are so many different itineraries and on-board options to choose from that you simply have to make certain that a travel agent presents all of the choices to you. Since so much of the world's history has developed along the great sea lanes used for trading, you can gain considerable perspective with your day trips into these old sea ports.

But if that's not your bag, then opt for the chance to visit developing nations where they lack good hotels and your ship becomes a comfortable, safe haven every night from your daytime explorations. On some of these trips you'll even fly to inland places in the morning and return at night. Or choose a theme cruise that focuses on one of your special interests or hobbies. I mentioned some possibilities earlier. Since the itineraries of cruise lines change each year, and more theme cruises come on line all the time, call a travel agent to find out about the latest offerings. Don't forget, if you feel pushed or a bit exhausted at any time, you can always close your cabin door and relax. Unlike an escorted tour, you never have to do anything on schedule.

8. You Know the Total Price in Advance

Like fully escorted tours, you have a fixed price for your room (cabin), meals entertainment and transportation (airfare to and from the port of debarkation) That's a real advantage. But be careful. Some cruise lines offer very low cruise prices but charge more for drinks, port fees, and shore excursions. We'll talk some more about saving money in the last chapter, "Travel Smarter, Not Harder." But if you don't go for lots of extras, you'll generally know what your vacation will cost. You'll usually have to add on some tips, but you do that for land based vacations also.

9. It's a Very Romantic Vacation

Cruising has always had romance associated with it. Some of the great movies of the '30s and '40s featured handsome stars sorting out their love triangles o board. Who can forget Fred Astaire and Ginger Rogers dancing magnificently i the ship's grand ballroom in the 1937 movie, *Shall We Dance?* The more recer and highly popular sitcom, "The Love Boat," also reinforced this image.

My data also indicates, as you would probably expect, that younger people rat this advantage more important than persons over 45. But, all consider it to be im portant. The romance of the seas enhances a romantic feeling on board.

10. A Chance to Do What You Want to Do When You Want To

Last, but still rating very strongly, is the fact that you really do feel like you hav no obligations to anyone when you're on board. Sailing the oceans of the wor creates a sense of isolation and a belief that time schedules no longer are impo tant. The wonder and awe that you'll feel when you look at the design and co struction of these magnificent ships add to a sense that you are experienci something special and quite unlike what you confront every day.

Where Should You Cruise?

If you haven't cruised before, you'll probably be most comfortable going to the traditional places first. As you gain experience and knowledge, even based on your initial cruise, you will become more adventurous and branch out in your choices. If you live east of the Rockies, you are most likely to choose destinations served by ports at Miami or Ft. Lauderdale, Florida. If you live to the West, you may also choose Florida ports or California (for the Mexican Riviera) or Vancouver (for Alaskan waters). But let's get a little more specific.

The Caribbean continues to dominate the market, with the ports of Miami and Port Everglades (near Ft. Lauderdale) embarking about 80 percent of cruise passengers each year. Of this, the Eastern Caribbean is the most popular, with such places as the U.S. Virgin Islands, Puerto Rico and Nassau. The Western Caribbean is next in order of importance and traditionally includes such ports as Cozumel, Grand Cayman, Jamaica and sometimes even Key West, Florida. Farther away is the Southern Caribbean where your cruise will usually begin with a flight to Puerto Rico and an itinerary that may include calls at St. Thomas, St. Maarten, Antigua, Martinique, Aruba, Curaçao or Barbados.

The Caribbean's broad expanse of islands and diverse cultures is perhaps the best place to begin your first cruise experience. With its unbeatable balmy weather, you are almost always assured of being lazily comfortable without having to worry about getting seasick because of its calm seas. Cruise prices are perhaps the lowest anywhere in the world because of the intense competition from old lines and quite a few new ones that initiated service in recent years. Finally, you have the greatest opportunity to choose a newer ship. These are more glamorous, comfortable, quieter, with less noticeable rolling motion from state-of-the-art stabilizers, and they have larger cabin windows (sometimes with floor to ceiling sliding glass doors) for better views. Also, new ship designers, such as the Norwegian architects Petter Yran and Bjorn Storbratten, concentrate on providing more outside cabins so that you won't feel claustrophobic looking at four walls and no view.

If you live in the Western states, for your first cruise you may sail down the Mexican Riviera from Los Angeles. Or, even more likely, you'll choose from the nearly 30 ships that traverse the waters of Alaska's inland waterway in the summer months and stop at quaint port cities as they head toward the magnificent glaciers of this five-star state (see "The Top 25 U.S. Destinations—And Why You May Be Surprised"). Strong competition also means newer, more comfortable ships among the bigger lines that serve Alaska, and favorable prices. You'll feel you entered an enchanted world where you view nature and wildlife in the raw, since your cruise will go places even beyond the reach of rural villages. However, don't rule out the Caribbean for that first big choice, even if you live in the West. Its warm, calm seas, crystal clear waters and huge array of cruise lines from which to choose provide the kind of comfort that many people look for on their first cruise. Then you may decide to take that Alaskan voyage the second time around.

If you have cruised even once, you have developed some expertise and may know where you want to sail next. I strongly urge consideration of the Mediterranean for anyone who is undecided. It also embraces you with great weather, offers spectacular scenery and amazes most first time visitors with its centuries of history that overlay almost anyplace you'll stop. You'll also have a chance to meet people from intriguing cultures. The Western Mediterranean includes popular ports in Spain, Southern Italy and parts of North Africa. The Eastern Mediterranean perhaps has even more interesting places because of the significant history associated with Greece, Turkey, Egypt and Israel. It's a fabulous way to travel because you don't have to pack and unpack as you venture forth on some of the history-oriented shore excursions. In some areas such as Egypt, you may also take an overnight inland trip to see something of special significance, such as the great Pyramids.

If you really get the cruising bug, you have endless choices. A transcanal voyage (through the Panama Canal), a trip up the New England coast to see the fall colors, a trans-Atlantic ocean crossing (steamship to England, fly back on the Concorde), or a passage to Bermuda. But it doesn't stop there. People who take leisurely barge trips through the waterways of France or Holland rave about them; the fjords of Norway capture almost everyone's imagination, and you can also select from various itineraries that cover many parts of Latin America. Meet celebrity guests on board, experience wine tasting festivals at their best, learn French cooking, or become part of a historical lecture series. If you get this far in your thinking, then be certain to locate an experienced travel agent who has booked clients on a couple of dozen different cruise lines. They should have brochure material on file for the most important cruise lines, along with their up-to-date itineraries.

Choosing a Cruise Line—Just for You

With more than 160 ships and at least 40 cruise lines marketing their products in the U.S., you have plenty of choices to satisfy almost your every whim. You do have to make choices: the price you're willing to pay for a cruise, where you want to go, the theme or ambience you want on board, the typical age of your fellow passengers, the specific ports-of-call you'd like, the time of year you want to sail, and the length of cruise. Sorting out the possibilities may seem overwhelming, but I'll try to make that easier in this section by putting some of the more popular cruise lines into perspective. Then you can decide which ones are for you. I'll cover most of the major cruise lines that you might consider, whether a first timer or a veteran. When you get more serious about choosing a cruise line and a specific itinerary, Fielding Worldwide publishes the largest selling guide, *Fielding's Guide to Worldwide Cruises*, which gives detailed information on 140 ships and their itineraries.

The primary way to distinguish between cruise lines is on the approximate per diem (daily) cost *per passenger*. I've divided it into some standard categories. You will notice, when you go to book a cruise, that price overlaps exist, as you would expect, particularly since the same cruise line may operate several different ships that command different pricing structures. Or the same ship charges different fares for inside cabins (no windows) vs. outside views, the deck you choose (upper decks cost more), the size of your cabin/suite, or your destination. We will not pay much attention to the parent companies of these cruise lines. You need only to focus on your wallet and the services you'll receive, not who owns the cruise line, to determine which one might be best for you.

CRUISE LINE CATEGORIES and PRICING

(Does Not Include Airfare)

Category	Daily Cost per Passenger
Ultra-Luxury	$550 to $800
Luxury	$450 to $550
Premium	$375 to $450
Standard	$300 to $350
Budget	$200 to $250

All prices listed above are for *standard* sized outside staterooms with two beds and shower/bath combinations. With a couple of exceptions, you can count on discounts in the range of 25 percent to 35 percent, and sometimes at the 50 percent level. In occasional circumstances, third and fourth passengers may also be allowed to go along without extra cost.

To help you choose a cruise line, I've developed what I call the Loyalty Scale. I ask previous passengers on cruise lines who plan to cruise again (in my American Traveler Survey) which cruise line they will probably select. In theory, this measure could vary from 100 (all passengers would choose it again) to zero (no one selects it). In practice, this never happens but the range of scores is much broader than I expected. However you look at it, this is a customer satisfaction index. Satisfied cruisers want to return to the same cruise line.

Overall, the Loyalty Index measures at 34. In other words, about one out of three passengers (34 percent) is considering sailing again on the same cruise line for the next cruise. Any percentage above this number means stronger than average loyalty, and below that suggests a less than average score. At the end of this chapter, I summarize the Loyalty Index ratings for all cruise lines reviewed.

Let's see how the cruise lines stack up.

Ultra-Luxury
($550–$800 Per Day)

The ultra-luxury segment has some advantages not often apparent to first time travelers. Aside from the fact that these cruise lines provide superlative service, a number of costs that other cruise lines charge extra for are included in their inclusive prices. You sometimes do not pay extra for drinks on board, your hotel night in a city at the beginning and end of the trip, tips for crew members who serve you, or extra for some of the sightseeing shore excursions. Sometimes, the costs are not as severe as they seem.

In early 1994, several cruise lines fit this category. Now confusion reigns following recent acquisitions and mergers as new owners attempt to develop their own positionings. I'll do my best to bring you up-to-date on everything in an effort to make it "perfectly clear." But ultra-luxury and luxury overlap to a great degree.

The ultra-luxury segment typically offers ships in the smaller to mid-size category, less than 200 to a maximum of 300 berths (passengers), with an emphasis on the maximum number of outside staterooms (rooms with windows). Only two cruise lines truly fit this category at present.

Seabourn Cruise Line

When it entered the market in December, 1988 with a stunning new ship, *Seabourn Pride*, it defined this segment. With the addition of the *Spirit*, it has set the standards that others entering this category must follow. It offers all outside staterooms. It caters to an older, wealthy audience who demand impeccable service in a more subdued and elegant manner. Prices range in the $700 to $800 per day category (plus airfare) for its all-suite configurations and spacious public areas. Lots of extras are included in its price, but not drinks or shore excursions. You'll pay extra for that.

In interviews with its passengers, they give it a perfect "excellent" score (all persons interviewed score it at 10 on a 10-point scale) for its quality of overall service. That is an extraordinary accomplishment. It also gets very high marks for its ships that are considered to be well-maintained with a crew dedicated to service and passenger support. The food on board achieves outstanding ratings, equal to some of the best restaurants in the world. But entertainment receives lower scores (small ships cannot support large casts or big name talent). Seabourn, based on my interviews with passengers, achieves an incredible vote of confidence: it has a Loyalty Index score of 92. In other words, 92 percent of its previous passengers who are considering taking another cruise within the next three years would like to return to Seabourn. No other cruise line comes close. I can't think of any other travel company that has generated as high a level of consumer approval. It confirms my earlier statements about going for quality: the higher a level of cruise experience you select, the more you are likely to return home satisfied.

Silversea Cruises

Silversea designed itself from day one to be a match for Seabourn and it hopes to equal or exceed Seabourn's success. With its first ship on the water in April, 1994 *(Silvercloud)* and the second in January, 1995 *(Silverwind)*, Silversea quickly caught the fancy of many travel writers and very upscale passengers. Its ships are also totally new, designed for the subdued tastes of the very wealthy, with most of its outside staterooms configured as suites with sitting verandas and floor-to-ceiling sliding glass doors. Although it takes time to establish a reputation, early indications suggest that it will at least equal the service standards of its primary competitor, Seabourn. By next year, I hope to have a Loyalty Index measure on Silversea.

Silversea follows a unique pricing policy. It does not advertise to the public, only through travel agents, and it passes on these savings to the consumer. Thus, its pricing structure tends to be about $200 per day lower than Seabourn's. But except for early booking incentives of 10 percent to 15 percent, Silversea does not offer discounts. That discount, in effect, comes from not paying for expensive advertising campaigns and passing the savings on to you. Thus, you can sail with the comfort of knowing that no other passenger received a lower price than you for the same type of cabin. Almost everything is included in the price, even the drinks you'll have on-board and one shore excursion. There's no tipping. The restaurants are elegant with single sitting dining service (you can go to dinner whenever you wish, rather than having to sit at a predetermined time). It offers a variety of entertainment, but again, on a much more limited scale than on larger cruise ships.

In summary, Silversea offers many advantages: a new line with elegant new ships, interesting itineraries, service standards that probably equal Seabourn's, and at a price below Seabourn's.

Luxury Cruise Lines

The luxury category established the image for the entire cruise industry in the 1930's and 40's by its high standards of service and through movie portrayals of the good life on board a transatlantic crossing. The luxury category generally has a solid reputation for delivering products of top quality, but you will usually pay extra for a number of the add-ons.

Crystal Cruises

Crystal Cruises (owned by NYK in Japan) demonstrates the interest and commitment of Japanese companies to enter the luxury cruise market. It inaugurated service in 1989 with is first ship called *Harmony*. Its second ship hit the water in May, 1995. It offers outside staterooms and sitting verandas for more than half of these. Although a relatively new line, Crystal's passengers give it very high marks in my surveys for overall quality. It also gets strong scores for its modern ships that are extraordinarily well maintained, and it provides superlative food, according to its passengers. Overall, it's a very strong cruise line that caters to mature, wealthy passengers. It is not seen as appropriate for young couples, families or middle class passengers because of its higher prices and more sedate service levels. However, it gets good ratings for its varied onboard activities and entertainment, primarily because its larger ships (nearly 1000 passengers) can support more diverse, quality entertainment. It also has a very dedicated group of ex-passengers. It has a Loyalty Index score of 62, *the second highest in the survey.* In other words, more than six out of 10 of its past cruisers are considering it again for a future cruise.

To summarize, you'll like just about everything about *Crystal*, its new ships, attentive crew, outstanding food, elegant dining, and even its on-board entertainment. Its ratings make it very competitive to the ultra-luxury category. Since it is still fighting to gain acceptance and recognition in the marketplace, you have a limited opportunity to gain an advantage in obtaining discounts.

Cunard Line

The *Queen Elizabeth 2 (QE2)*, which Cunard considers a category by itself, creates some confusion in people's minds because it has cabins that vary from luxury to premium (below luxury). Choice depends upon inside or outside cabin and, more importantly, on the level selected by the passenger. Guests in categories A, B and C can dine at the Queen's Grill; categories D and D2 only provide access to the Princess Grill. The ship's design also tends to separate passengers.

In spite of this potential confusion in people's minds, Cunard is well known in the industry but the *QE2* offers a traditional cruise experience that dates from the era of longer sailings with fewer ports of call. The quality of food rates favorably across most of the pricing categories for the *QE2*. It's generally seen by passengers in my interviews as catering to a more upscale and mature clientele.

The *QE2* is an older ship, built in 1967, although well maintained and constantly being refurbished. It underwent a $45 million remake of passenger areas in 1994, but it had some initial shakedown problems. Although problems have been handled since then, you can check with your travel agent for the latest update if you are concerned. The *Queen's* massive size, carrying 1864 passengers, means you can spend a week on board just trying to see everything. Surprisingly, entertainment gets very modest ratings, considering it's a mega-liner (larger ships can provide more varied entertainment and usually get stronger scores). It achieves a below average 23 on the Loyalty Index.

Cunard Royal Viking

As you have noticed, Cunard's name appears more than once in this category and in more than one category in this review because it brands its corporate name on each segment it serves (unlike many cruise lines). In 1994 it acquired the Royal Viking name and one of its ships, and added several of its own, to create the Cunard Royal Viking category. Cunard also added the *Sagafjord, Vistafjord, Sea Goddess I* and *Sea Goddess II* ships to the Royal Viking category. But all of these ships do not receive equal acceptance among passengers.

The *Royal Viking Sun* at one time set the standard for luxury service. It was owned by Kloster and sold to Cunard in 1994. It accommodates about 700 passengers with 96 percent of its staterooms having windows. It's a larger, older ship by today's luxury standards, but has a strong quality reputation.

The *Sea Goddess I* and *II* also get very strong marks for service and could be placed in the ultraluxury category. But, their smaller size (each carries slightly more than 100 passengers) and smaller, yachtlike staterooms make these appropriate for more experienced cruisers who want a unique level of onboard experience, rather than first timers.

The *Sagafjord* and *Vistafjord* are older ships (constructed in 1965 and 1973 respectively) and create more of an old world ambiance (originally owned by Norwegian America Line) with large staterooms and European style service and care for passengers. Each carries 600 to 700 passengers and receives good ratings for food and service levels. But these two ships are a notch below everything we've talked about thus far.

On my Loyalty Index, the ships of Cunard in this segment score in the average range, i.e., getting ratings from 30 to 33. The Royal Viking especially should achieve higher ratings because of its history and commitment to service (its current ratings are from when its previous owner, Kloster, operated it). Perhaps it will improve after it has settled in with its new owner, Cunard. Overall, these loyalty scores should be higher, to serve a discriminating clientele.

Radisson Seven Seas

What was a small player in the upscale market has suddenly become a bigger force through acquisitions and repositioning. Radisson Diamond, the ship management company owned by Radisson Hotels International, completed a marketing and management agreement with Seven Seas Cruise Line (which had earlier merged with the German tour company's Hanseatic Cruises). Collectively, this agreement controls about 10 percent of the luxury cruise market. But, it's a bit of a strange merger since none of the ships is similar, varying from ultraluxury to luxury and premium.

The 172 passenger *Song of Flower* ship of Seven Seas appropriately belongs in the ultraluxury category. It offers all the on board amenities and service levels of the best cruise lines in the world. But, it now becomes part of a larger marketing plan. Since it will take time for that plan to grab public attention, look for favorable pricing for the next year or two. It should be a strong contender in your set of cruising options. It's a new ship, with 100 percent outside staterooms, and it appeals to a mature, wealthy clientele.

The *Radisson Diamond* carries 350 passengers and has a stunning design. A twin hull (like a catamaran) helps it to ride out rough weather better than single hull designs. The *Diamond* hit the water in 1992 and meets most of the standards of the top cruise ships in the world (including single seating dining and formal wear for some events). But, it also depends heavily on what travel professionals call *incentive travel.* This refers to the travel rewards given to salespersons for exceeding quotas or to key employees for exceptional work. Thus, some cabin space on board is dedicated to meetings and conferences (a company can't deduct the expense unless some business is conducted), and you could find yourself occasionally with a more lively crowd because many of them know each other or they work for the same company. The *Diamond* typically features shorter itineraries of four or five days since its focus is on the incentives and meetings market (companies tend not to pay for long vacations). The *Diamond* belongs more appropriately in the luxury category, rather than ultraluxury.

The *German Hanseatic* ship does not fit this merger very well. It is supposed to provide a luxury "soft" adventure travel experience to people who want to explore less popular geographic areas while cruising. You won't see much advertising for this ship in the U.S. since it will primarily be based in Europe.

Renaissance Cruises

I would recommend this line only for more experienced cruisers, rather than first timers. Its eight small yachtlike ships (each carries about 100 passengers) focus more on destinations, rather than onboard cuisine and entertainment. Most sailings are at night, to allow daytime explorations of unspoiled and exotic places often unreachable by larger cruise ships with a deeper draft. Lecturers often add to the experience but, again, you should usually seek out on board ambience more than an exotic location for the first outing. However, it achieves a Loyalty Index score of 43 in my interviews, indicating that it does an excellent job in serving its self created niche. But that niche does not target the interests of majority of cruisers.

Premium Cruise Lines

Standards continue to be high in this category. It has some of the best known names in the cruise industry, including a few with long standing reputations for the quality of their products.

Celebrity Cruises

Celebrity represents another relatively new cruise line, formed in 1989 by Chandris Fantasy Cruises, to capture a more upscale market. It currently has two large ships (each carrying 1200 to 1700 passengers), one of which is a vessel converted with a $70 million makeover, two launched in 1990 and 1991, plus its newest 1995 ship. Two more will follow, one each in the years 1996 and 1997, indicating again the commitment and faith of many companies in the future of cruising.

It has a special focus on food, the top reason for taking a cruise by most passengers. It features menus planned by Michel Roux and perhaps offers the finest dining of any cruise line. Its passengers see it as catering to younger singles and couples, and somewhat less so to luxury passengers. However, it measures above average on my Loyalty Index (at 40 vs. 34 average), indicating that it has created an onboard ambience that pleases most of its guests. It should be a strong contender in your cruise options.

Cunard Crown

Cunard's focus on the premium market also causes a bit of confusion, especially since it created the Crown category only in 1994 after acquisitions and its own merger of ships and name. It operates two somewhat distinct lines, each with twin sister ships. The *Countess* and the *Princess* are older, and both launched in 1976. But like most lines, they have been refurbished more than once since that time. *Dynasty* and its sister came on line in 1993 under a long term marketing agreement with Crown Cruise Line. Each of the ships is in the 800 berth size, and each provides rather tight quarters for passengers.

Perhaps as a result of the smaller cabins, the Loyalty Index measures at a very low 16 (average is 34). However, public areas for relaxing and entertainment tend toward the impressive. You should be able to get favorable rates, particularly if you book quite early or very late. Most cruise lines in the Premium category provide good value for the money.

Holland America Line

It's one of the oldest lines around, carrying its first passengers in 1872. Carnival Cruise Lines completed its acquisition of Holland America in 1989 and has since allowed it to operate as an independent subsidiary. It has a mixture of older and new ships, with several on order because of its successful growth strategy.

If Alaskan waterways interest you, this is one of the companies to consider. Through its subsidiary, Westours, it has been a leader in opening that market. HAL also operates heavily in the Caribbean, includes the Mediterranean in its plans, and offers many unique itineraries and even 'round the world cruises.

In the premium category, passengers in my interviews rate it well above average for most service dimensions. Its ships get good scores for maintenance and cleanliness, presumably because it has Dutch officers who watch closely over its Indo nesian crews. It generally carries an older, luxury oriented but not extremely wealthy, group of passengers. Like most cruise lines that cater to mature markets, it is not seen as being particularly suitable for younger adults, singles or honeymooners. Its Loyalty Index score (35) comes in at about average, with one out of three of its former cruisers considering it for the next voyage. HAL's service scores have been slipping somewhat in my surveys over the past several years, possibly because of its rapid growth and its experiment with different onboard decors for its new ships. It has a distinctive blue bottom and white top color scheme to identify its ships.

Princess Cruises

In the premium segment, Princess stands above the crowd. In my interviews with past cruisers, it scores above average on a large number of dimensions, with none below average. Although upscale in image and service, it still appeals to a younger crowd, the 35+ group, rather than 45+. As a result, honeymooners like it, along with young couples in general. Its passengers believe that it offers good value for the money and it also fits the image of being an industry leader. It scores well above average on the Loyalty Index at 43 (the percent of past cruisers who are thinking about returning for another cruise). It also gets good marks for the quality of its food and on board entertainment.

The original "Love Boat" of the sitcom series has not rested on its laurels from the favorable publicity but has been innovative in developing new programs. It has a very large operation serving Alaska, and now offers interesting inland excursions that include rail car trips from Anchorage to Mt. McKinley or Prudhoe Bay. It alone carries as many cruisers each year as had ever cruised by 1970, demonstrating the tremendous growth of the cruise market. It also places ships around the world, often varying their schedules. It sails to Mexico, the Caribbean, parts of Europe, the South Pacific and Asia, India, Africa, Hawaii and the Holy Land. All in all, Princess can be considered a relatively good choice for most cruisers. Good service, good loyalty scores, and good value for the money.

Royal Cruise Line

One of two cruise lines owned by Kloster (the other is Norwegian Cruise Line), Royal Cruise Line (RCL) scores above average on almost all dimensions. Its clientele tend to be a bit older and wealthier, although not nearly as upscale or as mature as lines serving the ultra luxury segment. But it still is seen as being suitable for young couples and honeymooners—they won't feel out of place since it does not maintain a stuffy atmosphere on board. In my interviews, passengers report that it has superior food, well maintained modern ships, a crew that attends to the little details and quality on board entertainment. It develops very strong passenger loyalty, with a Loyalty Index rating of 45.

RCL recently installed new management and it has been aggressively pursuing what it believes today's cruisers want. It probably offers more exercise programs for the health conscious than any other line, including fitness classes, health lectures and a wide choice of low cholesterol and other health oriented meals. Its fleet, which is growing with new ships, serves most parts of the world. This includes the Caribbean, the Mediterranean and other parts of Europe, the Mexican

Riviera, the U.S. (including Alaska) and Canada, the Pacific and Asia, and longer voyages that can include the Panama Canal.

All things considered, Royal is a good choice for first timers and experienced cruisers.

Standard

The Standard category carries the largest number of passengers because its pricing appeals to the largest number of prospects. Carnival Cruise Lines dominates this category with most lines offering good value, along with a heavy concentration of sailings in warm Caribbean waters. Some well known names, including ships and their cruise line parents, compete with each other in appealing to the mass market.

Carnival Cruise Lines

They call them the "Fun Ships." With names like *Fantasy, Ecstasy, Sensation, Imagination, Fascination* and *Celebration*, you expect a party time, and perhaps some romance when you come on board. Expect lots of action if you sail with Carnival. It has more under-30 adults, with a high loading of singles, than any other line. These swingers want to experience a good time that they'll remember long after they return home. Where the ships sail is almost irrelevant because what happens on board is much more important. The casino opens at 8:00 A.M. and, along with the bars, it provides lots of action until the wee hours of the morning. Expect lots of activity, noise, dancing and drinking among this crowd. Because it operates some of the biggest ships in the industry, it offers a broad variety of entertainment. Its nightly stage productions feature about 40 entertainers, musicians and stage crew. You'll have a tough time finding a little old blue haired lady among this crowd.

Its recent entry, *Fascination*, came on the water in 1994, and carries more than 2000 passengers. The line has already committed to the construction of megaships (2600 berth vessels) that will continue to keep it ahead of the rest of the industry. It currently carries about 25 percent of the total passengers in the industry and will take delivery of ships through 1998, just based on current commitments.

Up to 70 percent of Carnival's passengers are first timers who focus on its low price and swinging atmosphere. It develops markets for the other cruise lines it owns (Holland America, Windstar and Seabourn, of which it owns 25%) and feeds passengers to many of its competitors. When passengers want to move upscale, it wants them to consider Holland America for the next cruise, or its boutique tall ship company, Windstar. In my surveys, its passengers believe that it offers good value for the money and has modern ships. In spite of its focus on glitz, glamour and an extroverted cruise life-style, its Loyalty Index measures at slightly above the industry average (36 for Carnival). It even equals the loyalty ratings for some of the more upscale lines.

Its itineraries concentrate on three, four, and seven day schedules, helping to keep the costs down and reducing the hesitancy of first timers who often don't want to try an extended cruise for their initial sailings. So, if you're young, single or married, haven't cruised before, enjoy lots of action and don't want to commit to a long cruise, Carnival may be the right choice for you.

Costa Cruise Lines

Costa at one time could claim the title of being the world's largest cruise line (it still has seven ships). It helped to pioneer sailing in the Caribbean. At present, however, it takes a back seat to a number of lines operating in the Caribbean, in terms of the number of sailings, and is increasing its presence in the Mediterranean rather than confront the tough competition off U.S. shores.

At one time Costa had some of the highest levels of service, but other lines have now taken on that mantle. In my surveys, passengers believe that it offers relatively good value for the money, catering primarily to a middle class, more mature market. But it rates somewhat below average on quality of food, of entertainment, attention to detail and in the upkeep and maintenance of its ships. Unfortunately, its ratings have been slipping gradually in recent years. On my Loyalty Index, it achieves a score of 20, a relatively low figure for a line that hopes to capture the broad market of cruisers. It should do better.

Costa can still provide a memorable cruise for you, however, and it participates in discounting. So, you may be able to get the right price for that first trip or the next one. It primarily covers the Caribbean and the Mediterranean areas, and it knows both of these regions very well.

Norwegian Cruise Line (NCL)

Serving the middle market, with a mixture of older and newer ships, NCL successfully caters to a broad group of passengers, from honeymooners to the mature, and middle income to the wealthy.

It rates at least equal to most cruise lines in its class and does not fall below average on any dimension. You can count on getting good food, quality entertainment, an attentive crew, well-maintained ships and an adequate number of onboard activities to keep you occupied during the daytime.

As one of the oldest lines serving the Caribbean, it knows those waters extremely well. It provides many three and four day cruises that are popular with busy people on tight schedules and with first timers. Its ships also sail the waters of Alaska, the west coast of the U.S., and some ports in Mexico.

Its Loyalty Index, at 39, measures above average. All in all, it can be a good selection for first timers or experienced cruisers who don't want to pay top dollar for a cruise on the high seas. Few lines provide above average service levels at value-based prices, making it a potential choice for many.

Premier Cruise Line

It serves the family market with the "big red boat" that anyone who has cruised with the line will remember well. In actuality, it has several red boats, each serving a limited number of ports in the Caribbean. It was the "official" cruise line of Walt Disney World, but severed its ties because Disney has plans to enter the family cruise market with two new ships of its own. Thus, your children will now be greeted by Warner Brothers cartoon characters (Bugs Bunny, Daffy Duck, Sylvester and Speedy Gonzalez) as they climb on board. But, you can still buy a package that includes three or four nights on the "boat," with the remaining portion of the week spent at Disney World.

Premier offers a variety of programs for children, sometimes educational in nature and often with an emphasis on sports. Its long standing relationship with The Major League Baseball Players Alumni Association brings ex-big leaguers on board some cruises. Adult activities are also planned, to make certain that parents stay happy. Its ships have casinos, several bars, big name entertainment and extensive facilities in their fitness centers.

In my interviews, it is seen as providing a good experience for all generations in a family, including grandparents, and it also is appropriate for younger couples and singles. Its Loyalty Index score is only a modest 24. That's primarily because its limited itinerary and shorter cruise length leads most people to seek greater choice for their next cruise. Its cabins do not create the comfortable ambience of a more sophisticated cruise line. But, if you're looking for a budget-priced family cruise, Premier is one of the first you should consider because of its dual focus on the needs of both adults and children.

Royal Caribbean Cruise Line (RCCL)

In this highly competitive world of cruise lines and cruise ships, RCCL does very well. It rates above the pack on most service dimensions and does not fall below average on any dimension in the studies I conduct. It gets good marks for its food, newness and maintenance of its ships, its efficient crew, the onboard entertainment and its overall attention to detail.

Like many traditional cruise lines, it carries an image of appealing to a more mature group of cruisers, although they tend to be middle class rather than the very wealthy. However, it also offers a number of three- and four-day itineraries that usually appeal to the younger set.

RCCL has been one of the leaders in building new mega ships, each having a capacity of 1600 to 2500 passengers. These provide an opportunity to put more dollars into superior on board entertainment, public lounge areas and upgraded fitness areas. But smaller cabins are a result of this commitment to grand sized common areas. All ships feature top Broadway musicals, further reflecting their focus on entertaining their guests.

Very important, it measures very high on the Loyalty Index: 57 percent of recent cruisers may select it again for their next cruise. That's the *third highest in my surveys*. To capture the interest of nearly six out of ten, you have to be doing something right. Its passengers also feel they get good value for the money.

RCCL covers most of the destinations that first timers, or those who are about to take their second or third cruise, would probably consider—Caribbean, Bahamas, Mexico, Alaska and Europe, and it has just added Asia. In addition, it has just put back on line a private destination that it built in Haiti, called Labadee, now that the country has political stability.

All in all, RCCL can be a good choice because of value pricing and high passenger ratings. Again, look for the right kind of bargains, particularly if this is your first cruise.

Budget Cruise Lines

This category provides what the name implies—lower pricing. If you don't have much money, or want to scrimp a bit on that first cruise, this may be your choice. But some of the services you want may be missing (fewer meal times, less attractive itineraries, smaller cabins). So, check with your travel agent before you make your booking. It may not cost that much extra to move up a category or two to a cruise line that includes more items in its price.

Dolphin Cruise Line

This line focuses on younger singles and couples who want to stretch their dollars. It also goes after families who desire to take their children along (Fred Flintstone and Yogi Bear frequently are on board), and it also tries to get honeymooners. It scores well for providing good value for the money, but below average on the quality of its food, on-board entertainment and activities, and the attentiveness of its crew. As a result, Dolphin gets a very low Loyalty Index score of 13 in my surveys. In general, expect low loyalty measurements among budget cruise lines because most passengers want to move upscale for their next cruise.

Regency Cruises

Positioned to offer good value, but not with the lowest fares in the category, Regency sends it ships to many ports throughout the world, depending upon the season. It covers portions of the Caribbean, Latin America, Alaska, the Mediterranean and even transcanal sailing.

It appeals primarily to middle income families and does a relatively good job with service levels and quality of food. Entertainment gets average ratings, a rather good score considering its focus on the value market. Since the Loyalty Index (30) measures at almost average levels, it could be one of the lines for you to consider if you're looking for more favorable rates.

Tall Ships and Specialty Cruises

No, I'm not talking about cruise ships now. Rather, this is a category of ships that have masts and sails, the so-called tall ships we all admire in photographs or have seen sailing into harbors around the world. In my surveys, they generally get high loyalty ratings, from average to above average scores, indicating that passengers like what they get. First timers probably should not consider them because they are so unlike a typical cruise experience. However, if you classified yourself strongly as an active venturer, this could be a cruise experience you'd like a lot.

I'll briefly review the four best known tall ship lines that dominate the market. I'm also including American Hawaii Cruises and Delta Queen Steamboat Company in this category because of their specialty focus.

First, all tall ships share some common characteristics that make them unique. You'll find life on board to be much more casual and informal than on a regular cruise ship. No one has a schedule so you eat and sleep when you feel like it, with lots of lounging around the deck during the daytime. At night, a partylike atmosphere often exists with late night dancing and lots of camaraderie between passengers and the crew. The ships typically are small, carrying from 70 to 150 passengers, which obviously restricts the amount of public area they can provide to passengers.

They all sail in warm water locales and feature watersports, such as scuba diving and snorkeling, water-skiing, and wind surfing. You'll also get a chance to visit some of the cities at various ports of call, although they often anchor off shore to allow passengers to choose between going ashore or diving into the water. As long as there's a good wind, you'll cruise leisurely with full sails. When it's calm, the engines take over. With a small ship, a limited number of passengers and a tendency toward somewhat longer cruise schedules (seven to 14 days), many people become close friends before the trip ends. Also, choices from the menus can be very limited, again because ship size does not permit elaborate preparations. Pricing tends to fit in the luxury category, around $400 to $600 per day per passenger.

Club Med Cruises

Noting the success of other tall ship cruise companies, Club Med decided to enter the operation on its own in 1992. It has two new, specially constructed ships (each carries approximately 400 passengers) that are much larger than those of its competitors. Their size not only allows greater operating efficiencies for Club Med, but also the opportunity to offer more services to passengers—two restaurants on board, a swimming pool, better entertainment, and more effort put into making the trip seem like you can drop all of your cares and inhibitions— a Club Med tradition.

It placed its first ship in the Caribbean and the second in the South Pacific, primarily around the islands of Tahiti. It has a strong emphasis on watersports, providing all of the gear you'll need, along with plenty of expert instruction. It has a very strong Loyalty Index score of 46. Passengers like what they get, and will come back for more.

Star Clippers

Its two new, modern ships carry 170 passengers and have the tallest masts among the specialty cruise lines. They rotate between Caribbean and Mediterranean waters and provide many of the amenities you expect on more standard kinds of luxury cruise ships. The line offers large cabins with modern bathroom appointments, two swimming pools—and 36,000 square feet of sail when all of it is unfurled. I have only a limited sample of persons who have cruised on it, but its Loyalty Index rates above average at 40. On board, you'll find a relaxed atmosphere and good service and food.

Windjammer Barefoot Cruises

The name may sound a bit odd, but it conveys the informality of life on one of these tall ships. This line started the trend and has been sailing the Caribbean since 1947. It features six restored classic sailing vessels, rather than the new ships of some of its competitors. Smaller in size, and not originally constructed as luxury yachts, they offer fewer services and amenities to passengers. Cabins are small, and even the food is described by the company's founder, Mike Burke, as "plentiful and wholesome, rather than gourmet and varied," (*Travel Weekly* 8/14/94). The atmosphere is even more relaxed than for the other lines, especially since passengers sometimes jump in and help to unfurl the sails. Like the others, it has a heavy emphasis on watersports.

Perhaps because of the smaller cabins and more austere nature of its older ships, it does not achieve the Loyalty Index score of other tall ship lines. Its rating, at 35, is right at average for all cruise lines.

Windstar Cruises

Acquired by Holland America, it became part of Carnival Cruises when it took over HAL. Until recently, Carnival left it alone to pursue its own path, but has now decided to give it a more firm focus on its path to future success.

It boasts modern ships with completely computerized control of the sails. Although its ships carry only 150 passengers, it provides a lot of creature comforts to its guests. CD players in every room, a hot tub on deck, a pool, a beauty salon with a massage parlor and a strong emphasis on cuisine planned by award-winning chefs. Its ships cover the Caribbean, the Mediterranean and South Pacific waters, depending upon time of the year.

In my surveys, it receives a very strong Loyalty Index score of 53. More than half (53 percent) of its passengers say they would like to take another cruise with Windstar. They're doing something right.

American Hawaii Cruises

Its name says it all. It sails only among the Hawaiian Islands, at a leisurely pace in the warm waters with stops at various ports. Its original concept was seven-day cruises starting and ending in Honolulu. But it now offers three- and four-day sailings. You can leave the ship and stay at an island resort to play golf on some of the grand courses, or to rent a car and drive around for a while. It's a great way to enjoy the islands, but you primarily should consider this cruise as an enhancement to a Hawaiian vacation, rather than as a first choice for cruising. However, it has good air/sea programs to encourage travelers to choose it as the best way to visit the islands.

It sails older ships, the *Constitution* and the *Independence*, that have been refurbished at various times. In my surveys, it is seen as appealing to a broad group of people, including families, honeymooners and people with moderate incomes. With shorter itineraries and smaller, older vessels, it does not rate well for onboard entertainment or activities. But, it shouldn't have to: when you sail between the islands, you enjoy one of the most tranquil locations in the world. It measures low on my Loyalty Index, at 19. But that's probably because you have to choose Hawaii as a destination first before you'll even consider taking a cruise with American Hawaii.

Delta Queen Steamboat Company

Consider it a very unique slice of American history, rather than a typical cruise experience. The ship (the company operates only one but has plans for more) has been around so long that a large number of people know about it and have cruised on it. It came on line in 1927, and has sailed up and down the Mississippi and Ohio rivers ever since, sailing from its home port in New Orleans. Although modernized at various times (especially with upgraded air conditioning), it still retains the original look and feel of what it truly is—an old paddlewheeler. Chippendale furniture and stained-glass windows add to its sense of timelessness. It recently added another, more modern ship, with the third to come online late in 1995.

It appeals primarily to experienced cruisers who want a change from their usual itineraries, and to those who simply are fascinated by the history of the old riverboat gambling era. First timers will also enjoy it, but don't view it as a typical cruise experience. My interviews with passengers indicate that standards for food, service and entertainment do not match the offerings of more conventional lines. Also, it's not appropriate for younger adults, especially those with children because the average age of passengers is higher. It measures very low on my Loyalty Index at 18 (less than one out of five say they might cruise again on it within the next three years). This low score most likely results from the fact that, once you've experienced it, you don't need to repeat that kind of a trip for awhile. Consider it a slice of Americana, not a typical ocean cruise.

What About the Kids?

Have you thought about taking the kids on a cruise? Probably not. The idea of being cooped up with dozens, perhaps hundreds, of other people's "little darlings" probably doesn't excite you. Rightly so. But, those thoughts may also keep you from enjoying one of your best family vacations ever. Besides, the family cruise market has grown faster than adults-only cruising, so something must be going on.

When you take a look at what's happening, you can see why. Traditional families (mother *and* father, plus children), single parents with their kids, and generational "splits" (grandparents with one or more children), have all taken to cruising in a big way. Three reasons contribute to cruising's new popularity. First with so much activity on board, all generations can find exciting things to do that interest them. You will have a tough time thinking of any land-based destination that offers as much diversity to capture the attention of various age groups. Second, it all happens in a contained environment. You don't have to worry about your children—where they are, their safety or whether they might be exposed to inappropriate kinds of experiences. Finally, it can bring people together from wherever they live throughout the U.S., and no one is stuck in the kitchen with all of the work. Great idea!

Think about it for a moment. If you are a traditional family, each of your various aged children has exciting activities to look forward to each day: supervised play times for younger children, skill learning and educational lectures on geography and sea life for pre-teens, and sports instruction, video arcades and social hours for teenagers. During all of this, you can be doing your own thing—much like you normally would on any cruise. You can be with your children for as much or little quality time as you choose. To find that combination of options on any land-based vacation is difficult, I'm sure you'll agree.

Single parents love it for similar reasons. Their children can have a great time while they can relax and get away from some of the pressures they feel on a daily basis. They can also be with their children to any degree they choose, participating in their games and play activities, or getting away from it all to think about life's choices or to socialize with others.

As for grandparents, what could be nicer. If they take a land-based vacation they typically must be with their grandchildren every waking moment to entertain them or to ensure that they don't get into trouble. That's a lot of responsibility, along with physical demands, for people who may not have the stamina they once enjoyed. With cruising, they can retreat to the quiet of their cabin while they grandchildren participate in supervised activities whenever the "old folks" need to rest or regain their energy. Refreshed and recharged, they can again keep up with the energy level of the very young. This situation even works well for single grandparents. No other vacation experience can compete as effectively.

Which Cruise Line to Choose for a Family

Let me make your choices relatively simple. As it turns out, you do and you don't have a lot of options when you think about a family cruise. Most cruise lines that sail larger ships (1000 berth capacity, or more) have family activity directors on board who focus on organizing and planning daily programs for children of all ages. But, on the other side of the equation, few choices exist to select a cruise line that caters only to families. An attempt to capture this market by American Family Cruises (an offshoot of Costa Cruise Lines) in 1994 failed after about nine months of operation. The company did not capture enough cruisers during the school months to stay alive. The Walt Disney Company will introduce two new, specially designed ships in 1997, and it will be interesting to see how well they succeed in what is a highly seasonal market.

In the interim, you can focus on a couple of very good choices.

1. Premier Cruise Lines, with its "Big Red Boats," concentrates heavily on the family market. They feature Warner Brothers cartoon (Loony Toons) characters on board, and a tie-in with Walt Disney World for split trip vacations—half of the time on the water and half at the theme park. This odd combination of Warner and Disney resulted from Disney deciding to go into the cruise business for themselves (until recently, Premier featured Disney cartoon characters). See the description of Premier in this section. It has lots of experience in satisfying both children and adults and wants to be known as the family-friendly cruise line. It's a good option for you to consider.

2. As I indicated, family activity directors sail along with most larger ships, particularly for cruise lines serving the standard market category. These lines will feel like a conventional cruise line to you, and children's programs will not be quite as obvious to guests. But, make no mistake, these lines provide entertaining activities that your children will enjoy. Quality supervision will help you relax because you know your offspring are both safe and happy. Although several lines have children's programs, Carnival and RCCL are the most active in developing onboard activities for younger passengers. Both of these lines score well on the Loyalty Index. But the luxury and ultraluxury cruise lines generally do not encourage young children on board. Their more sedate atmosphere does not lend itself well to the high energy levels of children.

If you shop well, family cruise vacations offer especially good value because children come along at deep discounts, and sometimes even for free. Your cruise specialist travel agent can tell you which lines currently offer good discounts for children. Then you can decide which line may be best for your trip by comparing Loyalty Index scores that are summarized at the end of this chapter.

It should be a great experience, so get going!

The Loyalty Index Summary

Since I reviewed so many cruise lines, many of which get scores above or below the average for their categories, it's worthwhile to present a summary of their ratings. Other factors will undoubtedly enter into your choice of a cruise line, but this at least provides a starting point for your review. Remember, the Loyalty Index is the percent of past passengers considering the line for their next cruise.

FIGURE 7
LOYALTY INDEX SUMMARY

Ranking	Loyalty Index Score	Cruise Line	Category
1.	92	Seabourn	Ultra-luxury
2.	62	Crystal	Luxury
3.	57	RCCL	Standard
4.	53	Windstar	Tall Ship
5.	46	Club Med	Tall Ship
6.	45	RCL	Premium
7.	43	Princess	Premium
7. tie	43	Renaissance	Luxury
9.	40	Celebrity	Premium
9. tie	40	Star Clipper	Tall Ship
11.	39	NCL	Standard
12.	36	Carnival	Standard
13.	35	Holland America	Premium
13. tie	35	Windjammer Barefoot Cruises	Tall Ship
15.	33	Royal Viking (Cunard)	Luxury/ Ultra Luxury
16.	30	Regency	Budget
17.	24	Premier	Standard
18.	23	Cunard Line (QE2)	Luxury
19.	20	Costa	Standard
20.	19	American Hawaii	Specialty
21.	18	Delta Queen Steamboat	Specialty
22.	16	Cunard Crown	Premium
23.	13	Dolphin	Budget

Not rated (insufficient data): Radisson Seven Seas; Silversea

Section III:
Travel Smarter, Not Harder

THINKING OF AN ESCORTED TOUR? HERE'S WHAT YOU SHOULD KNOW

Although guided tours have been around for centuries, explosive growth didn't occur until the early 1950s. At that time, airlines bought new piston engine airplanes that could get you to Europe from New York in 12 to 14 hours flying time vs. several days by boat. The cost of getting there and back dropped dramatically, while travel in Europe was extraordinarily cheap because of the very strong dollar.

But what really contributed most to the tremendous rise of foreign leisure travel was when some clever marketing executives recognized that millions of Americans might travel to Europe (and elsewhere) if their fears of the unknown could be removed. How to do that? Take care of everything that could bother them. Select the itinerary, arrange airline schedules, book all the hotels, choose restaurants that offer familiar tasting food, and provide tour guides whose intimate knowledge of local areas will make the tours interesting and who will also handle all language requirements.

It's been a winning formula! During the '60s and '70s, escorted tours accounted for as much as 30 percent of all leisure travelers to some countries. In fact, their popularity has resulted in considerable local criticism in some of the more popular tourist areas. The English now complain about increased traffic, congestion and pollution from bus engines in places such as Piccadilly Circus in London, and in the city center in Stratford-Upon-Avon, especially around Shakespeare's Old Globe Theatre. Italians mutter about tourist crowds ruining the majesty of the old ruins in Rome, and the Greeks believe that tour buses contribute to acid smog that has been destroying ancient monuments in Athens.

If they are this popular, they must be good. Well, usually, but not always. If you are considering taking an escorted tour, there are some things you should know about to determine whether it fits your personality type or not. You should also be wise about what to look for when selecting a tour program to make certain you get the most satisfying experience. Also, which countries consistently deliver the best tour experiences? On this latter point, just because a country gets high ratings from independent travelers who visit it does not mean that it also provides consistently good tour products, as we shall see.

What's an Escorted Tour?

A few simple definitions will help you understand the industry so that you will know more about how to decide what you want when you travel. You need to know these terms to effectively evaluate the alternatives offered to you by a travel agent.

F.I.T.

This abbreviation means "foreign independent tour." The traveler books airline flights, rental car arrangements, hotel accommodations and various city or countryside tours separately, based on specific interests, but usually through a travel agent. Nothing ties in directly to anything else, and the different travel providers may have no relationship to each other. The term "tour," in this case, means "trip," not a guided tour. F.I.T., as a phrase, has come into common usage among travel professionals because of the growth and dominance of escorted tours to foreign countries. At one time, it implied upscale travel—someone wanted to stay at better hotels, fly first class on the airlines and otherwise spend more money for a trip. No longer. It covers anything that means that the traveler makes individualized travel arrangements, regardless of level of quality.

Packages and Partial Packages

These have grown dramatically in popularity during the past two decades because they include the *essentials* that most travelers want, offered at a significant price advantage. A partial package might be airfare and hotel accommodations the first night or two after arrival and the night before departure. The more complete package might provide hotel rooms for the entire length of the trip and even a rental car, but no tour guide(s) and few, if any, meals.

In some destinations, such as places in the Caribbean and parts of Hawaii, 60 to 70 percent of all visitors arrive as part of a package. In Hawaii, for example, it has developed into a fine art. You might arrive on a charter airline flight leased entirely by your tour company, be greeted at the airport by local representatives of the company, given a lei for you and everyone in your traveling party, and provided with transportation to your hotel (and back to the airport at the end of your visit). At your hotel, you might receive a free breakfast every morning plus at least one luau during your visit. You can also enjoy featured entertainment a couple of evenings and a morning and afternoon tour to an interesting site or activity. It may have the appearance of a tour, but it's not. These travelers still have most of their time to themselves. Since these "packagers" deal with a simplified product and move thousands of people, they negotiate extraordinarily cheap rates for everything.

Fully Escorted Tour

The traditional program is called a fully escorted tour. Basically, it means that the tour organizer has accounted for almost all of your waking hours. You receive everything, and more, that is part of a package tour, but will probably move from city to city or country to country on almost a daily basis. Therefore, you may find yourself in a different hotel each night, never eating twice in the same restaurant, and shopping at places that tour organizers have selected as part of your rest stops. A sight-seeing bus picks you up each morning with a tour guide who typically stays with you during your daytime travels in the countryside, pointing out sights and interesting things to see and do. In the evening, you will probably be turned over to a local city guide who coordinates your nightlife activities and perhaps some daytime city tours.

This 24 hour care concept is sometimes abbreviated to include more free time for the visitor (not escorted by a guide), fewer meals (so that you can set your own schedule and eat when and where you want to), and less use of a daytime tour guide. In this situation, you have more free time to relax and set your own schedules and to shop at places not always selected by the tour organizer. These differences point to the distinction between a partially escorted tour and a fully escorted tour.

What Are the Advantages and Disadvantages of Escorted Tours?

Advantages

Although they have declined somewhat in market share in recent years, the tremendous historic growth of escorted tours is based on several advantages they offer:

- *Ease and Convenience.*—What could be nicer than to have someone arrange all of your hotels and other travel arrangements, pick you up at the airport and take you back at the end of the trip, and handle your bags in and out of the hotel every night? No question that it's a nice service, especially as you get older or if you're tired of schlepping everything yourself—the driving, carrying your bags in and out of hotels, selecting restaurants that turn out to be disasters, and so forth.

- *Removing uncertainty*—If you don't speak the language, and are uncomfortable in such situations, escorted tours offer obvious advantages. A multilingual tour guide gets you through all situations. Also very important, you know the guaranteed price of the trip. It can't go up after you've booked or while you're traveling just because the dollar has taken another nosedive against foreign currencies.

You also don't worry about what to order at night from a menu printed in a foreign language since escorted tours typically offer English version menus or the tour guide interprets everything for you. On a trip to Switzerland, my family and I stopped at a small Swiss/German restaurant. At the restaurant, with my poor German language skills, I ordered *trinkenwasser ohne kohlensäure* (drinking water without carbonation) for all of us. The waitress and I had a heated argument about this (she spoke only Swiss/Deutsch). Disgustedly, she finally brought us all tap water (rather than bottled water, which is most common in European countries), and which no one ever really orders. She then walked away, threw up her arms up in disgust and said to all assembled diners, *"Ganz Amerikanisch."* I knew enough German to know that she thought we were stupid and "typically American." I really wanted mineral water without carbonation, but she believed that I was a cheap American trying to avoid paying for bottled water. Without better language skills, I was trapped in an uncomfortable communications gap.

You can avoid these kinds of hassles and embarrassments with a fully escorted tour arrangement.

• *You won't miss a thing*—Another thing I can remember is the frustration I faced when I tried to find Neuschwanstein, the castle developed by the Mad King (Ludwig) of Bavaria that was copied in the *Sleeping Beauty* film by Walt Disney. My guidebook indicated that I was within 60 kilometers of its location, but my road map didn't pinpoint the spot. Somehow, in my inadequate German, I was not able to learn from the local people about its location, even though I asked many people. I never did find my way (It's in Füssen, Bavaria, I later learned).

With an escorted tour, all of the best sightseeing spots are usually included. You won't miss a thing. Interesting stories and historical perspective from tour guides add to your sense of enjoyment about each place on the tour. Most tour guides do an effective job and offer not only interesting information, but useful historical perspective in their presentations.

Disadvantages

Disadvantages also appear when you think about what tours offer. These need to be considered before you make your final choice.

• *Predetermined schedules*—You follow a fixed schedule when you travel on a tour, arising, eating and leaving according to the master plan. This can pose problems if you like to sleep in or often loaf around a bit, or if you don't feel very well because of what you did the day before. If you'd like to linger a bit longer at the museum or see that little village off in the distance, forget it. Your life has been preprogrammed for those two weeks, or for however long you committed yourself to the tour.

In Madrid, after I had spoken at an annual conference of the American Society of Travel Agents (ASTA), my wife and I went on a four-day, three-night tour of some of the most historic cities and villages in Spain. It was a wonderful experience because our tour guide explained it all in fascinating detail. But, as the tour bus sped by quaint, whitewashed villages tucked away in the nearby hills, I longed to have a car to explore these off-the-beaten-track places at my own pace.

Seat mates forever—When your travels include 40 to 60 other people who bought the same package tour, you will see them every day and know a lot more about them before you're through. If some of them turn out to be great people, you have developed lifelong friends. If not, a couple of loud mouths or other difficult people can detract from the enjoyment of your entire trip. Many people start traveling heavily when they retire. Some of my friends have complained about the rude or inconsiderate behavior of a few tour group members on their trips.

- *Pictures of people and more people*—Since you do everything as a group, when you take pictures of the places you visit you may get more people than buildings in your photos of historic monuments and other points of interest. Photos are an important part of your memories.

  I take travel photography seriously. I don't want a lot of people in pictures, particularly with the same seat mates showing up time and again in my photos. When I travel as part of an escorted tour, I feel the frustration of working hard to get the shots I want. Typically I wait until the tour guide and the group have moved on from the minilecture, take my photos sans people and run to catch up and hear a fragment of the next presentation. I lose much of the advantages of having a qualified tour guide lead me through what's interesting and important about the places I visit.

- *Cost*—Although tour operators get special pricing on all hotels, meals and other services offered, it still will cost you more to have a bus pick you up and cart you around everyday, and to provide a tour guide who will spend most waking hours with you. Obviously, you can tour more cheaply on your own, but you have to prepare yourself more carefully in order to ensure that you have a great trip. You can travel less expensively by buying a partial package.

Does Your Travel Personality Fit the Touring Type?

I made a brief reference in the chapter, "What Kind of a Traveler Are You: A Quiz" to the fact that not all types of people enjoy escorted tours. In reality, some will rebel openly at the thought of going on one, or will find themselves very unhappy on their first escorted tour.

Venturers, who want freedom in most areas of their lives and who retreat from the thought of crowds, generally do not fit the profile of a tour taker. They prefer F.I.T. travel (see, you've already learned some terminology) or a package that provides just airline flights, a rental car and perhaps a few selected hotels in busy cities. They like being on their own and setting their own schedules. They enjoy a sense of discovery as they accidentally wander onto interesting sights or cultural activities in a very unplanned manner.

But, no statement is always true. Some tour programs are organized with *venturers* in mind, especially for those who measure high on the active scale. These provide challenges that, through skill mastery, make that type of person feel more secure by having accomplished something when they travel. White-water rafting, treks to Antarctica or up Mount McKinley as part of an organized group, canoeing down the Brazilian Amazon, or bicycle touring through Europe all meet the psychological needs of many *venturers*.

Escorted tours best fit the personality of those individuals I call *dependables*. Their philosophy of "why make things more difficult when you can make it easy" leads them to choose tour programs, especially of the fully escorted type. They return home confident in the belief that they have had a much more complete travel experience, since little has been missed. They also learned much more than people who traveled without the assistance of a tour guide. So, if your travel per-

sonality fits the *dependable* type, you should seriously consider taking tour programs to some of the destinations that rate very well for you in this survey.

Centrics, as we've discussed, fall somewhere in the middle. They will enjoy
tours, but not always. More often they will want independent travel, with a package that includes airfare, a rental car and a few hotels.

One thing to consider as you become a more experienced traveler: your need
for an escorted tour and interest in them will probably decline. Travel, particularly to foreign countries, leads to the development of a great deal of self-confi-
dence. You will learn that in most foreign countries you can always find someone
who speaks enough English to help you find where you want to go or can inter-
pret the menu rather well. You don't need to have a tour guide with you all the
time because you might enjoy a greater sense of freedom from some of the restrictions that touring gives. However, when traveling to a third world country or
a nation that is just opening up to foreign visitors (such as China, Russia or the
Eastern Bloc countries), you almost always should consider becoming part of a
tour group. Choices for restaurants and hotels can be hazardous without expert
advice, and you may not be safe out on your own. Also, you will miss so much of
what is important without someone to explain everything. Therefore, it's very
worthwhile to check into some fully escorted tour programs.

If you think touring still fits your personality, read on to determine the types of
things that typically go right on a tour and what can go wrong (and should be
questioned before you sign up for the tour). I'll tell you which countries most
often deliver the best tour experience. I've concentrated on Europe and Israel,
the most popular places for tours. These areas have three to five times the number
of visitors of most Asian countries or other parts of the world. For tours in the
U.S., you generally don't have to worry about getting good meals, adequate hotels and other important components of a trip. U.S. standards are adequate. Just
be certain you like the itinerary and you selected a good tour operator.

What You Should Be Concerned About When You Sign Up for a Tour

My research points out the types of things that typically go well on a tour and
those areas that frequently get criticized as inadequate. Learn from this and ask
questions of your travel agent or tour company to make certain that you have
done everything possible to get the best travel experience while avoiding the
things that often go wrong. I've surveyed more than 14,000 tour takers, and
their comments provide some interesting tales. In this summary, I concentrate on
the most important elements of a tour program, although my surveys cover many
more items.

Figure 8 presents the results of an analysis that covers tours to nine different
countries in Europe and the Mideast, the most popular destinations for these
programs. It points out which things usually go well and get high ratings, and
which items you should be very concerned about when you start thinking about
taking a tour.

- *Motor coaches* consistently get the highest ratings of all items measured, even in those countries that otherwise may be rated poorly for a number of other items. Clean and comfortable coaches are the norm for almost all tours, and these add greatly to your sense of enjoyment. You need not be concerned about this aspect of your trip, as long as you sign up with a recognized tour operator.

- Most *tour guides* also receive very good scores in all countries. Typically, they are considered to be knowledgeable, friendly, helpful, and understanding of travelers' needs. Similarly, the itineraries planned for day trips get good scores, as do the city life/nightlife programs. The basics of your tour will usually live up to your expectations, i.e., you'll have a nice tour experience, with a good guide, while relaxing in a clean and comfortable coach— regardless of where you travel. That's why the vast majority of people return home saying they had a great time, even if not everything happened according to plan.

- Hotels selected for most tour programs usually receive adequate ratings for *cleanliness*, as can be seen in the chart. This general conclusion will be tempered somewhat when we look at differences between countries. But, at least on most tour programs, you don't have to worry about whether or not your hotel meets your standards for cleanliness.

- On an overall basis, however, hotels get rated at very marginal levels for their level of *quality*. They generally score at what can be considered unacceptable levels for *convenience of location*. If you start your vacation from where you sleep, as I've suggested elsewhere in the book, you need to examine the quality of the hotels offered in the tour package more carefully and determine whether or not they are close to the sightseeing and shopping you'll want to do on your own. Cross reference the hotels listed in the tour brochures with some standard hotel guides available at travel agencies to ensure that they meet your standards. Mark them on a map, along with the places that you'll want to visit. Are they close to the places of action, or do you foresee a problem?

- *Meals* included as part of a tour program pose an even bigger problem. Though most travelers state they are an important part of the travel experience, their quality gets rated below their expectations. Strong differences between countries exist for ratings of meals, as we will discover in a moment. Meals don't get talked about much, either by travel agents or in tour brochures. So you'll have to work a little harder at finding out whether you'll get the quality you want.

- Finally, the item that comes in for the most frequent complaints—*tourist shopping stopovers*. Typically in midmorning and midafternoon, the tour bus stops at a predetermined place and tour members have the opportunity to order some refreshment, use restrooms and shop at the local center. The frequent comments about these stopovers include that they are too touristy, have low quality items and everything is much too expensive. These are seen as rip-offs in which tour guides and tour operators get paid by the center's store owners for items purchased by tourists. For the most part, these suspicions are true. You will pay too much for non-authentic items, and a small portion of everything you buy will go back to the tour operator.

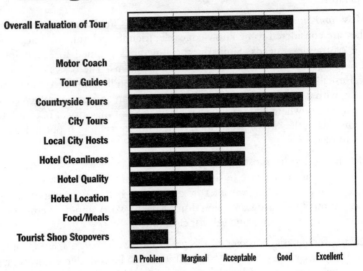

Figure 8

Ratings for Escorted Tour Services

Hotels deserve some special comment because of their importance when you travel. A poor hotel can ruin much of a trip since you view it as a place of refuge and retreat from the hustle and bustle of the day. You want it to be clean, of high quality and generally to meet the standards you maintain in your own home. Unfortunately, when I do this kind of research, I get letters back periodically from some people whose frustrations spill over. They feel they must write about their feelings and try to get someone to pay attention. Listen to some typical comments on problems encountered.

The brochure picture of the hotel looked so quaint and nice, but it was anything but that. It was in the wrong part of town and you didn't want to walk outside at night. It was just rundown. It shouldn't be part of any tour!

Physician, New York City

We saved a long time for this trip and it was very important to my wife and me. Since we are both well past retirement age, we can't afford nor can we take many more trips. Please look at the enclosed photo of our bathroom. The toilet was coming off the floor, the bathtub leaks and the whole thing was very unclean. There was no heat in the bathroom and the drip in the plumbing kept us awake much of the night. We complained to the tour guide and the hotel management, but they obviously didn't care. And, our bed was broken down. Why has anyone kept this hotel on the tour program? Our travel mates also complained.

Retired couple, Macon, GA

We had cockroaches in our hotel room, so many of them that we could never kill them all. Can you imagine trying to sleep not knowing where some of them still are? Doesn't anyone ever check out these hotels?

Middle management male executive, Dayton, OH

I looked forward to walking around a lot in cities where we visited to enjoy the sights and sounds of the people and their environment. But that couldn't happen. Our hotels were so far away from anything that it took a 25 minute, expensive cab ride to get back into the action. Obviously, I'm not going to do that every night. It's expensive and takes too much time!

Schoolteacher, Corvallis, OR

Quite a few complaint letters also come back to me and mention poor food, although the tone of the letters is milder and with fewer strong negative comments. Too often, food is considered to be of poor quality, unappetizing, without sufficient diversity, and insufficient in amount. For example:

I got tired of being herded around for most of the meals on the trip. When you come in as a big group you have to wait longer and you don't get very good service. And, we were given such limited choice compared to the individual guests of the restaurant that I saw around us.

Nurse, Chicago, IL

It seems like almost every place we ate in I would classify as a grade C restaurant. I just gave up for some of the meals and my wife and I went out and ate on our own. We enjoyed it more, but it added expenses I hadn't counted on.

Car salesman, Tucson, AZ

The food was poor and the entertainment in the restaurant mediocre. All in all, a pretty dull nightlife.

Business executive, Indianapolis, IN

When you consider why a tour operator would let these areas slip in an otherwise very good program, the answer becomes fairly obvious. The most expensive parts of a fully escorted tour are the nightly hotel bill for each couple and the costs for food. In the pressure to remain competitive on pricing, and still make a profit, negotiations between the land operator (the company that organizes the tours in each country) and local hotels and restaurants take on the highest degree of importance. Ten or fifteen dollars saved per night on a hotel room by the tour organizer (for each individual in the party) make a significant difference in the price that the tour program can be advertised for and whether or not the tour operator is able to make a profit. Similarly, savings on food can cut the costs of a tour program significantly. Hotels and restaurants that have had their rates negotiated down to the bare bones often have little incentive to maintain high quality standards since it's marginal whether they can make a profit or not on the relationship. You should check out the location and the quality of all hotels that are part of the tour package you may be considering. Since the hotels get listed in the tour brochures, you can cross-reference these to standard hotel guides available at your travel agency, if these are major hotels. Ask for the *Hotel & Travel Index International Edition*, the *Official Hotel Guide, Star Report*, or have your agent determine if information is available on their computer reservations systems. Checking on the food is more problematic. The standard restaurant guides typically do not contain references to the restaurants featured in tour brochures.

One further comment. Many tour programs divide into two levels of quality, i.e., a level often called "first class" vs. a mid-price or "value price" package or some similar term. Obviously, the value package costs less and you stay at less expensive hotels. You may also eat your meals at different places. However, ratings for food and meals are relatively similar, in spite of the fact that first class travelers often eat at better restaurants. It may be that "first class" tour takers, since they have paid considerably more for their trips as compared to value priced tours, have much higher expectations. Hotels may not measure up to their expectations, leading to a feeling that they have not received their full money's worth on the trip. Regardless, you get much better quality hotels and usually upgraded meals when you buy the higher priced packages.

When you're thinking about taking an escorted tour, you can usually count on sitting comfortably in a clean and quiet motor coach. Most often your tour guides will meet your expectations, including those who join you for the daytime excursions and the ones who take you on city tours. These basics should not concern you. Your hotels will probably be clean, but, do some background research on their level of quality and their locations. You could be disappointed if you don't. As for meals, no easy way exists to check on all of the unknown restaurants included in the itinerary, especially since most of these will not be listed in the tour brochures.

Which Countries Deliver the Best Tour Experiences

I have reviewed ratings for services received on a tour, regardless of the country in which a tour took place. But, some countries consistently deliver a better product while others often place at the bottom of the pile. For the most part, the rank ordering of these items remains the same from one country to another (you almost will never get a bad tour bus), but wide discrepancies exist in the absolute ratings. Quality of hotels and meals, two critical items on our list, vary greatly across borders. You can visit some countries with greater certainty that you will receive the quality of product and level of treatment you expect, while for others you should probably spend more time looking into what you'll be getting before you sign up for that expensive trip. Let's take a look at how countries vary on some of these important dimensions.

Figure 9 presents a quick visual summary of where countries place on an overall score that includes various dimensions related to hotels, food, meals, tourist shopping stopovers and tour guides. These dimensions contribute most to overall satisfaction with a trip. Let's look at each country to get a feeling for what makes it stand out or, to the contrary, why it has some problems. I'll review them in order from top to bottom, in terms of level of quality, beginning with Switzerland —the top rated destination—and ending with Spain.

Switzerland

Switzerland achieves above average scores on every characteristic. Even tourist shopping stopovers, typically the lowest rated item, score at acceptable levels. Hotels get good ratings for quality, cleanliness and even for convenient location. In contrast to most countries, Switzerland provides a level of quality for food and meals offered on most tour programs that is also quite acceptable.

In summary, there is very little you need to worry about when you book an escorted tour to Switzerland. The neat, punctual, hard working Swiss apparently do a good job in sending most of their guests home happy. Their tour programs also run like a Swiss watch. You get the quality you expect. If your escorted itinerary includes only Switzerland, you probably don't need to be as concerned about upgrading to first class hotels from the mid-priced or value-priced tour you have been considering.

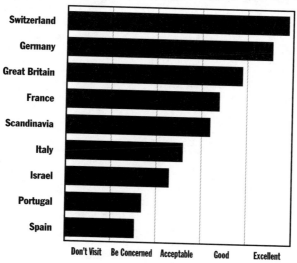

Figure 9
Overall Escorted Tour Ratings for Countries

Germany

Germany also gets above average scores on all dimensions, including achieving the highest ratings for cleanliness of hotels and for hotel quality. Convenience of location for most hotels also rates at acceptable levels.

Food and meals also rate quite well in Germany, but the country falls down somewhat for the quality of its tourist stopovers.

In conclusion, German citizens provide the basics for a good tour experience—good maintenance and upkeep of their hotels, and they usually do not slack off on the quality of food provided at the restaurants that serve tourists. In general, you do not need to worry about most of the tour elements that might be part of the tour package you bought to visit this country.

Great Britain

The English get a bum rap for food! That's what people participating in my surveys tell me. Their ratings on food and meals offered on a tour place above average, and well ahead of some countries noted for their gastronomic delights. These ratings also are consistent for what you will experience in other parts of the British Isles, such as Wales, Scotland and Ireland. I'd have to agree with this conclusion too. On a recent trip that my wife and I took across the countryside of Great Britain, we commented that we never had a bad meal in Ireland—even when we ate in what looked like very rundown pubs in working class cities.

Overall, England is one of the better rated countries. It gets very strong scores for quality of tour guides and for the diversity and quality of countryside tours. Even its shopping stopovers are rated above average, although this is not a popular item in any country. Cleanliness of hotels also rates well, but the location of where you might stay is often considered very inconvenient.

In summing up, as long as you select a good tour company, most of your experiences throughout the British Isles should be quite pleasant and enjoyable—measuring up to the standards you expect. You probably don't need to worry about the quality of the hotels selected, but check carefully as to their location. You may find yourself far removed from the action every night, leaving you with a feeling that you missed out on some things when you return home.

France

France provides variable ratings, with some aspects quite acceptable and others requiring a little more investigation by a potential tour taker.

The quality and cleanliness of its hotels both rate at acceptable levels for its guests. But, unfortunately, it faces a special problem in terms of inconvenient locations for many of these properties, according to tour guests. This problem is most severe around big cities, such as Paris, where most travelers express an interest in being close to the center of activity. But the same crush for good location also exists in many other cities in France.

Although France may be known for its food, wines and gastronomic delicacies, what escorted tour guests get on their trips often does not measure up to the advance publicity. French food, as experienced by the majority of escorted tour visitors, gets only average ratings—and generally below the level that most people expect. For the most part, you will not be impressed by the food you get as part of your tour of France. Tour guides, in contrast, get very strong ratings. They are informative, entertaining and interesting. But most tour shopping stopovers fall below acceptable levels.

If you're considering a tour of France, some extra effort should be put into checking out the location of the hotels and what restaurants are included in the program. If you don't eat well in France, you may feel that you didn't receive a major benefit that you expected. Although tourist shopping stopovers get low ratings, these simply are an inconvenience and not a major problem to the enjoyment of your trip. Plan to look at but not buy in most of these places. But your hotels and your meals are essential parts of your trip. These deserve some advance attention before you sign with an operator.

Scandinavia

Because of its relatively small population and the fact that most tour programs usually include several Northern European countries on the same itinerary (Sweden, Denmark, Finland and Norway), these are lumped together in our tour program evaluations. Scandinavia measures just a hair behind France and, therefore, literally is in a virtual tie for fourth place. Its hotels score very well for convenience of location and for cleanliness. However, the measures of quality for hotels score lower, primarily because some of its mid-priced/value-oriented properties do not meet the expectations for amenities desired by a majority of travelers. Scandinavia still demonstrates a quality of frugality and austerity that permeates its approach to life, resulting in some hotels that can seem to be a bit underwhelming.

It is second only behind Switzerland, however, for the quality of food and meals offered to its guests. You can accept the fact that most of the meals you'll receive on your tour program within Scandinavia will offer good taste and variety, regardless of whether you go first class or on a value priced program.

Tour guides and the quality of countryside tours also score relatively well but, again, tourist shopping stopovers drop below what can be considered an acceptable level.

The overall conclusion for Scandinavia, then, is that you generally will get a relatively good trip that offers few surprises or worries. But you may want to look into the quality ratings for the hotels included in your program if you select a value-priced tour package. Overall, however, you can feel comfortable about most items related to a Scandinavian tour.

Italy

With Italy, we begin to face some common problems in Southern European countries that are evident from my interviews in terms of the quality of tour experiences delivered to guests. For its hotels, cleanliness generally scores at acceptable levels, but the quality of the hotels falls below a standard I consider to be adequate. Further, the locations, even for some first class properties listed in tour programs, often are considered to be inconvenient by guests. Again, it's a problem related to the large, very popular cities (Rome, Naples, Florence, Venice, etc.). In these places, most people would like to be close to the famous monuments and historic sites to walk around and explore them on their free time. But not enough good hotels exist in close proximity.

Like the French, Italians are noted for good food, but you may not get much of that on your tour. This item rates well below acceptable levels, regardless of the price of the trip. Tour guides, however, tend to get very good ratings on almost all tour programs, although tourist shopping stopovers once more score very poorly.

For tour takers planning to visit Italy, the message is clear. Check carefully into the quality of hotels provided for your travels, although you probably cannot do much about getting a more convenient location because of the lack of good hotel properties near important sites. As for food and meals, ask some pointed questions of your travel agent or tour program organizers about this part of your program. But it may be difficult to get the consistent level of meals that you generally desire. Italy is a grand country to visit, but don't be surprised if some parts of the trip bother you somewhat.

Israel

Israel gets relatively good marks for convenient locations of its hotels, which generally are at acceptable levels. These properties tend to be close to where people want to be in modern day Israel, especially near some of the historic sights. However, quality of these hotels too often is below acceptable levels for persons on mid-priced tours. Cleanliness comes in second to the lowest level recorded in the survey. Hotels on first class tours do much better than those in the value priced category.

The food and meals in Israel, unfortunately, generally rate the lowest of the nine countries included in our ratings. The average rating is only between "fair" and "good." The tourist shopping stopovers get ratings that fall below anything we have looked at thus far. These are considered by most travelers to be big rip-offs. Tour guides, as is usually the case, receive very acceptable marks for their efforts, as do the countryside tours.

If your plans include a trip to Israel, I strongly recommend that you look carefully at the hotels provided on the trip and ask about the restaurants selected. These are the key components of any travel experience. Since Israel is a very expensive country to visit, there are few travel bargains offered to the public. You may want to consider spending the extra money and upgrading to a first class tour so that you can leave home with great certainty that you will enjoy everything.

Portugal

After years of being isolated from the world of tourism because of changing governments, varying from dictatorships to extreme socialism, Portugal has opened up and offers many advantages to tourists that countries with a steady stream of visitors for decades cannot match. It doesn't have a feeling of being overrun by tourists, its people are friendly and its relatively uncrowded cities and countryside cover over some other problems that guests notice after they arrive. Unquestionably, Portugal is a quaint, diverse and historic country that should be part of your travel plans before it gets too crowded with tourists.

Portugal has a large number of four- and five-star hotels. But what you get on a tour can be quite different. Although its hotels get relatively acceptable marks for cleanliness, their quality and convenience of location rate very poorly. Further, the meals provided, overall, score at what can only be considered unacceptable levels. What a shame, because the Portuguese can offer such interesting, tasty and varied food. Tourist shopping stopovers also rate at very low levels, even below what you'll typically find in other countries. Tour guides, however, continue to impress visitors. Even local city hosts, who take you on interesting day or night-time city tours, score well.

Portugal has launched an energetic program to improve itself as a tourist destination, and some of these scores may improve over time. However, persons considering a visit to this marvelous country, and who plan to go on an escorted tour, should be concerned about making certain their tour operator has chosen good hotels and that the quality of meals provided with the program also measure up to acceptable standards. Again, you may want to consider buying a first class tour program to ensure that you get the higher level experiences you want.

Spain

Spain scores very close to Portugal, but it still places in the last position out of the nine countries evaluated. Its hotels get relatively low ratings for cleanliness and inadequate scores for their quality and for their convenience of location. This combination of subpar scores suggests you could have a tour experience that will leave you dissatisfied. Spain is also a fascinating country, but you have to be vigilant in selecting a tour operator.

In examining the quality and kind of meals provided on tour programs, Spain scores only slightly above the very low ratings for food in both Portugal and Israel. Again, this is a surprising problem since Spanish food matches anything served around the world. Anyone who has tasted paella, prepared at your dining table, knows what I'm talking about. Its tour guides do quite a good job, however. But tourist shopping stopovers also get the lowest scores of the nine countries reviewed.

Thus, if you are considering a trip to Spain, you should demonstrate more than an average degree of interest in learning about the types and quality of hotels included in your trip package. You should also investigate the quality of restaurants selected for your meals. Do your homework and check everything out thoroughly. Or, as I've said before, perhaps you should buy a higher priced tour.

How to Select a Quality Escorted Tour

Unlike many industries, travel has never coalesced with just a few major players whose quality and reliability you can trust because their names are well known. It is mostly split into thousands of small companies, most of which never grew out of the "mom and pop" stage of entrepreneurship. Think about buying a new car. A dozen companies dominate market share worldwide. In packaged foods, commercial drugs, computer manufacturers and in a number of other categories, you can typically name on two hands the companies that control up to 80 percent of market share. Large companies typically take steps to protect their reputations and they establish separate departments to monitor consumer complaints.

In travel, however, 75 important airlines exist worldwide, and 160 significant hotel chains alone can be identified in the U.S. with several hundred more in other parts of the world. This does not count the tens of thousands of independent hotel operators not affiliated with a major chain. Nowhere is this problem more evident than in tour programs. Over 1500 tour operators provide various types of tours sold through travel agencies in the U.S. That number could double in size because of recent small startups serving special niches and offering unique kinds of programs. In this complex maze, let me suggest how to go about getting the greater certainty that you expect when you book your trip.

There are several ways to guarantee that you've selected a quality tour operator.

· A number of major airlines offer tour programs, both U.S. based carriers and large international airlines. Since they put their name on everything they sell, you can usually be more assured that they want to protect their reputations at all possible costs. Their offerings tend to be above average, with a select few providing some truly outstanding trips. They are not likely to go out of business while you're traveling, leaving you stranded in some strange land. If you have a complaint, they have procedures for handling these problems.

One word of caution, however. Airlines tend to look at their tour operations as a way to sell seats on their airlines, rather than as a way to build a tour business. Every seat sold to someone going on one of their tours guarantees that the person won't be flying on a competitor's airline. They often "farm out" their entire operations to another company, but maintain the airline's identity with the program. As a result, you still need to do your homework and check out the quality of the program, especially for hotels and meals.

2.   The U.S. Tour Operators Association (USTOA) is a nonprofit industry group that tends to be dominated by relatively large, well established tour companies with solid reputations. It has about 40 nonairline members now. Its rules for membership offer some important assurances to travelers. To be a member of the association, an organization must:

- have been in business for at least three years;
- have at least 18 travel industry recommendations to support its application;
- carry at least $1 million in professional tour operator liability insurance;
- meet specified minimums of passengers carried and dollar volume.

Further, the USTOA has established an insurance fund—a $1,000,000 bond from *each* tour operator—that will pay off individual travelers if that operator happens to go bankrupt after a trip was booked but not yet taken, or if it occurs during the course of the trip. This kind of protection is an important guarantee for travelers who do not necessarily know enough about an individual tour operator. You may want to ask your travel agent if the tour company recommended to you belongs to the USTOA.

You can contact USTOA directly to get a listing of their members by writing to:

U.S. Tour Operators' Association
211 E. 51st Street, Suite 12 B
New York, NY 10022

3.   Not all good tour companies belong to the USTOA, very often for their own business reasons. In these situations it's useful to ask your travel agent to make some very clear recommendations because they should know about the major operators with solid reputations. Be sure you select a travel agent who has dealt in escorted tours for at least three years, and preferably more. You want someone with perspective based on booking hundreds of people on a variety of tour programs.

4.   Very often, as is quite obvious, one of the best ways to verify anything is through word of mouth. You should raise questions with friends and relatives to see which ones may have taken a trip, particularly within the last two or three years. Recent experiences of travelers let you know if the company continues to enhance its reputation. However, it's doubtful that you'll get very clear perspective on a large number of tour companies. Most people travel infrequently with tour programs so that their base of experience is quite limited. Their ratings, therefore, may not be very reliable. As always, ask your most pointed questions about the quality of the hotels and the meals. Don't worry too much about the tour guides, whose ratings generally are quite acceptable. You probably wouldn't get the same guides anyway, but you might end up sleeping in the same hotels and eating at the same restaurants.

5.   Your church group may offer Holy Land tours with the pastor, or a Mideast scholar, serving as the tour director. In this case, most people com

back satisfied primarily because they travel with friends and learn about something of deep interest to them. Your hotel arrangement is likely to be a cruise ship. But, don't expect a top cruise ship. The best ones are usually in the fleet elsewhere, filled by higher paying nongroup passengers. The profit margins are better from that kind of traveler, so you're likely to get the second choice ship.

6. Here's some information you should think about getting from your travel agent, or the tour company itself, if you call them directly.

   • Request that they show you a description of the hotels, or a rating system on them, in one of the many standard reference documents available. Over 95 percent of travel agencies have the *Hotel & Travel Index* (including the International Edition), and a vast majority also receive the *Official Hotel Guide*, *Star Report*, and other review materials.

   • Also, more hotel descriptions are becoming available on the computer reservations systems (CRS) of travel agencies. With a few clicks of a button, your agent can locate a lot of information for you. Dig deeply to make certain you're getting clean, comfortable, well-located quality hotels in the cities you'll visit.

   • Surprisingly, many U.S. based tour companies have never sent their own representatives to foreign lands to check out the quality of hotels and meals provided on their tours. Rather, they rely on the recommendations and selections provided by their foreign operators. Since these foreign companies may have only an "arm's length" business relationship with the tour organizer (they operate the tours in the countries), they may make choices favorable to themselves (get the lowest cost) but not necessarily as good for you. Acceptable standards for hotels or meals, as judged by foreigners, may not be acceptable to many Americans, including you. So, ask the tour operator, or have your agent do it, as to who checks out the hotels and restaurants. If that's done only by people on site in the foreign country, you might have reason to be a bit concerned about the quality of tour program you'll receive. You'd like people from the headquarters of your tour company doing the checking. American executives should personally check out hotels and restaurants for their American guests.

   • Your travel agent can probably provide you with the names of some of their customers who have taken the same tour. Give them a call because you can at least judge their enthusiasm (or lack of it), even if they are not experienced tour takers. Your most important questions relate to hotels—cleanliness, quality and location—and to the quality and variety of the food. If these measure up, you can feel relatively comfortable because most other aspects of a tour will score at acceptable levels.

Taking an escorted tour is what's called a "big ticket" item in the travel industry since more dollars go into a travel agent's hands than is true for fully independent travel. Travel agents particularly like to book escorted tours because it takes
them less time (they don't have to look up and book individual hotels in different
cities), the overall price is higher, the commission level to the agency is about 15
percent (rather than 10 percent on F.I.T. bookings) and they can often get commission overrides as an incentive (extra payments back to the travel agency for
emphasizing one tour company over another). Since travel agents make more
money on a tour program, they can afford to give you a little extra service. Since
this is also a big ticket item for your pocketbook, spend some extra time making
sure you feel comfortable about the items that often get lower ratings, i.e., the
quality and cleanliness of the hotels, and the quality of the food and meals. Ask
more questions of your travel agent, the tour provider and friends and associates
who may have traveled with other programs. Consider upgrading the package
you buy to first class to guarantee the level of quality you want, particularly in
those countries where the research data shows some problems may exist.

CHOOSING AN AIRLINE

Let's be honest. Travel by air is the least civilized form of travel there is. A motor coach is more humane. On a train, you can get up and walk around regardless of the distance. You can stop a car whenever you fancy and have a breath of fresh air. But, when you're on a plane, come what may, you've got to stay there where you are for the whole damn journey. The seat is smaller than an average bus seat. Business Class may be better, but when you're in Economy, they really stick it to you. It is the least comfortable form of human movement.

This Londoner, participating in a focus group (10 to 12 people in a research setting discussing a common topic) says it all for people around the world. Leisure travel may be fun, but getting there and back isn't—especially if you fly to your destination, according to many people interviewed.

Regardless of where you're flying, your trip may begin a couple of hours in advance of the flight with a long drive to a major metropolitan airport (in heavy traffic) where you park your car a mile or two away and wait for the slow shuttle bus to take you to the airport. On the shuttle, you handle your own bags, step over everyone else's toes (or someone steps on yours) and sit patiently while it makes all of the airline terminal stops before it finally gets to yours.

At the airport, new problems set in: long lines to check in (how can it take so long in this computerized age to issue a ticket to that couple in front of you?), a stop at the security gate for scrutiny (empty your pockets of anything metal and hand them your camera and laptop computer for personal inspection so they don't get banged around) and proceed down the long, long walk to your gate, past dozens of airplanes, all the time struggling with your luggage.

Then the joys of getting on board. Enter by sections of rows, wait patiently as people in front of you stuff their belongings in the overhead bins before they can sit down and you can move on, and take your aisle seat—only to be asked twice to get out so that the window and middle seat passengers can take their places.

Your true pleasures will now begin. If you are six feet in height or over, your legs already touch the back of the seat in front of you, even before it reclines. You must turn your legs to one side when the guy in the row ahead decides to push his seat back or your knees will get crushed. Even average sized passengers can't get out of the way of the reclined seat in coach class on most airlines. When you finally land, you can thank your lucky stars because the most uncomfortable part of your flight has finished. All you have to go through now is the snail-like pace for deplaning, the struggle with your bags and the long airport walk when you are more tired and disgusted than before, again to catch a shuttle to your hotel or a taxi to downtown. Another small battle has been won, but no one awards campaign ribbons in this war.

How can air travel be made to feel so miserable? Well, you have to understand the business decisions of airlines, those who build airplanes, and the fact that you, the traveler, also contribute heavily to the choices made on your behalf.

If you can afford to fly First Class or Business Class, you can probably skip most of this chapter. But, if you fall into the category of 85 percent of those poor, unfortunate souls who get confined to coach (Economy Class), then there are a few things you should learn.

To begin with, you may have thought otherwise, but commercial jets are not built with passengers in mind. Engineers design them, not consumer research specialists, and they have a simple objective. Get the largest number of passengers flying through the air for the least cost. The larger the diameter of an airplane, the more air it has to displace and the greater its weight and, correspondingly, the more it costs to move that airplane. So, that means making the diameter as narrow as possible to carry passengers from one city to another. Now you understand why you sit so close to the fellow in the next seat because providing another inch or two of elbow room would increase the operating costs of that airplane.

But this does not explain why the seat in front of you also seems to nearly touch your bifocals, particularly when that person leans back. Now you enter directly into airline economics. A couple of decades ago, the standard seat pitch (the distance between two seats) was 36 inches. But, the airlines, in their efforts to make more money, reduced seat pitch to 34 inches so that they could get more people on board each flight and take home more revenue per flight. In the interest of passenger comfort, I convinced an airplane manufacturer to take a look at the seat design prevalent in small Japanese economy cars. They had gone to thin line seats to provide more interior room within the relatively small space available, yet these seats are relatively comfortable. Convinced, the airlines put in thin line seats and were able to reduce the seat thickness by half, from four inches to about two. That extra two inches saved could now get passengers back to a previous comfort level, i.e., the equivalent leg room of a 36 inch seat in a 34 inch configuration. But, airline economics won out over comfort. More seats were installed on airplanes to provide more revenue per flight since the equivalent of the 34 inch seat could be achieved in the new slim-lined 32 inch pitch. Score a touchdown and the point after conversion for airline operating efficiency and 0 points for flyers. Believe me, two inches more leg room in coach class is a dramatic improvement.

But, as a passenger, you share much of the blame. Airlines, and airplane manufacturers, will never do anything you don't want. Your constant message has continually been, "Give me a low, low ticket price and I'll fly with you." My studies indicate that most leisure travelers believe that airfares are often dirt cheap these days. So, you'd pay more for an airline ticket if you had to. But you recognize that you don't have to. If no fare wars currently exist, you (and others) wait a couple of weeks until the next one explodes on the scene. Since the rule is to follow the leader, other airlines soon match the new fares. Thus, the pressure continues to find ways to fly you less expensively to see Aunt Matilda or to take off on that dream trip halfway around the world.

A number of marketing experiments have been tried by airlines, most often by new carriers entering a market, where they offer more room and other amenities, either for no extra charge or for only a modest price increase. But you, as a passenger, usually turn them down. You stick with the airline you've been flying because you don't pay attention to the advertising of the new airline, or you're strongly committed to your airline's frequent flyer program. So, ultimately the final choice rests on your shoulders as a passenger. If you will always take the lowest price, or stick with a frequent flyer program, then you can't complain very loudly about the lack of comfort on board. Airlines watch how you buy tickets—what motivates you—and they will change in a hurry if you change.

Since the Gulf War in 1991, through 1994, the world's airlines lost nearly $16 billion—more than they made in profits over their 75 years of operation prior to that time. With improving load factors (percentage of seats filled), these carriers made about $1 billion in 1994—barely one percent on their total revenues, and a long way from paying off their accumulated debts. Conditions are improving for the airlines, but previous losses will keep them focused on making a profit for some time to come.

Cost pressures will continue. Southwest Airlines, the pesky gnat that buzzed around the heads of airline executives a few years ago, has grown into the street bully that dictates almost all thinking among today's airline executives. They experience heart failure when they hear that Southwest will enter one of their markets. It flies passengers at an average seat mile cost close to 7.5¢ (the total cost to fly a passenger for one mile). Other airlines vary all over the map, with the highest major carrier being at 11.5¢ per seat mile. Higher operating costs obviously have a dramatic impact on the bottom line of an airline and explain how most of them have lost hundreds of millions dollars over the last several years.

Every major airline is addressing the Southwest "problem" by trying to get increased operating efficiencies, primarily by getting rid of employees. Some are imitating Southwest's short haul, no frills service. New start-up airlines have once again come onto the scene and either copy the strategy of Southwest, or at least pursue most of it with a few add-on frills to set them apart from others. Since 1992, the U.S. Department of Transportation has authorized nearly 30 airlines to start up, most of them low fare carriers, with almost a dozen more applications still pending.

I'll take a look at U.S. and international airlines to help you decide which ones you would like to fly. However, less differentiation exits between airlines than can be seen for hotel chains, cruise lines or tour companies. Why? All carriers fly the same airplanes that come primarily from three manufacturers (Boeing, McDonnell Douglas and Airbus Industries), fly in and out of the same airports, follow safety procedures dictated by the federal government, typically have similar staff to passenger ratios, have meals prepared by the same small number of caterers and, with a couple of exceptions, crowd the same number of people onto similar sized airplanes. Subtle differences exist on their frequent flyer programs, the amount they pay for meals and in the selection, training and supervision of their customer contact personnel.

You hear many complaints these days, primarily from travel writers, about the decline in airline service since deregulation of the industry in 1978. They state that meal quality has gone down, flight attendants aren't as friendly as they used to be, the wait in lines has increased considerably and there are more flight delays. You may be surprised to learn that most of this has not happened. I track airline service on a regular basis. Deregulation first produced some lowered passenger ratings because of the confusion it caused in the marketplace with many new carriers and the adjustments that existing airlines had to make to discount pricing that became the norm. The major carriers cut staffs, readjusted their schedules, and otherwise had to determine how to save money and operate more efficiently. But, they also had to remain competitive. They have worked at getting passenger acceptance levels back to what they previously enjoyed and, by and large, they've done that. Specifically, my passenger data evaluating airlines indicate that:

- Evaluations of telephone reservations services have improved.
- Ratings of *helpful, courteous check-in personnel* remain relatively constant over this period of time, now scoring about 3.45 on a 4.0 scale (4 = "excellent"), a very high score, indeed.
- Departure delays have declined steadily since 1988 and, correspondingly, on-time arrivals have also improved during that same time, as noted in both our data and U.S. Department of Transportation (DOT) statistics. Most of this grows out of the fact that the DOT now publishes on time arrival data on a monthly basis for all major carriers, and airlines now compete to keep their numbers looking good.
- Flight attendant ratings have remained relatively constant on long haul routes (flights of four hours or more), my data points out, and have actually improved on medium haul trips (two to three hours in length).
- Ratings of the cleanliness of airplane interiors have improved, largely because airlines went on a huge buying splurge and picked up hundreds of new airplanes. Fresh carpet and paint and the latest in interior design improvements create a more comfortable and relaxed feeling on board.
- But, you may be right on one count. Ratings for the most frequently criticized item, meal quality, have not improved. But they haven't gone down either. The overall average for the industry is a relatively weak 2.6 on that same four point scale and has stayed stable over the years. But, who ever said it is possible to provide French cuisine from a convection oven at 35,000 feet?

In summary, food quality ratings are about at the levels they were before (at relatively weak levels); in-flight attendant evaluations by passengers have actually gone up in many situations; and on-time performance has improved rather dramatically because the U.S. Department of Transportation's monthly statistics have forced airlines to protect their consumer image by being on time.

Where the situation has gotten worse is in airports. Nearly three times as many passengers now go through airline terminals each year in the U.S. than when deregulation started in 1978, with only one new major jet airport having been built in the more than two decades since that time (the new Denver airport opened early 1995). Existing airports that have expanded tend to add new gates at the far end of the terminals (your walk gets longer). So, you're right again—airports are much more crowded than they used to be, less personal and more likely to make you feel hassled and uncomfortable. You also face added problems when fare wars hit, such as extra long waits in line to check in, difficulty in finding a place to sit before you board and the excruciatingly slow enplaning and deplaning procedures from high load factors. The bigger the bird you're flying on, the more you will probably feel out of sorts while still on the ground because of the added pressure of more people trying to do the same thing you are. We'll talk about how to manage your way through airports and make yourself more comfortable in the final chapter.

Choosing a Major Airline

Like people, airlines have personalities that are determined by the people who guide and direct them, and the impact of their unique histories as they each developed over the decades. Also like people, they can't escape their pasts. Policies and procedures set into motion today are reactions to what has gone on before. Once again, data from my American Traveler Survey provides information about passenger reactions to each airline, and I'll add some of my own knowledge gained over the years.

Alaska Airlines

Starting as a bush pilot operation, Alaska Airlines has grown into a successful regional airline that now covers the Pacific states from its headquarters in Seattle. Through most of the financial bloodletting by its larger competitors, it remained profitable, but not always. It did this by emphasizing quality. It provided about an inch more leg room in coach, better meals and an emphasis on customer service from its in-flight crew. Quirky, memorable advertising helped give the carrier the image of an upstart airline fighting the big guys by doing a better job. It's one of the few regional airline survivors. Most of the others have been bought out by larger carriers or have gone under.

Today Alaska fights for its life like most airlines because of brutal price wars and the downturn in passenger traffic during the several year period of the Gulf War and the recession. It has weathered most problems relatively well and will probably be an even stronger player in the future. It enjoys extremely strong passenger loyalty and Alaskans still feel that it belongs to them. Management tried to remove the face on the tail (an Eskimo in a fur collared jacket, in case you didn't know) to achieve a more contemporary design look, but strong passenger opposition forced management to backtrack. Alaska still has the highest overall scores of any airline in my passenger surveys, even though it has cut back on some passenger services. However, its frequent flyer program has limited appeal because of relatively few places that it flies to and fewer tie-ins with other airlines.

In sum, a great carrier confined to the western states.

American Airlines

It's one of three major airlines that consistently gets very high ratings from passengers on most dimensions (the others are Delta and Alaska). Its in-flight crew receives strong scores from passengers, its meals are above average and the interior decor of its airplanes creates a warm and cheerful feeling. Further, it has a strong frequent flyer program because it has the most members, many ways to earn miles (through credit card use) and lots of places to fly to.

Historically, American's management has made a commitment to being innovative in trying to stay a step ahead of other airlines. It started frequent flyer programs, was the first to make in-flight uniforms more casual and less military looking, added some of the first red coat customer contact people in terminals to direct passengers, and introduced the enclosed overhead bins on standard bodied airplanes (*727s*, *737s*, etc.). When I asked one of its executives why they had made various changes, he said, "We change before we have to." In other words, American never wants to play catch-up.

The bottom line: a quality airline with a long history of trying to be ahead of the pack in providing what passengers really want. They will continue to be leaders because they have built up a tradition of thinking that way. Its strong frequent flyer program and broad route structure add to its high level of passenger preference.

Continental Airlines

Continental shows the problems of its recent history and its distant past. Coming out of bankruptcy forced by the financial leveraging created by Frank Lorenzo (also owned Eastern Airlines), Continental has had a difficult time finding its proper positioning in the marketplace. It has experimented with providing three kinds of service, all at the same time—as a conventional airline in providing similar services to the other major carriers, as a Southwest clone (Continental "Lite"), and as a superior business class service airline on international routes. As a result, many passengers are confused about what kind of an airline it really is.

It wasn't always that way. At one time, a rough and ready airline exec, Bob Six, turned it into the preferred airline between Chicago and L.A. (it no longer flies this route) by emphasizing improved in-flight service and seeking out attractive young stewardesses, and approving catchy but controversial ad campaigns ("We really move our tails for you"). But Continental and its "proud birds" got bogged down in overly aggressive and leveraged expansion plans after deregulation. When Lorenzo took control, he lowered its operating costs by getting rid of the unions (he absorbed a strike) and seemingly was on the way to success, until he acquired Eastern Airlines. Eastern's union management refused to cooperate with his ideas and, ultimately, both airlines went under—with Eastern never to recover again. Lorenzo's gone, but a series of chief executives since that time have not been able to put the pieces of Continental back together again.

Today, Continental generally offers in-flight service that is competitive to other airlines, but it lacks a clear identity and specific reasons for flyers to choose it. Its frequent flyer program, once the best in the industry, has fallen behind most of the other major carriers. It's searching for the winning formula that even industry insiders hope it will discover soon.

Delta Airlines

During much of my professional life Delta was a regional airline confined to the southeastern states. It's now difficult to think of how big and international in spirit it really is. It covers most of the U.S. and serves more cities in Europe from the U.S. than any other airline, including foreign carriers.

At one time, its southern hospitality and attitude made it a memorable and strongly preferred airline among its passengers. It still has that gracious and caring spirit that is especially evident at its headquarters in Atlanta, but it faced special problems when it went on an acquisition binge. The takeover of Western Airlines in Los Angeles went smoothly because the easygoing attitude of Californians meshed with the charm of southerners. But swallowing Pan Am's European service was another matter. An airline whose passenger service personnel had grown haughty and disinterested (Pan Am) couldn't be charmed overnight into the Delta spirit and sense of commitment. The European venture did not go smoothly and cost Delta tens of millions of dollars. It also affected some of their domestic operations.

Most of that seems to have been worked through by now. The airline typically trades places with American Airlines in terms of which one gets the highest ratings for passenger service among the largest airlines in the U.S. It has recently improved its frequent flyer program to the point that it ranks ahead of many of its competitors.

Delta also operates one of the East Coast shuttles, between New York, Boston and Washington, D.C., and provides frequent schedules between these cities. It's not real low-cost, but you can get frequent flyer miles credit for each flight.

In sum, a very good choice for frequent or infrequent flyers because of its high levels of service and a good frequent flyer program.

Northwest Airlines

Many industry pundits thought it would be dead by now. It lost favor with so many passengers by letting its service standards slip, and tons of money as a result. KLM wrote off its entire $400 million investment in the airline with the thought that it probably would not survive. Northwest also suffered through a morale-bending acquisition (of Republic Airlines) with much bickering between pilots and in-flight crew about seniority and preferred assignments. A citizens' group in Memphis, one of its hubs, even tried to entice another carrier to serve the city. Many pundits did not expect the airline to last into the decade of the '90s.

But new management fooled all doomsayers. The emphasis now includes a focus on improved in-flight service, sticking to longer haul profitable routes, crafting closer ties with its international partner (KLM) and, more recently, improving its frequent flyer program. Its efforts have paid off. It is now one of the most profitable airlines in the U.S., is paying off its debts, and has a bright future.

It still does not get the service ratings in my surveys of the top carriers (Alaska, American and Delta), but it's not far behind and coming up. If you live in its cities, don't feel neglected. It's a strong competitor and your frequent flyer program competes well with the offerings of other airlines.

TWA

Poor TWA! It has such an interesting history, but it has been reduced to desperate times by financier Carl Icahn. Howard Hughes was associated with its early history and, with his contacts, it became the airline of the stars. More Hollywood and Broadway luminaries flew it, and it appeared in more movies in the 50s and 60s, than any other carrier. It had panache and class! It also had the prettiest planes in the sky, the Lockheed Constellations (although they were not as reliable as the ugly duckling workhorse *Douglas DC-4s* and *DC-6s*). It had a glamorous around-the-world flight that went both directions each day and that added credibility to its name.

Icahn came in and broke the unions to lower operating costs, and then proceeded to sell off its assets—primarily its gates at various airports and routes to different foreign destinations. Now it fights the problems of the limited number of cities it serves in the U.S. and other parts of the world, few nonstop flights between U.S. cities (you have to go through St. Louis to get to most places) and the fact that it no longer can land at the most important airport in Europe (Heathrow in London), an almost crippling blow for any airline focused on Europe. Icahn pocketed some cash for that too.

TWA has been in and out of bankruptcy and has had to be innovative to stay in the game. Its frequent flyer program has been extremely rich in offering awards for fewer miles flown, and it doesn't take away your miles if you don't use them within a specified period of time, a practice now common among many of its competitors. When it was coming out of bankruptcy, I convinced its management to give something back to coach passengers that they wanted most—more leg room—in order to gain popularity. It works! TWA's overall flight ratings by passengers on its comfort class exceed those of all other carriers. This feature also develops loyalty and, hopefully, will help TWA to survive. But is still is not one of the top preferred airlines.

So, for greater comfort in coach and a very strong frequent flyer program, TWA offers a good choice. Since its pricing is competitive, and sometimes leading the pack, you could come out ahead by choosing TWA.

United Airlines

Like TWA, United is partly owned by its employees, although flight attendants do not participate in the program. It originated as a mail carrier that organized (united) a group of small airlines into a bigger carrier to become a coast to coast competitor. It has again achieved its former status of being the largest airline in the U.S. (American held that mantle for a while until it cut back because of its huge losses).

United flies to more cities than any other airline, so its frequent flyer program allows you to earn miles more readily than some competitors. But the program is not one of the richest, requiring more miles to earn an award and dating those miles so that you can lose their benefit if you don't travel in time. It also does not rate at the top in the American Traveler Survey, but don't worry—it's always very close to the leaders. To emphasize again, differences between major airlines are very subtle. United has tens of thousands of passengers who think it's the greatest.

To answer the Southwest "problem," it began what is essentially a new airline in 1994 (Shuttle by United) offering cheap fares between northern and southern California. Now it's possible to fly to San Francisco from LAX, rather than to Oakland (as Southwest does), while still getting a reasonable fare. The shuttle offers the advantage of participation in United's more complete frequent flyer program.

The bottom line is that United is a good choice if it flies in and out of your city. You now have more ways to save money on their airline (its new shuttle service), while still getting frequent flyer miles.

USAir

USAir has had trouble finding its niche in the free-for-all fight for recognition among airline passengers. At one time it was a small regional carrier (Allegheny Airlines), but came to national prominence when it acquired PSA, a much copied airline that dominated the West Coast with frequent schedules, low pricing and a fun filled spirit. However, it lost all of its West Coast presence by failing to recognize that PSA's passenger loyalty came from being somewhat quirky and spunky, rather than formal and uptight like a conventional airline. Lacking a clear reason for choice among airline passengers, USAir has a difficult time developing loyalty. It is experimenting with an improved level of service for business flyers who typically pay the most for their ticket, to see if they'll choose USAir.

It also has experienced some image problems about its safety procedures after a couple of well-publicized accidents. However, its procedures are as safe as any other carrier and you need not be concerned about taking a flight with them. A top industry consultant, and good friend, R. Dixon Speas, was hired by the airline to review all operations to ensure that they exceeded all standards.

A more significant problem for USAir at present is that it has not yet lowered its operating costs to be truly competitive in today's marketplace. It flies for about 11.5¢ a seat mile (moving one passenger one mile in the air), vs. the target goal of 7.5¢ for most airlines. It has been losing lots of money, with no definitive turn around time in sight. British Airways, a part owner that invested heavily in the carrier, has refused to invest more money, so it must find its own way out of its problems.

USAir operates one of the two East Coast shuttles serving New York City, Boston and Washington, D.C. (the other is Delta), allowing you to pick up frequent flyer miles on short haul flights that provide good frequency and great on-time performance. Further, you don't even have to buy a ticket in advance. Just walk up to the counter when you're ready to go and they'll have space for you. Its frequent flyer program has been improved to offer some of the best tie-ins with hotel chains, rental car companies and credit card companies, and it offers good minimum number of miles credits when you fly on short hauls with it.

In sum, although not one of the top rated airlines, its service levels are quite acceptable, its frequent flyer program provides good opportunities to earn credits and it may be your primary choice if you live in one of its dominant East Coast cities.

The New Low Fare Airlines

Watching the success of Southwest in its fight against much larger competitors, a number of imitators have initiated service in the last few years. They either copy the Southwest formula exactly, or they attempt to offer low price with some added amenities. It's worthwhile to provide a brief review of a few of the more prominent ones to help you make a better selection when you have a choice.

Carnival Airlines

Carnival Cruise Lines' tentacles increasingly are reaching into more travel operations, such as hotel chains, tour operations and, recently, an airline. It primarily feeds passengers from the Northeast and California for its Florida cruise operations, but noncruise travelers can take advantage of its low fares. Its operation is bigger than a first glance might suggest, with 22 planes and 40 daily flights. It gives advance seat assignments, you can connect to other airlines (have your baggage transferred) and it has a frequent flyer program (for pets too!).

Frontier Airlines

Started by executives of the old Frontier Airlines that disappeared from Denver in the mid-1980s, it seeks to fill the empty space left by Continental as it retreated from parts of the western states. Frontier also offers advance seat assignments and cooperates with other airlines. Started in 1994, it's too new and too tiny to know at this moment what will be its ultimate level of success—or its level of service to passengers.

Kiwi International Airlines

Named after the New Zealand bird that can't fly, it also represents another airline start-up by employees of a previous airline. In this case, pilots from defunct Eastern Airlines and Pan American World Airways, rather than previous management, are behind the effort. It's a true bootstrap, self-funding operation. To work for them, you have to buy stock in the company—lots of it. Pilots who join each kick in $50,000 and get a yearly salary not much different from that. It failed to pass an FAA maintenance record-keeping inspection in early 1995 and had all of its planes grounded for a couple of days.

Although it does not interline (connect to other carriers), it offers more amenities than most low fare carriers, including advance seat assignments, flowers in restrooms and better passenger snacks. It operates on the East coast from its primary city, Newark, New Jersey. Employees are motivated to succeed, but it's too early to predict how it'll do.

Midway Airlines

Named after the airport it primarily serves (the original primary field for Chicago), it is attempting to pick up on some of the previous success of the relatively recent demise of the former Midway Airlines. Its fares are not quite as low as some of the start-ups, but it has the advantage of operating from its new low-cost hub airport, Raleigh-Durham. It interlines with only a few airlines (American, USAir and TWA), but does provide advance seat assignments. Its newness also does not indicate how successful it will be as competition continues to heat up.

Reno Air

Choosing an unlikely city for its hub, Reno has achieved the status of being one of the relatively new successful entrants. When it entered the San Jose, California market, American Airlines immediately withdrew, preferring not to compete with Reno's low cost structure. Now the two carriers have set up cooperative agreements and you can connect easily between the airlines and, more important, you earn American frequent flyer miles when you're with Reno. Its fares are higher than Southwest, but it also offers more on-board service and comfort. It looks like a winner.

Valujet Airlines

Perhaps even more successful than Reno Air, Valujet flies out of Atlanta to nearby cities. As a result, it gives fits to Delta, providing the primary reason why Delta wants to lower its operating costs to 7.5¢ a mile. Valujet doesn't interline and offers only modest service on board, but it offers very low fares and aims to keep it that way. Its name implies that it'll probably never be a high service airline.

Southwest Airlines

Ruling the roost, it would seem, Southwest has changed the plans of all major U.S. airlines. Its success (Southwest made money every year while other carriers lost their shirts) has forced an overhaul of the entire airline industry, and is even having an impact in Europe, Canada and elsewhere. Major airlines are lowering costs to compete. Almost every start-up carrier copies Southwest's operations. I'll spend a little more time on it because of its importance in the airline world.

Organized in 1967 during the days of a regulated airline industry as a carrier that flew in Texas, both Braniff Airlines and Texas International Airlines (TIA) were able to convince the Civil Aeronautics Board (CAB) to deny Southwest's application for four years on the grounds that air traffic demand in the state would not support another carrier. When Southwest finally started flying in 1971, its competitors slashed prices to 50 percent of what Southwest was offering to drive it out of business. It didn't work. Braniff and TIA no longer exist, while Southwest continues as the most profitable and successful airline around.

As a result of these battles, Southwest developed an attitude about the industry: it trusts no one and cooperates with no one. Herb Kelleher, the airline's chairman, has stated that he runs Southwest as though good times were bad times. That way, whatever happens to the airline, it's prepared. The airline follows the KISS philosophy (Keep It Simple Stupid). It saves money a hundred ways that other airlines never think about. Only recently did it agree to a limited form of participation in airline computer reservations systems (to save money). It doesn't interline (connect its flights with other airlines to provide for baggage transfer), it doesn't offer advance seat assignments (requires expensive computer back-up), and it doesn't provide meals on board (only peanuts and drinks for its short haul flights). Further, it only flies one type of airplane—the *Boeing 737*, thus reducing the number of parts stocked and simplifying pilot and mechanics training. It gets its planes out of the gates in 15 minutes or less for two-thirds of the time (the rest in under 20 vs. an industry average of 55 minutes), and it flies almost exclusively to secondary airports in major cities (reduces landing fees by up to two-thirds and helps on the turn-around time because of less congestion). Whew! That's a lot of differences from most of the airlines you fly on.

This philosophy has a major impact on you as a traveler. Southwest has consistently been the leader in pushing airfares down. When it enters a new market, it can double or quadruple that market in size within a year or two because of its low fare structure. Kelleher states that his major competition is the family car, not other airlines, as a reason for forcing down fares. Southwest trumpets the fact that it consistently wins the "triple crown" of commercial aviation, i.e., the DOT annual survey shows them to have the fewest passenger complaints, fewest delays and fewest mishandled bags.

It sounds like the perfect airline for you to fly, doesn't it? Well, before you make your final choice, consider a few factors that might influence your decision. In most airline passenger surveys, it typically rates below other major airlines in preference. With no advance seat assignments, busy people can get stuck in middle seats on the *B737s* because they arrive at airports late and get slim pickings. If you want to connect to another airline in a different city, you'll have to carry all of your bags because it doesn't interline with other carriers. You may not be able to connect at all because Southwest avoids the major airports where those connections usually occur. Its triple crown achievement deserves a closer analysis. Mishandled bags most often occur when they are transferred from one airplane to another and Southwest doesn't provide that service. Since it doesn't serve meals, you can't complain about that. Finally, if you compare its on-time record to major airlines that serve large airports, Southwest doesn't always win (competitors have gotten better). For example, look at the on-time performance of similar types of flights by shuttle services by the few major carriers that provide them (Delta and USAir). In some reporting periods, the Delta and USAir shuttles have no complaints, while Southwest always has a few. Shuttle operations seldom have complaints about lost baggage.

More important for you as a traveler, the major airlines are addressing the Southwest "problem." Several have initiated low cost, low fare operations that compete on routes served by Southwest. These include Continental Lite, Shuttle by United, and major efforts by American, Delta and TWA to reduce their cost and become competitive on various routes. These carriers can give you important advantages when you find that their fares are competitive. You can often get advanced seat assignment, the ability to connect to other airlines and, very important, participation in very meaningful frequent flyer programs. You can't fly many places in Southwest's program (they don't cooperate with anyone), such as Hawaii or foreign countries, and you'll lack good participating partners (mileage credit when you check into a hotel, rent a car, or even use an affiliated credit card).

The bottom line: all travelers can applaud Southwest's low fare structure. It has reduced the cost of air travel for most people throughout the nation. It is a very safe (never had a fatal accident), very reliable, still somewhat quirky airline that will save you money if it flies from your city. But, it now has competition from other major airlines. You may want to consider the additional advantages of flying with one of the traditional airlines that has learned how to compete with Southwest because of the advantages you'll get.

International Airlines

I'll briefly review some of the important international airlines that fly between the U.S. and Europe, the dominant international traffic routes, to provide a picture of the quality of service you can expect on board. As before, I have information from the American Traveler Survey. I asked people to indicate which airlines they had flown on internationally in the past 12 months and which ones they especially prefer. This provides a Satisfaction Index, a good way to compare airlines regardless of their size or the routes that they fly. The competition has a level playing field. Also, I will provide information from other ongoing surveys I regularly conduct among airline passengers.

Traditionally, foreign flag airlines (those whose base of operation is from another country) have set the standards of service. American carriers that flew overseas did not typically measure up to service levels of their foreign counterparts, perhaps because they didn't have to. Under bilateral airline treaties (agreements between two countries), the U.S. dominated most routes because the agreements were set in place after World War II when the U.S. was the dominant world power. Pan Am, TWA and a few other American airlines that serve these routes did not feel compelled to provide high levels of service.

Judging by the current interviews I've collected, all that has changed—dramatically. Airlines that fly the flag of the U.S. now dominate most of the preference choices of Americans in my American Traveler Survey. American Airlines, Delta and United recognized they had to improve their service levels in order to be competitive, and the impact can be seen in the results. With one exception, the dominant U.S. carriers also rate better than their foreign counterparts. That exception, as you will see, is Swissair—the gold standard for worldwide travel, regardless of class of service.

Airlines Serving Europe

Aer Lingus

Its satisfaction levels rate below average, but all of my measurements occurred before it improved its in-flight meals, redecorated the cabins and gave the in-flight crews new uniforms. I would expect these ratings to increase substantially the next time. Until mid-1994, they only flew to Shannon, Ireland. Now you can go to Dublin and on to London, typically at more reasonable prices than with most competing airlines.

Air Canada

Yes, you can catch Air Canada to Europe, sometimes saving a considerable amount of money through some of their supersaver fares. It gets relatively average ratings for its services primarily as a result of passenger reactions to the less effusive, more subdued personality of the Canadian in-flight crew. But it's a strong competitor and develops fierce loyalties among many Canadians.

Air France

Scoring below average, Air France has a somewhat bumpy history. Service levels in first class have usually provided food and flight attendant helpfulness that match the top levels offered by most carriers. However, coach/economy passengers have suffered. A similar situation holds true today, although the airline is improving because of its interest in privatizing (becoming publicly owned, rather than being owned by the state).

Alitalia

The national carrier of Italy has long been the butt of frequent jokes about their levels of service and style of flying. Perhaps that carries over today, whether or not it truly provides high standards of service. Its loyalty score is extremely low, with only half the number of people saying they prefer it to a competitor as is true for most other airlines.

American Airlines

American is one of four airlines that score at the top on the international Satisfaction Index. It improved service levels dramatically after it took on routes across the North Atlantic and this shows in its ratings. It gets good ratings for its flight attendants, onboard food and seating comfort—most of the essentials of a good flight.

British Airways

Also a strong airline (it rates above average on the Satisfaction Index), it shows a very unique pattern. Since it became private several years ago, it launched a massive publicity program to get out the message that British Airways had changed from an airline that was diffident and disinterested in its passengers to one that is much more alive and exciting in the air—and concerned about its passengers. However, it demonstrates the unique pattern that persons who have not flown it think more highly of the airline than persons who have flown it. It is still a great airline, but its PR and advertising may exceed reality at times.

Continental Airlines

Continental gets mixed scores on the North Atlantic route. What it calls Business First gets superior ratings, as compared to business class of competitive airlines. However, coach services generally fall below the average scores for competing airlines. Continental worked on, and improved, business class, but it has not developed its economy class to the same degree.

Delta Air Lines

Following a rocky start after it acquired Pan Am's European routes, Delta has straightened itself out to the point that it is also one of the four top rated airlines on the international Satisfaction Index. It gets good scores for meal quality, cour teousness of flight attendants, attractiveness and cleanliness of its airplanes, and for air quality (Delta went to a totally smoke-free policy in early 1995). Seating comfort in coach is not one of its virtues, however, but it gets very good scores for its in-flight audio and video entertainment.

KLM

It has developed an improved in-flight service that has resulted in only slightly above average scores on the Satisfaction Index. Its tie-in with Northwest Airlines provides similar ratings for the two classes of service, regardless of which airline you choose. In fact, they both score at very similar levels. You will experience a very acceptable and comfortable flight on board.

Lufthansa

The airline of Germany scores slightly below average on the Index. Its service operations (clean airplanes, audio-visual entertainment and food quality) score very well. However, the more formal German personality lacks the warmth that many Americans want when they are served by others. Make no mistake, however, your airplane will depart on time, you will be served your meal when it is scheduled and you will get all of the services you are supposed to get, according to their passenger service manual.

Northwest Airlines

This airline, which has formal ties with KLM, has a somewhat above average level of acceptance and offers a relatively seamless connection with its Dutch partner (KLM) to transfer to other European countries. Its improved frequent flyer program can make it a good choice for a flight.

SAS

This is the second carrier (along with British Airways) that demonstrates a very unique pattern. Its Satisfaction Index ratio scores are somewhat below average. Yet, those who have not flown it think more highly of it than those who have. Jan Carlzen also pulled a PR coup when he made the airline partly private and forced it to improve its level of service. His "empowerment of employees" idea caught the attention of the press and has led to the situation in which passengers expect more than they may actually receive when they step on board SAS.

Swissair

The quiet, polite Swiss have set the gold standard for the world in airline service. Swissair achieves a high satisfaction ratio. Its scores for in-flight service are unmatched by any carrier across the North Atlantic or elsewhere in the world, except for its business partner, Singapore Airlines. Swissair smothers its passengers in service to the point that they give it the highest ratings for seat comfort, even though seat pitch (distance between seats) in coach is not greater than that of other airlines flying across the North Atlantic.

TWA

TWA scores at average on the Satisfaction Index, putting it in the position of being lower than other American carriers on the North Atlantic route. However, it provides one advantage for coach passengers unmatched by any other airlines. It has Comfort Class, which provides from two to four more inches of leg room per coach passenger than any other airline. Ratings for cleanliness of the airplanes score lower however, as do some of the flight attendant and food scores. Some of this is because of its older fleet, which casts a somewhat depressing effect on other scores.

United Airlines

United also scores highly on the Satisfaction Index, along with the other American carriers. It is often selected because of its strong coverage of the U.S. market and a good frequent flyer program that allows it to "feed" many passengers to its overseas routes.

USAir

The Satisfaction Index for USAir places it above most European flagged carriers, and also well above average, but somewhat below its competing American rivals. As with its domestic airline system, USAir seems to lack a personality that can be carried on board and enthuse more passengers with the services it provides.

Virgin Atlantic Airlines

Richard Bransen, the billionaire developer of a record company, put together a somewhat quirky airline with a strong identity. Currently calling his cabin service Upper Class, and Premium Economy, (he has used other names in the past), Bransen has survived and succeeded where others have failed. His strong publicity and focus on giving more on-board services, provides him with a Satisfaction Index score that places him slightly behind the American carriers. Virgin Atlantic offers both competitive pricing and a high level of onboard service, suggesting that it can be a very good choice for your next flight.

TEN TIPS FOR GETTING THE MOST OUT OF YOUR NEXT COACH FLIGHT

When you ride in the back seat of a typical mid-sized car, you'll probably need to get out and stretch your legs after a couple of hours on the trip. You feel cramped and uncomfortable. Except for ceiling height, you've been sitting in an overstuffed chair compared to your airline seat. A Ford Taurus, the sales volume leader in the U.S., for example, has nearly 58 inches of width across the back. So, if three people are crammed in, you only have a little over 19 inches each. Seems tight, doesn't it? Well, compare that to an average airline coach seat. You can claim only 17 inches width all to your own. On most airlines, you get only 32 inches of seat pitch (the distance between your seat and the one in front of you). Your Taurus, or other mid-size car, typically provides 35 or more inches of seat pitch depending upon where the front seat passengers place their seats. Even the new Dodge Neon, Chrysler Corporation's small car answer to the Japanese, gives you more room than a typical airline coach seat. It offers about 25 inches of seat width for each of two people sitting in the back, with about 34 inches of seat pitch. Now you know why you're uncomfortable on an airplane. You never thought the back seat of a small car could feel so good, did you?

Why is it so tight? It's a matter of economics. It costs more to fly you someplace the more space you're given. So, to be competitive, airlines focus more on operating costs than on passenger comfort. They're all fighting to give you reasonably priced tickets. If you had your druthers, you'd rather fly in business class or first class, not coach. But, like a lot of people (including me), you don't want to pay multiples of your discount coach ticket just for a few hours of more comfortable sitting. You'd rather use that money for other things on your trip.

I can't get rid of all of the discomforts of coach for you. But, I can offer some suggestions that will improve most of your trips. I'll tell you what to do when it looks like your flight could be delayed greatly, or cancelled.

1. On long haul flights, my interviews with passengers indicate that the preferred airplanes are the *Boeing 767*, *Boeing 747* and the *McDonnell Douglas MD-11*, in that order. The *Boeing 767* is the *only* airplane designed with the

primary goal of providing coach passengers with extra comfort. I did the research that convinced Boeing to build the airplane. For the most part, it gets rid of the unpopular center seat in coach, as based on current configurations. It has two aisles and seven across seating, in this manner. Since some people (families or business partners, for example) travel in threes and want to be together, they will choose the three seat sections. The airplane literally has to have a load factor of over 95 percent before you are denied a choice of getting an aisle or a window seat.

The *Boeing 747* has long been a favorite. Passengers love it because its huge interior gives a feeling of spaciousness, helping to alleviate the claustrophobic feeling created in many standard bodied interiors. The big crossover areas provide a place to stand up or stretch, out of the way of others, when you get tired of sitting. You'll probably also enjoy talking with the cabin crew or other passengers in the open areas.

The *MD-11* of McDonnell Douglas has come in for a lot of positive comments since its introduction within the last few years. Quiet and smooth, yet still creating a sense of power, it also gets high marks for seat comfort because of good ergonomic design. As a wide body, it also receives high marks for spaciousness and offers places to stand and stretch.

For both the *747* and the *MD-11*, it's critically important to get seat reservations well in advance of the flight to get a window or an aisle seat. These airplanes have more middle seats and you can really get the packed sardine feeling on a long flight.

On short flights, the airplane you'll get will almost always be a standard body design (5 or 6 across, one aisle), so selection of a preferred airplane is less important. Besides, these smaller planes load and unload more quickly, helping to keep your trip short.

2. Which seat to choose? It depends. On long flights (three hours or more), think about taking a window seat. You can stake out more space for yourself because you can lean against the window—away from the passenger next to you and at an angle that gives you more stretching room. Leaning away from your seat mate creates a psychological barrier to conversations (if you don't want them) and isolates you a bit if that person has a cold. The *Lockheed L-1011* is the only airplane that has a contoured side wall on the inside cabin of the airplane, so it provides up to another three inches of shoulder room for window seat coach passengers. Since the interior is almost a Siamese twin to the dimensions of the *MD-11*, you'll also enjoy the *L-1011*—particularly in a window coach seat. On short flights (one or two hours), an aisle seat usually works best because you can get out more easily when the plane pulls up to the gate. You don't have to wait in an uncomfortable crouched stance under the overhead bins during the slow deplaning process if you're not next to a window.

If you're long-legged, or simply want more leg room, there are a couple of seating rows you should consider. The exit rows on all airplanes have a couple of inches more pitch/distance between seats—to allow passengers to escape through the rows in case of an emergency. And, the seats in front of the exit recline very little (you don't want to select those), again, to ensure an open area for passengers to get out quickly when needed. So, you'll have more leg room and less likelihood of having the seat back from the person in front of you hitting you in the face.   Also, a number of the exit seats in coach are over or by the wings, which is where the plane pivots (rotates) in flight. You will feel fewer bumps or turns than persons sitting at the back or at the front end of the fulcrum. One other little advantage: young children are not allowed to sit in that row. Thus, crying or squirming babies may be around you, but not next to you. But, you have to be in at least average physical shape to be allowed to sit there. The passenger closest to the window exit is required to open the small door and assist others out after exiting, according to FAA regulations.

The exit row also has a couple of negatives. Your seat also may not recline very much depending upon the airline and the specific airplane. And your seat tray will be three or so inches farther away since it typically is folded into the seat in front of you.

Another seat row worth your consideration that you may not have thought about before is at the bulkhead (a cabin divider). It has disadvantages—your feet can't stretch out as much and there is no place to put your under-the-seat bag or briefcase. But, no one sits in front of you, so they can't recline in your face, and it has a very open and comfortable feeling about it. Plus, you're sitting right behind the first or business class section and you can deplane right after them. If you don't mind sitting with your feet in a more typical office chair position, you can enjoy those other benefits. If you're by yourself, you may want to avoid this seat. Mothers with children often get assigned to that row because the bulkhead often has hooks from which to hang a bassinet.

Almost without exception, avoid seats in the rear of the airplane. Since the body of the airplane narrows in the tail (for aerodynamic reasons), seats can be more cramped. You get bounced around more in rough weather (again, you're at the end point of a fulcrum), and it's likely to be noisy (many airplanes have at least one engine, sometimes two, mounted on or near the tail section).

Whatever your choice, avoid seats near the galleys (food preparation areas) and lavatories, especially on wide-bodied airplanes. You don't want the smells, the noise or the passenger traffic. Your travel agent or the airline you call can confirm the selection of your seat—away from the noise and smell locations.

3.   Two items impact most on your comfort in coach—amount of leg room provided (defined as seat pitch—distance between seats), and the level of service provided on board.

Leg room can vary by airline. Although 32" seat pitch is standard for most airlines, Alaska Airlines typically offers one inch more and TWA provides up to three or four inches extra on its *comfort class* flights. Even one inch makes a difference, but three to four inches is dramatic, especially on long haul flights. Some of the recent startup airlines, as part of their positioning strategies, also offer greater room.

The other dimension impacting on your feeling of comfort onboard is service levels. Swissair and Singapore Airlines smother even their coach passengers with extra care and attention by flight attendants and with upgraded meals. As a result, they get higher passenger ratings for comfort on passenger surveys. They win awards from travel writers and from travel magazines that survey readers and report on the results. So pay attention to which airlines are winning awards. Even if it's last year's prize, they're still likely to be good.

4. On flights that offer full meals (not a snack/sandwich or peanuts), you will usually be much happier ordering a special meal. You must call at least 24 hours in advance to be certain you'll get it.

It's an obvious choice if you have special requirements—low fat, no salt, no sugar, kosher or vegetarian meals. But, if you have no restrictions, consider getting the seafood salad or fresh fruit plate. The seafood salad typically has fresh shrimp and crab, with spicy red sauce, lemon and some small appetizers. The most common fresh fruit plate is cut up mixed fruit and grapes, banana bread and a center of cottage cheese for protein. Your seat mates will look at you with envy as they compare their fried chicken or beef brochette (with noodles and gravy) to your fancy fare. You can also smile knowing that your meal cost the airline about double of what theirs did.

5. In an airline cabin, you fly at a pressurized altitude of about 11,000 feet with 15 percent humidity. You really don't notice it at the time, but you're literally sitting on top of a very high mountain in dry, desertlike air. To reduce the effects of jet lag and just the overall "blah" feeling when you deplane, drink lots of water because your mucous membrane tissues dry out. If you drink alcohol, take very little. It's very easy to get a slight headache and even a hangover when oxygen levels are that low. Typically you should also eat less in flight. When you eat, blood rushes to the stomach area, away from the brain—providing another reason to feel oxygen deprived.

6. Stay informed about differences in airline frequent flyer programs because some offer many more advantages than others, including more opportunities to be upgraded out of coach. Frequent flyers know that it's generally best to concentrate on one or two airlines so that you can get to a premium level. Then, you may receive automatic upgrades to business class or first class, even without having your account charged for the perk. Now you can avoid all the hassles and discomforts of coach. Even infrequent flyers need to focus on one airline as much as possible to increase the opportunity of getting a free ticket at some point.

The trend has been away from automatic upgrades recently with airlines distributing a somewhat limited number of upgrade coupons to their most seasoned travelers, and allowing them to buy additional upgrade coupons at relatively modest prices. The advantages of concentrating your flying on one or two airlines still exist. You can only earn free coupons and buy extra ones at reduced rates if you are counted among their more valued customers.

7. Another reason to pack lightly (see "10 Tips for Guaranteeing a Great Vacation") is so that you can take everything with you onboard in case anything goes wrong. If your flight is canceled, you don't have to wait for baggage delivery to get on another flight. You can jump off immediately when the pilot announces there'll be a two hour delay because of "mechanical problems." You can be long gone on another airline, provided you've got baggage in hand. Believe me, that flight may never take off. Once I landed in Boston on a flight from Los Angeles to New York because of weather problems in the "Big Apple." They said they'd be on the ground for an hour and a half. I jumped off the flight, rented a car, drove to New York City and was sleeping in my hotel room 45 minutes before the flight finally left Boston (I know, I called an airline friend the next day to get the results). *Always be ready to get on the move!* Even on international flights, it's best to take carry-ons with you. You'll often be finished with customs and immigration before your cabin mates have claimed their luggage. Some airports are notoriously bad for luggage delays (a 45 minute wait until you claim all of them). U.S. airports can also hold you up, with baggage delivery seldom less than 20 minutes and often double that time.

8. If you sit close to the front of the coach section, you can increase your options in the event of a delay. On a scrubbed flight, you can be near the head of the line at the airline's boarding gate to be assigned to another flight (theirs or a competitor's) before that flight fills up. If a lot of people get in line before you, you probably won't get the next most convenient flight. So, jump over to the phone and call *another* airline *before* your airline contacts competitors to handle its passengers from the scrubbed flight. Remember, that next flight could already be 80 percent to 90 percent full, which means they can't take many of the passengers from your flight. You can even call your own airline for confirmed space on their next flight, the one that people from your flight are standing in line to get on.

9. Carry a list of alternative flights with you for each of your destinations, whether in the form of the pocket sized *Official Airlines Guide* (OAG), xeroxed pages from the desktop OAG, or a summary given to you by your travel agent. Have the 800 telephone reservations number handy for all of the airlines you might take. You want to pick out alternative flight possibilities when the first announcement of a delay is made and make the reservation calls as soon as possible. Speed is the essence of success. You may get that last seat on the last flight. Be ready and act fast.

10. When you travel, take luggage on board with you that lets you have one hand free—to hold your ticket and loose papers, open taxi doors, put a key into a hotel room lock, carry an umbrella or whatever. Most business and leisure travelers usually take at least two bags with them. You have about three options to accomplish this goal, while still carrying two bags:

   • Get a wheeled, fold-up cart that allows you to put two or more bags on it. These allow considerable flexibility, and some of these are very compact and small. As I mentioned before, buy quality, rather than cheap, and you'll never be sorry. But you may get tired of the hassle of folding and unfolding the cart, placing the bags on it, putting the straps in place, finding a place for it in an overhead bin, and figuring out how to get on and off the hotel or rental car bus with it in tow.

- Select an under-the-seat type of luggage with built-in wheels and pull-out handle. These are very clever and very popular, but you lose a bit of packing space required for the recessed wheels and handle. Newer models have "piggyback" luggage you can purchase that hangs on the handle as a second suitcase. But the "piggyback" one may be too small in size to do you much good. If you select one, choose from the best brands.

- Over-the-shoulder valet packs/garment bags offer many advantages. They carry a lot, protect suits and dresses from wrinkles better, and are easier to pack and unpack. Some even have a mini-suitcase built into them, further helping to make packing easier and faster. When you buy one, choose a strong nylon (better than leather for traveling) and select the lightest one you can find that handles your needs. Since it goes over your shoulder, that arm's still free, even if you carry a briefcase or a suitcase with the other arm.

One final point, when you fly, pay attention to the safety announcements before the flight begins. Know how to use the oxygen mask (stretch the cord toward you and breathe deeply), locate the two closest exits, and figure on acting fast. Take a look at your safety card in the seat pocket because it provides a visual layout of the airplane you're on that can help mentally to prepare you for an emergency. Major airlines in the U.S. have incredibly good safety records (as do most large international carriers), but the wise always prepare for any emergency. Your safest clothing usually is natural materials, wool, cotton or leather. Man made fibers, such as polyester, have a tendency to absorb heat more and to melt on your skin, causing serious burns.

CHOOSING A HOTEL: THEY'RE NOT ALL THE SAME WITH THE LIGHTS OFF

Why should you care where you spent last night? When you're asleep, you can't see anything so why pay extra for just a bed and four walls? For the amount of time you use a hotel when you're awake, it seems pretty expensive to pay for the glitz and glamour of a place that has a big lobby and a fancy restaurant. Why not get a cheaper place instead and save your money for the things you really want to do when you're on vacation? That makes sense to many people and they plan their trips that way.

But, think about one thing: your hotel is part of your vacation—an important part! I've ruined more than one vacation by getting a bad hotel. Once, my younger son and I went to a weekend air show at Los Baños, California where a group of aviation buffs had bought an abandoned WWII Army Air Corps cadet training base. They put on a live action show to recreate some of the excitement of that era. I called some of the local, non-chain hotels and selected one that was reasonably priced and whose owner sounded nice on the phone. What we got when we arrived was an unshaven desk clerk in a dirty undershirt, a room with bugs and spider webs (we found a black widow), and only lukewarm water. We didn't sleep well that night, and didn't enjoy everything as much the next day because we were tired.

The example may be extreme, but the reality exists that a poor hotel can ruin much of your well planned trip. Since a good vacation is so important in your life, don't let that happen to you. Hotels are not all the same when you've turned out the lights. I'd like to give you ten reasons why you should think about making certain you've chosen a nice place to stay, even if it costs more. You're likely to feel better the next day and enjoy more of your trip.

Ten Reasons for Choosing a Better Hotel

1. **A Quieter Night's Sleep:** Ever been bothered by noisy people in the halls, or the TV left on by the guy next door when he fell asleep? Better hotels protect your rest more because they pour more money into construction by building thicker walls, and they are more likely to put sound deadening insulation into the walls. The seal between the top of the wall and the ceiling will probably be much tighter (a major source of sound transfer between rooms), again because of higher quality construction. You're also less likely to hear the maid vacuuming the hall when you're trying to sleep in.

2. **A More Comfortable Night's Sleep:** You'll always sleep better on quality beds. Hotels that try to keep their guests happy not only buy more expensive beds, but they also change them more frequently. You're less likely to wake up with a backache because of the bow in the center of the bed, or feel like you spent the night trying not to fall out of bed.

3. **Cleaner rooms:** I just feel better going to sleep at night in a cleaner room, and one that's not frayed at the edges with paint coming off of the walls. I've been in places where I've gotten up in the middle of the night and you can feel dirt on your feet in the bathroom. Not a pleasant experience. Bad rooms can depress me so that I don't enjoy my trip as much as I could the next day. It's not worth ruining a vacation with a bad hotel.

4. **A Safer Sleep:** You may not always think about it, but a place that has someone at the desk 24 hours a day has safety procedures in place to protect you in case of an emergency, such as a fire or other important problem. Hopefully that will never happen, but you'd like to be alerted by someone who's awake while you're sleeping.

5. **It's location, location, location:** If you pay more for a room, you expect to be in a nicer neighborhood, and undoubtedly you will. Other than looking prettier, better surroundings have some important advantages. If you drive a car, it's less likely it'll be broken into or stolen because fewer robberies occur there and the parking lot will have better lighting, someone may patrol it (or monitor it from a TV camera), or it might even be fenced. If you don't have a car, you might want to stretch your legs before you turn in and nicer neighborhoods make that possible. A mall or major shopping center might also be close by to allow you to do a little browsing and take your mind off of the pressures of the day.

6. **Helping you stay on top of things:** Whether traveling for leisure or business, most people want to keep a link with home or the office. If someone needs to reach you, a quality hotel will do a better job of follow-up. They have more staff to do such things, and they have more intensive training programs for their staffs. A couple of times on trips, I was very glad one of the hotel employees worked harder at making certain I got an important message.

7. **When you need a place of refuge:** When I've had a very busy or stress filled day, I feel like retreating. My hotel room is my only place of refuge. I can just relax or take a nap. The nicer the surroundings, the better I feel. What about

you? I bet you have some similar needs. Just knowing that it's there any time you want to return to it during the day is a comforting feeling.

8. **Helping you when you need it:** With more staff available, and better training for that staff, you can get more services when you need them. At the simplest level, you may want a sandwich or a bowl of soup when you arrive late at night. Room service can provide that (cheaper hotels don't have restaurants, or don't provide room service). At a more serious level, if you happen to get very sick, better hotels have physicians on call. Even if you need it only once, it could be worth all of the other times that you paid extra to enjoy more comfortable surroundings. The staff in the best places can sometimes be extraordinary in their support when you need it most.

9. **Little things mean a lot:** Sometimes the extras that go with nicer rooms become the subject of stand up comic routines. Who needs the fancy soaps, shampoos, bath gels, and shower caps they leave in the bathroom? You usually bring your own when you travel anyway. But there are some other little niceties that can get overlooked. You're more likely to have a larger cable TV selection, free in-room movies, a much better shower head and plenty of hot water (Oh, how I hate cold showers in the morning!), and a doorman to get you a cab when no one else can (when it's raining) because cabbies always hang around places where more people use cabs, such as better hotels. One little thing, I sure like the big, thick towels they give me at quality hotels, rather than those little skimpy poor excuses for a dish rag at so many other places. If you're into exercise, you can just about forget it if you took the low priced place. Not only are quality hotels more likely to have a workout room and perhaps a jogging path (or they can tell you where to run nearby), very often the fitness center is free for guests. Some of the services of a nice place are worth the extra money, and even provide very good value.

10. **The feel good phenomenon:** An intangible benefit of staying in a nice place is that I just feel better about myself and the world. I've always assumed that's one of the reasons for taking a vacation—to feel like you're a more important and valuable person. Personally, I face a lot of pressures during a regular week and sometimes get the mild blues at the end of a difficult day or week. Vacations are supposed to bring me back to the land of the living and make me feel charged up again so that the little things don't bother me so much. A great place to stay always charges me up. Even forgetting about problems of safety or being in nice neighborhoods, I also sleep better when I go to bed in a place that I know will do more to take care of me.

Ratings of Hotel Chains:
The Good, the Bad and the Ugly

During the past 10 or 15 years, hotel chains have multiplied like rabbits. We now have more than 160 recognizable hotel chains in the U.S., and even more large hotel management companies that may operate as franchisees for several chains at the same time. I can't talk about individual hotels—there are more than 60,000 hotels and motels in the U.S. But I can review the more important chains,

52 of them, that account for perhaps two thirds of all hotel bookings. Some of them do an excellent job in maintaining the kinds of standards that you expect when you check in. Others aren't as consistent, or they simply haven't gotten the message that pleasing customers is good business.

My research evidence for this is substantial. The more than 13,500 interviews in my American Traveler Survey provide tremendous perspective on which chains focus more on their guests' needs. This forms the basis for most of the conclusions I'll present in this chapter. In addition, I also interviewed more than 2000 senior travel agents for this review—professional counselors who make more than 1 million hotel bookings a year. They deal directly with all of these chains, and they hear back from their clients—a good way to become well informed.

Like the chapters where I rated destinations, a couple of simple indexes will help you quickly understand how good or bad a chain is. My basic measure is straightforward. I asked people to tell which hotel chains they stayed in during the past 12 months and which ones they especially like. I also asked which ones they try to avoid because of poor service or the properties are inconsistent in quality from one location to the next. By subtracting the negative votes from the positive ones, I have a Satisfaction Index. What I get is very revealing. Perhaps most surprising to me is that some chains get more negative votes than positive. Wow! That's not a good way to stay in business. I'll add comments from my travel agent interviews to these ratings, when useful, to provide some more perspective. All in all, I think you'll find it informative.

For ease of use and convenience, I've divided hotel chains into five categories—then I compare hotel chains with each other only within a category. If you decide to choose a lower priced hotel, you'll know which ones usually do the best job, as compared to their competitors. Otherwise budget chains would almost always lose out to higher priced competitors because they don't attempt to provide the same level of service, and you could never find out which ones stand tall in their own circles.

The five categories (which are standard classifications in the industry) are:

1. Budget/economy
2. Mid-price
3. First class
4. Luxury
5. All suites

Obviously, the progression goes from budget to luxury on the pricing scale. But, all-suite hotels stand by themselves. They are growing in popularity, but their quality and pricing vary greatly.

As you would expect, the rating scores improve as we move up the scale. If you pay more for a room, you expect to have a more pleasant experience, and that's usually true. But, an occasional budget chain can equal the scores of first class hotels, quite an accomplishment when you consider how much less you are paying for that room.

What you learn here can make that next trip more pleasant when you have greater certainty about the quality of each night's stay. I'll give you a Satisfaction

Index score for each chain based on the ratings of people who have stayed there during the past year.

How the Hotel Satisfaction Index Was Developed

In my American Traveler Survey, I ask which hotel chains my travelers used during the past year, which ones they especially like, and which ones they try to avoid. By subtracting the number of "try to avoid" mentions from the "I especially like this chain" references, I get a Satisfaction Index score. Most hotel chains come out on the positive side, but a few actually end up in the negative column. More complaints than compliments come from their guests. So, beware of those claims that don't meet adequate standards.

An interesting relationship can be seen in the data. As you move up from one segment to the next, you double the number of people who are satisfied with their stay at a chain. Specifically, on my Index, about 12 percent of the people who visit a budget/economy chain are very satisfied with their stay. This figure jumps to 25 percent for the mid-price segment, and about 50 percent for the first class group of hotels. In the luxury category, nearly everyone had a good experience. Again, quality leaves its mark on how good a trip you're likely to have. All suite hotels vary widely in price and quality and these statements don't apply to them.

Let me emphasize again, these averages don't tell a complete story. Wide variations in ratings exist within each category. If you want to save money and still have a very enjoyable trip, then look for the best hotels at your price range.

Within each category, I'll give you the ranking for each hotel chain and its Satisfaction Index score on a 10 point scale where 10 = best quality and 1 = worst. That score compares it to others within that category only. Otherwise, the best chain in the economy/budget segment would always lose out to first class or luxury class hotels, for example.

I will also add some information, when relevant, from interviews I conduct regularly among 2000 senior travel agents asking them to evaluate chains. Collectively, as I mentioned, these agents make over a million hotel bookings a year representing a lot of experience. The important thing is that they hear back from their customers as to which chains they prefer and why. We have even more verification of the best places to stay.

Ratings of Economy/Budget Hotel Chains

More variability exists in this category than for any other, indicating that you need to be more selective in choosing the right place. In addition, a few chains get ratings that indicate they can compete effectively with hotel chains placed in the mid-price or first class categories. You can get both good value and a good travel experience, or a night's stay that you will wish you did not have depending on the choice you make.

Hampton Inns—Ranking: #1. Rating: 10

Hampton Inns is helping to redefine this category. Its scores are extraordinarily strong: many compliments and very few complaints from its guests. Its concept is to build new properties, with a standard look and feel about them, and locate these in more suburban, nonprime locations. Established as a businessman's ho-tel, it also grabs many leisure travelers. A breakfast bar is set up each morning fea-turing juice, coffee, rolls and, typically, cold cereals. It offers the best value for the money of all the hotel chains rated, based on travelers' comments, although its rates have been going up recently because it has been so successful. In fact, it may soon belong in the mid-price segment. It has been expanding very rapidly so that you're more likely to find one where you're heading.

Comfort Inns and Suites—Ranking: #2. Rating: 8

Three hotel chains tie for this #2 spot, the first of these being the 1000+ Com-fort Inns and Suites chain. Although an older, more established group of hotels, Comfort Inns and Suites has maintained its quality and consistency. It also offers a morning breakfast that goes beyond traditional coffee and danish, making the room rate seem even less. In the same city, you might find Comfort Inns priced somewhat below Hampton Inns.

Fairfield Inn—Ranking #2. Rating: 8

Marriott Corporation doesn't get into anything unless it does it right. Its entry into the low priced segment, through Fairfield Inn, demonstrates that it would like to be a leader. Its properties tend to be newer, with a homelike atmosphere. Fairfield also ties for second place in this segment.

Vagabond Inns—Ranking: #2. Rating: 8

Also a more established property, Vagabond has been able to hold its quality up, as judged by the ratings of its guests. It's a smaller, San Diego-based chain, so you will not see its properties in many cities, but it manages to be the third chain to lay claim to second place.

La Quinta Inns—Ranking: #5. Rating: 7

Two hotel chains tie for the fifth spot, with La Quinta as one of them. One of the more important players in the economy segment, La Quinta also has done a relatively good job of satisfying its customers. In general, you'll get a good, clean, comfortable room and at a very reasonable price. It also will be located away from city centers.

Red Roof Inns—Ranking: #5. Rating: 7

Red Roof also ties for fifth spot, a newer company with 210 properties in 30 states, primarily east of the Mississippi. It has been on a slower growth program, but its new owner (a real estate firm) plans to expand it from coast to coast. With its rating, you can be more assured of greater consistency and delivery of a com-fortable night's stay for a reasonable price.

Super 8—Ranking: #7. Rating: 6

Its name demonstrates the age of the chain, named for when they could give you a room for $8 a night. In spite of its age, it has been able to maintain better standards than a number of its competitors. It now has a breakfast program in more than half of its 1000 hotels, and that number is expanding all the time.

Friendship Inns—Ranking: #8. Rating: 5

A smaller chain that is trying to make a name for itself, it scores in the middle of the category. It needs a bigger base of hotels established around the country before it can develop a loyal following.

Days Inn—Ranking: #9. Rating: 5

Days Inns has an inconsistent mix of individual hotels, some newer, well constructed and they receive very good ratings. Others are older and in need of repair. In addition, it has a tendency to take over some of the hotels that mid-priced chains drop because those no longer meet their standards. Therefore, you should have firsthand knowledge or a reliable reference source before you make a booking.

Rodeway Inns—Ranking: #10. Rating: 4

Another smaller hotel chain, it has failed to develop a very loyal following in my surveys. Check it out before you book.

Econolodge—Ranking: #11. Rating: 4

Like some of the other hotels and motels in this category, Econolodge's name implies what it is. However, it is ranked below average for the category, primarily because of some inconsistent properties, in terms of quality and guest services.

Red Carpet—Ranking: #12. Rating: 3

Red Carpet is the first of several lodgings that has more people in the surveys who indicate they prefer not to stay there than who state they like to. It is sometimes confused with the higher rated chain (Red Roof), but it does not measure up on quality.

Motel 6—Ranking: #13. Rating: 2

You've heard the Tom Bodett ads on radio with his country humor inviting you to stay at Motel 6, and "we'll leave the light on for you." He has done a magnificent job in bringing in new business. But, unfortunately, many of those customers won't return very often because of poor properties, especially the older ones. It receives more negative votes than positive in my ATS survey. Its name also implies its age, i.e., when you could be given a room for $6 a night. Be selective for which Motel 6 you visit.

Scottish Inns—Ranking: #14. Rating: 2

A smaller chain, it rounds out the bottom of the list for the economy/budget segment. It also has more people who indicate they avoid it than who select it as a place they would like to stay. Therefore, be very selective on which specific hotel you would like to use, if you consider Scottish Inns.

Mid-Priced Segment

The image leaders in this category are two chains developed by Marriott with favorable ratios of preferred vs. try-to-avoid scores more than double those of the nearest competitors.

Residence Inn by Marriott—Ranking: #1. Rating: 10

This chain is designed for longer term stays among people on assignment for companies. But, it is also used by leisure travelers and it gets very high scores from them. You can expect some of the amenities that often go with an apartment.

Courtyard by Marriott—Ranking: #2. Rating: 10

Marriott's entry into the mid-price segment with Courtyard was an almost instant success. Typically located in suburban business parks, these low-rise properties also have many of the amenities of first class chains. It's a favorite with many business and leisure travelers. They usually have attractive buildings and well landscaped grounds.

Best Western—Ranking: #3. Rating: 9

Starting out as a collection of loosely franchised motels under a common name, and relying on AAA listings in their guidebooks, Best Western has since developed many properties that are more upscale and it has worked on greater consistency on what it offers to the public. As a result, its ratings have come up in recent years. However, you may want to check out a few of its properties through AAA listings to ensure that you'll get the consistency you demand.

Holiday Inn—Ranking: #4. Rating: 9

This chain established the concept of offering a consistent product to travelers about four decades ago. Now it faces the task of reinventing itself as it progressively goes about weeding out franchise locations that do not measure up to its current, higher standards (some have gone downhill over the years). It now goes after only newer, better managed franchisees. For now, be selective in which Holiday Inn you choose. In time, you will probably get the consistency in hotels that you desire because of the intensity of focus by its management team.

Quality Inns—Ranking: #5. Rating: 8

This chain has conventional hotels/motels, inns (smaller properties) and suites in its collection. Because of its value oriented pricing policies, it could also be placed in the economy/budget segment. But it competes effectively in this segment and generally offers a relatively good experience for most travelers. However, some of its properties are also older and might deserve a check in a AAA book before you commit.

Forte Travelodge—Ranking: #6. Rating: 6

A British company (Trusthouse Forte) took over an American company (Travelodge) and not only put its name on that chain but acquired other properties as well. Some of the Forte acquisitions provide a very good room and good value for the money. But, quite a number of the Travelodge motels are leftover roadside locations that serve the lower end of the market. Therefore, I suggest making certain of the quality of the hotel/motel you are considering before you make your final commitment.

Ramada Inns—Ranking: #6. Rating: 6

Considering some of the quality locations and hotels owned by Ramada, it should place higher. However, its guests are obviously experiencing some very inconsistent, lowly rated hotels as they visit them around the country. In general, Ramada offers very conventionally constructed hotels, much like Holiday Inn, but it faces the need to upgrade. At present, it does not have the most active and aggressive program to upgrade its properties.

Howard Johnson—Ranking: #8. Rating: 3

This is the only hotel chain in the mid-price category to get an overall negative score. More people say they avoid it than indicate they like to stay there. It has gone through several ownership changes in recent years, with none of them apparently able to upgrade its properties. Be very selective when considering a Howard Johnson.

First Class Segment

First class hotel chains dominate the market in terms of advertising, name identity, and their overall share of the wealth. They generally receive very strong ratings from both their guests and travel agents who book in this category. A number of these chains offer half-price weekend specials that allow you to experience the good life during a short mini-vacation and at rates that put them in a mid-price category.

Walt Disney Hotels and Resorts—Ranking: #1. Rating 10

Almost everything with the Disney name on it means quality, including its hotels and resorts. However, it has a limited number of hotels, located primarily near its theme parks. Travel agents have the same high opinion of them as do leisure travelers.

Marriott—Ranking: #2. Rating: 10

These are the flagship properties of the Marriott chain and their dedication to providing quality and consistency shows in all of our surveys of both travelers and travel agents. Expect a pleasant stay at almost any hotel with a well trained and supervised staff.

Hyatt—Ranking: #3. Rating: 10

Hyatt competes neck and neck with Marriott and has been able to do this on the basis of improving itself each year for most of the past decade. The "Hyatt touch" results in a strong focus on guest services and consistent standards. You can expect quality at all of its locations whenever you travel.

Canadian Pacific—Ranking: #4. Rating: 10

Its name implies its roots; it comes from Canada. It has developed into a quality chain with a number of grand old historic lodges and inns in our northern neighbor's provinces. Although not as well known, nor having a large number of properties in the U.S., it will typically provide you with the kind of experience that you want.

Westin—Ranking: #5. Rating: 10

Westin has changed ownership a couple of times in recent years, but it has maintained its high standards. It has some excellent hotels, but it lost some of its identity in the marketplace when it changed its name from Western International several years ago. However, it typically ranks up there with other quality hotel chains.

Hilton—Ranking: #6. Rating: 9

Hilton offers an extremely broad diversity of hotel types, from its resorts (a heavy player in Hawaii), gambling (a major emphasis in Las Vegas), its city center business oriented hotels, and its somewhat smaller suburban properties located in business parks. However, it provides good consistency across most of its offerings and generally does a very good job in keeping its guests happy. It also features weekend specials for a number of its hotels located in suburban business parks.

Sonesta—Ranking: #6. Rating: 9

Also tied in sixth spot, Sonesta is a smaller chain that primarily serves the northeast. Still run by the founding family, it has maintained a relatively low profile and has not been as aggressive in expanding as some of the other chains. It generally offers good quality and value for the money, however.

Stouffer/Renaissance—Ranking: #6. Rating: 9

The third hotel chain to tie in sixth position, it was acquired recently by the Hong Kong based Renaissance hotel chain. In 1996, it will drop the Stouffer name to just have an identity as Renaissance. Its U.S. properties are primarily from the Stouffer chain that has experienced some difficulties trying to get the acceptance and identity that it wants in North America because of its smaller size. It also offers specials on weekends and off-seasons, and sometimes special incentives for business travelers to stay more frequently.

Doubletree Hotels—Ranking: #9. Rating: 9

Doubletree has been combined with Guest Quarters Suite Hotels and has made the decision to use only the Doubletree name. You need not be concerned about quality, although it is not one of the top ranked chains in the category. With its strong rating of 9, you can't go wrong. Call ahead to get a better priced room than at some of its competitors.

Wyndham—Ranking: #10. Rating: 9

It has been around a lot longer than its relatively poor identity in the marketplace would suggest. It simply does not have enough hotels to be well remembered. It places at about average for a first class hotel chain and is quite acceptable for your travels. Most of its properties are relatively consistent in their level of quality.

Red Lion Inn—Ranking: #11. Rating: 9

Primarily a chain in the Northwest, Red Lion now is expanding into other states. Its style is a bit more informal in trying to create a warm atmosphere for both business and leisure guests. Look for special rates and weekend/off-season bargains.

Omni—Ranking: #11. Rating: 9

Also tied at eleventh spot, Omni offers some inconsistent properties, with a flagship property in the Turner Broadcasting Center in Atlanta setting the standards that it hopes its newer properties can emulate. It primarily operates as a franchisee, rather than aggressively seeking to develop new properties on its own. Because of its small size, you will be less likely to encounter it, except when heading to major cities.

Sheraton—Ranking: #13. Rating: 8

This large chain also operates a variety of different types of hotels, including its newly designated Sheraton Resort and Vacation Hotels (25 resorts in North America and a heavy emphasis in Hawaii), a mid to first class priced hotel chain primarily for business travelers (207 properties), a large gambling hotel operation in Las Vegas (Desert Inn), a riverboat casino (Tunica, Mississippi), and as the official government casino operator in Nova Scotia, Canada. With the acquisition of the luxury Phoenician Resort in Phoenix (built and went bankrupt under convicted S&L executive, Charles Keating), it is now in a very aggressive program to upgrade its image. It suffers from inconsistent properties, but it plans to weed out all franchisees that do not live up to its current standards. It also promotes a considerable number of weekend discounts. However, spend a little more time making certain that you've selected one of its better properties.

Hilton International/Vista—Ranking: #14. Rating: 8

Although it bears a similar name, it has no current relationship to the Hilton Hotels. It has some hotel locations in Canada and the Caribbean, with a few in the U.S., but it primarily serves Europe. In the U.S., its Vista chain is best known, especially the New York hotel that received major damage from the World Trade Center blast of April, 1993.

Before the blast, Vista had become a bit tired and this impacts on its current ratings. However, the new hotel is magnificent and it can be expected that the ratings will increase for Hilton International/Vista on the next survey. In general, the chain offers excellent quality on an international basis.

Crowne Plaza—Ranking: #15. Rating: 8

This hotel chain is also better than its reputation. It recently dropped the Holiday Inn designation that preceded the Crowne Plaza identification, primarily because the Holiday Inn name has probably been holding down its overall image. It offers good quality and acceptable pricing in the first class segment and it too will probably improve its ratings as it establishes a truly independent identity.

Radisson —Ranking: #15. Rating: 8

Also tied at fifteenth spot, Radisson is owned by the mega-travel agency, Carlson/Wagonlit. In time its position will probably improve, but it currently faces the all too familiar problem of inconsistent hotels that it offers to the public. It's a good idea to check out the specific location through a hotel directory with your travel agent.

Outrigger—Ranking: #17. Rating: 8

Blanketing the Hawaiian Islands with 27 properties, Outrigger has a large supply of rooms with a pricing that places it between the mid-price and the first class segment. It typically offers very good value for the money in this segment and it has established a strong feeling of trust among travel agents. Outrigger can provide reasonably priced rooms or deluxe accommodations when you travel to Hawaii. Although it gets a good score, it would rank even higher if it had a presence on the mainland because travelers would become more familiar with it.

Clarion Inns, Hotels and Suites—Ranking: #18. Rating: 7

Clarion has been repositioned by its owners, The Comfort Group, from a mid-priced chain to compete in the first class segment. However, it lacks prime locations, quality construction for the most part, and top levels of service. You may want to check out a specific chain with your travel agent before you make the booking.

Luxury Segment

Obviously, when you move into the luxury segment you don't have to worry about the quality of the hotels. However, differences still exist that are important. These differences can result in a good stay or a superlative one. You can actually get good value at some of the top ranked hotels when you consider all of the little extras that they provide.

Ritz-Carlton—Ranking: #1. Rating: 10+

At one point, the Ritz competed neck and neck with Four Seasons for the top spot but, through consistent attention to little details, management has moved it into a consistent first place position over the past several years. It also has several five-star/five-diamond properties in the U.S.

Expect everything to go right when you stay at a Ritz. If it doesn't, then expect someone to correct it very quickly. What may surprise you most is the number of nice things and services that come with your room or because you are their guest. Don't miss their breakfast or luncheon buffets (every day) at most properties. These are reasonably priced and fabulous.

Four Seasons/Regent—Ranking: #2. Rating: 10

The Four Seasons hotel chain, a superlative group of properties that originated in Toronto, now also operates the Regent Hotels in the U.S. Four Seasons also provides all of the little niceties that go with a top quality hotel, and rates only slightly behind Ritz-Carlton. In addition, Regent International offers outstanding service, but not quite with the consistency that Four Seasons provides. Therefore, its level of service will upgrade gradually as the impact of Four Seasons becomes more prominent.

Meridien—Ranking: #3. Rating: 9

By most measures, Meridien deserves a 10 except that it's competing in a very tough segment. Its service levels are excellent, but not quite at the same consistency of the two other primary chains in this category. It is the smallest in size in the category, but it also offers some good specials from time to time. With one of these discounts, you can experience true luxury at very good value.

All Suite Segment

As a category, all suite hotels do very well with no chain getting below a 9 rating. Their popularity derives from the extra room they provide, making a very pragmatic and useful selection for leisure travelers who can separate their families into separate rooms for the price of one.

Embassy Suites—Ranking: #1. Rating: 10+

Travelers think extremely well of Embassy Suites as judged by the very high rating they give. It dominates the category in terms of size and image, with the largest number of properties. It has set the pattern for what suites offer that other chains attempt to emulate or exceed. Consistent quality of its hotels provides good assurance for all of your trips.

Homewood Suites—Ranking: #2. Rating: 10

This is a lower priced hotel chain, but it achieves very good scores. It offers extraordinarily good value for the money for travelers.

Guest Quarters—Ranking: #3. Rating: 9

Now combined with Doubletree, Guest Quarters All Suite Hotels is positioned as a first class property. Its hotels do more to isolate the sound between the two rooms in its suite properties. It is attempting to please both the business (weekday) market and the leisure market (weekends and summer vacation times). It offers consistent quality and attractively designed buildings.

Crown Sterling—Ranking: #4. Rating: 9

With a pricing often in the mid-range, Crown Sterling can also provide good value for the money. Although it maintains consistent quality, some of its properties have very a different look and feel from each other, but still all quite acceptable. It can offer good value for the money, especially with some of its off-peak rates.

Aston Hotels—Ranking: #5. Rating: 9

This is the second Hawaiian company I've reviewed (along with Outrigger). Its 29 properties include hotels and condos, some constructed as standard hotel rooms but with Aston's primary focus on suites or kitchenette units. It offers a wide range of pricings, from the mid-price segment to luxury. Because of its diverse offerings, your travel agent can select the best unit for you. Its overall score is strong.

Bed & Breakfasts/Small Country Inns
Ranking: NA. Rating: 10

With thousands of B&Bs scattered across the country, and almost all of these independently run, one of the bigger surprises to me in the study is the very strong ratings for this very diverse group of places to stay when traveling. Apparently most travelers like B&Bs and small country inns, probably because of the homey atmosphere and the chance to talk with the friendly folks who run them. For the most part, you will experience an evening wine and cheese session, with a grand send-off breakfast in the morning.

B&Bs used to be relatively inexpensive, costing less than a standard hotel room. Over the years, however, prices have increased to the point that they now compete directly with many first class hotel chains. Get a good B&B guide before you make your selections because they can be quite variable, both in terms of quality and the services offered. Some locations are also very poor. You generally want places that are situated in nice surroundings, either historic villages or residential neighborhoods.

FIGURE 10
Summary Data on Hotel Chains

Chain	Ranking	Rating
Economy		
Comfort Inn/Hotel Suites	2	8
Days Inn	9	5
Econo Lodge	11	4
Fairfield Inn	2	8

FIGURE 10
Summary Data on Hotel Chains

Chain	Ranking	Rating
Friendship Inns	8	5
Hampton Inns	1	10
La Quinta Inns	5	7
Motel 6	13	2
Red Carpet	12	3
Red Roof Inns	5	7
Rodeway Inns	10	4
Scottish Inns	14	2
Super 8	7	6
Vagabond Inns	2	8

Mid-Price

Chain	Ranking	Rating
Best Western	3	9
Courtyard-Marriott	2	10
Forte Travelodge	6	6
Holiday Inn	4	9
Howard Johnson	8	3
Quality Inns/Hotels/Suites	5	8
Ramada	6	6
Residence Inn by Marriott	1	10

First Class

Chain	Ranking	Rating
Canadian Pacific	4	10
Clarion Inns/Hotels/Suites	18	7
Crowne Plaza	15	8
Doubletree Hotels	9	9
Hilton	6	9
Hilton Int'l/VISTA	14	8
Hyatt	3	10
Marriott	2	10
Omni	11	9
Outrigger	17	8
Radisson	15	8
Red Lion Inn	11	9
Sheraton	13	8
Sonesta	6	9
Stouffer/Renaissance	6	9
Walt Disney Hotels & Resorts	1	10

Chain	Ranking	Rating
FIGURE 10		
Summary Data on Hotel Chains		
Westin	5	10
Wyndham	10	9
Luxury		
Four Seasons/Regent	2	10
Ritz-Carlton	1	10+
Meridien	3	9
Suites		
Aston Hotels	5	9
Crown Sterling	4	9
Embassy Suites	1	10+
Guest Quarters	3	9
Homewood Suites	2	10
Bed & Breakfasts/Small Country Inns		
all locations	NA	10

CONFUSED ABOUT TIPPING IN FOREIGN COUNTRIES? HERE ARE THE BASICS

I'll admit it. I've never quite settled in with tipping. Why isn't the price of a tip included in the price of a meal, or as part of a bellhop or doorman's wages? Why am I supposed to give a tip to a taxi driver who has just charged me an extraordinary amount for a 15 or 20 minute ride? The airport pickup bus driver for the hotel or rental car company should be recognized too. Even maids now leave their cards in the room telling me their names so that I won't forget them when I check out.

Do I tip? Of course. But I feel that someone has put a surtax on almost every service I receive, in addition to the heavy local, state and federal taxes I must pay as part of my travel experiences. I resent that, but there's no good way out. In many countries of the world, they don't hide the fact that it's a surtax; they automatically add it on to your bill. In the U.S., that doesn't happen, but you are supposed to follow the informal rules (tip about 15 percent of your bill).

I'll keep this chapter short and sweet because you shouldn't spend a lot of time memorizing rules about tipping. For the most part, they're pretty simple and you should not be made to feel uncomfortable. Most people are confused when traveling in foreign lands and worry that they'll do dumb things. To overtip can make you feel stupid; but you also don't want to seem like a cheapskate.

You should always remember that, in the U.S. at least, tipping is voluntary. It should be a reward to someone who provided good service, either at an acceptable standard or above and beyond the expected. If you do not get the courteous, helpful service you expect, you may want to leave only a token amount, such as five percent of the bill. A colleague made it his personal cause one year at Christmas time and he gave most of his friends a set of wooden nickels with the inscription, "No, I didn't forget to tip. You deserve this because of service I got." We should all think about varying our tipping, giving more to the best people and less to the inadequate ones. Otherwise, we have not done our part to improve service levels as we travel or eat out at local restaurants.

Tipping in the U.S.

Although this chapter says it's about tipping in foreign countries, we have to start with the U.S. One pattern exists here that is gradually being adopted in various parts of the world, especially in developing tourist areas, but the pattern contrasts with rather standard practices in Europe.

Nothing could be simpler than to follow U.S. practices. Tip waiters/waitresses 15 percent of the meal price, before tax is added. Fancy restaurants often give a bill with separate places to tip the waiter and the captain. I object to that because it always comes across as another way to get more money out of a diner. They want you to leave 15 percent for the waiter and another 5 percent for the captain. I believe they should figure out how to split the money, the same way that waiters routinely give bus boys something for clearing tables for them. So I'll sometimes just put in a 15 percent tip for the waiter, nothing for the captain, and let them divide it up. The high meal price in these restaurants results in a good sized tip, so why should I have to add 20 percent on to the bill (15% for the waiter plus 5% for the captain). Remember the voluntary nature of the tip. You may want to give less if the waiter or waitress deserves less, or consider offering more (20%) for those very special people who treated you well beyond the ordinary.

Cabbies get about the same amount—15 percent of the bill, but not counting bridge tolls and other extras. If service levels don't measure up, think about giving less. You may get lots of squawks from a taxi driver if you give less, but that can be fun too. Once I gave a New York cabby a 10 cent tip. After he stopped yelling for a couple of seconds (I heard about how he has to feed his wife and four kids), I explained that his tip was eaten up by the extra fare charged for going two blocks beyond my destination before he circled back (since it was on Park Avenue, he knew exactly where to turn around).

For doormen, usually give a dollar for getting you a cab, and two dollars on a rainy day when the task is more difficult. If he carries your bags in when you arrive, another dollar will suffice. Bellhops get about 50 cents a bag, but never less than a dollar. In fancier hotels, you'll usually want to tip two dollars, even if they carry only one bag. Remember, you don't have to use a bellhop in most hotels. Since I travel light, with only an over the shoulder valet pack on both business and leisure trips, I very seldom ask for assistance. I hate waiting for a bellhop to get free, and the meaningless chatter that goes on with them while you ride up in the elevator bothers me when I'm tired from a long flight. I simply want to get to my room and relax. But, four and five star hotels typically insist on having a bellhop take you to your room. They consider that to be part of the high level of service they provide.

Concierges receive a regular salary from the hotels where they work, so you can ask questions of them without feeling you have to tip. But, if they do something special, such as get you theater tickets, arrange a meal in a popular restaurant on a busy night, take care of a number of faxes or whatever for you, a five dollar tip and occasionally more is appropriate.

Tipping in Europe

For most of central Europe, you'll see the words "*Service compris,*" (France and Belgium), "*Servizio compreso*" (Italy), or "*Trinkgeld Inbegriffen*" (Germany and Switzerland) on your restaurant bill, and very often on your hotel charges. This means that the service charge (tip) has already been added to your bill, usually in the range of 15 to 17 percent. You need not add anything, except in those exceptional situations of service beyond the ordinary (then leave about 5% additional). If you tipped when the bill already included the phrase "*service compris,*" you'll quickly be identified as a naive American traveler. These rules apply to most of France, Germany, Austria, Switzerland, the Scandinavian countries, Italy, Spain and Portugal. In those special situations where the service charge was not added to the bill, tip according to American standards.

It's more common to tip the room maids in Europe than in the U.S., usually about a dollar a day for an average hotel and up to two dollars a day for better quality properties. Sometimes you'll find people lined up outside of your door when you check out, particularly in Southern Europe. Unfortunately, you're supposed to give something to each of them—your usual tip for the maid, and about half of that to each of the others. Taxi drivers on the continent usually get smaller tips, in the range of 10 percent.

England generally doesn't add on service charges, so follow the American practice of adding 15 percent. Bartenders in pubs don't get tips directly; at some point, you simply say, "I'd like to buy you a drink" and he'll take out the price of a half pint for himself (but without pouring it). Tip your taxi driver on the same scale, about 15 percent of the total.

Most countries in Eastern Europe, including Russia and its former satellite states, have not yet developed standard practices related to tipping because tourism is a relatively new phenomenon. As I've said earlier, you generally will have a better trip by traveling with a tour program. However, when you're on your own time, or if you decide to travel independently, few of these countries include service charges as part of the bill. Following standard American practices gets you by in most situations, except that you often do not have to be quite as generous. A tip of 10 percent usually is adequate. In Romania, tip only for special assistance or service beyond the ordinary since tips are not expected.

You'll find helpers in restrooms throughout much of Europe. They should get between 50 cents and a dollar, depending upon the quality of the establishment. Bags carried to your room in hotels by porters also follow that pattern, about 50 cents a bag but never less than a one dollar minimum and hardly ever more than two dollars maximum.

Tipping in Asia

Western influences have changed things in a number of Asian countries. You still shouldn't tip in Japan. But, 10 percent will usually be added to your hotel and restaurant bills in Hong Kong and Korea, and more recently in Vietnam. So, you do not need to add to this, except in those situations of unusual service. Only five to ten percent is required in mainland China, and small gift items from the U.S. often will be appreciated more than money (cigarettes, portable radios, toiletries, etc.). In Thailand, you can follow American practices. It has a long history of catering to visitors from around the world.

Tipping in the South Pacific

Oh how Americans have changed the world. Until recent years, good service was always expected without having to pay extra for it. Now you can add ten percent to most things in Australia and New Zealand, such as for meals and taxi rides. If the service rates extra special notice, you might want to increase the amount to 15 percent. Porters carrying your bags should be tipped according to the standard practices outlined above (one to two dollars total).

For most of Polynesia and Melanesia, tipping is not expected. You may be surprised that they still treat you with all that friendliness, but it's part of their cultural heritage to welcome guests to where they live.

Tipping in the Rest of the World

Practices vary so much in other parts of the world that it is difficult to give more common rules that don't have so many exceptions that the advice becomes confusing. Generally, you're better off to check before you leave for a country in Africa, the mid-East or Latin America about what should be done where you will visit. Some parts of Africa still reflect their French influence and you will see a "service compris" added on to your bill. Elsewhere on the continent, tipping is usually expected, but usually no more than 10 percent. You can count on tipping in Egypt, Israel and Morocco, but use common sense in how much you leave.

Latin America varies greatly, even sometimes within the same country. In Brazil, you might see a service charge added to your restaurant bill. If not, add about 15 percent, but no more than 10 percent for taxi drivers. But you don't tip cabbies in Chile and Venezuela, and you only leave 10 percent for waiters in these countries, including Argentina.

In cases of uncertainty like these, you can seek out several sources of information on appropriate tipping practices. At the airport, look for a travelers' information booth. If none exists, ask the person at the airport bank where you change your money since these people are usually quite good in English. If you end up taking a taxi to your hotel and still don't know the rules, ask the doorman about what you should give to the driver before you leave the cab. Once inside the hotel, you have your best sources of information—the manager/assistant manager or concierge. In a pinch, even the check-in persons or cashiers (who often seem young and inexperienced) may be able to give you enough information.

Special Situations

You'll also encounter other situations where tipping is expected. A brief review will help to put these in proper perspective.

Cruise Lines

On most cruise lines, expect to pay the standard 15 percent for the extras you order—drinks, the hair salon, and personal services such as a masseur. Your cabin and dining room stewards can get $3 or more a day each, depending upon the quality of the cruise line. Busboys get $1 to $2 a day. In total, it comes close to $10 a day per person paid at the end of the cruise. For many lines, you can write a check or use your credit card and they'll distribute the money. Several upscale lines have an inclusive price, no tipping policy, such as Silver Sea, Seabourn, and Sea Goddess I and II. Don't tip officers or cruise directors. They have full salaries.

Escorted Tours

You're taxed once more when you take a fully escorted tour. You're expected to give something to several people who have served you during your trip. Usually this happens at the end of a trip, not on a daily basis.

Tour Guides: The person who travels with you every day explaining the history and wonders of what you see will get from $2.00 to $5.00 per day per passenger, usually closer to the $5.00 amount. Europe will be toward the high side, less developed parts of the world toward the low side of that figure.

Bus Drivers: One to two dollars a day is appropriate for the bus driver.

City Hosts: In various cities, a local host will take you around and show you the nightlife and excitement of their cities. A couple of dollars per person is appropriate.

Tour guides and bus drivers get paid at the end of the trip; city hosts receive their money each night because you won't see them again.

Safaris

Not many of you will probably take a safari. But a quick review will help to place tipping practices in perspective for those considering such an adventure trip.

Camp Based Safaris: Tipping usually runs about $10 to $12 per day per person, paid at the end of the trip in a lump sum. This money then gets divided up between various staff members, guides, porters, drivers and trackers/walkers.

Hotel Based Safaris: An increasing number of safaris use small hotels located in the bush country that have been built just to serve these groups. In these situations, guides get about $5.00 a day, trackers/walkers the same amount (when you have them), drivers $2.50 a day, and porters about a dollar for handling two bags—when you arrive and when you leave.

TRAVELING SMARTER

By now the central message of this book should be imprinted indelibly on your mind. You need a great vacation trip. You deserve it, you earned it, and you should take it! But, be sure it's a fabulous one by making the right decisions about the important things that will impact on your travels. So let's review a few suggestions that have already been covered, and I'll add some tips about how to travel smarter than other tourists you'll meet along the way.

Understand Yourself and Your Travel Companion

To enjoy yourself to the maximum, learn more about your travel interests, including why you like to travel. If you didn't take the little travel personality test in Chapter VI, go back now and spend a few minutes to complete it. You'll learn something about yourself, the places you enjoy the most when you travel, and the kinds of things you like to do on a vacation. You'll avoid a lot of common mistakes that can ruin a trip.

Someone else is an important part of this equation, however, and should be considered in your plans. If your travel companion's personality characteristics match yours, you're in great shape. Both of you will like the same places, will enjoy participating in the same activities while you're there, and the two of you will generally find yourselves compatible throughout the trip. If you have different needs and interests, however, then either or both of you could have a disappointing trip. There are ways to prevent that outcome which I'll cover in a minute. The important point for consideration is that your travel companion should also take the travel personality test. Then you'll know whether you will both enjoy the same places and things to do, or perhaps you should make some adjustments to accommodate each other's needs.

The advice to "know thyself" may be a couple of thousand years old, but it still holds true. You can have a better time wherever you travel by understanding more about your own interests and motivations. When you follow that advice, you'll come back from your trips not only refreshed, but better able to handle the pressures you feel in your daily life.

Understand What the World Has to Offer And Then Prepare and Enjoy

The more you travel, and the further from home you get, the more you will believe we live in a world that offers excitement, beauty and interesting things to do. You'll meet interesting people, see fabulously beautiful scenery, savor the delights of exceptional foods and enjoy sports and entertainment activities you probably never knew existed. To maximize your chances, you have to prepare yourself well and then "let it all hang loose" when you're on the trip.

Getting ready for your next great trip is a bit like becoming an accomplished jazz musician. Before someone can become creative enough to play great jazz, he must achieve exceptional facility on his horn. That means lots of discipline and hard work in order to develop a good sound, be able to play high and low, achieve dexterity in going through major and minor scales (in all keys) quickly, and intensive study of the patterns and phrasings of great jazz masters. Similarly, to get the most out of your next trip, you need some discipline too. Read all you can and plan your trip well—where you want to go, what you want to do while you are there, and how much time will be required so that you don't schedule yourself too tightly.

Then, when you travel, relax and enjoy everything to the maximum. Be carefree because you know that you have thought about everything in advance to the maximum degree possible. In fact, even do some silly things that don't seem to fit with your character because those events may be your most lasting memories. If you did your homework in advance, then all you have to do from that point on is to let things happen. Ben Hogan once said that to be a good golfer, don't practice your golf swing on the golf course. Do that on the driving range. Similarly, don't get in the habit of figuring out what to do after you've arrived someplace. You'll waste valuable time, miss out on some of the most interesting things you could have experienced, and probably arrive home not quite as happy and satisfied as possible if you had only done more planning before you left town.

What to Do If Your Traveling Companion Has a Different Personality

If we believe common wisdom, opposites attract. We've seen that in lots of marriages. We wonder how two very different personalities ever got together. Yet, they seem to complement each other to make a very complete relationship that most of us can admire. That's fine and dandy for day-to-day getting along, but it can cause problems on trips. If personalities don't match, a couple may not agree on where they want to go on a vacation, or what they want to do while they're there. Or perhaps, without forethought and planning, they selected a location that one of them thoroughly enjoys while the other is bored, uncomfortable, or tired from the strenuous activity required.

Not to worry! There are ways to handle these kinds of problems. I cover that in this section, but you have to start at a common point. Again, let me emphasize that both of you must take the travel personality test because what I'll say is geared to that.

In the chart below, I have outlined some of the differences in vacation interests that I have seen in my research, along with possible solutions. You may even have additional thoughts, which is O.K. At least you are now focusing on the need to take into account the interests of both people on your trips. Let's take a look at how you and your travel partner can work it out if you find yourselves talking about different kinds of vacations.

Working it Out Between Different Personality Types

Situation	Dependables	Venturers	Solution
Beach/Sun n' Fun Vacations	Generally like very much	Only moderately like	Some beach and sun spots have lots to do for venturers, and they like the place too. Consider Hawaii, Florida, Arizona, and Southern California in the U.S. Or, international destinations of Bermuda, U.S. Virgin Islands, Cayman Islands or Australia. All of these destinations get high ratings from both groups.
Active Vacations	Generally want only moderate activity	Usually prefer as much activity as possible	Again, choose places that each person can enjoy pursuing his or her own interests, from high energy to complete relaxation. Some spots that offer this include Colorado, Vermont, Maine, the Carolinas, Northern California, Washington State, and New York City. Internationally you may want to consider the English countryside, Ireland, Switzerland, Paris, Rome, Israel and parts of Canada (British Columbia and Ontario especially).
Cruises	Strongly like, especially warm Caribbean cruises	Only recently trying some cruising, usually try to avoid.	Take a cruise since both will enjoy it. But choose larger ships (over 1000 berths). These have more activities on board to please the interests of both personalities. The Mediterranean would be a good destination choice (warm & exciting), or other unique sailings (as trans-canal).
Adventure Travel	Generally do not like	Have strong interest, particularly hard adventure travel (high activity level with some potential risk of injury).	Agree upon a soft adventure trip (less activity and low risk of personal injury), such as a bicycle tour of New England or a group rafting trip down the Grand Canyon's Colorado (includes some white water). Otherwise you may have to take separate vacations.

Situation	Dependables	Venturers	Solution
Foreign Travel	Relatively low interest, especially to countries with very different customs and habits or that speak a different language.	Strong interest, especially to places not really discovered yet or at least that are not too touristy. They feel comfortable even when they do not speak the language.	Both should take these trips. Allow the venturer personality to take the lead while traveling—finding the way around, deciding where to go, negotiating hotel rates, talking to foreigners, etc. Always make certain you have arranged for a good hotel room at night with a bath and/ or a shower.
Fully Escorted Tours	Love them.	Hate them with a passion.	Not much hope of reconciliation here, except to take short escorted tours. A venturer can last 3 to 4 days before "going bananas" from the regimen and control imposed by tour guides or feeling the oppression of being around 30 to 50 other tour members. Solution? Let the venturer become the tour guide by arranging everything for just the two of you. Perhaps also include a couple of short tour packages in that trip (city tours and 3-day tours).
Drive vs. Fly Vacations	Prefer family car vacations	Prefer to fly then rent a car.	Do both because each type is enjoyable. Nothing can beat a good car trip, but some of the best places can only be reached by air.
Shopping	Typically love it— the more the better.	Generally bored and shop only by necessity.	No problem. Venturers can agree to do some shopping, especially at interesting locations. Dependables can also do some shopping on their own.
History and Culture Trips	Prefer more familiar places for culture trips, as in the U.S. (southern plantation tours, New England history vacations, etc.).	Like unique and unusual history trips, such as explorations of ancient Mayan ruins or visits to relatively unknown art or technology/science galleries.	Do both because each type is enjoyable. Vary the focus of the trip to satisfy one or the other's wishes on an "equal time" basis.
Wilderness Trips & Bush Safaris	Mostly can't stand them	Many *venturers* strongly enjoy backpacking trips and photo safaris.	No hope here for reconciliation. You may have to agree on separate vacations if these kinds of trips are important to the *venturer.*

Traveling Easier

Sometimes travel involves so much struggle and planning that it hardly seems worthwhile. Let's get rid of some of the hassle and put more enjoyment into your trips.

Should You Use a Travel Agent?

What? You don't use a travel agent? Well, you're not alone. Surprisingly, even some sophisticated travelers do not. They either assume that the travel agent's services cost a lot or that they work for their own benefit, not yours. Let's clarify both points.

On the first point, travel agents historically never directly charged you, the traveler, a cent. Airlines, hotel chains, rental car companies and cruise lines paid commissions for all business that agents booked, amounting to 10 percent or more of the total ticket price, room rate, etc. But that all changed recently. In late 1994, Delta Airlines announced that they would reduce commissions to eight percent (from ten percent or more) on international flights. Then they fired their biggest salvo in January, 1995 when they said they would pay only a flat fee on all tickets, dramatically reducing commission revenue to travel agents. Travel agencies now face difficulties that compound their current problems and will force many out of business. A common reaction has been to begin charging fees directly to some clients. Thus:

1. You might pay a consulting fee to a travel agency if you book only a low cost, discounted airline ticket with them. But that fee will be deducted from the cost of a future trip.

2. You probably will not have to pay that extra charge if:

   a. You are a regular customer of theirs, or

   b. You also have them make the hotel and rental car bookings in addition to purchasing your air tickets through them.

On the second point, you now must be a bit more concerned than was true in the past about whether travel agents you use are keeping your best interests at heart rather than their own. For the most part, they will. But, in order to stay alive, more travel agencies will now push their own travel packages (or a package offered by what is called a wholesaler). A common type of package is a trip that includes airfare, hotel room and rental car. They can get commissions of 15 percent or more on these programs, much higher than for selling airline tickets and hotel rooms. From your perspective, however, you will still save money on these packages, but be sure to do some price comparisons on the costs with and without the package.

The bottom line? You should use a travel agent, but select a good one. You need their "smarts" and assistance to help you plan a better, easier and cheaper trip. If you choose well, they have more knowledge than you and more resources at their fingertips to answer questions. They'll handle all the little travel details, like booking the hotels and rental cars, coordinating your schedule, and confirming all arrangements. Let them do everything for you so that they can get a comfortable commission and don't need to charge you a fee. Your best bet is to look for a Certified Travel Counselor (CTC), a travel agent who has achieved certification from the Institute of Certified Travel Agents (ICTA) in Boston, Massachusetts. These agents generally are the most knowledgeable and professional because they completed a two year study course, with exams that dramatically expand their expertise.

If you plan to buy just a discounted airline ticket, such as a flight on Southwest, then you should call the airline directly because you may have to pay an extra fee to the agency. That would turn your cheap ticket into something less than a bargain.

Take Care of the
"Oops, I forgot" Items Early

It's obvious that you need a passport if you plan to visit a foreign country. What's not so obvious is that you may also need a visa. I forgot about that requirement in visiting a client in Brazil once because their visa is only good for ninety days and it had been three and a half months since my last visit. During two frantic days filled with anxiety and extra effort, I finally got one through a visa service in San Francisco. But, it cost me $140.00 extra and made my trip less relaxed and comfortable. Get the requirements checked out and completed early.

Also, it's useful to get museum passes and tickets to major events you want to see while you're still at home. Your travel agent can probably arrange these for you, particularly because they may have a preferred access program for obtaining such items. This advance planning could save you hours of standing in line at vacation cities as you try to pick up those important theater/concert tickets. By getting these in advance, you won't discover too late that what you wanted to see is not open because of a national holiday or other event.

Packing for a Trip

Following a few simple rules will help to make your trip easier because you'll avoid some common hassles.

Pack Light

I've said it before, but let me emphasize it again: pack light, light, light. Backpackers can teach us a lot since they can live for ten days or more with what they carry in their packs. To save weight, the experts even cut the corners of their maps and trail guides. You should have a similar sense of dedication to carrying no more than you absolutely need.

Copy or tear out important pages from your guidebook for the places you'll visit, rather than taking along the entire directory.

Stay Flexible

For your clothes, take color coordinates and mix and match items. Today you can buy pants with zippered legs that serve as shorts in the afternoon and become full length for the evening. If at all possible, get by on two pairs of shoes—a pair of dress-ups and some casual shoes for walking or running. An all-weather coat can double as a robe, and you may want to carry an extra light-weight bag with you—a packable one made from nylon that you can use to put things in that you buy on your trip.

Leave the doo-dads at home. Use every inch of packing space so that you don't have to take a bigger bag or an extra one. That means stuff socks into your packed shoes or shirt collars, roll up handkerchiefs to fit in corners or around objects, and get travel-sized supplies of all toiletries. If you know which hotels you'll visit in Europe or elsewhere, you may not have to carry along a D.C. or A.C. electricity converter and plug adapters because most hotels have special converter plugs in the bathrooms. Check in advance for information. Leave everything at home that might be nice to have on a trip, but not essential, such as extra reading materials or more than one camera (a good zoom lens covers almost all situations).

Getting In and Out of Airports, or To and From

In some respects, I almost have to throw up my hands in resignation when I talk about large metropolitan airports. Their massive size precludes any easy adaptation or rules on how to win the game to make it easier. However, a few suggestions can help:

Get out of the Rut—It's Easier

Whenever possible, choose smaller, off-line and often older airports that serve major cities. You can get in and out of them more quickly and, typically, they are located closer to downtown or other areas you want to visit. This includes Hollywood/ Burbank, Long Beach, or Orange County airports around Los Angeles; La Guardia, Westchester, or Stewart/Newburgh in the New York City area; Love Field in Dallas; Hobby airport in Houston; San Jose in the Bay area of California; Gatwick in London, etc.

Plan Your Escape

When the inevitable happens, and you have to go through a large airport that's unknown to you, get a map of its layout before you arrive. The Official Airline Guide (OAG) has a good array of airport diagrams in the front of the book that you can copy. Or, the airline you are on has maps of its major airports that you can look at in the in-flight magazine during your flight. You can also take it with you (the magazines are free).

In getting to and from an airport in your home city, you probably already know the best way. However, even some sophisticated travelers haven't learned about the convenience of various local transportation services, either operated by the airport authority or by a company licensed by the airport, or a private transportation service that uses private cars and station wagons rather than limousines. Look in your yellow pages under transportation services, especially airport transportation, and call to get information about the costs and limitations of some of these companies. Brand name services, such as Super Shuttle, can be relatively inexpensive, but it may take you much longer to get there because they typically pick up several people and you wait while they go to each of these places.

Find Friendly Helpers

To learn about the best way out of an airport and into your city where you've just landed, look for one of the Traveler's Aid stations. Staffed by volunteers, they know the area and usually have no loyalties to any particular form of transportation. They'll tell you how to get a subway or train into town that may be cheaper and faster than the airport bus, taxi or limousine. They also can tell you the cost for each and how long it will probably take you.

The best ways to get around town can often be determined from the people you plan to visit in other cities, either in the U.S. or in foreign countries. They can tell you about subways, trains, taxis, or rental cars—and give directions on how to get to where you want to go.

Beat the Crush

Arrive at the airport early so that you don't have to worry about traffic delays or otherwise face a last minute frenzy that can spoil the start of a good trip. Before you board, have a snack and use the restroom. You may not know it, but airport restaurants have improved rather dramatically in the last three or four years since many of them have turned their concessions over to major chains with well established reputations they want to protect. Boring cafeteria lines have given way to sit-down meals that still can be served quickly.

Board the plane early, as soon as your section is called. With more and more people carrying their luggage on board, the overhead bins fill up quickly. To get your share of that space, you want to be one of the first to arrive at your seating area.

For your rental car, use express check-in and check-out. For express check-in, you typically have to be a member of the rental car company's preferred club. Almost every rental car company has the capability for express return, even if you don't belong to their priority club. An employee will either meet you at your car when you arrive or you can drop the contract in a box and they will send you a summary later. I have never found an error on any of those summaries, at least the ones I have received from major rental car companies.

If you have a morning flight, particularly in a foreign city, it's usually best to stay close to the airport the night before. Traffic tie-ups (traffic congestion in foreign cities can be horrendous) could make you miss your flight. Otherwise, you might have to leave very early in the morning just to make certain you get there on time.

Other People Also Own Samsonite

For your bags, you obviously need identifying tags that have your name, address and phone number on them, in case you check your luggage. But, with the dominance of some manufacturers in the market place (such as Samsonite), and the tendency for so much carry-on luggage to look similar today, you should tie an identifying ribbon or other object on each handle. That way you can spot it on the baggage carousel more easily and someone else won't inadvertently take one of your bags. Put a personal card inside in case your luggage tag gets torn off.

The Little Things

It's easy to forget some of the small things that can become hassle factors. Take care of them in advance to make your trip more enjoyable.

Use a telephone credit card for most of your long distance phoning. AT&T, MCI, Sprint and other long distance companies allow their customers to dial toll free access numbers and they can complete the call by charging it to their telephone credit card, or they will get an English speaking operator who will complete the call for them. Usually these rates are much less than for using overseas telephone services. Also, carry a lot of small change to make local telephone calls. When visiting a foreign country, get some money converted at the U.S. airport in the currency of the country you plan to visit, including small change so that you can make telephone calls after you land. The new telephone debit cards are very useful when traveling in the U.S. and can save you from having to get a private telephone credit card number. These debit cards allow you to buy a predetermined amount for long distance calling. You can get $50.00 worth in advance. To use it, insert your card into a slot in a telephone and, every time you call, the amount of that call will be deducted from the amount remaining on the card. It's all handled electronically, making it very easy on you, the traveler.

- Take along an envelope large enough for the receipts that you'll receive from hotels, rental car companies, taxis, etc. Keep all receipts for items purchased in foreign countries because, in many situations, you get the value added tax (VAT) refunded at the airport. You also need to have proof of prices paid for the goods you purchased when you return and face the customs officials in the U.S.

- When you take long trips, you probably know which friends you will write to so why not preaddress some labels to them before you leave town. It makes it very easy to send off a letter or a postcard from wherever you are (you don't have to open your address directory or ever get out a pen). If you're in the U.S., buy the stamps before you leave town. If you're in a foreign country, pick up some when you're walking around town and pass a post office. Or, get them from your hotel. It's one of the few items that hotels typically don't mark up.

Traveling Cheaper

To understand the craziness of airfare wars, or hotel pricing, and when you can probably get the best discounts, you need to know a bit about how industry leaders think about their costs.

In the airline industry, a passenger seat is called a *perishable* commodity. If it isn't filled when the door closes, revenue for that seat is lost. Like a spoiled tomato, it is thrown away as useless. So, not too many people stayed up late at night to come to a simple conclusion: "If we can get some revenue for that seat, even at a deep discount, we come out ahead because we don't have to add to our costs." The idea developed to offer heavily discounted prices for the perishable seats to get you to take unplanned trips just because the flight seems so cheap. Sophisticated computer systems project when travel will be lighter than normal and, therefore, it's time to crank up another fare war. Restrictions get placed on when you can leave town or return so you don't load up heavily booked flights and to prevent business flyers from taking advantage of your super low fares (Saturday night stay usually required; travel on Tuesday, Wednesday and Thursday may be restricted).

That answers the question about low fares, but have you ever wondered why an airline starts a fare war since competitors almost always match the offer? Simple. A one day lead time in announcing an offer can put $50 to $100 million extra in the coffers of the fare war leader. That kind of "small change" makes a lot of airline execs think hard about starting the next fare war. But they've learned that the benefits of being first quickly diminish after a couple of days, and you find that the duration of fare wars is getting shorter and shorter. If you want to take advantage, you must be ready to act quickly.

What about hotels and rental cars? Have you noticed that they never seem to offer discounts as large as the airlines, even though their commodity is also perishable? Again, the reason is easy to understand. Every time travel gets soft, the airlines start new price wars. The unplanned trips stimulated by super low airfares bring people to cities all over the country. Many of these fliers need hotel rooms and rental cars. The airlines have done a free sales job for hotel chains and rental car companies. During the Gulf War and the recession of the early 1990s, a number of large airlines went bankrupt. No large hotel chain nor rental car company faced a similar fate because the airlines discounted their fares heavily, while hotels and rental car companies gave only modest price reductions.

This review of how some travel companies make money, or lose it, provides perspective to help you understand when you can expect to see the best offers.

Traveling costs a lot, but there are also hundreds of ways to save money. One thing I discovered quite clearly in the American Traveler Survey that I've quoted throughout this book is that persons from all income levels consider it very important to get good value for their money. High income couples may stay in better places, but they also want some kind of a price break on their rooms.

Airfares—Get the Best Price With the Same Quality

Unless you're a business traveler and can't control your schedule, you should never pay full fare these days for your airline tickets. In fact, your friends will probably consider you a fool if you do (92% of all air tickets today are sold at discount). Let's review a few of the more common ways to protect those precious dollars of yours.

- Almost every airline offers discount tickets throughout the year that simply require a Saturday night stay. These fares are for times of the day or days of the week when business travelers don't travel. These discounts are usually significant, but not typically the lowest.

- If you can be flexible in your travel plans, particularly when you want to leave and return—or even the destinations that you will visit—you can really save a bundle. The great fare wars I mentioned above come at soft times for the industry. Every time someone thinks things will settle down, a new pricing war breaks out. Stay alert, watch TV, read your newspaper, and you'll hear about them.

The best times to expect bargains are during anticipated soft seasons. Discounting usually begins in earnest for most places right after Labor Day, especially to Europe, since the summer crush of travelers has gone. It will end by mid-April to May. Some places follow a seasonal opposite pattern, such as Arizona, Florida and the Caribbean. Super sales may begin on April 15 and end by October 15.

- Most travel sections of major city newspapers have weekly ads promoting incredible bargains available through a variety of sources. But, look to see whether these ads include major airlines and prominent hotel chains. If they don't, it could be a bad trip. Look for the disclaimers; there may be too many for you to live by.

When you call the advertised number on Monday morning, ask lots of questions. What is the airline or hotel chain, and is it a charter flight or a regularly scheduled flight (for the most part, stick to scheduled flights on major airlines). If the company you've called tries to "sell up" (discourage you from taking the advertised price to buy something more expensive), most often you'll be better off by hanging up and looking for another bargain. That agency or discount shop probably can't be trusted. The advertised price leader either doesn't exist, or you wouldn't want it anyway.

- Find out if your travel agent deals with consolidators. These organizations collect unsold space on airlines (and cruise lines and hotel chains) and resell it, primarily through travel agencies. It may also be the same discounted trips you see advertised in the Sunday paper. Discounts can be as high as fifty percent. Sometimes you can deal directly with a consolidator, but it's usually wise to go through your travel agency. You expect them to be knowledgeable about the financial stability of the consolidator since they are in the business of knowing the companies that serve the public. Ask some pointed questions of your travel agent about the consolidator you're considering, such as how long they have been in business, their financial stability, and how many times that travel agency has booked with them.

When you buy a consolidator's trip, pay for your tickets by credit card. It's a form of protection for you. If you have any problems with the consolidator at a later date, credit card companies most often take the side of their customers (you) in such disputes. Remember, tickets from consolidators typically are nonrefundable. You can't change your travel plans. That's why you get them at such a low price.

- Beware of "travel scams," the so-called "free" or bargain trips that seem too good to be true. Unsolicited telephone calls, and an unwillingness to provide their complete company name, address and phone number suggests that something is wrong. You may be pressured to make a quick decision, provide your credit card number on the spot, and told you must make full payment on the trip before receiving complete information. A refusal to name the hotels where you will stay, the cruise lines you'll use, or the specific airlines (other than saying a major airline) are further clues about trouble ahead. Don't buy anything for which it will be 60 days until you get confirmed reservations, or if you can't take the trip before that period of time. It just so happens that two months is typically the time period in which you can challenge any disputed bills with your credit card company.

- A few consolidators deal directly with the public and have 800 numbers for you to check out their airfares. They book major airlines and it's worth a call to see if they have tickets to where you want to go. Try the following:

  Travel Bargains: ☎ *(800) AIRFARE*

  Ridgewood, Macks & Olsen: ☎ *(800) FLY-ASAP*

How to Get the Best Deal on Lodging

Few leisure travelers object to the cost of airline ticket prices today. They know that if they shop around, they can get tickets that are unbelievably low in price—often cheaper than driving to a destination. However, you hear many complaints about room rates at hotels. Why does it cost as much money to stay in New York City for one night as it does to fly there from Los Angeles? Instead of just fuming, there are some things you can do save money on hotels.

- Look for advertised specials, both in the U.S. and in other countries. These cover weekends or soft periods for the hotels with discounts up to fifty percent. Sometimes they throw in a free breakfast or a bottle of champagne in the room. If you call the 800 number and they say that no space is available at the hotel you want, then get the number for the hotel and call them directly. The 800 number staffs only get a specific number of rooms released to them, but the local property usually does not want to turn away business and will take you at the discounted rate. Also, many of the 800 number reservation services are not run by the hotel chains. They contract this out to independent companies that handle multiple chains. So, the reservationist you reach has little incentive to close a deal.

  The off-season for resorts is one of the best times to get super deals on rooms at hotels or inns. Ski areas scramble to fill space during the summer months. Winter sun 'n fun places are grand just after the season ends (as April 15th for Arizona) or before it begins (October 15th). Seldom can you get so much for so little from a hotel.

- Look for new hotel openings, or those that have gone through major refurbishment. Almost all of these have what is called a "soft opening" in which their goal is to have some visitors test out their procedures and operating systems before the grand opening announcement brings a large rush of business. Rates at those times also can be dramatically lower, often as low as 50 percent of the "rack rate" (standard room price).

- If you call the hotel directly, continue to press the person you talk with for a lower rate. Sometimes the person is instructed to provide the lowest rate only after the caller has made three or four inquiries. Some travel agencies, because of the volume of business they do with certain hotel chains, get very special rates not available to the public or to most travel agencies. These go under special names that are specific to each hotel chain, such as "great rate," "premium discount," "room savers," etc. Ask your travel agency if they have any of those special rates. You may at first be offered a "corporate rate." It sounds good, but it typically amounts to only 5 to 10 percent off of the standard rate.

- See if the hotel offers discounts for membership in professional organizations. Mid-price and budget hotels typically give ten to fifteen percent discounts if you're a member of an automobile club or AARP (American Association of Retired Persons), but more expensive properties frequently do not.

- Ask the hotel, if not beforehand, then at least at time of check-in, if the rate includes a breakfast—either full or continental. More hotel properties are doing that these days for a couple of reasons. The budget/economy group usually does not have restaurants in their hotels and, as a convenience for their guests, they offer a spruced up continental breakfast that includes juice, coffee, cold cereals, sweet rolls and, very often, some fresh fruit. More expensive hotel chains now sometimes throw in a breakfast or a Starbucks-type coffee stand with rolls because current tax laws only allow a company to write off half of the cost for meals. If it's included in the price of room, the full amount is deductible, a preferred option for many companies whose personnel travel a lot. You can also take advantage of that.

- Don't forget all of the alternative forms of lodging. These include staying with friends and relatives, using your camper or mobile home (or renting one), camping, and scanning the rental and condo ads in your newspaper's classified section. If you're taking a longer trip, you may even consider a home swap. You can also search for these in the newspaper classified ads for vacation rentals, but also ask your friends as to whether they know about any swap clubs.

- Discount coupon books are common these days. You probably know about the ones that offer two-for-one deals on restaurants in and around your city. But a number of these also include special deals on hotel rooms, locally and nationally. For a fee, usually $20.00 to $50.00, you can get up to half off on rooms at hotels that are part of national chains (and occasionally in foreign countries). You'll save a lot of money if you do enough traveling. Check the hotels listed to make certain they are the ones you want to stay in for the cities you will visit. Too often only lower class properties are included or they are in out-of-the-way locations.

- Finally, consolidators exist that deal directly with the public and specialize in excess hotel space. Their growth coincided with the recent recession when hotels were burdened with unfilled rooms, but they probably will have a permanent place on the travel scene. Call them directly to see if they have anything you want in the cities you'll visit. Some of the bigger ones include:

  Express Reservations: ☎ *(800) 356-1123*

  Hotel Reservations Network: ☎ *(800) 96–HOTEL*

  Quikbook: ☎ *(800) 789-9887*

  RMC Travel Center: ☎ *(800) 782-2674*

  Room Exchange: ☎ *(800) 846-7000*

Getting the Best Deal on a Cruise

Probably over ninety percent of cruise passengers now travel on some kind of a discount. So, if you paid full price, many of your fellow passengers may wonder about your naivete.

Many different types of discounts are available, including:

- Your travel agent should be aware of quite a few. They get faxes, special mailings, and sales calls from cruise line representatives that constantly keep them informed about the latest special offers.

- The Sunday travel section of your local newspaper, again, should be mined for the rich offers that cruise lines present. Review the chapter on cruising to determine the cruise lines you most want to travel with, based on previous passenger ratings, and then select an attractive offer from a good cruise line. Fielding's *Guide to Worldwide Cruises* has the most complete review of the ships of major cruise lines, so you can even be certain that you will sail on a ship you'll like.

- If you can be flexible on the timing of your cruise, you can sometimes get unbelievable bargains. Not only can you get half price tickets, but occasionally a third and a fourth passenger can go free. Cruise lines sometimes find that they have excess space available for selected sailings, and they'd rather let that space go at deep discounts than to have it "perish." Consolidators are a good source for these discounts but, as before, check out the consolidator very carefully. Your travel agent can keep you well informed on that.

- Sometimes you can get "stand-by" cruise prices. Your travel agent can get up to a two-thirds discount on a cruise price. The travel agency adds on their costs and profit, and sells it to you. You may be required to put down a $100 deposit and indicate three cruise selections you would accept. Your advance warning will be 10 to 30 days.

- Anytime you travel off-season, you'll get discounts. If you travel during the "shoulder" months (just before or after travel seasons), make sure it's not too cold or too hot for the area you'll visit. For the most part, you should not have to worry since cruise lines will not put a ship on the water at an inappropriate time of the year. They simply cannot get the number of passengers they need if they make that mistake.

- You pay a "penalty" if you travel alone on a cruise because you occupy a cabin that is priced for two. So, see if you can find a friend to be a travel companion and share the costs but, obviously, choose someone you feel can adapt to your idiosyncrasies.

- Cruise clubs have appeared as the industry has matured. If you can locate one in your area, or get on their mailing list, you can save a lot. These usually consist of previous cruisers who especially like the activity. They get together to compare notes about the best cruise lines and the best ships, and they are astute at searching out the deepest discounts. You could learn a lot and save even more.

Getting a Good Rental Car Rate

It always amazes me how variable rental car rates can be in the same city, or even at side-by-side locations in the same airport. Typically, you'll have to do a bit of work to get the cheapest car in town.

- If you see an advertised rate for one of the rental car companies on a special deal that involves either a small car or perhaps their largest luxury car, clip the ad before you call. Surprisingly, you may not get the discount unless you make a specific reference to the ad. As in the case of hotels, if you don't have a special rate advertised in hand to call about, continue to press for a cheaper rate because some of these agents also are instructed to offer the lowest rate only after several inquiries by the caller.

- If your company has a special rate with a particular rental car company, try using that company for your vacation rental. Show your company identification but use your personal credit card.

- If you don't have any special relationship with a rental car company, almost always call several rental car companies at the airport or city you plan to visit. I suggest sticking with the well-known, major national chains, including Hertz, Avis, National, Budget, Dollar, Alamo, and Thrifty. Except for Thrifty and Alamo, most of the others are on-site at all major airports, with the big four on the grounds of virtually every airport of importance. By calling several different companies, you'll find that you can save as much as $30.00 a day.

- I suggest renting a subcompact car because, if they're out of them when you arrive, they will upgrade you to a larger vehicle without cost. If they have a subcompact available when you show up and you really don't want it, you can typically upgrade at that time without a penalty for the discounted rate on the larger car.

- Unless you have other reasons for doing so, don't take the collision damage waiver (CDW), personal accident insurance (PAI), or other forms of insurance add-ons. These can add 50 percent to the price of your rental and they are not necessary. Carry a gold credit card since it usually provides insurance coverage for your rental car, provided you use that card for your rental. Verify the coverage by calling your credit card company. Your own insurance policy also stands as a backup to the charge card insurance, although it may require a deductible that you must pay.

Reach Out and Touch Someone

One of the big surprises to Americans who don't travel overseas very often is the cost of calling home or the office. A few suggestions on this will help.

- Get a telephone calling card from a discount phone company. If it has an 800 number that you access first, you are probably saving the maximum amount on rates. Sometimes you can save as much as 90 percent of the cost of placing a call through conventional calling methods.

- Whether in the U.S. or overseas, never charge a long distance telephone call to your hotel room. You can face astronomical add-on charges, especially when dialing overseas, for telephone calls charged to your room. Use your charge card after you get direct access to long distance lines (punch "8" for most U.S. hotel telephone systems). You may have to pay a fifty cent access fee for each call you place, but you can sometimes avoid that by punching the # sign between calls.

- Overseas, I recommend that you use some form of calling through an American telephone company, rather than using a local telephone company. You will save dramatically on your telephone charges and also be able to get an English speaking operator who can help you. AT&T and other phone companies, such as Sprint and MCI, offer such programs. Call them to get a list of the codes that you would utilize in each country to reach their operators.

- Again, have small change available in the denomination of the country you're visiting for local calls. To put any of that on your credit card might give you heart failure when you return.

Saving Money on the Little Things

- Get traveler's checks before you go. Usually you can get these for free at a local bank or savings and loan, or from the auto club.

- Americans are not used to riding trains because ours can be slow, often dirty and uncomfortable. But most developed nations in the world (even Canada, just north of our border) have excellent trains. Therefore, a good form of travel, and very inexpensive for vacationers, is to buy a rail pass before you leave. The Eurail Pass for Europe lets you get around almost anywhere and is offered at a discount far below what local residents can buy it for. What a joy to sit there in relaxed comfort as beautiful European countryside unfolds before you.

- Once you get comfortable with taking subways, the elevateds, or other local forms of transportation in many cities throughout the U.S. and the world, you will probably find that you can not only save money but also get around more quickly and easily. In many countries, their public transportation systems are efficient, cheap and very safe. Even in the U.S., a number of major cities have very good public transportation systems, such as Boston, New York City, Washington, D.C., and Chicago. If you've never taken the London underground, that should be a priority just to have the experience, in addition to the savings and convenience you'll get.

- Most of your money exchange should be done at banks in foreign countries. But still get a small amount for cab fares or bellhop tips before you leave the country. Hotel exchange rates always work against you, but don't be afraid to charge your room and expenses on your credit card since those charges are posted that day at the current exchange rate. You can also use cash machines (ATMs) in most developed foreign nations now. The exchange rate at these also is acceptable.

- Buying entertainment/restaurant discount books is often a good way to save a considerable amount of money. These will provide meals at selected restaurants, hotel discounts, and shopping incentives. But be sure to look through the book carefully to make certain that it has discounts for the cities you want to visit and with hotel chains or restaurants you would be willing to use.

- If there is one consistent piece of advice on how to save money, it is to be flexible. Discounts on travel for airlines, cruise lines, rental cars, and hotel rooms crop up at unexpected times. If you can be ready to travel on short notice, you can save a bundle. If you want to plan your trip while still saving a lot, think about going during the off-season.

- When you travel, you'll find that film is expensive at resorts and doubly so in foreign countries. Buy your film at home and take plenty of it with you. You may want to consider using mailers so that, when you finish a role, you can pop it into the bag and it will be ready for you to look at when you return. This is even more important if you take transparencies (slides) because they can take a week to ten days for processing, depending upon who does them. However, quality one hour developing stores for color print film are available in Europe. It will cost you more, but you'll be able to look at your pictures while on your trip. When you rewind your film, wheel it all the way into the film container so that you don't later put an exposed roll of film back into your camera.

One important, often overlooked item. Always present your camera and all film for hand inspection at airport security gates. In spite of assurances that the X-ray machines do not harm film, the fact is that multiple exposures can diminish the quality of your pictures.

Traveling Smarter

We all make mistakes when we travel, little ones that don't mean much and some big ones that we will always remember because of how dumb we seemed to be at the time. Here are a few suggestions covering different situations to help you avoid some of those trouble spots.

Managing Jet Lag

We all know about it and anyone who uses airlines can't avoid it. When you fly north/south, you don't cross a time zone and you don't feel its effects. But when you go east/west, it typically takes about one day to catch up for every hour time zone you crossed. If you fly to a time zone different than what you're in, it's going to take you somewhat more than a week to feel normal again. About the time you feel great, you'll probably head home and start the process all over again. Flying east creates the biggest problems; flying west is somewhat less difficult.

You can read lots of suggestions about what to do. The latest hope centers on melatonin, one of the body's hormones that helps to regulate the sleep/wake cycle as related to light and darkness. Tests now in process suggest that mild doses of it may help to give you a good night's sleep in your new time zone. Until its effects are proven, some of the things you can do include:

- I reset my watch to my new time zone as soon as I board the airplane. That way, my psychology of when I should sleep and be awake begins to adapt a little sooner.
- Eat lightly, especially carbohydrates rather than meat, and drink lots of water, but very little alcohol, when flying. Con-

trary to the assumption of many, alcohol tends to interfere with restful sleep, rather than make you feel relaxed and comfortable.

- Unwind for an hour or so before you go to sleep doing whatever relaxes you—reading, watching T.V., or walking. Follow your normal meal patterns. If you eat your biggest meal at noon time, continue to do that. Or if it comes at the usual dinner hour, enjoy it. A change in your stomach, either bloated or feeling empty, can interfere with your ability to go to sleep, or it may wake you up.

- Consider using a mild relaxant, either one prescribed by your physician or an over-the-counter sleep medication.

- Flights to foreign countries such as Europe typically land in the early morning or late afternoon. Although, I may feel very exhausted because I have had little sleep on the plane (I envy people who can grab four hours or more of sleep during a flight—I usually get about twenty minutes), I check into the hotel, take a shower, and go out and walk around, and sightsee or shop. I don't take a nap at that time because I find I cannot go to sleep at night. But I will go to bed between seven-thirty and eight-thirty the new local time after a relaxing dinner, and can usually get up to seven hours of sleep before waking. That way, I am more adapted and adjusted to the next day's time. My sleep is more likely to be a bit more regular from that time on. That's my pattern; it may or may not work for you.

Making Your Hotel Stay Safer and More Secure

When I check into a hotel, regardless of its class or category, I am always concerned about safety and security. I've been in three fires and, since I once slept through the sound of the fire trucks and the yelling in an apartment next door, it has bothered me that I might sleep through the next one if not adequately warned. The other two fires involved the Bonaventure Hotel in Montreal, (a smoldering cigarette started a trash can fire two doors away that caught the drapes and then engulfed the room), and the third was in a small San Francisco hotel. An intoxicated guest next door went to sleep smoking in bed. He set his mattress on fire, burned himself, and forced evacuation of the floor.

For fire safety, you can do several things for self protection:

- Always bring a small flashlight with you and keep it by your bed in case the lights go out and you need to find your way around.

- Before you go to sleep at night, check the location of the closest fire escape. Go into the hall and walk to the escape door counting the number of doors on that side of the hall. You can always find your way if there are no lights or smoke is so bad you can't see very far in front of you. Also, check out the fire escape to see what the stairs look like. Most escapes have lights operated by battery packs that will continue to shine even if the hotel electricity goes out. Never consider taking the elevator; always use the stairs.

- If the fire alarm goes off, or you hear someone yelling about fire, feel your outside door first to see if it's hot from a fire. If not, open it slowly before you exit to make sure that you won't get trapped in a burning hall.

- If you are confined to your room because of fire in the hallway, immediately put towels at the bottom of the door to stop smoke from coming into your room. Break the window, unless fire is lapping at its edges, so that you can wave to firemen below to let them know that you are in your room. Draw water into the bathtub (with the stopper closed) that you can use to soak towels to put around you. If smoke enters the room, breathe through a wet towel to control smoke inhalation.

In most fire situations in hotels, you'll get out safely if you use your head.

As for security, you should also take several steps because more criminals now prowl hotels looking for easy hits.

- Don't leave valuables in your room—take them with you or put them in a safe provided by the hotel, either in your room or behind the front desk. When you check in, ask if your room has a personal safe.

- At night, use all the locks on your door, usually a dead bolt of some type and the chain lock.

- If someone knocks and says they are part of the hotel staff, particularly in the evening (a maintenance man, security officer, etc.), tell them to wait a minute while you call downstairs to verify that they are supposed to be serving your room. If they don't belong there, they will leave in a hurry.

- Except when I leave in the morning and the room has not been made up, I always hang out my "Do Not Disturb" sign. When I'm gone, the wrong kinds of people assume that someone is in the room.

- When you leave your room, take your passport, traveler's checks, cash, and all valuables with you. You face difficulties if you lose these or they are stolen. If your suitcases have locks, by all means, lock them.

Safety and Security in Cities And Foreign Countries

Some U.S. and foreign cities are so safe you can walk almost anyplace without fear. In others, you have to be careful, even when you're in popular spots. But here are a few things you can do to improve your chances wherever you are:

- If you have expensive jewelry, including Rolex watches and gold rings or pins, leave them at home. Thieves look for visible signs of wealth and they target those individuals.

- Similarly, unless you must dress up for a business meeting or a nighttime dinner/theater engagement, you're better off not dressing too ostentatiously. Again, you've made yourself a visible mark for the wrong kinds of people.

- Generally, avoid conversations with unwanted strangers or children who approach you on the street. While they engage you in conversation, one of their buddies may bump you to steal your wallet or purse. They took note of where you keep it when you pulled it out to give the stranger a business card or write down some information. These kinds of conversations can even happen in major cities. I was accosted this way in a major hotel in New York City recently and, even before I cut off the conversation, I backed toward a corner so that no one could get behind me to steal my wallet. This person claimed they knew me but hadn't seen me in some time and it was good to make my acquaintance again! All a lie! Read Fielding's *The World's Most Dangerous Places* to learn about which places you must be most concerned about and the kinds of tricks strangers can pull on you.

- When you carry large amounts of money with you, never put it all in one spot. If you get hit, you don't want them to take more than about a third of everything you have.

- Before you leave town, put your driver's license, passport, credit cards, and plane tickets face down on the glass of a xerox machine and copy them to carry with you as a record. That way, if you lose anything, or it's stolen, you have all of the information you need as backup to make a report.

- When walking in a city, stay a few feet away from the curb. Persons on motorscooters or coming by in cars cannot quickly jump out and grab your purse or packages and make a fast getaway.

- It's strongly advisable to carry traveler's checks with you or use an ATM to get money so that you don't have to carry too much cash. Remember, also keep a copy of traveler's check numbers in a separate place.

- One other item: be certain to protect yourself from "shoulder surfing." When you punch in your telephone credit card number or ATM number, someone can look over your shoulder ("surf") to get your card number. These problems can be real. In my company, we once had a problem where one of the telephone charge card numbers of an employee was copied and we received over $9800 in international telephone charges the following month. None of these were ours. When you are about to phone, look around to see if anyone seems to be standing close to you or could even use binoculars to read your finger's movements. One of the best things you can do is to rotate from side to side in your telephone booth as you punch in the numbers so that an observer cannot get the complete listing of all digits.

Protecting Yourself Medically

Obviously, you can get sick while on a trip. So, there are some simple things you should think about:

- Be very careful about what you eat. It's easy to forget that, if the water is unsafe where you are, so are the ice cubes—and the washed fruits and vegetables. Bottled water and soft drinks are better options, by far.

- You should carry along your own minor medical kit because some of your items can be hard to find, particularly in foreign cities. Typically, this will include your own supply of aspirin, ibuprofen or other pain medication, vitamins (if you take them), cold medicines, diarrhea suppressants (if you have problems when you eat strange food), your light-sleeping medication, insect repellent (if you're going to tropical countries), and some mixed sizes of bandages. Keep these in the original packaging for sanitary reasons.

- Obviously, before you head overseas, ask your physician for prescriptions of any vital medicines you need.

- If you have some concern about health when you travel, you may want to become a member of the **International Association for Medical Assistance to Travelers** (IAMAT) that provides weather and climate charts, booklets on dietary matters, and a worldwide list of IAMAT physicians. They can be reached at *417 Center Street, Lewiston, New York, 14092,* ☎ *716/754-4883.* But, if you stay in a quality hotel, they probably can get you a physician more quickly than you would be able to find someone through IAMAT. You may also want to call the Center for Disease Control (CDC) in Atlanta, the federal agency that provides health advisory updates. They can be reached at ☎ *(404) 332-4555.* Your own physician should also be consulted.

The Little Things

Taking into account many small things as you travel can help to make your trip more pleasurable and save you grief and frustration.

Carry Essentials

In addition to the first aid kit mentioned above, carry along a Swiss army knife or some such tool with a combination scissors, screwdriver and can opener, or a comparable, fold-up tool sold in luggage shops or sporting goods stores. I use my Swiss army knife virtually every day to cut things out of the paper, tighten up a loose screw on something, or file down a rough fingernail. You need a small, handy sewing kit of the type you can find as a bathroom give-away item in most upscale hotels. You should also include some lightweight slippers with hard soles in case you have to get out of your room in a hurry. These are sold in travel stores as specialty items. You may want to take along an inflatable pillow to use when sleeping in-flight. Not only can these be more comfortable than conventional airline pillows, but a lot more sanitary. Pillow covers are not changed after every flight regardless of what most airline crews tell you.

Verify Hotel Location

A hotel chain can have several properties in the same location, even in the downtown area of a city. In a visit to the Mall of America, I booked a Holiday Inn from an ad in the Hotel & Travel Index that indicated that it was the closest hotel to the Mall. But, when I called from the airport for a van pickup, I had to check several Holiday Inns to get the right one. Surprisingly, the chain has several hotel properties around the airport that also serve the Mall. I also got on the wrong hotel shuttle bus. Don't make the mistake of taking a taxi to the wrong place. Expensive and time consuming!

Get a Tour Guide

When you want to explore a foreign city, hire a qualified tour guide. Don't rely on a cabby to be your guide. They know very little about any city, other than how to get from one place to another, and they possess almost no sense of its history and heritage. The concierge at your hotel can help you find a guide, or look in the yellow page directory for guides and tour directors. If you can't seem to find someone, you can call or walk into a local travel agency. They should be able to point you in the right direction, even though they won't pick up a commission.

Get To Know the Hotel Manager

If you visit a city regularly, or come back periodically to the same place, make certain you introduce yourself to the hotel manager. You may find a situation at some point in the future when the hotel is booked and you want to be there. A call to your "old friend," the manager, can usually secure a room for you even when things are sold out. He or she is a handy person to know.

Wear Comfortable Clothes

You should wear loose fitting clothes when you fly because your body tends to swell at higher altitudes (that's why you have trouble getting your shoes back on when the plane is about to land). Pants that are a size too large or with an expandable waist can help. One of the best things you can do is to wear a shirt with two pockets that button. It's a great place to put a lot of loose items that you might be using, such as receipts, extra film, pencils, portions of maps, etc.

Plan Your Itinerary

Don't overschedule your trips. The purpose of travel is to relax and enjoy yourself. If you feel you must rush from place to place, you've destroyed many of the benefits of a grand tour. See fewer sites and participate in fewer activities, but enjoy them more.

Check Travelers Advisories

Want to know about security alerts, medical requirements, or updated passport and visa requirements? You can get information free, just for the cost of a long distance call by contacting the **State Department Citizens Emergency Center** at ☎ *(202) 647-5225* for a menu and a twenty-four hour a day recording of all current travel advisories. If you have a computer modem, the **Consular Affairs Bulletin Board** provides similar information accessible by calling ☎ *(202) 647-9225*. This information can also be downloaded and printed for distribution to others who are traveling with you.

Getting Bumped and Lost Bags

Airlines routinely overbook because they expect a certain percentage of "no-shows." However, sometimes more people arrive than they expect and the flight can't handle all passengers. Your seat can be legally given away if you have not checked in from ten to twenty minutes before flight departure time. At that point, the airline has no further obligations to you. But, if you are there on time and they say that they don't have space, you have a couple of choices. You can demand a seat and the airline will try to get someone to wait for a later flight by giving them compensation, or you can also take that option. The compensation is typically in the form of a confirmed seat on the next flight out and up to $200.00 in cash. Or, if you would land more than two hours late on that next flight, you are entitled to twice the value of your one-way ticket up to a maximum of $400.00. Sometimes you can even keep your original ticket for a refund or future use. A "240" rule also allows you to demand passage on another airline.

In terms of baggage delays or lost baggage, airlines typically will pay for items that you need until your luggage arrives. But, you have to request that privilege. If your bags are very late, they will deliver them to your location (hotel or residence) free of charge. If the bags are totally lost, they will pay you a maximum of $250.00 for the depreciated value of the contents (which you must itemize). You might even get less than that on international flights, so make certain you don't put anything valuable in your bags if you must check them.

Sharing Your Insights

I've provided quite a number of suggestions about how to make your next trip easier or buy it cheaper, or just avoid some of the dumb mistakes we all make. I can't think of them all, however, and you may have some good ideas that you've learned about over time. If you'd like to share them, drop me a line. If they are used in the next edition of this book, I'll give you credit (unless you want to remain anonymous). I can be reached at:

Stanley C. Plog
c/o Fielding Worldwide
308 South Catalina Ave.
Redondo Beach, CA 90277

Au Revoir, Auf Wiedersehen, Arrivederci!

Well, it's time to say goodbye. I've covered a lot of territory, more than you can remember at any one time. But, you can always go back and look up the characteristics and descriptions of any destination or other item in the book at any time.

If I was asked to summarize the main theme of the book, it is that travel is lots of fun—to the degree that you take control of it. If you do not, it may take charge of you and reduce the amount of enjoyment you could have had. For anything that costs a lot of money, you should spend time researching its many aspects to make certain that you make the right decisions and get the best value for your money. If you buy a new house, you'd like to be in the best neighborhood you can afford with a house that will serve your needs. You also want to get it at the right price. Similarly, buying a new car usually involves shopping around for the kind of car you like and negotiating a good deal. The cost of travel these days means that you should not take any trip too lightly. Think about it, plan for it, and make well informed choices. Once you have selected a destination that suits your personality and your needs based on the descriptions you've seen here, then buy guidebooks that provide more information to help you get the maximum enjoyment when you're there. Don't forget to look up which hotels you might want to select in this book and the best airlines or cruise lines.

You'll find that your life becomes richer the more you travel, and you'll also feel more relaxed and at peace with yourself and the world. It can put a little more meaning into your daily existence. As we rub elbows with people and cultures throughout the U.S. or around the world, we gain perspective that cannot be gathered even through reading literary masterpieces. Truly, leisure travel has become a necessity, not a luxury. It elevates us to new intellectual and emotional highs on which we get hooked. Like a drug, we want more and more. Fortunately, the benefits are overwhelming; the drawbacks few.

As you plan your next important vacation, I wish you bon voyage, hasta la vista and, in plain old American, have a good trip and hurry back. See you soon, you all!

INDEX

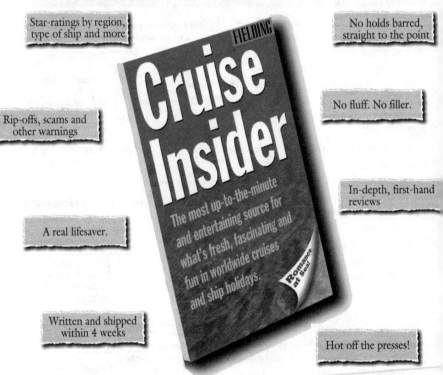

Order Your Fielding Travel Guides Today

BOOKS	$ EA.
Amazon	$16.95
Australia	$12.95
Bahamas	$12.95
Belgium	$16.95
Bermuda	$12.95
Borneo	$16.95
Brazil	$16.95
Britain	$16.95
Budget Europe	$16.95
Caribbean	$18.95
Europe	$16.95
Far East	$16.95
Freewheelin' USA	$19.95
Hawaii	$15.95
Holland	$15.95
Italy	$16.95
Kenya's Best Hotels, Lodges & Homestays	$16.95
London Agenda	$12.95
Los Angeles Agenda	$12.95
Malaysia and Singapore	$16.95
Mexico	$16.95
New York Agenda	$12.95
New Zealand	$12.95
Paris Agenda	$12.95
Portugal	$16.95
Scandinavia	$16.95
Seychelles	$12.95
Southeast Asia	$18.95
Southern Vietnam on Two Wheels	$16.95
Spain	$16.95
The World's Great Voyages	$16.95
The World's Most Dangerous Places	$19.95
The World's Most Romantic Places	$16.95
Vacation Places Rated	$19.95
Vietnam	$16.95
Worldwide Cruises	$17.95

To order by phone call toll-free 1-800-FW-2-GUIDE
(VISA, MasterCard and American Express accepted.)

To order by mail send your check or money order,
including $2.00 per book for shipping and handling (sorry, no COD's) to:
Fielding Worldwide, Inc. 308 S. Catalina Avenue, Redondo Beach, CA 90277 U.S.A.

Get 10% off your order by saying "Fielding Discount"
or send in this page with your order

Favorite People, Places & Experiences

ADDRESS:	NOTES:

Name

Address

Telephone

Name

Address

Telephone

Name

Address

Telephone

Name

Address

Telephone

Name

Address

Telephone

Name

Address

Telephone

Name

Address

Telephone

Favorite People, Places & Experiences

ADDRESS:	NOTES:

Name

Address

Telephone

Name

Address

Telephone

Name

Address

Telephone

Name

Address

Telephone

Name

Address

Telephone

Name

Address

Telephone

Name

Address

Telephone

Favorite People, Places & Experiences

ADDRESS:	NOTES:

Name

Address

Telephone

Name

Address

Telephone

Name

Address

Telephone

Name

Address

Telephone

Name

Address

Telephone

Name

Address

Telephone

Name

Address

Telephone

Favorite People, Places & Experiences

ADDRESS:	NOTES:

Name

Address

Telephone

Name

Address

Telephone

Name

Address

Telephone

Name

Address

Telephone

Name

Address

Telephone

Name

Address

Telephone

Name

Address

Telephone

Favorite People, Places & Experiences

ADDRESS:	NOTES:

Name

Address

Telephone

Name

Address

Telephone

Name

Address

Telephone

Name

Address

Telephone

Name

Address

Telephone

Name

Address

Telephone

Name

Address

Telephone

Favorite People, Places & Experiences

ADDRESS:	NOTES:

Name

Address

Telephone

Name

Address

Telephone

Name

Address

Telephone

Name

Address

Telephone

Name

Address

Telephone

Name

Address

Telephone

Name

Address

Telephone

Favorite People, Places & Experiences

ADDRESS:	NOTES:
Name	
Address	
Telephone	
Name	
Address	
Telephone	
Name	
Address	
Telephone	
Name	
Address	
Telephone	
Name	
Address	
Telephone	
Name	
Address	
Telephone	
Name	
Address	
Telephone	

Favorite People, Places & Experiences

ADDRESS:	NOTES:
Name	
Address	
Telephone	
Name	
Address	
Telephone	
Name	
Address	
Telephone	
Name	
Address	
Telephone	
Name	
Address	
Telephone	
Name	
Address	
Telephone	
Name	
Address	
Telephone	

Favorite People, Places & Experiences

ADDRESS:	NOTES:
Name	
Address	
Telephone	
Name	
Address	
Telephone	
Name	
Address	
Telephone	
Name	
Address	
Telephone	
Name	
Address	
Telephone	
Name	
Address	
Telephone	
Name	
Address	
Telephone	

Favorite People, Places & Experiences

ADDRESS:	NOTES:

Name

Address

Telephone

Name

Address

Telephone

Name

Address

Telephone

Name

Address

Telephone

Name

Address

Telephone

Name

Address

Telephone

Name

Address

Telephone